A History of

Modern

Britain

ELLIS WASSON

A History of
Modern
Britain

1714 to
the present

WILEY-BLACKWELL
A John Wiley & Sons, Ltd., Publication

Library of Congress Cataloging-in-Publication Data

Wasson, Ellis Archer, 1947–
A history of modern Britain : 1714 to the present / Ellis Wasson.
   p.   cm.
   Includes bibliographical references and index.
   ISBN 978-1-4051-3935-9 (hardcover : alk. paper) – ISBN 978-1-4051-3936-6 (pbk. : alk. paper) 1. Great Britain–History–1714–1837. 2. Great Britain–History–Victoria, 1837–1901. 3. Great Britain–History–20th century. 4. Great Britain–History–21st century. I. Title.
   DA470.W37 2009
   941.08–dc22

                                        2008054077

A catalogue record for this book is available from the British Library.

Set in 10.5/13pt Minion by SPi Publisher Services, Pondicherry, India
Printed in Singapore by Ho Printing Singapore Pte Ltd

3   2012

For Joey

Contents

Figures

Illustration Credits

0.1   Reg Speller/Hulton Archive/Getty Images

1.1   Credit: *Reapers*, 1795 (enamel on Wedgwood biscuit earthenware) by George Stubbs (1724–1806), Yale Center for British Art, Paul Mellon Collection, USA/The Bridgeman Art Library

1.2   Heritage Image Partnership/City of London Libraries and Guildhall Art Gallery

1.3   John Ker, third duke of Roxburghe, by Pompeo Girolamo Batoni, Scottish National Portrait Gallery

1.4   Tate Gallery, London 2008

1.5   Courtesy of The Holkham Estate

2.2   The Election IV: *Chairing the Member*, 1754–55 (oil on canvas) by William Hogarth (1697–1764). Courtesy of the Trustees of Sir John Soane's Museum, London/The Bridgeman Art Library Nationality

2.3   © The Trustees of the British Museum

2.4   © National Portrait Gallery, London

3.1   Library of Congress

3.2   Library of Congress

4.2   Reproduced from M. J. Daunton, *Progress and Poverty*, Oxford University Press, 1995. Source: (i) *A Short History of the Steam Engine* (Cambridge University Press, 1938) and (ii) *A History of Technology, IV: The Industrial Revolution c.1750–c.1850* (Oxford University Press, 1958)

Tables

Maps

Biographies

Preface

I

A photograph that brings a lump to my throat every time I see it portrays the front balcony of bomb-scarred Buckingham Palace in London on **VE Day** (words in bold are defined in the Glossary), May 8, 1945. King George VI and Queen Elizabeth stand on either side of Winston Churchill, with Princess Elizabeth (later Queen Elizabeth II) and Princess Margaret framing the group. Anyone who has read about that day or seen newsreel footage can envision the massive crowds that formed in Trafalgar Square and flowed up the Mall to stand in front of the palace cheering in hoarse voices all day and long into the night, calling on the royal family to appear repeatedly as patriotic songs and the national anthem were sung over and over again (Figure 0.1).

Many things make that scene poignant. I can remember seeing the building in its smoky, near-black shroud when my parents took me through the streets of London only a few years after it occurred. Churchill was again prime minister and Princess Elizabeth had recently succeeded her father as queen. I remember the rubble of bombsites scattered through the city. Empty lots where buildings had once stood still could be seen from trains crossing viaducts. I have returned to the city throughout my life, lived in it for substantial periods, and followed the triumphs and tragedies of the men and women who stood on the balcony that day. I watched the moving live television coverage of Churchill's funeral in 1965, an occasion many feel was the coda for the years of Britain's greatness, and I have seen in person on various occasions the others on the balcony, except for the king. Now only Elizabeth II still lives.

The photograph is a remarkable testament to the durability of the traditional elements of British society. The monarchy and Parliament managed to bury the hatchet after 1688 and have worked more or less in concert ever since. Each still supports the other and, like Siamese twins, cannot function independently even in 2009. Hereditary power was not just represented by the royals. Churchill was a member of one of England's greatest landowning families, and at one point in his life heir to the **duke**dom of Marlborough and Blenheim Palace. He was also the last Englishman ever to be offered a dukedom. In many ways he was a man out of the past, a full-blooded aristocrat who had the passion and genius to achieve the leadership of the nation in spite of the dynamics of change and the triumph of egalitarian values.

Figure 0.1 "Balcony, Buckingham Palace, VE Day, 1945"

Tradition in Britain sustained inequality and promoted an unhealthy obsession with class. It also contributed to the creation of one of the most tolerant, peaceful, free, and stable societies in modern history. Paradoxically, that society was also a volcano of innovation, especially in the field of technology and industrialization. Britain was able to save itself from defeat by Hitler in part due to the genius of its scientists and the willingness of a conservative society to embrace creativity and change.

On the balcony that day in 1945 stood the last emperor of India. George VI was also king of Canada, Australia, New Zealand, and a vast array of other colonies straddling the globe, the head of an imperium larger than any other ever assembled by humans on this planet. The story of how such a small place was able to construct such a huge dominion, how the oak grew in the flowerpot, is extraordinarily interesting and vital to an understanding of the modern world.[1] British history is global history. Two years after appearing on the balcony Princess Elizabeth pledged her life to the service of the empire while she was on a tour of South Africa. She remains to this day queen of Canada and Australia (in the latter case winning a continued right to reign in a democratic referendum) as well as, improbably, queen of Jamaica, Gibraltar, and other unlikely places. No one speaks more highly of her than the African statesman Nelson Mandela. India, Nigeria, and 51 other countries still acknowledge her as head of the **Commonwealth**, a far-flung organization that exercises comparatively little influence yet stubbornly refuses to disappear. Indeed, countries that were not even part of the British empire now clamor to join it. Elizabeth II probably has been seen in person by more human beings that any other figure in history during her 60 years of travels around the globe.

What moves me about the balcony scene with all of its trappings of yesterday is its meaning for today. It marked the triumph of freedom and democracy over a depraved dictatorship. In 1940 it was Churchill who convinced his countrymen to fight Hitler even if that meant entering the most dangerous passage of arms ever faced by the nation. Defeat would have meant at best submission to German rule and the murder of all the Jews in Britain, and at worst could have led to mass destruction and the extinction of representative government around the world. The British people followed him literally into the valley of death with no obvious means of winning the battle and with no more than a sporting chance of clinging to survival. His courage and theirs is one of the most remarkable stories of modern times, to which all free people owe a debt of gratitude.

The image of Churchill also reminds me, however, that history can be consciously shaped. Our understanding of World War II will never entirely escape the imprint Churchill put on it in his triumphal memoirs written after the event.[2] All who come to study the past must do so with a sense of awe at the remarkable achievements of our predecessors but also an awareness of the need, so far as it is possible, to cast off the blinkers imposed on our view by previous accounts and present concerns. The eighteenth-century literary critic Dr. Samuel Johnson reminds us: "We must consider how very little history there is. I mean real authentic history. That certain kings reigned and certain battles were fought we can depend upon as true. But all the colouring, all the philosophy, of history is conjecture."[3] Objectivity is perhaps impossible; getting as close to the truth as we can is worth making great exertions to achieve. As we sift through the views of historians we will find many different interpretations. This should not dismay us. History is an ongoing conversation, not a finished product. We need to bring modesty to our task but ask hard questions.

II

Two personal experiences have also helped to shape my vision of Britain. The first took place in a movie theater in Edinburgh when I was a schoolboy living in the city while my father was on a sabbatical. A newsreel image of Queen Elizabeth II was projected on the screen, and several voices contradicted the narrator with cries of "Elizabeth I" (Scotland was an independent country during the rule of the Virgin Queen in the sixteenth century, so technically the present monarch is the first Elizabeth to reign north of the border). As a seven-year-old, I barely knew that there was a queen, let alone a dispute about her ordinal. Only later did I grasp the extent to which Scottish society was distinct from England in ways more substantive than kilts, sword dancing, and royal suffixes, but I have never forgotten the vehemence of those voices in the darkness.

As a graduate student in Cambridge during the early 1970s, I first visited my cousins in Northern Ireland. My grandfather was born and raised in County Antrim, north of Belfast, and we have maintained transatlantic family links ever since.

I found it hard to grasp the extent of the destruction that IRA terrorist bombs had inflicted on the province. The center of Londonderry looked as if the Luftwaffe had recently returned to finish the job it began during World War II. I learned that one of the subtle signals used to identify a **Nationalist** or a **Unionist** in a population that on the surface seemed indistinguishable was whether they used the Roman Catholic "Derry" or the Protestant "Londonderry" when speaking of the city. What seemed a minor distinction was freighted with huge significance and offered a pathway deep into centuries of bitterness and conflict.

These two experiences remind me that even minor shifts of emphasis and definition can be of importance. Historians have to be as careful in their dissection of terminology as anatomists are in separating layers of tissue. Students need to be mindful that reading too rapidly or too carelessly can lead to missed opportunities of understanding. My visits to Scotland and Ulster also taught me the importance of looking at the British Isles as a conglomeration of peoples and not simply as "England" writ large. London's grip on Ireland was never completely secure, Scotland was for long a formidable rival, and the Welsh have preserved a language and culture that resisted absorption. England was larger than the other constituents of the Atlantic archipelago but never alone.

One can suggest many reasons why every North American should know the history of Modern Britain. We were one of the parts of the British empire in the eighteenth century, and although Canada and the United States took different paths in the nineteenth century, both remained profoundly influenced by the Atlantic relationship. This textbook will help students understand those underlying structures of which many people today are almost wholly unaware. Understanding British history is to be able to identify the qualities, institutions, traditions, and values that developed in the United Kingdom over the two or three centuries prior to the great emergency between 1939 and 1945 that gave it resilience and the will to win. It is a tremendously exciting story. It touches on topics as diverse as the slave trade, the novels of Charles Dickens, the Irish Famine, the legalization of homosexuality, coalmines in south Wales, Antarctic exploration, Nelson's death on **HMS** *Victory*, and the invention of the computer. If we can understand the rise of modern Britain, we will be a long way towards understanding what constitutes modernity, the strengths and weaknesses of the developing world, and the reason why democracy survived the mid-twentieth-century onslaught of the Nazis and Marxism.

III

I have tried to be conscious of the needs of students who have neither lived in Britain nor previously read extensively about it. The Glossary has already been mentioned. Maps and illustrations should provide alternative ways of looking at the material. History unfolds as narrative, but it is worth stopping for periodic overviews, which is the way this volume is organized. From time to time I also stop the march of the story to consider examples of individual lives because they can sometimes illustrate important points better than anonymous generalizations.

The title of this book embraces "Britain" as the key denominator of the subject of study. From 1707 Scotland was directly incorporated into a "Union" with England and Wales, and Ireland was subsumed in 1801. Although it is possible to write the history of any single element in the United Kingdom, for the last three centuries the story of the whole is necessary to understand the role it played in the modern world. The overseas empire must also figure largely in the narrative because it was so closely integrated into what happened in the "home" islands.

I welcome feedback from anyone who reads this book. Students and teachers are encouraged to let me know the ways they think it could be improved, send notice of errors of fact that they catch, and, if in a particularly benign mood, comments on the strengths that they see (ewasson@towerhill.org).

Ellis Wasson

Notes

1   C. W. Pasley, *Essay on the Military Policy and Institutions of the British Empire* (1810), 54, cited in L. Colley, *Captives*, New York, 2002, 10.
2   See D. Reynolds, *In Command of History*, New York, 2005.
3   J. Boswell, *The Ominous Years 1774–1776*, ed. C. Ryskamp and F. A. Pottle, London, 1963, 151 (April 18, 1775).

Acknowledgments

No survey covering three centuries can be written without heavy reliance on the work of colleagues. I have made use of the most up-to-date standard accounts, especially the *Blackwell Companion to British History* series, the *New Oxford History of England* series, and the *Oxford History of the British Empire*, as well as recent studies by leading national historians of Ireland, Wales, and Scotland and work by historians such as Wilfrid Prest, Frank O'Gorman, Linda Colley, W. D. Rubinstein, José Harris, Martin Daunton, Michael Thompson, Peter Mandler, R. S. Searle, R. F. Foster, T. M. Devine, Bruce Lenman, Peter Clarke, and others too numerous to name. I have not used large numbers of footnotes, but the citations acknowledge my debt to them.

No scholar flourishes without help from others. I owe much to David Spring, who first urged me to read Halévy and G. M. Young. At Johns Hopkins he and Wilfrid Prest fired my interest in British history. At Cambridge my supervisor was George Kitson Clark, who encouraged me to learn enough about my chosen period so that I could pick up a collection of nineteenth-century caricatures or cartoons and be able to identify the characters and get all the jokes. Spring and Kitson Clark were strong political partisans on the left and right respectively, which, perhaps, made them especially conscious of bias. They set an admirable example for young historians in making sure opinions never overwhelmed the facts. Over the years Michael Brock, Geoffrey Best, Lord Blake, and Rick Trainor showed me kindness. Others who were helpful along the way were Bill Rubinstein and Dan Duman. The latter's early death was a serious loss to the profession. The brilliant company of historians at Cambridge, ranging from Sir James Butler, who published his book on the Reform Act of 1832 in 1914 (!), to J. H. Plumb, Maurice Cowling, Jonathan Clark, Henry Pelling, Derek Beales, and Boyd Hilton, all helped along the way.

Michael McCahill's meticulous scholarship and keen critical eye were invaluable. David Stedman's editorial skills and enthusiasm are much appreciated. My family provided the perfect place to write and much helpful support.

Stone Harbor, NJ
August 2008

Part I

Uniting the Kingdoms

Chapter 1

The British Isles in 1714

Contents

Map 1.1 British Isles

History is about change. Rises and falls come naturally to peoples and states. Wars and revolutions have convulsed the modern world. Britain was not isolated from these events and was often a prime actor in them. Big changes place enormous stress on societies, and only those that have powerful and resilient cores survive rapid innovation or decline without losing their balance. Strong institutions and deep traditions allow countries to transform themselves without extreme breaks with the past that usually end in disorientation and great suffering. Britain is the only major European state not to have had a revolution in the last three centuries. Most of its neighbors have undergone traumatic episodes that have produced terrible self-inflicted wounds under the rule of tyrants who rejected the constraints of law and morality that protect us from the abuse of power. Britain has been a center of innovation and change in the modern world but also stable and peaceful. Patterns of behavior, attitudes of mind, conditions of living, and seemingly anachronistic institutions have persisted over the centuries at all levels of society. Some argue these continuities have caused a kind of societal constipation, making it harder for the country to achieve a fair distribution of healthcare, education, and wealth. On the other hand, Britain was spared the Terror, gulags, and the Holocaust.

Before we begin to look at the narrative of British history over the last three centuries we need first to study the underpinnings: the geography, the economy, the social order, religion, and ways of life. Herein lie the origins of stability and the engines that drive change. Over time these forces helped shape national identity, the class structure, and empire.

Geography and History

Remember above all else that Britain and Ireland are islands (see Map 1.1). The archipelago which they form on the northwest coast of Europe is cut off from the Continent by a narrow strait that is often unpleasantly rough. Once an heir to the English crown drowned in it, and a large modern ferry sank without a trace during a storm in the Irish Sea as late as 1953. Northerly winds driving the Atlantic into the shallow and confined waters of the North Sea create huge waves that can make it dangerous to venture out of port. Over the last thousand years mainland armies intent on invasion have only succeeded in making the crossing to England twice. A threat always lingered that Spain, France, or Germany might land men or arms on the remote west coast of Ireland where only seals stood guard. Britain was vulnerable to attack from the rear. Ireland's tragic fate was that England came to associate oppression in Dublin with safety at home.

The second most important fact to remember about the archipelago is the fortunate proximity of the Gulf Stream, a warm current originating in the tropical Caribbean that flows northeastwards across the Atlantic passing close to the southern and western coasts of England and Ireland. Palm trees can be seen in Cornwall and Cork, and the general climate is so mild that pipes were often attached to exterior

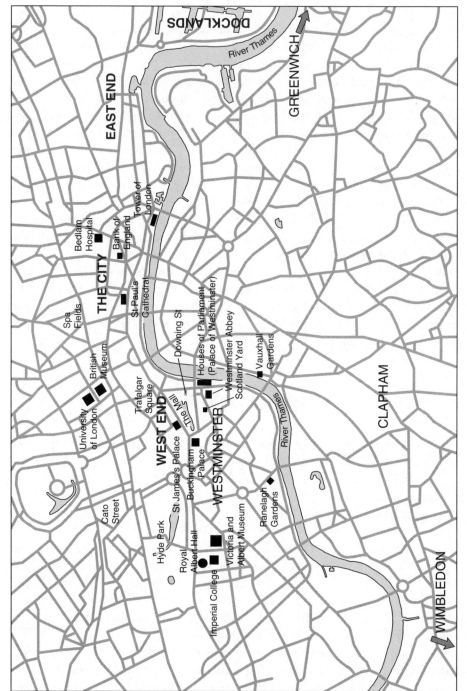

Map 1.2 London

walls when modern plumbing came to be installed in old buildings because there was little chance of sustained deep freezes during the winter. Aside from the mountainous areas in Wales and Scotland and some of the higher elevations in northern England snow is comparatively rare and usually disappears quickly. Even though the islands lie in the same latitude as Labrador, Britain and Ireland are encased in a thermos-like oceanic environment that keeps the weather cool in summer and temperate in winter. Winds from the Atlantic push a steady flow of rain across the islands, which makes drought infrequent.

The third striking characteristic of the archipelago relates to size. Britain is tiny compared to Russia. England is half the area of the Italian peninsula and one-fourth that of France and could be fitted within the borders of a number of US states. Once roads had been surfaced with durable materials in the eighteenth century and railroads were built in the nineteenth, people and goods could move and be moved around the place with remarkable rapidity. Almost all the important population centers came to be connected by trips of a few hours. Even northern Scotland could be reached from London in less than a day. No one lives more than 70 miles from the sea. Once outside London visitors from North America often feel they have tumbled into Lilliput. Edinburgh and Dublin seem like miniaturized versions of what one expects capital cities to be. In the countryside, narrow lanes linking quaint villages with names such as Lower Slaughter and Steeple Bumpstead lead one into a world that even today appears taken from a storybook. Rivers are small in Britain, but there are many of them. They are often navigable for lengthy stretches, and provided a natural system of transportation for heavy goods that eased the movement of food and manufactured items even before the water courses were connected by a man-made network of canals.

The feel of a miniature world can be misleading. Forty years ago, before the decline in industrial output became precipitate, a train journey between Manchester and Sheffield impressed on the traveler the giant scale of what was once the workshop of the world. The sea entrance into the ship channel of the port of Liverpool, now largely abandoned but once the center of the Atlantic passenger and cargo trade, still conveys the impression of penetrating a nodal point on the globe. The Scottish **Highlands** remain one of the most awe-inspiring landscapes in Europe. London (see Map 1.2) exudes the feel of an imperial city, vast in size, with some of the most grandiose and elaborate royal and civic architecture in Europe. It has no single building to match the Forbidden City of Beijing or the ensemble of structures found along the Mall in Washington, but the sum of museums, palaces, concert halls, processional routes, riverscapes, churches, government offices, and sprawling suburbs is unique. Dotted around the countryside in all parts of the archipelago is a remarkable collection of medieval cathedrals, lovely market towns, splendid regional capitals, and enormous aristocratic palaces surrounded by far-flung walls and thickly timbered parks that have no equal in their numbers, continuity of ownership, and beauty anywhere.

If being an island has been central to the development of England, the greatest single fact in the histories of Ireland, Scotland, and Wales was their proximity to England. Four distinct peoples inhabited various parts of the archipelago. They in turn encompassed numerous further divisions and fragments. The Highland Scots were very different from their brethren in the **Lowlands**; Cornwall, a peninsula at the southwestern tip of England, had distinctive traditions and even its own language; before 1922 Ireland was ruled by a Protestant elite largely recruited from Scotland and England, while the native population was Roman Catholic among whom Gaelic speakers were once predominant. The diversity of peoples and cultures within the confines of such a small physical capsule makes it hard to write a single narrative about their development over the last three centuries. The relative size of England skews our perspective. There is no doubt that it was a Goliath among a much smaller and weaker collection of entities. Yet, a Scottish army invaded England in 1640, and subsequent incursions reached deep into the south in 1715 and 1745. The English repeatedly suppressed rebellions in Ireland that threatened, or at least were imagined to be the harbingers, of mortal danger.

The royal family of Scotland, the Stuart dynasty (spelled Stewart in Scotland), inherited the English throne in 1603 and ruled jointly over the two countries, although increasingly this proved to be like having one leg each on the backs of two unharnessed horses. A constitutional merger took place in 1707, which opened up a golden age of economic and intellectual expansion for the smaller partner. On the other hand, the fragile Union between Ireland and Britain, concluded in 1801, never "took."

Much of the time the smaller nations were required to cooperate only at a grand strategic level, leaving the decisions of everyday life largely to local governors. Nevertheless, the overwhelming nature of English prosperity and its eventual global hegemony had a subtle, undirected homogenizing force that gradually drew the disparate cultures closer and closer together. The Welsh preserved their own language, though most of them eventually came to speak English as well, while Cornish died out and Irish and Scots Gaelic have largely disappeared. The English were glad to see traditions that encouraged independence evaporate and sporadically attempted to stamp them out, but, in the case of native languages, for example, the gravest danger to survival was not London-inspired campaigns to eradicate difference. English was so convenient and valuable to learn that its adoption became impossible to halt. People voted with their tongues.

The physical geography of the British Isles shaped the direction that events took and channeled economic, social, and political forces. Britain was thrust into the Atlantic as a launching pad for seaborne exploration, trade, and empire. The rich seams of coal and iron ore, the navigable waterways, the abundance of ports, and the location of the islands are fundamental to this story.

Readers also must keep in mind "negative space" in the historical record that arises from geography, the things that did not happen because of the physical environment. For example, the existence of the moat-like Channel meant there was no need for a large standing army that would have endowed the central government with the means to crush opposition. This allowed challengers to whittle away royal power. The difficult terrain of the remoter parts of Scotland and Ireland meant that English authority became stretched quite thinly as one traveled farther from London. On the other hand, lack of significant physical barriers within the core areas of England and lowland Scotland explain the absence of local customs and laws inhibiting trade that plagued the economic development of France, Italy, and Germany. These and other aspects of the archipelago that will become evident as the story progresses were as much a part of modern British history as inventors, politicians, or the workforce in factories.

One note on a delicate point of nomenclature requires mention. The term "Britain" is generally accepted to apply collectively to the island on which England, Scotland, and Wales are located. For much of the period under review here it also more or less included Ireland. In this book, for the sake of clarity, Britain and Ireland will be used as separate designations.

The Economy – Agriculture

By modern standards the population of Britain in 1714 was miniscule and thinly scattered. No official census was conducted until 1801. Thus, data for the eighteenth century are based on assumptions, extrapolations, and guesses. The population of England stood at about five million, Wales between 300,000 and 500,000, Scotland one to one and a quarter million, and Ireland two or two and a half million. Within a few years the British Isles as a whole would pass the 10 million mark. The combined white and black population of British colonies in America was about half a million in 1710.

For the first time in history the average age people could hope to attain rose consistently over the three centuries under review except in Ireland. Political and economic disturbances had kept living standards low in the seventeenth century. On the other hand, after 1666 the plague no longer made terrible visitations. Famine remained a problem in parts of Scotland, and hit Ireland both in the 1740s (when it was estimated to have killed up to 400,000 people) and the 1840s, but otherwise ceased to harrow the British people. In the 1720s England was able to feed itself and export wheat. Infant mortality remained high, which kept the *average* age of death low. In fact, people did not all keel over while still young. If they made it past the vulnerable early years, a normal lifespan could carry them into their sixties. Of course dangerous microbes lurked everywhere, and temporary setbacks still occurred.

The majority of people lived in the countryside and worked in agriculture or related employment. New agricultural techniques were developed. Farmers and landowners sought increased yields to offset falling agricultural prices. In England 15 to 20 percent of the land was owned by the **grandees** (**peers** and greater **gentry** who were known collectively as "aristocrats"), 45 to 50 percent by the middling and lesser gentry, 25 to 33 percent by small owners, and 5 to 10 percent by the Church and state.

The tripartite English land tenure system was a unique and critical factor in economic growth during the eighteenth and nineteenth centuries. Large landed estates

Figure 1.1   Agricultural laborers – *Reapers* by George Stubbs, 1795

that could reach 100,000 acres or more in size were subdivided into units rented out to rural entrepreneurs called "farmers." By 1700 a system of traditional holdings tended by families had been largely replaced in much of England by agrarian capitalism.[1] Landless wage laborers, a rural proletariat, carried out the physical tasks of raising crops and tending animals (Figure 1.1). The surplus income left over after paying the rent allowed the "farmer" to live in comfort. Large landowners employed stewards or agents to coordinate relations with the tenant farmers. Lesser gentry acted as their own managers. Big estates operated like rural corporations designed to increase the profits of both landowners and farmers. Large farms ensured that tenants could achieve economies of scale. Good tenants were not always easy to find. Landowners were willing to be moderate in their demands so long as the farms were well managed and the rents paid on time. Aristocrats and gentry focused on maximizing output, which often included the production of bricks and lumber or the extraction of mineral resources such as coal or tin. Ireland was economically and socially the most backward of the three kingdoms. An alien ruling class with little legitimacy ruled over the confiscated land of a subject people by force. Subsistence farming was practiced by peasants who rented small plots from grasping middlemen, who in turn were the tenants of subdivided big estates.

The agricultural system in England and Lowland Scotland not only encouraged expanded food production but also social stability. Paternalistic practices lingered.

Many landlords took some responsibility for the welfare of laborers, who except on "home" farms were not usually their direct employees. Opportunities to appear beneficent and to avoid direct confrontation over wages and conditions of employment helped the elite escape dangerous resentment. Cottages were rented at below market rates; ladies from great houses would distribute charity to the sick and needy; projects such as building walls around parkland were designed to provide employment in times of dearth. Special arrangements were made for rebates of rents to tenants in years with poor harvests. The mutually beneficial relationship between the aristocracy and gentry on the one hand and the farmers on the other was the foundation of England's and southern Scotland's social peace and security. Farmers and landowners participated together in rural recreations, and social occasions were arranged for the entertainment of both tenants and laborers with the roasting of whole oxen and oceans of beer.

The Economy – Business

Bernard Mandeville (1670–1733) published his famous *Fable of the Bees* in 1714. He doubted that the pursuit of material success was compatible with virtue. This challenge to unrestrained greed was largely swept aside and forgotten in a rush towards prosperity. The British landed elite's strong sense of self-interest was a key to economic growth. The energy and ingenuity of the middle classes expanded commercial wealth to unprecedented proportions. Great merchants became landowners. Both groups were represented in Parliament and devoted the resources of the state to plunder the riches of the world and protect their own interests. While England still derived approximately 37 percent of national income from farming during the first half of the eighteenth century, it had developed a more complex mixed economy than its close neighbors. A fifth of its income came from industry, 16 percent from commerce, and a fifth from rent and services.[2]

During the seventeenth century local industrialists supplied regional needs. They were small-scale operators such as millers, shoemakers, weavers, and metal workers. Consumption increased slowly but inexorably. Manufacturing was still primarily rural. Fast-flowing water and surplus seasonal labor made the countryside attractive. Centers of production were distributed all over, although what were to become the great industrial hubs of modern Britain – Birmingham, Leeds, Manchester, Sheffield, and Belfast – were emerging as important manufacturing cities. Liverpool and Glasgow were on their way to serving as the key ports in the Atlantic trade. Wool had long been the major product of England's manufacturing system. To remind politicians of this fact the presiding officer of the upper house of Parliament sat on a sack of wool that looked like a mutant purple beanbag. Production of woolen cloths and clothing continued to play a major role in the economy until overtaken by cotton textiles and iron production in the age of coal and steam. Much of the English woolen manufacture took place in the southwest and the eastern areas.

Figure 1.2   London and the Thames, 1760. Compare with the illustration of London in Chapter 11

Gradually, as wool declined in importance and manufacturing shifted north, these regions lost population and prosperity. Like the skeletons of huge dinosaurs, cathedral-size churches still loom over what are now modest villages that were once able proudly to proclaim prosperity with richly embellished stained glass and stone towers.

Historians have questioned whether the designation "revolution" is appropriate when discussing the transformation of industry that took place in the eighteenth century. We will reserve the discussion of this question for Chapter 4. What can be said is that pottery was already being manufactured on an industrial scale, and English coal production had outstripped the combined output of the entire rest of the world by 1750. Steam pumps helped drain mines as early as 1699. Abraham Darby (1678–1717) discovered a means of smelting iron with coke rather than charcoal in 1709. The industrial growth rate remained slow, however, and there was little or no increase in the number of workers engaged in manufacturing during the second half of the century, when the traditional "revolutionary" advance in industry was supposed to have taken place.

The growth of urbanization in England was rapid. "Heightened specialization in and interdependence between … economic regions, greater agricultural productivity, and the willingness of people to abandon traditional ways of life" drove the expansion forward.[3] Exchange, production, ideas, and fashion met in towns. The proportion of the English population living in centers with at least 5,000 people rose from *c.*8 percent in 1600 to 17 percent in 1700 to 21 percent in 1750. The number of cities with at least 10,000 in population increased from five in 1670 to 20 by the middle of the eighteenth century.

The size and growth of London was extraordinary (Figure 1.2). During the seventeenth century it had doubled its share of the national population from 5 to 10 percent. At half a million people in the early eighteenth century, 675,000 in 1750, and 1,000,000 by 1800, it dwarfed all other cities in Britain, and was in the process of surpassing Paris as the largest metropolis in Europe, a position it has retained to the present day. Daniel Defoe described it in the 1720s: "New squares and new streets rising up every day to such a prodigy of buildings, that nothing in the world does, or ever did, equal it, except old Rome in Trajan's time."[4] In the rest of the isles, the Scottish and Irish capitals of Edinburgh (*c.* 30,000) and Dublin (*c.* 60,000), London's only competitor in size, also grew, but few other Scottish, Irish, or Welsh towns were of much significance in 1714.

The Economy – Trade and Empire

European merchants from the time of the Renaissance triggered what C. A. Bayly has called "a continuous chain reaction of commercial innovation."[5] The first half of the eighteenth century was a period of quickening growth. The Dutch retained primacy in European seaborne trade until the 1740s, but Britain's rapid expansion outstripped them. The French remained a world-class mercantile power longer, but the rise of the **Royal Navy** and military victories in Canada and India discussed in the following chapters placed Britain in the lead. The most dynamic sector of the economy was overseas trade.

The expanding empire was crucial to the British economy. By 1732 almost half of all imports came from the colonies and nearly a quarter of exports went there. The English had arrived in the West Indies at about the same time as they colonized the North American mainland. The Caribbean islands, however, were of far greater commercial importance than the Thirteen Colonies even though the latter were much larger in population. The range of products flowing into Bristol, Liverpool, London, and Glasgow was phenomenal: coffee, chocolate, rice, furs, fish, spices, and textiles. What had once been luxury goods were enjoyed by a wider and wider range of people. Sugar was the key commodity. The British rapidly developed an insatiable addiction as prices dropped. Consumption rose one thousand times between 1660 and 1753.[6]

The dark side of this prosperity was the nature of Caribbean agriculture. Growing, harvesting, and processing sugar cane was labor intensive. The indigenous populations of the islands had been largely wiped out by disease in the early stages of European conquest. Slaves imported from Africa were the essential element in making sugar cheap. The trade in human beings also brought further profits. Between 1662 and 1807 nearly three and a half million Africans came to the New World as slaves transported on British ships. That was over three times the number of white migrants during the same period. Only a comparatively small portion of slaves went to the mainland colonies. A "triangular trade" evolved whereby English manufactured goods were shipped to Africa to pay for the purchase of a human cargo; the slaves then crossed the Atlantic; and plantation sugar went on to North America and Britain. Accounts of the slave trade are often horrific. The death rate during the "middle passage" averaged up to 20 percent. However, this was not much worse than the fate suffered by white prisoners being "transported" to the colonies from Britain or the crews of the ships that carried them. Even paying passengers died at rates that would put an end to air transportation if they were sustained by today's transatlantic fliers.

Trade with Asia was on the increase under the aegis of the East India Company, a peculiar entity established in 1600 as a joint-stock enterprise given a monopoly on trade in the region. Cottons, silks, spices, and porcelain came from India and China. The British people added to their lengthening list of addictions that included gin, tobacco, and tea, the beverage with which their culture would become most famously associated. The Company's territorial base was not large. In India it was able to operate due to the sufferance of local rulers; attempts to use military force often met with resistance and failure. China was so huge and power-ful that it was not until 1840, after the Royal Navy acquired the advantage of steam-powered vessels, that Britain could begin to challenge the authority of the Qing emperors.

Trade across the Irish Sea expanded greatly in the eighteenth century. Claims that the Irish economy was restricted by England have been exaggerated. Not being able to trade directly with the American colonies was inconvenient but did not stop considerable exchange through British ports. Trade with Britain in textiles and foodstuffs prospered. Later exports of agricultural products boomed.

The state was an active agent in promoting the commercial growth of the British economy. The establishment of the Banks of England in 1694 and Scotland in 1695, the Act of Union with Scotland, enactment of laws favorable to business, charters enforcing monopolies, encouragement of expanded communication and infra-structure development, and even the waging of commercial wars helped promote investment and knock out the competition. England tied colonial trade to its own interest through a series of Navigation Acts passed in 1651, 1660, and 1696 and subsequent legislation. (Scotland until 1707 and Ireland until 1801 were kept out-side this system.) The colonies were rarely allowed to trade with any country other than England, and commerce had to be conducted in British ships with British or colonial seamen.

Not all was right with the British economy. Consumption taxes were too wide-spread and too high. The Royal Mint failed to keep sufficient silver coins in circula-tion for everyday transactions. The slow and costly legal system required reform. Laws to prevent profiteering in foodstuffs and price fixing, regulations governing the production and sale of bread, beer and other basic commodities gummed up the works. Poor relief provisions discouraged the free movement of labor. Yet, from the late seventeenth century onwards, leading officials demonstrated an under-standing of the importance of allowing market forces to operate freely. Growth was sustained.

The Shape of Society

Belief in the Great Chain of Being, a medieval system of hierarchy that was part of God's plan for the world, had been shattered twice in the seventeenth century: by the execution of King Charles I in 1649 and by the overthrow of King James II in 1688. Yet, in 1714 Britain remained a society in which everyone had their place. People thought in terms of "orders," groups with rights and responsibilities, and not yet in terms of "class" with its economic focus. The king and queen headed the royal family in a carefully defined line of succession. Beneath them stood two hierarchical systems. One was the leadership of the state Church with archbishops followed by bishops, archdeacons, vicars, and curates. The other hierarchy was topped by the peerage, who stood at the head of civil society. They, too, were elaborately graded from **duke** down to **baron**. Within that system each titleholder had a place depending on the date of the family's first elevation to high rank and on whether their title was English, Scottish, or Irish.

The English and Welsh peerage was tiny: 173 in 1700 rising to 267 by 1800. No more than 1,003 persons held titles during the whole eighteenth century.[7] The Scottish nobility was larger, but members had lost an automatic right to sit in the Parliament after the abolition of the Scottish legislature in 1707 (Figure 1.3).

Figure 1.3   A Scottish grandee: John Ker, third duke of Roxburghe by Pompeo Batoni, 1761

Some magnates and a good number of substantial landowners were not lords. The Irish peerage retained its own **House of Lords** in Dublin.

Few legal privileges accompanied a title, certainly not the exemption from paying taxes so fondly cherished by foreign noblemen. Peers did have the right to be tried in criminal cases by the House of Lords, and, if condemned to death, they were launched into eternity by a silken rope, a privilege last exercised by **Lord** Ferrers in 1760. Yet, to be a lord was something special, and to gain a title remained the supreme goal for most men of affairs in British life until the twentieth century.

Peers held automatic access to the royal court. Peeresses set fashion and regulated social functions in the capital cities. Usually, **county** societies were headed by the resident nobles, and untitled gentry looked to local magnates to protect and foster their interests in London, Dublin, and Edinburgh. Peers understood that social and political leadership required them, however much this might necessitate dissimulation, to be open and agreeable to people much below them in rank. For every instance of aristocratic arrogance, tales often told because of their rarity, one finds dozens of instances of what the eighteenth century called, approvingly, "condescension." They lived amphibiously, moving back and forth between rural and urban environments to which they adapted with equal interest and skill.

Social boundaries remained important but became blurred below the peerage. **Baronets** and knights enjoyed titles, but what were once prestigious categories of people became very mixed in social status. Knighthoods came to be given automatically to civic office holders even if they did not own a yard large enough to walk a dog. The social gradient in England and Ireland was measured by the amount of land somebody owned. Distinguished ancestry counted for little without wealth. In Wales and Scotland lineage carried some weight, even if the family had seen better days, but great names tended to fade into insignificance if bankruptcy loomed.

The greater gentry were easy to identify. Like the nobility they lived in enormous houses, extended lavish hospitality, were memorialized with heraldic tablets and tombs in their local churches, attended Parliament (as **MPs**), and partied with the peerage. Tribes of servants, sometimes 100 or more indoors and outdoors, catered to their every whim. The houses were not built to evoke the awe of yokels, who were taught to pull their forelocks by the realities of their employment and dependency. The grand houses were meant to impress the lesser gentry, political clients, professionals, clergy, and others who had to scuttle down long corridors enriched with gilt furniture, family portraits, and precious possessions in order to pay homage to the owner. About 1,000 families constituted the English governing class who were regularly represented in Parliament.[8]

Social navigation got trickier as one descended the scale into the lesser levels of landownership. The "county" gentry might be modestly endowed but still rich enough to attend important political and social gatherings. "Parish" gentry, or in Scotland lesser "lairds" (lords), tended to be confined by low incomes to their comparatively humble homes and near neighborhood. No official body succeeded in regulating who was in and who was out. For this reason it is almost impossible to estimate the size of landed society accurately. Counts in England range from 5,000 to 25,000 families.

The younger sons of landowners, even of peers (or at least their grandsons), merged rapidly into an amorphous mass of "gentlemen" who might own little or no landed property. The practice of primogeniture (in which the bulk of an estate was given to the eldest son at the expense of his siblings) among the landed elite meant that younger sons drifted into occupations where they had to earn a living in some form of business. This might be the more "genteel" profession of the law or socially less elevated commerce. In either case they sank or floated according to luck and ability. The lower borders of this category became more and more ragged as the century progressed and the mass of gentlemen became larger and larger. Someone who spoke reasonably grammatical English and dressed to look the part generally passed muster unless other evidence emerged of depraved character or employment as a manual laborer. Most bankers, merchants, doctors, and attorneys came to be accepted as "gentlemen."

The tiny Welsh elite clung longer to traditional practices and met with fewer members of the middle class attempting to gain access. They numbered no more than 500 or 600 families with about 50 regularly represented in Parliament. Bards still wandered from mansion to mansion as late as 1720 and some gentle families did not adopt a surname until the same period. There was a sharper division between a handful of remote, Olympian magnates who rose like high rock formations out of the flat plateau that constituted the rest of the elite. The more gentle, sloping effect in social pyramids found elsewhere was absent.

In Scotland a core group of about 1,500 families held much of the land in the kingdom of whom 175 to 200 were regularly represented in the **Westminster** Parliament. Fifty or so magnates of ancient lineage such as the Campbells, Douglases, Hamiltons, and Stewarts composed a group of "national" families whose histories were in a real sense the story of the country.

Three to five thousand families formed the **Ascendancy** in Ireland, of whom perhaps 350 were regularly represented in Parliament. The top elite lacked the vast resources of the great English and Scottish families. To be well-to-do in Dublin was equivalent of holding a modest social position in London. Later, the Irish would fall further behind as British magnates profited from the mineral and other resources on their estates that helped fuel industrialization. The Ascendancy formed a mongrel elite with far more mixed origins than elsewhere. The origins of the O'Neills may stretch back to the fifth century AD, but most families rose as English and Scottish immigrants in the sixteenth and seventeenth centuries. They lived as "a garrison in a hostile land," in fear of a seething mass of dispossessed Roman Catholic natives beneath them.[9]

The "professions," as traditionally defined, included the better-bred clergy, military officers, and upper-level lawyers and judges. By 1700 the clergyman ranked second to the squire in the parish and even lived on friendly terms with greater landowners and peers. An increasing number came from landed families themselves. The many substantial rectories and vicarages built in the eighteenth century attest to their status. From about 1680 university-educated doctors (though not barber surgeons) gradually established professional status.

Lawyers in England, Wales, and Ireland were divided into three groups: barristers (called "advocates" in Scotland) who argued cases in court (at the bar), solicitors (in Scotland "writers"), who advised clients, drew up documents, and managed cases, and attorneys, local purveyors of legal advice of varying quality. Outstanding barristers and advocates promoted to judgeships could gain excellent incomes and

Figure 1.4   Even a middle-class artist such as William Hogarth could afford to maintain a large household. *Heads of Six of Hogarth's Servants* by William Hogarth, *c.* 1750

in some cases found great aristocratic families through accumulation of fees and prerequisites. In the Church, bishops sometimes had incomes as large as important landowners. Making a career in the army, and to a lesser degree the navy, became more and more fashionable in the eighteenth century. The navy required more brains and more difficult living conditions, but a system of rewarding captains and admirals with prize money raised by the sale of captured ships could make them rich.

The professions stood on the border between landed society and the "middling orders," an expanding body of families in the eighteenth century. This category was immensely varied and ranged from great merchants to modest businessmen. Successful farmers and tradesmen were entering from below and aspired to social recognition and comfort. The middling orders were increasingly assertive and entrepreneurial in outlook. As incomes rose, they also became consumers of material possessions on a grand scale and adopters of Enlightenment values.

Lesser farmers, shopkeepers, and tradesmen remained among the "lower orders" in the company of artisans and other skilled manual laborers. These men were literate and held responsible offices, like Thomas Turner (see Biography 1.1), in the localities. Upper servants such as butlers and housekeepers were quite superior people. Like farmers and shopkeepers, they were themselves waited on by servants (Figure 1.4).

Biography 1.1

Thomas Turner
1729–93

Thomas Turner kept a modest shop in the village of East Hoathly in Sussex in the south of England. He also wrote down his thoughts and cares in a rare instance of an eighteenth-century diary kept by a modestly situated citizen. It is probable that Turner went to school. His reading – from sermons and history to classics such as Homer's *Odyssey* and the plays of Shakespeare – suggest considerable intellectual development. In addition to running his shop Turner acted as a middleman in the sale of sheep wool. He wrote letters for the illiterate, drew up wills, and intervened on behalf of villagers with the local peer in the distribution of patronage. Regular income was provided by serving as undertaker at funerals. He was a druggist, stationer, and dispersed personal loans. He made periodic trips to London and regional towns to purchase goods and conduct financial transactions. For a time he served as the village schoolmaster, was a conscientious member of the local church vestry, and occupied offices such as churchwarden, overseer of the poor, collector of window taxes, and surveyor of the highways.

Turner's interests and activities constitute a unique window into the lives of ordinary people in the eighteenth century. He was an assiduous churchgoer and connoisseur of preaching. He visited country houses, military fortifications, cockfights, and concerts. He loved to play **cricket** and would travel considerable distances to witness matches. "Curiosities" such as five-legged sheep and two-headed turtles delighted him. He went to the horse races, smoked tobacco, and had a distinct partiality for the bottle, often coming home drunk. He was regularly thrown off his horses. He loved to play cards, especially cribbage, and gambled.

Turner's diary described a society participating actively in self-governing institutions that managed local affairs. The villagers celebrated military and naval victories with bonfires and services of thanksgiving. They followed the doings of the royal family and Parliament in newspapers. They lived lives largely free from overt oppression, usually in comfortable enough circumstances to avoid hunger. They delighted in small luxuries, pub crawls, gossip over garden fences, and the emotional attachments that made life both bearable and rich.[10]

Below this category, the servantless world began. This included footman and scullery maids, farm laborers and ditch diggers, gardeners and the mass of propertyless people who survived on wages. Regular soldiers were often seen as bad and dangerous, ranking below paupers. In Ireland and Highland Scotland peasants lived in the most harrowing and squalid conditions, largely unseen and ignored by those above them, little better than slaves.

Joseph Massie, who in the late 1750s attempted to update Gregory King's famous 1688 table of data on social categories and income in England, believed some 81 percent of all families had annual incomes of less than £50 (50 **pounds**). It has been suggested that £40 to £50 was the absolute minimum annual income required by those aspiring to respectable "middling sort" status.[11] The number of people who described themselves as Mr. or Mrs. increased substantially. A noted historian observes: "This debasement of gentility is one of the clearest signs of social change in the eighteenth century."[12] They aped the manners and morals of the gentry as soon as they possessed the means to do so. The aspirants sought incorporation in the class above them, not collaboration with those below them. This kept society stable and growth dynamic.

Paul Langford notes, "in a modern consumer society, things are cheap, people are expensive. In the eighteenth century, the reverse was true."[13] The lives of the common people were rarely easy and often grim, full of hard labor with modest protection against accident, illness, old age, or bad luck (Table 1.1). However, they came to enjoy little luxuries such as tea and sugar imported from halfway around the globe. Many had some education, were alert to the world around them, and took pride in the accomplishments of their country. Unjust prices or attacks on customary rights could provoke violent protests. If they lived in or near a county town or parliamentary **borough** they followed the course of elections and went into the streets to register their discontent or approbation. It did not occur to most people that any significant change in the social structure was possible.

Table 1.1   The annual expenditure of an Oxfordshire laborer with three children near the end of the eighteenth century

Bread	13 pounds 13 **shillings**
Tea and sugar	2 pounds 10 shillings
Butter and lard	1 pound 10 shillings
Beer and milk	1 pound
Bacon and other meat	1 pound 10 shillings
Soap, candles, etc	15 shillings
Rent	3 pounds
Coats	2 pounds 10 shillings
Shoes and shirts	3 pounds
Other clothes	2 pounds
Total expenses	31 pounds 16 shillings

As a carter and digger he earned 8 or 9 shillings a week. His expenses thus exceeded his income by over eight pounds a year. Contributions from the parish partly made this up; but he was five pounds in debt.[14]

Social Mobility

No fixed barriers stood in the way of movement up or down the social scale in British society except religion and gender. Non-**Anglicans** and women were for all practical purposes excluded form holding civic office, a key means of social ascent. In Ireland harsh penal laws aimed at the destruction or at least containment of the Catholic population, although these rules were often not enforced or could be evaded. However, discrimination against the majority of the population by the Protestant elite constrained the careers of able men who otherwise would have risen in rank and wealth. In England it was largely **Dissenters** who were held back. However, as in the modern world, forces such as lack of educational opportunities, dysfunctional families, cultural prejudices, ignorance, and bad luck injured many people. Being in the right place at the right time was critical. One ducal family began its ascent when a young apprentice jumped into the Thames to save the life of his master's baby daughter. Notable instances of rags to riches stories tended to delude people then as now into believing social mobility was more real than it actually was. Downward flows, on the other hand, tend to be neglected because people who sink rarely wish to advertise their adversity. It is also worth noting that our knowledge about social mobility in comparable Continental societies is primitive.[15]

That said, much traffic up and down took place in British society. New blood entered even the upper reaches of the elite and many younger sons of the gentry, failed merchants, and unsuccessful artisans tumbled downwards. The dynamic quality of British politics, culture, and economic growth during the eighteenth and nineteenth centuries was the product of social fluidity.

Lawrence Stone argued that most new families entering the upper elite came from landed backgrounds or via the traditional routes of office, law, and military service. He believed that businessmen did not buy as much land nor aspire to the trappings of gentility in the way that men from more genteel backgrounds did. Only in the second half of the nineteenth century did business entrants become more "than a thin trickle."[16] According to Stone, social mobility cannot be used to explain the unique experience of modern Britain. Analysis of Stone's data has demonstrated that he misinterpreted some of his own statistics. The most serious flaw, however, is that he did not include new entrants from business to the lesser gentry. For a majority of families this was the first step on the way up. Commercial wealth had been flowing into the elite since the Middle Ages. This legitimated the existing social order and kept the relationship between land and capital a close and harmonious one.[17] Stanley Leighton, who descended from an ancient and broad-acred dynasty, wrote in 1901: "It may be said, without fear of contradiction, that every landed family is indebted to commerce for some of its wealth, and every family which has existed for three hundred years has some of its members enrolled on the Trade guilds of our towns."[18]

Some historians have argued for very rapid turnover. That underestimates, however, the continuity of landed families. In England at the very pinnacle were a core group of 140 or so grandee dynasties largely impervious to decay and rarely added to. A tiny dense apex stood at the top, but it had fluid flanks. In Ireland many members of the Ascendancy rose rapidly in the seventeenth century, but further entry grew more difficult as the eighteenth century progressed. The landowning elite in Scotland turned over more slowly and in Wales hardly at all.

Poverty

A majority of British people in the early eighteenth century experienced poverty at some point in the lives. The country "was full of the spectacle of pain."[19] There is evidence that destitution was becoming more prevalent in towns. The slow growth in population during the first half of the century, however, meant that more resources were available to society due to improvements in industrial and agricultural production and commercial growth, so a modest rise in the standard of living for the poor was likely. However, significant regional variations existed in wages and prices. A lot depended on weather and good harvests.

The poor were believed by those above them to be idle, improvident, and undisciplined. Yet, provision was made for the elderly, infirm, and destitute. England was the only country in Europe with a system of poor relief financed from taxation, although private charity also contributed support. Perhaps a quarter of households had some relief in the course of a year. Payments were made to cover periods of ill health and provide medical treatment. It was not necessary to fall into extreme poverty before turning to the parish for assistance. Poor Law payments were relatively high compared to workers' wages, but this situation deteriorated over time.

In parts of Wales no public system of support for the poor existed in spite of English legislation, though charity picked up most of the slack. In Scotland each parish or town had responsibility for their own poor funded by fines and collections taken at **Kirk** services, fees, and endowments but not direct taxation. The system served the poor in a reasonable way, though after mid-century **outdoor relief** was increasingly eliminated. In Ireland there was no state provision for the poor, and they often wandered the country looking for work or begged. Much was left to private charity. A visitor from Europe in 1732 was appalled by the condition of the Irish peasantry, and thought them "as great slaves to the Irish lords and gentry as the Russians are to the [nobles]."[20] However, this condition was not reserved just for Roman Catholics. The large majority of Protestants in Ireland were also poor.

Crime

Poverty was likely to breed crime. Illegal activity was severely punished, if the perpetrators could be caught, but no general police force existed. Rates of indictments for crimes were very low by modern standards. The disorderly were whipped or given short jail terms. The list of capital crimes, many relating to property not personal violence, grew longer and longer as the eighteenth century progressed, but in fact many among the condemned were reprieved. Judges and juries often mitigated the severity of punishments or mercy was recommended to the king based on the character and circumstances of the prisoner.

English law also developed a wider range of options for sentencing. "Transportation" to the North American colonies (and, when that became unworkable after the War of Independence, to Australia beginning in 1787) was increasingly adopted by the government as a new alternative to hanging. The condemned were shipped off, usually for seven or 14 years. This provided underpopulated colonies with labor. The chance to start life anew actually began to erode the deterrent effect of the punishment. This may have contributed to a renewed spate of laws creating more capital crimes and to the 1752 Murder Act that allowed a condemned corpse to be hung in chains or given away for medical dissection, which frightened people and made them uneasy.

The Scots took pride in the preservation of their legal system based on Roman/ Dutch ideas rather than the common law of England and Ireland, although they shared the practice of using juries. Both the Scottish and English legal systems contributed greatly to the formation of national identities. At the heart of both, social equality before the law became a revered principle that made Britain unique in eighteenth-century Europe.

Local Government

The governance of Britain largely depended on amateurs. Kirk sessions composed of elected community leaders regulated schools and morals in Scotland. The church vestries in England and Wales oversaw the poor and mundane matters such as sewers and roads. Parish offices were filled by "respectable" people like Thomas Turner: shopkeepers, farmers, and artisans. The churchwardens, elected on a regular basis, were responsible for collecting national taxes. Local taxes (called **rates**) were levied upon the better-off members of the parish, though the statutory labor to maintain roads (traditionally six days annually) fell heaviest upon the poor. Above the parish stood the county, at whose pinnacle was the lord lieutenant.[21] He nominated justices of the peace (**JPs**) and took command in emergencies, but otherwise day-to-day management fell to the JPs. They constituted "the bench" of the quarter sessions held four times a year to deliberate about county-wide projects and serious crimes. Sheriffs supervised elections and conducted county meetings. The size of the commission of the peace (the bench) grew during this period, more than tripling in number in some counties between 1688 and 1727. Many viewed the office of JP as honorific and not participatory. The lack of active JPs led to the appointment of less prosperous men to undertake the donkey work of ordering and regulating local society. Property qualifications were set low and gradually clerics were also appointed to help pick up the burden. Local government was idiosyncratic and paternalistic but yet remarkably flexible, democratic, and efficient. David Eastwood has shown how historians have been too ready to swallow uncritically the invective against the old system by radicals bent on its reform or overthrow.[22] There was much in it that was vibrant and responsive.

After 1747 the Scottish landed elite had their legal powers curtailed. JPs and quarter sessions played a much less important role there than in the rest of Britain. The burden of local government was distributed among sheriffs, **burghs**, Kirk sessions, and the central government. The Irish aristocracy was less present in the countryside than was the case in England and Scotland and gave less leadership, although that began to change somewhat later in the eighteenth century. Authority rested on a very narrow foundation. With 75 percent of the population debarred by law from holding office, not enough qualified Protestants were available to fill all the jobs. Much of rural Ireland had no Protestants at all. The few resident property owners were obliged to carry many burdens.[23] Nor were the 12,000 or so troops stationed in the country a formidable force to rule the whole island. It is testimony to the determination of the Ascendancy to retain control of their property that the country remained largely at peace for as long as it did.

Men, Women, and Children

The nuclear family was the fundamental unit of eighteenth-century British society. Lawrence Stone argued that parents in the early modern period remained psychologically detached from their children due to high rates of infant mortality. The pain of frequent loss of babies was so great, his reasoning went, that adults had to insulate themselves from nearly continuous grieving. This situation was supposed to have changed beginning around the middle of the seventeenth century due to the rise of more companionate marriages based on free choice, warmth, and intimacy which spilled over into enhanced affection showered on children.[24] Recent research suggests that human emotions are too deeply imprinted in the core of our beings to be easily overridden by circumstance. Parents loved their babies even though the infants faced frighteningly high rates of death. That did not mean, of course, that children avoided harsh conditions. Among the poor they might be set to work earning their keep by age seven. Being from a family prosperous enough to afford schooling did not protect the child from savage discipline and mind-numbing recitations. The notion that children were not merely miniature adults whose moral and spiritual failing should be treated accordingly gained acceptance only late in the eighteenth century.

Evidence of the new style of companionate marriage can be found in the records of the time. For example, a 1779 letter from an Irish landowner to his heir contains admonitions about how to treat his spouse: "Endeavour to make Home agreeable to each other by making your amusements domestick. Two people who really love each other can never be at a loss for amusement together. Time can never lye heavy if you wish to employ it to each other's satisfaction."[25] Stone may be right that family composition and interactions change significantly over time, but most historians are now more cautious than he was in making generalizations, especially for the lower orders about whom few records survive. Many observers believe that patriarchal and companionate marriage were not successive stages in the development of the modern family. Rather these were, as Keith Wrightson has argued, "poles of an enduring continuum in marital relations in a society which accepted both the primacy of male authority and the ideal of marriage as a practical and emotional partnership."[26] Co-dependency was probably the prevailing condition of most happy unions. Unfortunately, there was also much incompatibility, unhappiness, and violence. No doubt members of the upper levels of society demanded more personal privacy, cleanliness, and delicate manners as the eighteenth century wore on. Whether this was a product of greater emphasis on rational thought and behavior, the whims of fashion, or a larger body of people who could afford the luxury of elaborate sets of cutlery, lice-defying wigs, and corridors rather than enfilades of rooms in their houses remains open to debate. The rise of sensibility led to more respect for women and redefinitions of femininity and masculinity.[27]

Another belief that prevailed among scholars for a time was that large family sizes were the norm in the days of high infant mortality. In fact the number of children was smaller than has been previously assumed. We now know that fertility was significantly limited by late marriage and sexual abstinence as well as by the large numbers of babies who died. People waited to marry until they could afford to establish their own households. Most people in the eighteenth century married for love. Even among the elite, where the transmission of property and titles made alliances of great economic and political importance, parents increasingly exercised vetoes rather than force their children to marry incompatible partners. Occasionally, the daughters of dukes would run off with men judged unsuitable by their parents and get away with it, although the rare elopements with servants or actors almost always ended in tears.

Understanding of sexual knowledge was shaky at best. Many believed it was possible for a pregnant woman to produce rabbits rather than human progeny. It was long thought that females had to enjoy sex in order to conceive. Prostitution and a homosexual sub-culture existed in London and some provincial centers, although various organizations led by puritanical "do-gooders" waged war against commercial sex and "deviancy."

Most women worked. In the country this meant both farm labor, tending family plots, spinning and weaving, as well as maintaining the household and raising the children. Later, factory work employed large numbers. For many thousands of unmarried women domestic service was their fate. Generally wages were two-thirds or less of what men earned. Women in the middling and upper orders found expanding opportunities to take the lead in the public sphere by organizing concerts and social assemblies. Educated women achieved prominence in the arts, and many aristocratic women were influential in politics. On the other hand, women were excluded from government and judicial service, university educations, apprenticeship in most trades, and the vote.

In spite of its being a "man's world," women were more valued for their intelligence and abilities than is sometimes supposed. The inscription on a funerary monument for a woman from a gentry family suggests a complex picture of respect and condescension.

> She was an Woman of Excellent Sense and Spiritt
>   Prudent and Frugall
> As well as a true ffriend To the family She married into.
> And was moreover endued
>   With all Those Graces and Virtues
>   Which distinguish and Adorn
> The good Wife The good Mother and the good Christian[28]

Religion

Religion remained a dominant element in the lives of British people and a central concern of politicians, scholars, and monarchs. Church buildings were the centerpieces of most villages and towns. The great landmarks of life – baptism, confirmation, marriage, and burial – were conducted and recorded by its ministers. The notable celebrations of the year such as Christmas and Easter were high points in people's lives. The universities were citadels of clerical and religious life as were the numerous cathedral hierarchies dotted around the country. Religion was a central theme in the arts, music, and literature. Western Europe was emerging only slowly from an age when thousands of people were killed for their religion. It is essential to keep in mind the centrality of spiritual beliefs and religious practice in daily life, political activities, and national identity during the eighteenth century.

Each kingdom had a state Church. The large majority of people in England, Scotland, and Wales were members of the established Protestant Church. In Ireland about one in five was. Because of England's separation from Rome in the sixteenth century and the disruption of civil war in the seventeenth, beliefs within the "broad" Anglican (a term that only entered common usage in the nineteenth century) Church had become variegated, the "high" church remaining nearer to Catholic practice while the "low" church approached Protestantism most closely. The king appointed the bishops of the **Church of England** and the Church of Ireland. First among equals was the Archbishop of Canterbury. Bishops sat in the House of Lords in London or Dublin and so were political decision makers as well as shepherds of their flocks. Convocation, the assembly of the established Church, ceased to meet between 1717 and 1852, leaving theological decision making moribund.

In Scotland Protestantism was Calvinist, although a much smaller "Episcopal" Church also existed. Religious practice and architecture were austere. Emphasis in services was on the sermons not ritual. An annual General Assembly determined theology and governance. The Scottish Kirk was fundamentalist, but gradually shook off its most bigoted and vengeful habits as the eighteenth century progressed. Comparative "moderates" gained control of church governance. Kirk discipline in the parishes crumbled slowly. Interference in areas not directly connected with sexual license or keeping the Sabbath progressively dwindled although clergy and elders remained influential moral arbiters in their communities. Civil law was progressively ascendant over religious regulations in parts of Britain and Ireland.

Roman Catholics were despised. They were associated both with attempts to establish despotism and the "papist" powers of the Continent, especially the evil French. Much hostile legislation was passed against them not only in Ireland but also in Britain. However, the tiny numbers of the Catholic community that had survived in the latter island gradually made prejudice towards them seem unfair, especially once the threat of a Stuart restoration passed. Pressure from the London government anxious to win loyalty or at least civil peace also ameliorated their condition in Ireland, over the objections of the Protestant minority. Nonetheless, hostility to the religion of the mass of the Irish people constantly provoked irrational fear across St. George's Channel. The Anglican clergyman Sydney Smith noted in 1807: "The moment the very name of Ireland is mentioned, the English seem to bid adieu to common feeling, common prudence, and common sense, and to act with the barbarity of tyrants and the fatuity of idiots."[29]

In 1689 limited toleration was granted to Protestant Dissenters in England and Wales. These were people who objected to governance by bishops and felt that even "low" church theology was not genuinely Protestant enough. The Dutch prince who came to the throne in 1688, King William III (1650–1702), was a Calvinist and the subsequent German "**Hanoverian**" monarchs Lutherans (see Chapter 2), so the established Church had to be flexible. In England and Wales the Test and Corporation Acts (1661 and 1673) restricted civil and military office holding to communicants of the established Church. This meant that many Dissenters and all Roman Catholics were excluded from power and position in society. Some Dissenters took the Anglican communion annually ("conformed") in order to hold municipal offices, and a few Catholic lawyers made nominal conversions in order to practice at the bar. No official accommodation was offered to Jews (readmitted to England in 1656) and Quakers. Some wealthy Jewish financiers and merchants were received at the royal court but anti-Semitism continued to exist.

Historians long thought that the Church of England slumbered through the eighteenth century. Revisionists have demonstrated that, in fact, it was alert and lively. New religious societies were founded to promote morality and missionary work. Their members threw themselves into charitable activities and the persecution of vice. Much attention was paid to upgrading the qualifications of the clergy and building more churches. Sermons poured off the presses by the hundreds of thousands to be read with earnest pleasure. Many members of the Church, even among the leadership, were undogmatic. Enlightenment ideas wore off some of the sharp edges of orthodoxy, but core beliefs remained strong.

--------------------   **Manners, Knowledge, and the Arts**   --------------------

Eighteenth-century written English was often ponderous, wordy, and convoluted. In polite society, however, methods of thought and understanding were becoming recognizably modern. Free speech grew to be an accepted right, and the thirst for knowledge and the critical spirit of its pursuit led to a rapidly expanding understanding of nature and human behavior.

Literacy had spread fairly widely in England, with nearly half of the men and a quarter of women able to read, though fewer could write. The rate was higher in Scotland and much lower in Ireland. Many towns and charitable organizations offered schooling for a wide range of students, some of it free, but only children of the middling and upper orders could afford more than a short period of education. English Dissenters and Scottish Calvinists always put a high value on schooling in order to promote religious goals. Increasingly through the century elite children (mostly boys) were sent off to boarding schools. A few institutions gained a national reputation such as Westminster, Harrow, and Eton. The curricula of these schools concentrated on the mastery of Classical languages. Schools serving the middling orders sought to offer more "practical" subjects such as mathematics, geography, and science.

Higher education was largely the preserve of the well-to-do, especially those preparing for the professions. In the past, English and Welsh landed gentlemen had "finished" their studies with time spent at one of the law schools (inns of court) in London, which was a good preparation for their role as magistrates. During the eighteenth century they tended to go to a university. England had only two such institutions, Oxford and Cambridge, although these were federal organizations with many constituent colleges. Young magnates were likely to take a "grand tour," a lengthy stay abroad seeing the world. Scottish universities, where teachers relied on fees paid by students rather than endowment income for their salaries, were livelier and more seriously academic.

Boys in Scotland with modest economic resources were far more likely to gain access to a university education than anywhere else in Britain thanks to low fees and scholarships. There were no confessional tests for admission, which meant Englishmen and Dissenters from Northern Ireland frequently attended. Edinburgh became a key center in Europe for the study of medicine, drawing students even from North America. At the summit of the Irish educational system stood Trinity College in Dublin, a bastion of Ascendancy pride and bulwark of Anglican doctrine.

Literary life in eighteenth-century Britain was turbulent, fecund, and brilliant, matching the dynamism of the urban culture developing in towns and cities around the country. Reviews, magazines, and pamphlets were produced in increasingly large numbers. London newspapers were widely disseminated around the country, and local ones arose in the provinces. The press was largely unbounded by censorship unless the editors slipped into blasphemy. Governments repeatedly tried to restrict circulation by imposing taxes that raised the purchase price, but copies were always available in public places such as coffee-houses, taverns, and inns, and the papers were read aloud so that even the illiterate could follow events.

Literary publications found a wide audience as more and more prosperous families enjoyed the funds and leisure for recreational reading. Daniel Defoe's *Robinson Crusoe* of 1719 was arguably the first English novel. He also produced works on economics, history, and travel. Satire reached a high point in the early eighteenth century with Alexander Pope's *Dunciad* (1719–28) and Jonathan Swift's *Gulliver's Travels* (1726). Romances and adventure stories became popular. The romantic novel was first mastered by Samuel Richardson in *Pamela* (1740) and *Clarissa* (1747). Feelings and emotions were unbuttoned. The famous critic Dr. Samuel Johnson (1709–84) noted: "Why, Sir, if you were to read Richardson for the story, your impatience would be so much fretted that you'd hang yourself. But you must read him for the sentiment."[30] A glittering train of novelists followed, ranging from Henry Fielding (1707–54) to Jane Austen (1775–1817). The Scottish Enlightenment and the work of many great masters of new methods of analysis, such as Edward Gibbon's (1737–94) historical treatises, added luster to British literature. Shakespeare was revived and raised into place as a great national icon. Theater life was vibrant in London. Italian opera, combining music and drama, became popular.

The arts embraced the values of neoclassicism: balance, order, restraint, and complex simplicity. In architecture the work of the Scottish Adam family contributed magnificent public buildings and country houses. The rural "seats" of magnates were rebuilt, embellished, and surrounded by enlarged parks. Palaces such as Stowe, Blenheim, and Wentworth Woodhouse were comparable in grandeur and size to medieval cathedrals. The austere magnificence of the **earl** of Leicester's Holkham Hall required 2.7 million bricks and more than 30 years to build (Figure 1.5).

Culture became more rational and organized. For example, Dr. Johnson's dictionary of the English language was completed in 1755 and the British Museum opened in 1759. The Royal Academy, sponsored by George III in 1768, gave shelter and order to the world of painters and sculptors. William Hogarth (1697–1764) was the great artist of the first half of the century, and Sir Joshua Reynolds (1723–92) reigned supreme in the second half. The master of music was the German immigrant Georg Friedrich Handel (1685–1759). His oratorio, *Messiah*, is one of the masterpieces of the eighteenth century and was immediately recognized as such. He was much patronized by the royal family. His coronation anthem "Zadock the Priest," which raises the hair on the back of one's neck, has been played at every coronation since George II's in 1727.[31]

The propertied classes suffered fewer and fewer moral and cultural restraints on enjoying themselves. Fashion ruled; prostitution and gambling flourished. In London great pleasure gardens at Vauxhall and Ranelagh emerged and prospered in the 1740s and 1750s. Assemblies for socializing and dancing were more personal and private and could be managed by local groups. They arose all over the country and new rooms were built to accommodate them. In some places both tradesmen and gentry intermixed.

Figure 1.5   Holkham Hall, Norfolk, built 1734–60

Gin for the lower orders and wine and brandy for the rich flowed copiously. Accounts of heroic drinking bouts flavor contemporary diaries, although bottles were smaller in size than now. One elderly country gentleman advised another who was ailing: "It is not fit for you and me at our Time of Life to drink Water. ... I beseech you not to drink less than a Bottle of good Claret [red wine] in condition after your Dinner and a Pint of old Port [fortified wine] after your Supper."[32]

Time for leisure was generally sparse among the lower orders, although the rhythm of the agricultural year produced periods of comparative ease. Religious traditions and celebrations of national events such as the birth of a prince or great naval victory provided even the poor with occasions to enjoy themselves. Local traditions, often involving unique rituals or games, some of which survive down to the present day, added spice to rural life. Horse racing attracted the elite, but ordinary people also liked a day out at the racetrack. Some of the most famous stakes races were established in the later eighteenth century, including the Derby in 1780.

Among the elite organized fox **hunting** was of growing significance, indeed on its way to becoming the quintessential activity enjoyed by English and Irish (but not Scottish) landed society. Fox hunting is exhilarating and dangerous, "the image of war without its guilt and only five and twenty per cent of the danger."[33] It served well as training for soldiers. Young members of the elite were brought up to take risks, endure pain, and compete. Another preoccupation of landed society was shooting, a sport that became more enjoyable as technology improved. In 1671 a Game Act limited the shooting or capture of wild game to gentlemen with substantial property. These rules remained in place until the nineteenth century. However, much poaching went on. The poor resented the Game Laws, and they became a serious source of social tension in the countryside.

Travel was easier to undertake as roads improved. Spas, seaside resorts, and watering places thrived. Though fashion and wealth contributed to this trend, it was the need to escape clogged and smoke-filled London and the inability of eighteenth-century medicine to cure most ailments that stimulated the growth of Bath and its many lesser satellites. Later, the fashionable Gothic revival that harkened back to more romantic and effusive ideas and feelings promoted journeys to remote and previously unvisited areas. Tourists sought scenes that were totally different from ordinary life – wild and simple.

Science

Britain had produced outstanding scientists in the seventeenth century such as Francis Bacon, Robert Boyle, and Robert Hooke. Two English geniuses bestrode the world of Western thought. The philosopher John Locke (1632–1704) put emphasis on the importance of acquired knowledge rather than innate ideas and applied this concept to all aspects of life and government. The physicist and mathematician Sir Isaac Newton (1642–1727) was among the first uncommon commoners to be buried with special ceremony in Westminster Abbey, the coronation church. In the early eighteenth century the astronomer Edmond Halley (1656–1742) made a series of remarkable predictions concerning heavenly events, most famously about the return of the comet that now bears his name.

These men were working out the achievements of the previous century or often were cataloguers and describers of stars or plants. The age was more curious about the mechanisms of the natural world than previous times. More and more people could appreciate the achievements of science and technology and the usefulness of empirical research. Many of the achievements of the eighteenth century were practical and commercial, from charting oceans to making steam engines. The importance of seagoing trade was emphasized by the passage by Parliament in 1714 of an Act establishing a prize of £20,000 for discovering a reliable means of measuring longitude. The adoption of the **Gregorian calendar** was enacted in 1752. Gradually science moved away from mathematics, physics, and astronomy in the direction of the study of the organic world.

Superstition was increasingly condemned. Laws against witchcraft were repealed. The last conviction took place in 1712, though old-fashioned beliefs lingered among the lower orders later than this. Even educated people did not always find it easy to draw a clear line between the rational and irrational. Newton took alchemy seriously.

When the parson James Woodforde (1740–1803), who had been educated at Oxford, suffered from a swelled and inflamed eyelid, he recorded in his diary the following nostrum. "As it is commonly said that the Eye-lid being rubbed by the tail of a black Cat would do it much good if not entirely cure it, and having a black Cat, a little before dinner I made a trial of it, and very soon after dinner I found my Eye-lid much abated of the swelling and almost free from Pain … Any other Cats Tail may have the above effect in all probability – but I did my Eye-lid with my own black Tom Cat's Tail."[34]

Medical care was administered, mostly to those who could afford the fees, by a phalanx of apothecaries, barber-surgeons, midwives, and university-trained physicians, none of whom knew much about how to assist patients other than through what they learned by experience. Much was known about anatomy but nothing about microbes and viruses. The great breakthrough of the eighteenth century was inoculation for smallpox. In 1717 **Lady** Mary Wortley Montagu (1689–1762), wife of the British ambassador to the Ottoman Empire, brought the knowledge of Turkish practice in combating the disease back to England. In 1721 some criminals condemned to death were used as guinea pigs for the new treatment, and the **Princess of Wales** lent her support. The father of King George III was among the first to be inoculated, but it was not until the 1760s that the practice became widespread.

Otherwise diagnoses were based on a false science of "humors" that involved "bleeding," "cupping," and other gruesome treatments. Surgery was performed, and people survived amputations, removal of gallstones, and even the removal of cataracts, but because sterilization of instruments was not practiced patients often perished due to infection. Many also died of shock caused by pain that could only be partially relieved by copious imbibing of brandy or gin before the cutting began. Hospitals existed, but were dangerous places to stay. If you did not die of your original complaint, there was a good chance you would catch something else that was fatal. Mental illness was not understood. "Bedlam" (officially the "Bethlehem") hospital in London was really a prison where the public could come and gaze openly at the demented in their chains.

An English Empire?

On the Continent conglomerates of nations held together by dynastic bonds have been called by historians "composite states." The British archipelago and its dependencies in 1714 were at best an unequal partnership. The English watched their neighbors and colonies with a distrustful eye, anxious about internal and external security. Enemies abroad sought to exploit rebellion and the Scots and Irish were only too happy to oblige. Highlanders still looked to their clan chiefs for leadership, not the alien German king. The colonies were seen as valuable but vulnerable.

The English regarded the Welsh as generally cooperative. Concern about the Scots and Irish was more serious. From time to time virulent anti-Scottish feeling erupted.

Hostility towards the Irish was more akin to racism. Unreasoning hatred of Roman Catholicism contributed greatly to this, as did Irish nationalists looking to France and Spain for succor. The Irish were seen as superstitious, untrustworthy, lazy, and liable to breed like rabbits. Yet, talented Scots and non-Catholic Irishmen who moved to London could rise high in English society.

Many people in Scotland, Ireland, and Wales did not speak English. Ireland retained a separate Parliament and Scotland an independent Kirk and legal system. Both Dublin and Edinburgh, capital cities that were genuinely independent cultural, social, and political centers, had begun to undergo extraordinary transformations in design. The New Town in Edinburgh, as a single ensemble of buildings, has few equals in grandeur anywhere in Europe, while the new squares, rows of houses, and public buildings in Dublin asserted a strong sense of separate identity.

The aristocracies were superficially becoming more alike, but this was patina and not at the native cores. Most historians too readily assume the idea of a merger of elites at the top of society.[35] Homogenization did not take place quickly. Diverse interests remained a powerful prophylactic to inclusion. Alternating belief in their "British" identity and fear of betrayal left the Irish Ascendancy in a kind of love–hate relationship with their English counterparts. The great Scottish magnate, the third duke of Argyll (1682–1761), was a strong supporter of the Hanoverian dynasty and delivered Scots MPs as **lobby**-fodder to the London government, but he demanded in exchange that Scottish interests be looked after and promoted. Highland chiefs were still going to the Tower of London to be beheaded for treason as late as 1747. Eighteenth-century Scottish MPs saw themselves more as a representatives of their families than of their constituencies.[36]

Wales continued with its own language and culture even though it was closely connected with England and possessed no separate capital city, parliament, or laws. The Welsh elite had strengthened their position by leading their country into the world of English speech and accepting the Reformation, but this advantage began to dissipate as they detached themselves from the values and language of the national culture in the eighteenth and nineteenth centuries. Some continued to speak Welsh but education and marriage became increasingly an English experience for the aristocracy and gentry. The growing strengths of **Nonconformist** religion created a wide gulf of misconception and ultimately made communication between the elite and the people difficult.

In the seventeenth century Scotland had already been limited in its independence. Foreign policy had been directed from London since 1603, often pursued exclusively in England's interest. The nation was virtually bankrupted by a hare-brained scheme of colonial development in Panama. After the Union of 1707 all existing Scots laws remained in force. The legal system and Kirk were held sacred. The country retained its own banking system. The common Scots dialect was gradually converging with English, though pronunciation to this day remains distinctive. Gaelic survived in the north and west while poets of the south such as the great Robert Burns (1759–96) still wrote in the Scots vernacular. The division and mistrust between Highland and Lowland Scots remained significant throughout the eighteenth century. Unlike in

Ireland all of the chief posts in the Kirk and state remained in the hands of natives. On the other hand, Scotland was allocated fewer seats in the Westminster Parliament than their proportion of the British population justified. In addition, from 1711 until 1782 the House of Lords excluded Scottish peers who also held English or British titles from taking their seats. This act of discrimination was deeply resented.

Ireland was even more distinct an entity than Scotland. The majority of its population remained Catholic and many were Gaelic speakers. The kingdom was connected to England by the rule of a lord lieutenant who became known as the "**viceroy**" (almost always an English grandee) and the appointment of Englishmen to high positions in the established Church and civil administration. The Ascendancy elite still gathered each year for the meeting of Parliament in Dublin and owned large urban residences there. Even after the Union in 1801 the viceroy's court held balls and functions attended by many aristocrats, who formed a separate social circle from the London elite.

The Protestant Ascendancy was an odd mixture of cruelty, venality, prejudice, courage, and culture. They built some of the most lovely buildings of the eighteenth century and seemed to have an instinctive taste for the chastely beautiful. The Irish playwright J. M. Synge called them a "high-spirited and highly-cultivated aristocracy."[37] Others, less friendly, saw them as oppressors. The alien elite monopolized law, politics, and society. Like slave owners in the American South, even decent people were so deeply immersed in evil that many could not see it. They were, however, conscious of living on top of an active volcano. The harsh penal laws against the Catholic majority were deeply resented by the victims. Reliance on force to protect their property made the elite more militaristic, more rigid, and less confident than the Scots and English landowners. They were also conscious that their Parliament wore an English collar and leash. Edith Johnston-Liik observes: "The confident British MPs looked pragmatically to the future, while their Irish counterparts remained shackled by the past."[38]

The Irish elite had a tendency to "go native," at least to the extent of adopting a distinct Irish identity along with their British one. They increasingly thought of themselves as "Irish patriots." The earls of Kildare, who headed the premier aristocratic family in Ireland, "encouraged recollection of the past when they had ruled the kingdom and resisted meddlesome English politicians."[39]

Shared imperial interests did not produce identical aristocracies. Nor did the colonies in North America grow closer to the motherland as the century progressed. Part of the problem was that they were filling with African slaves, Huguenot refugees, Dutchmen, Swedes, and Germans. The British and Irish inhabitants had often fled the archipelago for reasons that did not endear it to them such as religious persecution and economic deprivation. Convicts "transported" there may have held no fond memories. The colonists were left much to their own devices. The isometric threat of the French to the north in Canada helped keep them securely under England's wing. These peoples did not develop a sense of Britishness of the kind that emerged in the archipelago.

The ramshackle arrangements that held together the distant empire and the near abroad of Ireland and Scotland suggest serious and fundamental weaknesses. Britain was a disunited kingdom with dangling dependencies and a ruling elite opposed to strong standing armies. Opportunities abounded for invasion forces to land on remote shores. The exiled royal Stuart family, with considerable claims to legitimacy and foreign support, was bent on overthrowing the "usurper" Hanoverians (see Chapter 2) and placing themselves back on the throne.

Integration and Stability

In 1714 the three kingdoms of England, Scotland, and Ireland and the principality of Wales were by no means welded together as a single unit. They preserved separate cultures and identities. The colonial populations overseas began to mature into unique societies with interests distinct from the mother country. Britain was like the "Tin Man" in the *Wizard of Oz*, with a new Hanoverian head bolted onto a clanking and squeaking English-Irish-Scottish body. What forces drew these disparate entities together? The requirements of the great century-long struggle with France for global mastery required Britain to maximize unity to achieve victory. Political and military integration was essential. The shared prejudice against, and later fear of, France among large segments of the population helped keep the Hanoverian head in place.

After the abolition of the Council of Wales in 1689 institutional harmony between England and the principality was achieved, and the end of the Edinburgh Parliament obliged the Scots to focus their political life at Westminster, tied by language, the Protestant religion, and a common commercial structure after 1707. Economic integration helped. The removal of all barriers to trade with England and the colonies was an enormous boon, as was the opportunity to link directly with the agricultural and industrial revolutions and be part of the empire with opportunities in military and commercial service.

The state was active in promoting the Irish economy, setting up the Linen Board in 1711, backing canal ventures and colliery schemes, and founding the Bank of Ireland in 1783. Immigration of Scots and Irish looking for opportunities began to lead to a sloshing around of populations in the isles, although relatively few English people moved to the other kingdoms. The Irish constituted the largest group of foreigners in England and Scotland. Many originally arrived as seasonal harvest workers. Their Catholic religion combined with a willingness to undercut prevailing wage rates, however, made them unpopular with English laborers.

Judged by the moral standards of the time, Britain was humane and just, and Ireland not worse off than many other eighteenth-century societies where alien elites lorded it over subject peoples. The ties holding British society together were strong. That strength ensured that the bubbling pot of innovation and change did not boil over. The social and economic systems were flexible but rested on a foundation of exceptional stability. This pattern of core continuity combined with dynamic change became the hallmark of modern British society.

Signs of a "British" identity or at least a sense that everyone was in the same boat together emerged, although this could be weak or even non-existent in remoter areas. Historical anniversaries and royal birthdays were celebrated widely. Efforts to create a patriotic spirit can be seen in the figure of John Bull (the equivalent of Uncle Sam), first drawn to represent a "British" persona in 1712. The Scot James Thomson's poem "Rule Britannia" was put to music around 1740.

> When Britain first at Heav'n's command
>   Arose from out the azure main*;
> This was the charter of the land.
>   And guardian angels sung this strain;
>
> Rule Britannia! Britannia, rule the waves:
>   Britons never will be slaves. (Chorus)
>
> The nations not so blest as thee,
>   Shall in their turns to tyrants fall;
> While thou shalt flourish great and free,
>   The dread and envy of them all.
>
> To thee belongs the rural reign;
>   Thy cities shall with commerce shine;
> All thine shall be the subject main*,
>   And every shore in circles thine.

(*ocean)

Despite corruption and elite control Parliament was willing to distribute the tax burden more rationally that any other country in Europe, and with its rollicking, public, and competitive electoral system achieved consensus on the big issues of war and peace, religion, and kingship. The royal house produced three reasonable kings who ruled in succession for over a century. They were not brilliant or flashy, they were sometimes stubborn and crazy, but British monarchs worked to achieve good government at low cost.

Chapter 2

A New Beginning, 1714–62

In England landowners stopped building castles once the Wars of the Roses (1455–85) were over, although having one handy turned out to be useful during the Civil Wars (1642–51). The last fortified house in Scotland was built in 1660. Most Irish mansions of the eighteenth century lacked barbicans and drawbridges, although strong shutters and heavy doors were still put to use when the Catholic peasantry grew restive. With a few exceptions the island of Great Britain has preserved civil order successfully since the mid-seventeenth century. This fortunate outcome was the result of flexible and resilient political institutions.

The Constitution

The constitution was a mixture of legislation passed by Parliament and agreed to by monarchs, along with conventions and traditions not all of which were written down. Parliament could switch royal families or dispossess small farmers with ruthless efficiency. However, in 1689 it had also enshrined ancient rights and established new ones which set Britain on an different course than its Continental neighbors. Theoretically, the new system could be swept away again, but underlying everything were assumptions about power and liberty shared by a wide spectrum of society. With some restrictions and exceptions, free speech, freedom of the press, trial by jury, an independent judiciary, taxation only with parliamentary consent, and an executive with limited powers made eighteenth-century Great Britain one of the freest societies in the world. Constitutional conventions were not always clearly established and sometimes much negotiation was necessary between various politicians and/or institutions to achieve a resolution of conflicts. Considerable head butting and horn locking took place from time to time.

Politics is about who gets what when, where, and how. The Glorious Revolution of 1688–9 was engineered by aristocrats who were set on attaining supreme power. They reshaped the institutions and laws to permit this, although only their own continuous effort and commitment of energy could make the system work. They were not guaranteed power; they held it only so long as they were successful in responding to and satisfying those elements in society that had the leverage to challenge them. The king remained a formidable force in eighteenth-century politics, and it was in alliance with him that the aristocracy secured its power.

The Monarchy

Key to the success of the Glorious Revolution of 1688 was the provision that the monarch must be Protestant like the majority of his or her subjects in Britain. The settlement was placed in jeopardy by the failure of Queen Anne, the last Protestant Stuart sovereign (see genealogical chart), to produce a child who survived to adulthood. Her personal tragedy led to national problems that would rumble on for decades after her death in 1714. The divine cord ordaining the royal succession had been decisively severed in 1688. Now the pieces were to be ritually burned in 1714. On the former date, the king and his heir had been deposed because of their religion, but there was uncertainty surrounding the latter's legitimacy, and his sister, who was next in line, was made queen. In 1714 54 heirs with better hereditary claims were leapfrogged in order to place a Protestant prince from a small German state, who spoke broken English, on the British throne.

King George I (1660–1727), who also continued to reign as "elector" of Hanover, a title of the Holy Roman Empire, became the first of his line resident in Britain. His hereditary credentials stretched back, through his mother, to a daughter of King James I (and VI of Scotland – see genealogical table). In accepting the throne the family agreed to a number of restrictions on royal authority. The vision of a more limited "constitutional" monarchy took root in a way that it had not during previous dynastic renovations of 1660 and 1689. The position was summarized in typical eighteenth-century prose when a prime minister wrote to George III: "The Parliament have altered their sentiments, and as their sentiments whether just or erroneous, must ultimately prevail, Your Majesty having persevered, as long as possible, in what you thought right, can lose no honour if you yield at length ... to the opinion and wishes of the **House of Commons**."[1] (See Figure 2.1 showing the structure of government.)

Nonetheless, the early Hanoverians were skilful enough politicians to fend off serious interference in foreign policy and other matters important to them. They still called elections, shut down sessions of Parliament, commanded the army, appointed and fired ministers, vetoed legislation (pre-emptively and in private – Queen Anne was the last monarch to cast a public veto after the fact), regulated the creation of peers, and gained their choices as bishops, judges, generals, and admirals. Members of the royal family held active senior commands in the British army and navy well into the twentieth century. If monarchs were adroit politicians, as the first three Hanoverians proved on occasion to be, they could change the course of national policy. Only at the tail end of the dynasty in the early nineteenth century, with the preoccupied George IV and inept William IV, did royal political power decline into intermittent influence.

Parliament

Parliament became indisputably supreme only after the Glorious Revolution, when it also began to meet regularly for the first time. Annual gatherings were called that lasted an average of 20 weeks. Along with the increased frequency and length of parliamentary sessions, the volume of legislation grew. The fulcrum of parliamentary power was control over annual appropriations for the military forces and payment of interest on the National Debt, money borrowed by the government, usually to conduct wars. Responsible payments made to creditors were vital to ensure access to future funding of national policy. The Triennial Act of 1694 limited the length of each

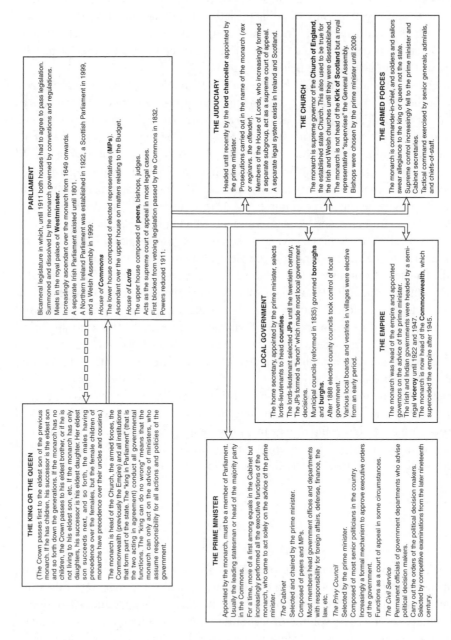

THE KING OR THE QUEEN

(The Crown passes first to the eldest son of the previous monarch. If he has children, his successor is the eldest son and so forth down the generations. If the monarch has no children, the Crown passes to his eldest brother, or if he is not living to his eldest son, etc. If the monarch has only daughters, his successor is his eldest daughter. Her eldest son succeeds next, and so forth, the males having precedence over the females, but the female children of monarchs have precedence over their uncles and cousins.)

The monarch is head of the Church, the armed forces, the Commonwealth (previously the Empire) and all institutions that form part of the state. The "king in Parliament" (that is the two acting in agreement) conduct all governmental functions. The "king can do no wrong" means that the monarch can only act on the advice of ministers, who assume responsibility for all actions and policies of the government.

PARLIAMENT

Bicameral legislature in which, until 1911 both houses had to agree to pass legislation.
Summoned and dissolved by the monarch governed by conventions and regulations.
Meets in the royal palace of **Westminster**.
Increasingly ascendant over the monarch from 1649 onwards.
A separate Irish Parliament existed until 1801.
A Northern Irish Parliament was established in 1922, a Scottish Parliament in 1999, and a Welsh Assembly in 1999.

House of Commons
The lower house composed of elected representatives (**MPs**).
Ascendant over the upper house on matters relating to the Budget.

House of Lords
The upper house composed of **peers**, bishops, judges.
Acts as the supreme court of appeal in most legal cases.
First blocked from vetoing legislation passed by the Commons in 1832.
Powers reduced 1911.

THE JUDICIARY

Headed until recently by the **lord chancellor** appointed by the prime minister.
Prosecutions carried out in the name of the monarch (*rex* or *regina* vs. *the offender*).
Members of the House of Lords, who increasingly formed a separate subgroup, act as a supreme court of appeal.
A separate legal system exists in Ireland and Scotland.

THE CHURCH

The monarch is supreme governor of the **Church of England**, the established state Church. This also used to be true for the Irish and Welsh churches until they were disestablished.
The monarch is not head of the **Kirk of Scotland** but a royal representative "supervises" the General Assembly.
Bishops were chosen by the prime minister until 2008.

THE ARMED FORCES

The monarch is commander-in-chief, and soldiers and sailors swear allegiance to the king or queen not the state.
Supreme control increasingly fell to the prime minister and Cabinet secretaries.
Tactical command exercised by senior generals, admirals, and chiefs-of-staff.

THE PRIME MINISTER

Appointed by the monarch, must be a member of Parliament.
Usually the leading statesman or head of the majority party in the Commons.
For a time, more of a first among equals in the Cabinet but increasingly performed all the executive functions of the monarch, who came to act solely on the advice of the prime minister.

The Cabinet
Selected and chaired by the prime minister.
Composed of peers and MPs.
Most members head government offices and departments with responsibility for foreign affairs, defense, finance, the law, etc.

The Privy Council
Selected by the prime minister.
Composed of most senior politicians in the country.
Increasingly a formal mechanism to approve executive orders of the government.
Functions as a court of appeal in some circumstances.

The Civil Service
Permanent officials of government departments who advise political decision makers.
Carry out the orders of the political decision makers.
Selected by competitive examinations from the later nineteenth century.

LOCAL GOVERNMENT

The home secretary, appointed by the prime minister, selects lords-lieutenants to head **counties**.
The lords-lieutenant selected **JPs** until the twentieth century.
The JPs formed a "bench" which made most local government decisions.
Municipal councils (reformed in 1835) governed **boroughs** and **burghs**.
After 1888 elected county councils took control of local government.
Various local boards and vestries in villages were elective from an early period.

THE EMPIRE

The monarch was head of the empire and appointed governors on the advice of the prime minister.
The Irish and Indian governments were headed by a semi-regal **viceroy** until 1922 and 1947.
The monarch is now head of the **Commonwealth**, which superceded the empire after 1945.

Figure 2.1 The structure of government

Parliament to three years. In the wake of the traumas of the seventeenth century it was believed frequent elections would guarantee honest debate and representative government. The system came to be seen as costly, time-consuming, and divisive, so a corrective Septennial Act was passed in 1716, which made it easier for the dominant party to stay in power longer by extending the period between elections to seven years.

Parliament was bicameral. The upper chamber, known as the House of Lords, was composed of bishops and a small number of great landowners (called peers) who sat by right of inheritance, occasionally augmented by the promotion of outstanding diplomats, generals, and ministers, which brought men of great ability to its deliberations. Judges were recruited to compose a panel that served as the final court of appeal in the legal system. Increasingly the Lords encompassed most of the richest men in the kingdom. Gaining a title was often made easier by acquiring control over the election of members of the House of Commons, the lower chamber of Parliament that numbered 558. Of these, 489 were from English constituencies and the remainder Scottish and Welsh. The lower house had established the sole right to initiate legislation that required expenditure of money. This gradually gave it ascendancy over the upper chamber. However, the Lords could block important legislation and continued to do so into the twentieth century. Monarchs, whose wishes were generally deferred to by the peers on important occasions, had a readily available brake to apply to the forward motion of government unless a powerful prime minister with a secure majority in the Commons demanded submission, a very rare event.

Gaining entrance to the Commons was not guaranteed by some law of inexorable inheritance as was admission to the Lords. A conscious effort had to be made, and in the eighteenth century this was neither cheap nor easy. Aristocrats who wanted to win a contested election in a prestigious constituency had to be prepared to spend on a grand scale, not just on bribery and entertaining voters, but also on the philanthropy and favors necessary to win friends and influence people year after year over decades and even centuries while a family represented a county or borough. Except in the case of a few absurd constituencies with hardly any voters at all, no seat was absolutely safe, and many slipped from the grasp of inattentive families. Riding around a large county during a preliminary canvass to call individually on prospective voters was arduous, boring, and time consuming. In the final days of polling (in contested elections it could take up to two weeks to cast all the votes) candidates were expected to deliver coherent speeches. Crowds rewarded inadequate performances by assault with dead cats, swung overhead by the tail to gain acceleration.

This electoral process had a number of important consequences. First, it meant that MPs had to mix with a wide social range of people. Even dukes sat around in taverns drinking with all sorts of men to help secure the election of a son or brother. Second, successful candidates had to pay attention to and tend the interest of various groups in the constituency. For example, an MP from Northamptonshire, where footwear was a major product, needed to know a lot about the shoe industry, work to stave off excise increases on leather proposed by governments desperate for new revenues, and help resolve labor troubles between workers and employers. Third, participation in electoral politics required drive and ambition. Members of the elite were bred to compete. The membership of the Commons, while oligarchic in nature, was filled with men of ability.

Of course, monarchs and their ministers strove to put as many MPs in their pockets as possible. Appointment to offices in their gift helped gain leverage in both houses of Parliament. In the Lords new peers could be created and compliant bishops appointed. Yet the corps of royal supporters never gave the government an unchallengeable dominance. Once a peer was created, he could not be unmade, and he or his successors might very well have independent views that were not subject to control. Queen Anne was the last monarch to create a block of peers purely for the purpose of gaining her way in the House of Lords. The threat of such action was to be mooted several times at critical junctures in the nineteenth and twentieth centuries but never actually implemented. As the size of the peerage increased, the number of new titles necessary to win by this means became so large that it would have destroyed the social exclusivity of the order. This was a "nuclear option." Monarchs were increasingly obliged to shape ministries tied to the support of Parliament.

Outward signs in the political system could be deceptive. Attendance in both houses was spotty, the turnout of voters could be low, and campaigns in many constituencies were not fought down to the poll. Governments did not change as a result of general elections. The absence of an open contest in a constituency, however, did not mean lack of conflict. Elections were often determined by private pressure applied by each side. Candidates who judged their loss at the polls likely withdrew or did not even put their name in nomination in order to avoid the expense of the campaign and the humiliation of defeat. Politics in provincial towns could be vibrant where members of the middling and upper orders worked out compromises and fought for influence often in the presence of an active and sometimes belligerent crowd in the streets (Figure 2.2). The party composition of the Commons could shift after an election.

In the counties only property-owning adult males could vote. In the boroughs a variety of franchises were based on wealth and status. In a few constituencies something close to universal male suffrage existed, but in most the electorate was confined to prosperous townsmen or in the "pocket boroughs" to the henchmen and creatures of large landlords. Over a third of boroughs had fewer than 100 voters. The total number of English and Welsh voters stood at somewhere between 300,000 and 500,000 in 1700. About one-fifth to one-quarter of adult males enjoyed the franchise, although the size of the electorate failed to keep pace with population increase during the first half of the eighteenth century. Nonetheless, recent research has demonstrated the substantial impact of non-voters on the English electoral system exercised through a variety of channels. The system was more open than was once thought.[2]

The Scottish electoral system was far more restrictive. In 1708 little more than 3,000 voters were qualified to elect the 45 MPs sent to Westminster, which rose to about 4,200 a century later. Scottish government under the Hanoverians was essentially about patronage. The great masters in extracting respect for Scottish interests and delivering votes in Westminster under the first two Georges were the second and third dukes of Argyll and their associates. The Argyll supremacy was succeeded by other managers including Henry Dundas (1742–1811), eventually Lord Melville,

Figure 2.2   A victory parade after a parliamentary election. The system encouraged mass participation even by those who did not cast a ballot. *Chairing the Member* by William Hogarth, 1754

who was both king of patronage in Scotland and a formidable politician in London. He passed on the role to his son Robert. As sleazy as all this sounds, Bruce Lenman argues: "It was no despotism. Rather it was an enlightened manipulation of the existing system to facilitate Scottish participation in the advantages of an incorporating union, while still upholding that distinct Scottish identity which nobody denied that the first two **Viscounts** Melville and the Argylls always showed."[3]

The Irish Parliament that met in Dublin survived until 1800. Its upper chamber was largely a rubber stamp. Furthermore, no Irish legislation could be enacted without prior English consent. The Dublin legislature could only pass or reject bills, not amend them. In 1720 a Declaratory Act asserted the superiority of legislation passed by the Westminster Parliament over laws enacted by its junior partner and declared that the British House of Lords was the final court for appeals, not the Irish one.

The Irish House of Commons was elected exclusively by a group of Protestants who numbered between 3,000 and 5,000, a tiny fraction of the minority privileged order. Knocktopher had one qualified voter in 1783. Usually, local powerbrokers, called "undertakers," delivered a majority of MPs compliant to the wishes of the English government in exchange for a say in policy making and patronage. Viscount Townshend (1724–1807), appointed lord lieutenant in 1767, was commissioned to counter the power of the undertakers and establish a ruling party dependent upon the **Crown**. He found this could be achieved only by recourse to the patronage system he had been sent to stem and took to drink.[4] The Irish representative system has been the subject of much tongue-clucking among historians. The bewigged mafia of Dublin are seen as irredeemably oligarchic. J. H. Plumb's judgment that Ireland's Parliament "was utterly servile" is a typical specimen of a widely held view.[5] In 1783 peers and large landowners returned over two-thirds of MPs. Yet, as in England, Irish representatives did have to show responsiveness to the electorate, and some constituencies were comparatively large and produced vigorous contests.

As the eighteenth century progressed the British House of Commons relaxed its policies on permitting journalists into the public gallery. Both London and provincial newspapers devoted increasing column inches to reporting debates, often half or more of the space not given to advertising. This omnipresence of Parliament in the newspapers was testimony to the seriousness with which its deliberations were held. In the depths of the age of patronage, Parliament, both Commons and Lords, was seen as the council of the nation. Many people came to hope that it would more accurately reflect public opinion.

The aristocracy defined their interests broadly and made available to many elements in society the opportunity to gain economic advantage. The landed elite was distrustful of kings and ministers with too much power concentrated in their hands or interference by central authority in local affairs. This, along with the intense public scrutiny imposed by Parliament, helped to keep government cheap and efficient. Furthermore, only men with administrative powers of the highest order could win respect from MPs and peers.

The Fiscal-Military State

Why did Britain rise to the rank of the dominant world power during the eighteenth century? The answer lies in its aptitude in fighting successful wars. One should never underestimate, of course, the capacity of its enemies to overreach and make unforced errors. Louis XIV and Napoleon were megalomaniacs who contributed to their own failures. However, the emergence of a ministerial system that gradually produced two innovations contributed to effective government. First, the **Cabinet**, a collection of senior politicians who acted increasingly as a solid phalanx, reduced the chances of the king making serious mistakes. Though "Cabinet responsibility" did not emerge until later, it became harder for the king to cherry-pick his senior officials, isolate them, and play them off against each other to gain his own ends. Second, from the 1720s one man, the first lord of the Treasury, usually took the lead in shaping the structure of the administration and persuading the king to adopt its policies. The office of prime minister was still in its infancy, but it gave more cohesion to government than had existed before.

Force of arms and commercial capitalism were at the heart of a winning strategy. Going against the grain of their instincts, MPs funded an increasingly large and professional army and navy who accomplished the heavy lifting of conquest and security. Brilliant commanders were raised to stardom; ruthless punishment was meted out for defeat. One aristocratic admiral was executed on his quarterdeck for being overly cautious while the son of a **marquess** died in prison after being court-martialed for making snide remarks about his commanding officer.

To pay for the increasingly large armies and navies necessitated by the nearly constant state of warfare in the eighteenth century, a revolution in state finance was required. The costs of keeping armies in the field and building a strong navy were high. The military consumed 61 to 71 percent of all government expenditure between 1702 and 1783. For more than half the years between 1713 and 1785 payments on the National Debt absorbed more than 40 percent of all revenue. This was a greater burden of debt than that which provoked the revolutionary crisis in France in 1789.[6]

Thanks to an expanding economy Britain was able to pay for its own troops and subsidize the armies of European allies both through current taxation and borrowing. Taxes went up, and the debt went through the roof. Yet neither development seriously impeded continued economic growth, and the policy paid vast dividends in the long term by sweeping France aside and opening the globe to British trade and empire. The unintended consequence of war was a rapid growth in the size and power of the state as the bureaucracy necessary to collect taxes and expend newly acquired revenues lifted the government to unprecedented levels of activity and authority.

John Brewer has made a convincing case that the hidden sinews of the British fiscal administrative management of government and taxation were the secret of the superpower status. The British could raise funds better and faster than anyone else and they could spend more efficiently. Much of the structure of what has been termed the "fiscal-military state" was already in place by 1714. After 1688 Britain's bureaucracy grew as never before; new boards and offices were created. By the 1720s approximately 12,000 permanent employees worked in civil government. This rose to 16,000 by 1760s. The greatest increases were in the departments of revenue, the fiscal bureaucracy. Customs employees almost doubled between 1690 and 1782, while Excise officers quadrupled.[7]

On the whole, the expanded government was remarkably free from corruption compared to its European counterparts. Modern career ladders for advancement of Excise officers motivated the ambitious. Internal monitoring systems maintained probity. Many people worried about the 10,000 or 20,000 eyes prying into every nook and cranny of the land. The legal expert William Blackstone (1723–80) expressed alarm: "the rigour and arbitrary proceedings of excise laws seem hardly compatible with the temper of a free nation."[8] Yet the system was so successful that when further reforms were proposed in the 1780s, they achieved only modest advances. The triumph of this revolution in government was to provide the state with a secure and predictable income at low cost.

Map 2.1   Europe in the Eighteenth Century

The British government survived on mixed financial streams derived from a land tax, tariffs on imports, and excise taxes on items such as tea, sugar, beer, salt, and liquor along with increasingly large long-term loans. The burden was not equally distributed. Landowners escaped relatively lightly as taxation shifted to excise duties on consumption. However, the rich paid more heavily for wax candles and imported wine while the poor managed by using inexpensive tallow candles and drinking domestic beer. Taxes on necessities rose less than those on other commodities. The elite understood that a tolerable distribution of the burdens was important. During the war years (1799–1816), when expenditure rose to unprecedented levels, the ruling class picked up the main burden by enacting an unprecedented income tax. The Irish elite, on the other hand, successfully resisted efforts by the English to have their taxes spent outside Ireland. Nor would they establish a land tax, which meant they were more lightly burdened than their peers in Britain.

King George I (1714–27)

Queen Anne died on August 1, 1714. Her successor, George I, was a rather dull but not stupid monarch. His heart lay in Hanover, and he spent as much time there as he could. He spoke some English and was able to converse readily with most of his ministers in French, which was his own first language. A flock of German courtiers and advisors wafted behind him on his travels. After 1717 he rarely attended the meetings of the Privy Council, an ancient element in the constitution that consisted of most of the monarch's chief advisors, and he never met with the entire Cabinet, a gathering of ministers that gradually took shape under the leadership of the king's great servant, Sir Robert Walpole (1676–1745 – see the appendix for a list of prime ministers). None of the Hanoverians ever established a court of the kind to be seen in France, Austria, or Russia. With the sole exception of George IV (1820–30) they lacked style and preferred simplicity. Unintentionally, this contributed to the gradual diminishment of royal authority.

George I's chief interest was foreign policy, about which he was well informed and contemplated from a Continental perspective (see Map 2.1). At age 54 he was an experienced war leader who had participated in his first military campaign against France at age 15. Three of his brothers were killed in battle. He was anxious to uphold his adopted country's interests, but also he attended to the security of Hanover, always vulnerable to invasion by the armies of the surrounding great powers in a way that Britain was not. The death of the king of France in 1715 removed the chief disturber of the peace in Europe. George I was fortunate to reign during a relatively quiet period before Britain again faced the financial stresses and physical threats of war.

Late in her reign Queen Anne's ministers were Tories, sympathetic to legitimate royal succession, religious orthodoxy, and royal authority. The 1715 rebellion in favor of the Stuarts, precipitated by George I's accession, confirmed the new king's darkest thoughts about this party. He had been keeping an eye on British politics ever since the Hanoverian succession was ordained in 1701, and he was convinced that the safety of his dynasty rested with the Whigs, who strongly supported the Protestant cause and became the party of government for the next two generations. The Whigs won large electoral majorities in the House of Commons so that the monarch and Parliament stayed in reasonable harmony much of the time.

The **Jacobites** could not abide a "false" king on the throne. They were left with the following options: conceal their true feelings and participate openly in politics as Tories, cease to play a role in conventional politics, go into exile, or rebel. Hence we remain uncertain as to their number and importance. Because their goal was to overthrow the existing constitution, it is hard to know how many of them there were operating within it. Exposure meant disgrace, degradation, or death. Even during outbreaks of rebellion in 1715 many English Jacobites remained hidden, waiting to see how viable the military campaign would be before showing their true colors. Some English politicians may have kept up Jacobite links as an insurance policy in case the Hanoverians faltered. They were strongest in Ireland after 1688, and grew stronger in Scotland and England due to the unhappiness with the policies of William III and Anne. Some were romantics and others pragmatic. Perhaps as much as a quarter of the English gentry had Jacobite sympathies, but some did little more than commemorate "the little gentleman in black velvet" (a mole that was said to have dug the hole that tripped William III's horse and precipitated the king's death in 1702) or pass their glasses raised in toasts to the exiled **Pretenders** across a bowl of water to signify sympathy with the Stuart dynasty. Others were ready to kill for their rightful king.

The first Jacobite rising, which began in Scotland in 1715, was slow to get under way, poorly led, and fizzled out like a defective firework. The second duke of Argyll, chief of the powerful clan Campbell, and other key Scottish magnates stayed loyal. The earl of Mar was able to raise a considerable Jacobite following. However, the French had been obliged to withdraw their support for the Stuarts at the Treaty of Utrecht (1713). No foreign army accompanied the returning Pretender. The English government took sensible precautionary actions. Only a small sympathetic reaction in the north of England accompanied the Scottish rebellion. A Stuart army reached Preston in Lancashire on November 10 but met determined resistance from government forces and surrendered. In Scotland an indecisive battle was fought at Sherrifmuir, but support melted away and "James III" (1688–1766) fled back to the Continent in February 1716.

Although some confiscation of property and executions took place, including two Scottish lords beheaded at the Tower of London, retribution was as modest as the rising itself. A few of the most prominent English Tories such as Viscount Bolingbroke fled to France. From 1717 the Pretender became a distant and discredited figure living far away in Rome. An army was sent to open up the Highlands with roads and to tame the inhabitants. Attempts were made to stimulate the Scottish economy. Scots joined the army and diplomatic service and Scots MPs and peers became part of London life. The ruling dynasty's future was by no means secured in 1715, and the danger of another rising lingered, but what threat there was helped bind forces who might otherwise have stayed aloof to the new order.

A new treaty with France was concluded in November 1716. This was a diplomatic revolution brought about by the conjunction of the Hanoverian succession, the Jacobite threat, and the emergence of a new regime in France after the death of the warmongering Louis XIV. George I negotiated the alliance from his palace in Hanover. Several Whigs, including Robert Walpole, the leading minister in the Commons who had made his reputation with proposals for a "sinking fund," a mechanism to repay war debts, and his relative and ally, Viscount Townshend (1674–1738), resigned from the government because of their disagreement with the terms. Initially, the new outsiders went into opposition. This division in the Whig Party was eventually resolved, but in the short term it would have momentous consequences.

About this time the emergence of a rival political center surrounding the king's eldest son, the Prince of Wales (1683–1760), heralded a new development – the "heir apparent syndrome." Despite the fierce party battles since 1688, it was still considered somewhat unseemly directly to operate a systematic opposition to the king's ministers, and hence rallying around the heir removed the tincture of disloyalty to the Crown. From this time forward until the death of George III in 1820 ambitious politicians excluded from office tended to gather under the patronage of the king's eldest son. Relations between generations in the Hanoverian family were notoriously bad. The prince and his popular wife, Caroline (1683–1737), made great efforts to provide a focal point of society especially during his father's frequent absences abroad. In an age when life expectancy was considerably less than now, the son of a king near 60 could reasonably expect to come to the throne sooner rather than later. Politicians intimate with the heir could count on rapid promotion once his accession occurred.

In July 1718 Britain entered a quadruple alliance with Holland, France, and the Habsburg Emperor. Soon they were at war with Spain. In 1719 Madrid sent two invasion forces towards the archipelago, but neither met with any success, and war was soon over. The geopolitical position of Britain was strong. The exhaustion suffered by the Dutch during the wars of the second half of the seventeenth century had removed as a rival the nation most like Britain itself in its dynamism and "modern" commercial life. A critical early triumph for the British was the acquisition of a permanent naval base at the point where the Atlantic and Mediterranean meet. Charles II had tried to establish a colony at Tangier on the nearby north African coast but failed. England lacked the military resources to hold out against hostile local rulers. But the seizure of the gargantuan rock of Gibraltar at the southern tip of Spain in 1704 gave Britain such a huge advantage in the deployment of its naval forces that it has retained the harbor and fortress there ever since. British naval mastery of the Atlantic became increasingly dominant. The British fleet was outnumbered by the French as late as 1700, but never again (see Table 2.1).

The dissident Whigs continued to ally with the Tories in thwarting government measures, celebrating their victories at the house of the Prince of Wales. Facing further defeats, the king reconciled with his son in 1720, and the Whig divide

Table 2.1   Size of navies 1689–1815[9]

	1689	1739	1779	1790	1815
		Ships of the line (large battleships)			
Britain	100	124	90	195	214
France	120	50	63	81	80
Spain	–	34	48	72	25

disappeared. Robert Walpole emerged as the fixer. He gave his support to measures close to the royal heart, enabling their passage. He played a leading role in reuniting the royal family through the agency of Princess Caroline. The Whigs in power recognized that they were badly in need of his skills at financial management.

The absence of Walpole and Townshend from government between 1717 and 1720 meant that they were unconnected with the political chicanery that led to the madness of the South Sea Bubble, a scheme to privatize the National Debt. A get-rich-quick mania had quickly emerged, followed by a disastrous bursting of the balloon. Solving the crisis of the public finances consequent upon the collapse of the Bubble was beyond the capacity of those in office. From outside the Cabinet Walpole devised a means of rescuing the situation by relieving the South Sea Company of some of its obligations and involving the Bank of England and the East India Company in the management of the Debt. This had the effect of re-establishing confidence in public finances, and Walpole's presence in government came to reassure **City** interests. In 1721 a ministry headed by Walpole and Townshend was appointed. The general election of March 1722 demonstrated the continued support of the political nation for the Whigs.

J. H. Plumb argued that party conflict diminished under George I, which brought political stability.[10] Other historians point to the resolution of religious and constitutional issues lingering from the seventeenth century. Rising living standards may have brought civil peace. Walpole provided cheap and stable government. He successfully kept Toryism and the Jacobite cause connected in the public mind, most notably in 1722 following the discovery of a treasonous plot. He possessed enormous talent as a politician and genuinely feared for the security of the dynasty. Walpole survived ferocious attacks by his rivals and Tory satirists and mounted formidable counter-attacks of his own (Figure 2.3). The give and take of this battle helped to awaken in the nation a fresh level of political attention to parliamentary affairs.

George I established a new dynasty that would last for the next 300 years. It was by no means a foregone conclusion that he could pull this off, and some doubts lingered in his son's reign. The king set precedents that became established practice. Largely unintentionally, George I voluntarily surrendered some of the monarchy's power by ruling with a prime minister and spending much of his time abroad. He made little deliberate attempt to win the hearts and minds of his people since he could rely on his religion to keep them loyal. It is important to note, however, that

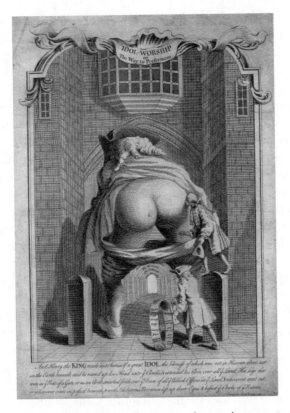

Figure 2.3 Here it is suggested that the only way to gain appointment to government office was by kissing Walpole's backside: "Robert Walpole Straddling the Gates of the Treasury," 1740

he chose not to assert the more absolute style of power he enjoyed in Germany. He made a conscious choice to play by the constitutional rules and work in harmony with Parliament.

King George II (1727–60)

On June 11, 1727 George I died while on a visit to Hanover. Walpole was able to ingratiate himself with the new king partly through his close friendship with the queen and partly by providing a larger income for his new boss. Walpole's command in Parliament was indispensable, and George II had the wit to grasp this. The administration continued in office. The Old Pretender, isolated in Rome and without the support of the French, was unable to act. The general election necessitated by the succession of the crown gave Walpole a massive majority in the Commons as he moved towards peace with Spain. He then set about shrinking spending and giving tax relief to the landed classes. Among other things he revived excise taxes and raided the sinking fund he had been instrumental in founding in 1716. The acceptance of the National Debt as an ongoing burden that was to be managed rather than all paid back as soon as possible marked a fundamental change in British fiscal policy. Now the big question was simply how to reduce the rate of interest on what were perpetual loans, all of this made possible by an economy that continued to prosper.

Walpole was forced by popular reaction against his proposals to withdraw the new excise rises in 1733 and fight an acrimonious election in 1734. The Tories did a bit better than usual, and in open constituencies where men of modest resources could vote the government suffered heavy reverses. Though he lasted in office for much of another decade, he was often on the defensive and relied on the king's influence to survive (see Biography 2.1).

German-born George II was, despite his quarrels with his father, a chip off the same block. He loved Hanover just as much and spent long periods abroad, to the dismay of his ministers. He also fancied himself a soldier. He was unloved by his subjects and frequently ridiculed. As usual, a rival political center sprang up around his eldest son, Frederick, Prince of Wales (1707–51). The two courts growled at each other perpetually.

Walpole's pacific foreign policy paid great dividends, but was harder to sustain as the 1730s progressed. Relations with Spain deteriorated in 1738. When a ship's captain appeared in the Commons holding an ear purportedly chopped off by wicked Iberians, patriotic fury knew no bounds (or skepticism). Walpole was unable to resist the drive to war. Campaigns to capture Cuba and Panama proved costly failures. Walpole's authority in the Commons began to evaporate. The duke of Argyll, so influential in managing Scottish elections, openly defected in 1740, taking his train of MPs with him. The death of the prime minister's most influential ally at court, Queen Caroline, was also damaging, while the Prince of Wales waged all-out war against him.

Walpole's fall from power in February 1742 was precipitated by the general election in 1741. His masterful parliamentary performances in the new house, speeches as good as any that he had ever given, were not enough to save him as his majorities sank to a few votes. He left the Commons for the Lords in full retreat. He could no longer guarantee passage of legislation, and he resigned in February 1742. Some of his opponents desired old-fashioned vengeance, but he was allowed to retire rather than be stripped of his assets, imprisoned, or executed. A corner had been turned; politics had become "modern," at least in that respect.

The War of the Austrian Succession (1740–8) drew Britain and France into conflict, a pattern repeated with frequency in the years ahead. The king was interested in protecting Hanover and committed troops to Continental warfare for the first time since the reign of Queen Anne. The war was surprisingly popular. Henry Carey's "God Save the King" was first publicly performed in 1745, and later became the national anthem, sung, rather disconcertingly to Americans, to the tune of "My Country 'Tis of Thee." It is an assertion of patriotism, not enthusiasm for George II, who was personally unpopular.

Biography 2.1

Sir Robert Walpole
1676–1745

Robert Walpole, first Earl of Orford, is said to be the first British "prime minister" in the modern sense. He served longer than any other man in that position, from 1722 to 1742. Often depicted as corrupt, avaricious, and unprincipled, he was one of the most brilliant politicians ever to hold the post. He was cautious, phlegmatic, pragmatic, down-to-earth, unaggressive, and fond of the finer things in life.

Walpole was born into an old and prominent gentry family. He combined vaunting ambition with a genuine desire for peace and prosperity for his country. Walpole profited greatly from manipulation of the perquisites of office. His regime became known as the "Robinocracy" (implying robbery of government funds). He was also referred to as "The Skreenmaster," referring to his role in screening or whitewashing those guilty of corruption. Walpole used traditional methods – patronage and bribery – and more innovative subsidies to newspapers and journalists to secure his rule. His own lavish lifestyle and huge building campaign at Houghton, where he erected one of the most elegant and beautiful country houses of the eighteenth century, led people to believe he had his hand in the till.

Walpole studied politics minutely. He understood the reasons for political instability in the post-1689 era and by careful planning and adaptation reversed the trend. Above all, he grasped and accepted that the House of Commons had become the pre-eminent element in the constitution, and that attaining and maintaining a majority there was crucial to successful government. Thus he refused promotion to the House of Lords until the end of his career. He also played the pedals and stops of the patronage system with the genius of a great organist. He used the Lords as a means of resisting measures that he did not want to appear to be blocking in the Commons. Yet for all his brilliance in managing Parliament, he was even better at managing kings, especially the stubborn George II whose feet seemed sometimes to be set in concrete.

God save our noble King,
God save great George our King,
God save the King!
Send him victorious,
Happy and glorious,

Long to reign over us;
God save the King!
O Lord our God arise,

Scatter his enemies,
And make them fall;
Confound their politicks,
Frustrate their knavish tricks,
On him our hopes are fixed,
God save us all!

Though a victor on the battlefield, the king could not keep an administration of his personal favorites in place. The great orator William Pitt the Elder (1708–78 – his son is known as William Pitt the Younger) made his reputation by denouncing the special attention paid the "despicable electorate" of Hanover.

George was forced to turn to a new ministry built on a "broad bottom" foundation under Henry Pelham (1695–1754) that even included a Tory. The king was furious, but all he could do was block the addition of William Pitt, because of his offensive speeches. The coalition failed to flourish. The king had no intention of cooperating. Whig ministers read him long lectures on the nature of his duties. "In response he offered robust abuse."[11] The "old corps," as the Pelhamite Whigs were called, gained in popularity from the capture of Cape Breton, the key to French Canada, in June 1745. The victory overseas could be portrayed as a concession to the "blue water" strategy advocated by the Tories, although in fact the foreign policy of the "broad bottom" was little different than the king's desire to intervene in the fighting on the Continent. There an army under the command of George II's son, the duke of Cumberland (1721–65), aged 25, lost to the French in a crushing defeat at Fontenoy.

The situation was transformed within a few weeks of Fontenoy, when the Young Pretender, the Catholic Prince Charles Edward Stuart, known as Bonnie Prince Charlie (1720–88), landed in the Scottish Highlands in July 1745. The clans rose. Edinburgh surrendered to the rebels. The royal army in Scotland was put to flight. By December the Jacobite forces had crossed the border and reached Derby, 130 miles from London. The ministry was in some disarray. A run on the Bank of England was said to have been stopped only by paying all demands in small coins. Expected support from English Jacobites did not emerge, however, and the prince decided to retreat. Cumberland was sent to Scotland, where he butchered the Highlanders at the Battle of Culloden near Inverness on April 16, 1746. He then commenced a campaign to repress further outbreaks of violence against his family's regime, prompted at least in part by the mustering of some clansmen even after the defeat at Culloden. The west of Scotland saw pillage and burnings supervised by the army and supported by the navy. More military roads were built and Highland dress proscribed. The legal authority of landowners in private courts was abolished. The clans would never rise again.

No Scottish magnate joined the rebellion. Fewer clans were "out" in 1745 than in 1715. Many of the leaders were bankrupt or in financial trouble. Yet the situation would have been grave if the French had invaded. The government did not have enough troops to cope with two attacks at the same time. The "Forty-five" was unquestionably a civil war in Scotland, though not in England, but it never shook the foundations of the state. The still formidable clergy of the Scottish Kirk assailed a Stuart restoration. The romanticism of modern Scottish nationalism has cast a gauze of sugar candy over a weak cause. As the Scottish historian T. M. Devine points out: "The heartlands of Presbyterian Scotland greeted the news from Culloden with relief and celebration."[12]

About 120 rebels were executed, a third of them deserters from the British army. Sir Robert Strange was saved, when soldiers conducted a search of his house, by his wife hiding him under her hooped skirt. Three Scots peers were beheaded, although the earl of Cromarty was reprieved in part due to the remarkable efforts of his wife, who was reported to have feigned pregnancy ("brought to bed of a cushion," gossips said), despite the fact that when captured he had been found in the arms of another lady.[13] Jacobitism imploded; the Hanoverians showed steadiness of purpose and judicious choice in their advisors. They even produced a prince of their own skilled enough in generalship to defeat his cousin on the battlefield. His victory inspired Handel's great march, "Hail, the conqu'ring hero comes!" (1747). The bonnie prince fled into permanent exile and alcoholism disguised as a servant.

Disgusted by his interference with their policies, the ministry resigned and dared the king to form an administration of his own. He tried and failed. The "old corps" showed extraordinary unity. George II was cornered and he capitulated. He reinstated the government and, feet dragging, appointed William Pitt to the post of paymaster-general. This moody and erratic man of "wild ambition" consolidated his reputation for personal integrity by ostentatiously refusing the huge profits customarily enjoyed by the occupants of his new office, but he exercised little influence over policy, which was controlled for the next decade by the bland but hardworking Henry Pelham, partnered by his brother, the neurotic Thomas Pelham-Holles, first duke of Newcastle (1693–1768). The latter joined the Cabinet in 1724 and would hold high office for over 40 years, the greatest worrywart ever to become prime minister. Walpole's son, Horace, called him a "ridiculous creature" "who never lets slip an opportunity of being absurd."[14] He lacked insight, imagination, and decisiveness, which he made up for by obsessive labor and occasional shrewdness. The Pelhams formed an able team, with Henry Pelham providing steady, competent leadership and the duke, a detail man, masterfully deploying the intricate patronage machine to support his brother's policies.

Party differences gradually moderated after 1745 as the Jacobite threat receded into the far distance. Unexpectedly, the Prince of Wales died, which left dissident politicians with no safe harbor. The new heir, aged 13, could not be expected to mount a full-scale opposition to his grandfather's ministers. Moreover, Pelham was less of a lightning rod than Walpole. He was the only premier in the eighteenth century to leave office by death rather than dismissal or resignation. Pelham came close to blending the various Whig factions into a smoothly operating unit.

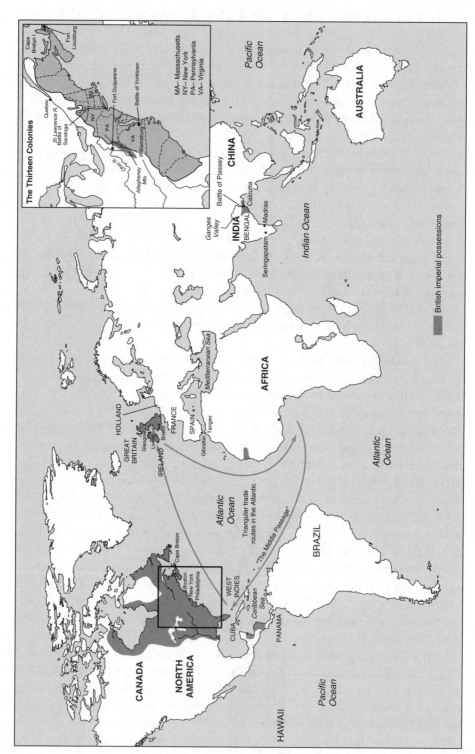

Map 2.2 Britain and the World in the Eighteenth Century

The first priority of the ministry was to bring to a close the expensive and unsatisfactory war that had resulted in a stalemate. The French elephant prevailed on land and the British whale at sea. Pelham negotiated the peace of Aix-la-Chapelle (1748). He then turned his attention to reducing military costs and the interest on the National Debt. This belt-tightening could only last for a few years, however. France and Britain were both ambitious and distrustful. Territorial interests in the Caribbean, India, and North America led to renewed conflict. Both sides sought allies on the Continent to help leverage their power elsewhere.

The Pelham administration also produced some important domestic reforms to regulate crime, marriage, consumption of gin, and to remove some restrictions on Jews, although the latter had to be rescinded in the face of public outrage. On Pelham's death in 1754 the duke succeeded him as prime minister. However, he could not lead the Commons from the benches of the House of Lords. Yet he was too jealous of the ablest men in the lower house, Henry Fox (1705–74) and Pitt, to concede the premiership to either of them. Disputes over strategy let the government fall into disarray. In 1755–6 Pitt proposed himself to the Commons in a series of brilliant speeches as a "patriot leader" who had the true interest of the nation at heart. He rose above party to appeal to the Tories and achieved widespread support outside the walls of Parliament as well as inside the chamber. His call also appealed to the young heir to the throne.

War came in 1756 with a successful French expedition against the strategically important western Mediterranean island of Minorca where Britain had maintained a naval base since 1708. In India a major East India Company outpost at Calcutta surrendered to the forces of a native prince. The Seven Years War (1756–63 – known to the colonists as the French and Indian War) was a struggle for global supremacy between Britain and France, which decided the fate of North America and Asia. It also heralded an almost perpetual state of war fought between France and Britain around the planet that lasted until 1815 (see Map 2.2).

Pitt briefly forced himself on the king and became a senior minister in an administration headed by the fourth duke of Devonshire (1720–64). George II could not bear the situation for long and dismissal came swiftly in April 1757. But by this time Pitt's bellicose policies had made him a patriotic hero. In June he was back in office in a coalition with Newcastle as the dominant partner leading the "old corps." Considerable debate surrounds the degree to which Pitt's undoubted genius contributed to victory. Beyond his capacity to articulate a vision of national greatness it is hard to say what he actually achieved. The contribution of the king and Newcastle to war strategy is often underestimated. Moreover, Pitt's volatile nature and serious mental depressions made it hard for him to concentrate on the day-to-day decision making upon which winning the war depended. The French continued to contribute greatly to Britain's achievement by trying to win on land and sea at the same time. This overstretched their resources and left them vulnerable to defeat by Britain's allies on the Continent, while the Royal Navy enabled comparatively small British armies to achieve decisive victories elsewhere. Robert Clive's (1725–74) triumph over the Indian prince Siraj-ud-Daulah at the Battle of Plassey was achieved in 1757. In 1758 Jeffrey Amherst captured the great fortress at Louisburg commanding the mouth of the St. Lawrence River in North America, and Anglo-American forces successfully attacked Fort Duquesne, which controlled the Ohio River. Islands were seized in the Caribbean, and Quebec was conquered by General Wolfe (1727–59). At Minden in 1759 the British allies inflicted a humiliating defeat on the army of Louis XV. Decisive naval victories against the French fleet followed.

On George II's death in 1760 a contemporary observer, Elizabeth Monatgu, offered this assessment: "With him our laws and liberties were safe."[15] Like his father he chose to accept the restraints that had become fixed constitutional practice limiting his powers. He showed good judgment in the selection of ministers, steadiness of character, and was willing to play the political game to achieve his goals. If offended, he would give as good as he got. When he met with cooperation, he was willing to compromise.

King George III (1760–1820)

George III came to the throne in October 1760, aged 22 (Figure 2.4). He was the first British-born monarch since Queen Anne and proud of it. Hanover receded to secondary status. His reign was to be revolutionary in many ways. The Tories were welcomed at court and many Whigs were not. No serious politician now contemplated any challenge to his dynastic right to rule, and parties could no longer credibly form along those lines. Future fights would center on the exercise of the royal prerogative.

As a young prince, George had been convinced by his tutor, the Scots nobleman, the third earl of Bute (1713–92), that the monarchy was unconstitutionally held in the thrall of the "old corps" aristocrats and that it was his duty to set it free. The king was determined to reign without submitting to party, which he thought of as malicious "factions." The magnates who had dominated government for more than half a century not unnaturally took this amiss. Some selfishly and some sincerely saw the king's naïve attempt to change the government as a plot to impose royal absolutism organized by sinister forces "behind the curtain." Bute had little experience with politics and had none of the attributes of a statesman. His family name was Stuart, and he was reported to be having an affair with the king's mother. This controversy, in which the principal actors passed each other in a fog of misunderstanding, threw politics into years of upheaval and crisis. Eight ministries followed one another between 1757 and 1770 with the rapidity of *coups* in a banana republic.

No one now seriously believes that the inexperienced and blundering young George III intended a royal revolution or that Bute slept with the dowager Princess of Wales and wanted to establish Scottish tyranny in England. That a sincere belief in a malign royal conspiracy existed is far harder to disprove. Just as

Figure 2.4 *King George III* by J. C. Stadler, 1812

the American colonists became increasingly paranoid about British intentions to extinguish liberty in the 1770s, so Whiggery was reshaped and energized by a belief in the menace of resurgent royalism. When George III began to dismiss from government magnates such as the duke of Devonshire, he aroused a deeply imbedded distrust of monarchical authority among men who thirsted for news of the ancestors who had died on the scaffold at the hands of a tyrannous king in the 1680s.

Not all of the trouble was the king's fault. Popular opinion had begun to play a more continuous role in shaping political process. In part this was due to the demagoguery of Pitt and partly the continuing rise in the importance of the press. Voter turnout increased from the 1740s onwards and the number of contested elections rose after 1761. Those without the right to vote petitioned Parliament and rioted.

Thus in an atmosphere roiling with controversy the Seven Years War was ended by the new Bute ministry in 1763 with Newcastle now in full opposition. Parliament supported the treaty concluded at Paris because of the heavy cost of the war in taxes and trade. Britain retained Canada, but returned other captured territories to France and Spain. Pitt fulminated without immediate effect.

———————————   **The Enlightenment**   ———————————

Changing understandings of the world helped Britain become more dynamic and powerful but, unlike in France, without experiencing destabilization. The legacy of the scientific thinkers of the sixteenth and seventeenth centuries was to place emphasis on rational thought. This process unleashed a European-wide phenomenon called the Enlightenment. Central to the movement was a desire to use scientific discoveries to achieve progress through human reason. Tolerance and advancement based on merit not hereditary privilege were other important values. On the Continent the writers who developed and disseminated the ideas associated with the movement were often unwittingly or deliberately hostile to the established order and particularly the Church. The theorists and savants in Britain, on the other hand, worked largely within the constraints of established religion, custom, and tradition. Some prominent thinkers were themselves clergymen. Aristocratic patronage also gave the movement a conservative cast. The middle classes embraced the Enlightenment without seeing the need for revolutionary change. Limited monarchy, parliamentary government, religious toleration, and free speech allowed the Enlightenment to flourish; at the same time the structure of British society did not offer the target of a dark and irrational regime unworthy of preservation. British *philosophes* and their followers saw routes to improvement; the basic system was worth the effort to change, not to destroy.

Scottish Calvinism embraced the notion that God was rational and therefore nature must be too. The system of university professorships at Edinburgh and Glasgow encouraged high-quality research. The prevailing party in the General Assembly encouraged moderation and toleration. The leading lights of the Scottish Enlightenment broke new ground in the study of society and the natural world. They became sociologists, historians, and philosophers of the first rank. Adam Smith's (1723–90) *Wealth of Nations* (1776) is still the foundation text of modern economics. James Hutton's *The Theory of the Earth* (1795) helped launch the science of geology. David Hume's work had a profound impact on religion and politics. Sir John Sinclair's massive *Statistical Account of Scotland* published in the 1790s provided a minute analysis of the nation's social structure.

A great British hero of the second half of the eighteenth century was James Cook (1728–79), whose epic voyages around the world beginning in 1768 opened up whole new sectors of human knowledge. He began life in humble circumstances, the son of a laborer. The navy promoted him to higher and higher ranks, and he gained the fame accorded in the later twentieth century to astronauts. Like his modern counterparts, assertion of national pride and power was an additional fillip to scientific achievement. Cook's unveiling of hitherto unknown Polynesian cultures lent credence to the idea of "noble savages." A new sensibility emerged based on expanded knowledge of remote societies that had never encountered "civilization" as Europeans defined it. All was not quite as it first appeared, however. Cook was killed in an affray with natives in Hawaii.

The greater understanding of human behavior that emerged out of the Enlightenment stimulated important advances in education and respect for human diversity. Society became more humane. This spirit ranged from increasing concern about corporal punishment, campaigns to save small children from abuse as chimney sweeps, better living conditions for the insane, attempts to curb brutal treatment of animals, and ultimately control over the hours and safety of workers. The most notable movement of this kind to arise in Britain towards the end of the eighteenth century was stimulated by a combination of religious and humanitarian thought. It became the first organized mass political campaign in history. The Committee for the Abolition of the Slave Trade was founded in 1787, although men such as Granville Sharp (1735–1813), both a devout Anglican and impassioned believer in the Enlightenment value of human liberty, had begun to agitate earlier. The former slave Olaudah Equiano (*c.*1745–97) was also a notable figure in the campaign.[16] An early victory was Lord Mansfield's ruling in 1772 that a slave, James Somerset, could not be held in that condition any longer while on English soil. Though the verdict was narrowly defined, it was quickly taken both popularly and eventually by the legal establishment itself to mean that slavery could not exist in England.[17]

William Wilberforce (1759–1833) carried the abolitionist standard in Parliament, but the drive for change came above all from the young Thomas Clarkson (1760–1846), who had a roadside epiphany in 1785 while coming down from Cambridge to London after winning a university prize for an essay against the trade. That experience led him to devote the rest of his life to ending slavery. The involvement of the "land of liberty," as the British liked to think of their country, in the slave trade inevitably caused tension and anxiety. Many people were aware of the paradox. Like the Germans during the Nazi era, most ordinary people simply averted their gaze from something that seemed distant from ordinary life. Increasingly, however, educated, thoughtful, and powerful men and women expressed unease, then denounced the practice and rallied to the cause. A combination of Enlightenment ideas about natural rights and ardent Evangelical (see below) humanitarian zeal created a powerful new political force to British life. The ardent abolitionist and industrialist Josiah Wedgwood (1730–95) fired thousands of porcelain seals for the campaign showing a kneeling African with the legend: "Am I Not a Man and a Brother?" Even the deep-dyed Tory Dr. Samuel Johnson gave a famous toast: "Here's to the next insurrection of the Negroes in the West Indies!"[18]

Religious Resurgence

Intellectual ferment was to be found in many areas of British life. Two great movements erupted within the Anglican establishment during the mid-eighteenth century. These were the Evangelical revival and Wesleyan Methodism. The former movement, which can be traced to the 1720s and became widely influential from the 1770s, never created a unified organization. People embraced it in a variety of ways as its influence spread over a lengthy period. Leaders such as Charles Simeon (1759–1836) at Cambridge and the "Clapham Sect" in south London later aroused much attention and interest.

Evangelicals emphasized piety, simple living, spreading the Gospel, and good works. "Evangelical theology rests on a profound apprehension of the contrary states: of Nature and of Grace; one meriting eternal wrath, the other intended for eternal happiness."[19] To glorify God one must take action in this world. The establishment of Sunday schools was one of the most important outcomes of their work. Eventually, the movement penetrated deeply into aristocratic society. Along with the Whigs and Quakers, Evangelicals became the heart and soul of the anti-slavery campaign. John Newton (1725–1807), a slave ship captain who wrote the celebrated hymn, "Amazing Grace" (*c.*1772), was turned into a campaigner against the trade by his Evangelical conversion.[20]

> Amazing Grace! How sweet the sound
> That saved a wretch like me!
> I once was lost, but now am found;
> Was blind, but now can see.
>
> 'Twas grace that taught my heart to fear,
> And grace my fears relieved;
> How precious did that grace appear
> The hour I first believed!

Evangelicals could be sanctimonious, narrow in vision, and obsessively self-disciplined. Among people with generous hearts and sophisticated minds, however, the movement led to many humane and liberal acts.

Methodism was part of a great awakening. The name comes from the biblical "method" by which followers lived their lives. It arose out of a group of pious students at Oxford in the 1730s that included the Wesley brothers and George Whitefield (1714–70). In 1738 John Wesley (1703–91) experienced a profound religious conversion. He was both an organizational genius and a charismatic preacher who spent a lifetime on horseback converting souls all over the British Isles. Whitefield was equally electrifying and drew as many as 50,000 at a time to hear his sermons. Charles Wesley (1707–88) composed many stirring hymns. Whitefield leaned towards Calvinism and ultimately split with the Methodists, but the Wesleys were determined to stay within the established tradition, which the movement did until after John's death. His work was complemented by a "connexion" established by the Countess of Huntingdon (see Biography 2.2) and a strong awakening in Wales.

Many churchmen disliked the revivalist style and unworldly simplicity of Methodism and tried to suppress it. Emotional outbursts and female preachers also provoked antagonism. By the 1750s the Methodists themselves were debating whether to secede from the Anglican communion and ordain their own ministers and bishops. Most Methodists came from the lower orders: artisans, textile workers, coalminers, and the like. They were against drink, gambling, and most forms of fun. E. P. Thompson

---

Biography 2.2

Selina, Countess of Huntingdon
1707–91

Selina Shirley was the daughter of the second Earl Ferrers and in 1728 married Theophilus Hastings, ninth earl of Huntingdon. She had seven children in the next 10 years. In 1739 she joined with a dozen other aristocratic ladies who opposed the Walpole ministry's foreign policy in noisily disrupting a debate in the House of Lords, shouting down the speakers with whom they disagreed. In that same year she embraced Methodism and initiated a relationship with the Wesley brothers.

Although she preached privately to groups of friends, she did not approve of women delivering sermons in public. However, she spent the rest of her life developing a strictly Calvinist church that became known as the Countess of Huntingdon's Connexion. It still has 23 chapels and a theological college in operation today.

Lady Huntingdon broke with the Wesleys over the doctrine of predestination, and George Whitefield served for a time as her private chaplain. She was also a source of continual irritation to the established Church. As a woman, she had to work through remote control but was able to launch her church successfully against powerful opposition in a strongly paternalist culture. A number of important aristocratic families stood by her.

Lady Huntingdon's personality was not attractive. She was sour, rigid, obsessive about money, and paranoid. Her elder daughter found life with her mother "void of every thing agreeable."[22] Not all her fellow aristocrats were enthusiastic supporters. The duchess of Buckingham objected to the democratic nature of sin: "It is monstrous to be told you have a heart as sinful as the common wretches that crawl on the earth."[23]

---

described their chapels in the industrial districts as "great traps for the human psyche."[21] Wesley was politically conservative and had no notion of overthrowing the existing social or political order. He was on a mission from God against sin.

Dissenters appeared to be splitting into a number of camps. Anti-Trinitarian rationalists tended to decline in numbers and find support from well-to-do and intellectual followers while Methodists were more affected by the Evangelical movement and emotive in their worship. In Scotland the Kirk experienced a sympathetic revival of mystical rapture. From 1760 Dissenting aims subtly shifted from a defense of the toleration they enjoyed under the Revolution settlement to the destruction of the Church–State alliance.[24] Dissenters became and remained a chief source of criticism of the existing social and political order.

An Aristocratic Age?

Many historians have seen the emergence of modern Britain in terms of a rising bourgeoisie whose values and influence gradually began to drive the economic, social, and political agendas. So can the 1700s be called, as it often is, an "aristocratic century"? Paul Langford rejects term. "This mistakes appearance for reality." He argues that blue blood and rank counted for very little.[25] The British were fundamentally a commercial people. In his view the period witnessed a triumph of the values of the middling orders. The aristocracy was bowing to bourgeois interests and morality. Jonathan Clark, however, argues that the *ancien régime* was still intact, its progress hardly ruffled by the advent of economic, social, or political change.

Imposing overarching theses of the kind Langford and Clark have attempted is stimulating but can obscure a more complex reality. Clark is right to argue that part of the problem is that bourgeois scholars tend to assume aristocrats were anti-capitalist and exclusively paternalistic in their thinking. There is much truth in his caricature of those who have an unshakeable belief in "the middle class always rising, the aristocracy always about to disintegrate."[26] Many years ago Herbert Butterfield rightly brought attention to the simplistic view that Britain was on a triumphant march to democracy and liberal values, what he identified as the "Whig interpretation of history."[27] In fact Britain was more complicated, more regionally diverse, more riddled with exceptions and idiosyncrasies than single, overarching models can accommodate. Langford and others correctly argue that British society adopted a new conception of manners in social relations during the eighteenth century, what he has called the "progress of politeness," intended to control and discipline the spreading forces of prosperity.[28] This change affected tastes, fashion, consumption, and conceptions of respectability. Both the elite, who could absorb what was relevant and new, and the middle classes, who were interested in innovation and cultivation, shaped this evolution.

As British society worked its way towards a lasting political and religious compromise, while parties raged and Jacobites rebelled, the state found a means to work out differences without violence. The secret of success lay in a number of factors. These included the vigor and growth of the middle classes, and the willingness of the aristocracy to accommodate change. The openness of the landed elite to newcomers meant they could co-opt talent and diffuse pressure from those who aspired to rise from below. The new working relationship between Parliament and the monarchy came to be accepted as a foundation on which to build a stable and prosperous society.

Chapter 3

War and Revolution, 1763–1814

The end of the Seven Years War in 1763 proved but a short respite. Within little more than a decade, Britain would again be fighting overseas. These wars that lasted intermittently until 1815 were of enormous consequence for modern Western civilization and for the peoples of North America, Africa, and Asia, whose histories were radically transformed by independence or conquest. Not only did the American Revolution give birth to what became a vast new state, but also it embodied ideas that reverberated in Europe and ultimately around the world. The struggle with France echoed the dangers of the earlier conflict with Spain in the sixteenth century, in which the very existence of a distinctive way of life in the archipelago seemed in danger. These wars were no minor skirmishes but became a struggle for ascendancy over the planet. By the second half of the eighteenth century Britain had become the most dynamic state in Europe. Its rulers understood this, and also that they could no longer think purely in terms of their immediate neighborhood and the Atlantic empire. As the duke of Newcastle put it: "Ministers in this country, where every part of the World affects us, in some way or another, should consider the *whole Globe*."[1]

Ministerial Instability

The earl of Bute's administration did not long survive the efforts to conclude peace. A combination of anti-Scottish feeling, distrust of the king's intentions, and dissatisfaction over foreign policy, all amplified by increased press coverage, brought him down. Much of the criticism was mean-spirited and savage. The earl was a classic case of a cook who could not stand the heat in the kitchen. As the king gained in maturity, he came to rely less on Bute's advice, although their enemies did not – or chose not to – notice.

On Bute's resignation in 1763 the king turned to George Grenville (1712–70), an English aristocrat, as his new prime minister. Grave in manner and cautious in policy, the head of the administration turned out to be obsessed with cheap government and reining in the National Debt, which made him popular with the independent country gentlemen. Unfortunately, Grenville possessed a tin ear for politics, knowing neither how to propitiate the king nor listen to the grievances of the American colonists. Like the more advanced Whigs, led by the second marquess of Rockingham (1730–82), he assumed the king's increasing hostility was due to the influence of Bute "behind the curtain." This was wrong, and he was even more in error in his imperial policy.

Virtually all British politicians were concerned about the expense of maintaining the military security of North America. France had by no means been made incapable of waging future wars by her defeat in 1763, and many people correctly believed she would soon be seeking revenge. Westward expansion across the Alleghenies could also provoke new and expensive wars with the Indians. By the later stages of the Seven Years War over 30,000 British regular soldiers were serving in the Americas. The British taxpayer was paying 26 shillings a head for imperial defense as against one shilling a head paid by some of the colonists.[2] Not unreasonably, London felt that the costs of fighting had been inequitably distributed and that in the future the Americans would have to bear a greater part of the burden. Grenville proposed a Stamp Act in 1764 that was supposed not to raise huge sums of money but to make it clear that Parliament had the right to impose taxes in North America. These and associated measures unexpectedly provoked fierce resistance. In American eyes the colonists' connection with the home country was through the king and not the legislature. Furthermore, they rightly feared that London wanted to impose tighter restrictions on trade with other European colonies and strengthen the bonds of imperial control that appeared to be weakening. The politicians in London did not grasp how deeply the Americans distrusted their intentions and resented their methods. The attempt to erase any misunderstanding about the right of Parliament to legislate for North America by the passage of a Declaratory Act failed to dissolve the illusions of the colonists. They remained loyal to the king as "free" subjects, believing that his reign guaranteed the consent of the governed.

Grenville and the king had never hit it off. George complained that the prime minister lectured him unmercifully. "When he has wearied me for two hours," the king remarked, "he looks at his watch to see if he may not tire me an hour more."[3] In the spring of 1765 the king fell gravely ill with what we now believe to have been the first onset of the rare genetic disease porphyria that had the effect of making him appear mentally unstable. The uncontrolled language and actions of a man who lived by strict moral standards was a personal and national tragedy. The cruel and prolonged sieges recurred with increasing frequency over the course of his long reign and left him totally disabled for the last decade of his life. On this first occasion he recovered quickly, but it seemed prudent to provide for the possibility of permanent incapacitation. The king wished to determine the choice of his own replacement or "regent," but he was challenged by his ministers. Grenville had to go.

The Rage of Party?

The king's choice to head the new government in 1765 was the young Whig grandee, Lord Rockingham, who lived in the largest private dwelling in the British Isles, Wentworth Woodhouse in Yorkshire. His appointment raises the question of the extent to which parties based on ideological principles existed. There is no question that Rockingham thought so, and that his band of followers, at least in their own minds, represented a tradition that stretched back to the seventeenth-century martyrs executed by the Stuarts. The Whigs had fragmented in the years after 1750. No heir to the throne was available to give cover to the opposition from accusations of disloyalty. On the other hand, the disappearance of Jacobitism made it harder to brand opposition as treasonous.

For many decades the dominant view in the historical profession, as established by Lewis Namier, was that eighteenth-century politicians operated within the closed world of great estates and royal intrigue. He argued for "the purely personal character of politics. Parties, if ever mentioned, appear[ed] merely as combinations of men with no definite principles to bind or divide them."[4] That picture has been largely overturned for the period 1688 to 1750, but it is still persuasive to some historians as the image of mid to late Hanoverian practice. Well-developed structures of popular politics may have existed, it is argued, but they rarely exerted pressure on the elite, who were primarily interested in procuring jobs for family and friends and whose behavior was governed by considerations of pragmatism and custom rather than by concern for society or commitment to principle.[5] Experts stand in almost total disarray on the configuration of party politics between the 1770s and the 1810s.

The world of parties was certainly not the modern one of mass fund raising, annual conferences, and tightly organized discipline. The groupings were informal and blurred. The Whigs emerged as an aristocratic coterie with an extra-parliamentary following that attempted to block James II from succession to the throne between 1678 and 1681. A great cousinhood, which included descendants of Parliamentarians who had fought against Charles I during the Civil War of the mid-seventeenth century, kept alive for a century or more the memory of the executions of their ancestors in the 1680s. The Whig grandees were among the principal engineers of the Glorious Revolution in 1688–9. Today we tend to underestimate the feelings of men whose very identities were entwined with an "historic" conception of honor and pride in the deeds of their lineage. Even in the 1820s Whig noblemen could work themselves up into frenzies of antagonism against a moderate Tory ministry appointed by a king (George IV) who was more interested in the color of fabric to be used in his dining-room curtains than he was in parliamentary debates. The hereditary hatred of the Stuarts and a distrust of monarchical/ministerial tendencies towards absolutism, and especially standing armies, remained at the heart of Whiggism until the mid-nineteenth century. The Whigs argued for the supremacy of Parliament and strict limitation of the royal prerogative. A strand of **republicanism** also snaked its way through Whig thinking. They were anti-Catholic but sympathetic to Protestant Dissent and advocated religious toleration. Even though they came from landed families they supported the interests of the great merchants. They aspired to office both to implement what they considered vital objectives in foreign policy and to ensure that the kings they served remained constitutionally restrained in power. Men spoke, wrote, and believed in the "Whig cause." Division lists in the Commons show more consistency than those skeptical about the existence of party will allow and more followers of Rockingham than was once realized.

Defining and identifying a Tory Party is more difficult to do during the eighteenth century. The term derived from one used to denote Irish bandits in the seventeenth century and royalists in the 1650s. On balance Tories were more ready to defer to the king, more assiduous in defending established religion, and more rigid in asserting Westminster's prerogatives in the empire. Later, the French Revolution and all its works became anathema. Pitt the Younger (1759–1806) embraced many Whiggish causes such as Catholic Emancipation and abolition of the slave trade, but the majority of his followers upheld slavery and were for keeping the state's boot on the necks of Catholics.

Although there were Tory magnates, the strength of that party lay among the lesser elite. Many parishes had small gentry, who were kings in the locality but carried little weight outside it. They traveled less and tended to be more devout Anglicans and politically more old-fashioned than larger landowners. They rarely visited London, which they considered a sink of iniquity. It was said that "the shires were full of trout and Tories." The party placed faith in a strong monarchy, supported the supremacy of the state Church, favored a "blue water" foreign policy focused overseas and not on the Continent, and to a lesser or greater degree hankered for legitimacy in the royal succession. In 1714 the last principle became inoperable without embracing treason. They could not convince the first two Georges that they were genuinely loyal.

Aside from the complications introduced by concealed Jacobites, a secondary set of political dividers confused the picture of parties. The terms "court" and "country" were an undercurrent flowing crosswise against Whigs and Tories. When Whigs who lost "court" favor ended up sharing the opposition benches with "independent" country gentlemen fond of mantras about good government and criticizing official corruption, they merged, some have argued, into a "country" alliance. Detailed analysis of the division lists, however, reveals that in Parliament many "country" Whigs chose not to vote with the Tories. When it came to the point they simply could not trust them. Too many were thought to be tainted with Jacobitism. In elections it was also rare for electors to split their two votes between a Tory and a "country" Whig. There was a "country" platform, but there was no "country" party in the early Hanoverian period. During their lengthy proscription from office the Tories maintained a notable cohesion but they and opposition Whigs retained their separate identities, clubs, and whipping arrangements. Although occasionally they acted together, they were never able to sustain unity.[6]

Holding office for a long period without a serious chance of being toppled from power is always dangerous. Being permanently excluded from power also has a deleterious effect on oppositions. Party discipline and spirit atrophy. Leaders get lazy and careless. Although party labels were still in use in the late 1750s, Tory organization was ghostly by 1760 and the Whig Party was in an unhealthy state. Confusion and fragmentation reigned for a time. However, conventions had been established and ways of thinking became customary that led naturally to the continuation of party politics in the new framework. Party systems arose renewed, not only in England but also in Scotland and Ireland, which drew the three kingdoms together and shaped the practice of politics that emerged in the nineteenth century.

The marquess of Rockingham helped to rejuvenate and reinvent Whiggism. The grandees metamorphosed from upholders of the status quo during the first half of the century into advocates of change and reform in the second half. Under Rockingham, W. M. Elofson argues, the party "moved away from its earlier court Whig background just far enough to accept that the system could in fact be changed for the better."[7] The Whigs became slowly but surely the party of progress and improvement. Though not politically adept, Rockingham's conviction that only a united Whig Party stood between liberty and absolutism laid a strong foundation for unified political action. Three times, in 1766, 1767, and 1780, he refused to enter coalition ministries. More and more, however, the Whigs also became a permanent opposition.

Edmund Burke (1729–97), Rockingham's aide, articulated the substance of their concerns in his *Thoughts on the Causes of the Present Discontents* (1770). His support for the idea of party solidarity and Cabinet responsibility were crucial underpinnings to the restoration of a unified Whig tradition. Under their joint efforts the party arose refreshed. Like the Anglican Church, it had to be a big tent that held many differing personalities and points of view. It survived the deaths of powerful leaders such as Rockingham and Charles James Fox (1749–1806), which demonstrated that it was held together by more than personal loyalties. Whigs embraced the idea that education, toleration, and prosperity would help everyone become better people and better citizens. They came to conceive their duty as aristocrats as being, L. G. Mitchell has argued, "to lead the people in their aspirations, to make contact with them, and to give practicality to their hopes."[8]

The new administration was inexperienced, indeed out of its depth when confronted with the crisis brewing in North America where the Stamp Tax was being defied. Rockingham wished to be conciliatory and decided on repeal of the offending legislation. The king's doubts about the wisdom of this course were dismissed as part of Bute's lingering malign influence. The Commons gave the prime minister his first victory: 275 to 167 in favor of repeal.

Rockingham tried to bring the Elder Pitt, who was showing renewed signs of activity, into his orbit, but the great man was not likely to serve under so young and inexperienced a prime minister. Both had strong ambitions to lead and both could not squeeze through the door at the same time. Rockingham was obliged to resign. The king then embraced the man who had so deeply antagonized his grandfather with denunciations of Hanover. Pitt moved to the House of Lords as earl of Chatham, and became the chief minister under the nominal leadership of the third duke of Grafton. Some of the young Whigs who had followed Rockingham stayed in office, but the marquess went into full opposition, ably served by Burke's skills as ideologist. The Whig Party stayed independent and aloof from Pitt, who was not a party man. In the Lords Chatham found that he could not exercise his extraordinary powers effectively once he had been removed from the elective chamber. His mental state, never on a secure foundation, became rocky.

The **chancellor of the exchequer**, Charles Townshend (1725–67), became the leading figure in the government as Pitt's strength waned. He proposed taxing a number of commodities imported into the colonies from Britain: glass, lead, paint, paper, and tea. These were to be collected by a Board of Customs in Boston and used to pay official salaries in North America. The British believed that the colonists were opposed only to internal not external exactions. Thus a way had been found to keep Parliament's right to tax alive without arousing serious resistance. As usual, London misread the situation in Boston and Williamsburg. A non-importation campaign of

British goods was organized. The colonists were in no mood for any kind of interference with their liberties. Ministers and MPs could not grasp that many North Americans had decided that only directly elected assemblies held the legitimate right to taxation. Townshend died in 1767 and the unstable ministry collapsed, although Grafton managed to cobble together a new edition without including Pitt. During this interval an unprecedented political crisis burst on the scene in the unlikely character of John Wilkes (1727–97).

John Wilkes

Wilkes was a businessman who had entered the Commons under aristocratic patronage in 1757. He was a "patriot" supporter of Pitt, with deeply flawed personal habits and disreputable friends. His paper, *The North Briton*, heaped abuse on the Scotsman Bute as a threat to English liberty. Issue "Number 45" unwisely asserted George III's direct responsibility for what were seen as the failings of the Peace of Paris. Grenville had Wilkes committed to the Tower of London, the celebrated jail for traitors and state prisoners. In characteristic fashion Wilkes succeeded in challenging his arrest on constitutional grounds. The popular response in his favor rallied around the slogan, "Wilkes and Liberty!" A country shopkeeper, Thomas Turner (see Biography 1.1), a loyal supporter of the monarchy, nonetheless wrote of Wilkes's *North Briton* in July 1763: "I really think [it] breath[s] forth such a spirit of liberty that it is an extreme good paper."[9] Then in 1764 Wilkes threw away his victory by publishing obscene material in his *Essay on Women* and fled to France to escape a second bout of incarceration.

By returning from exile in 1768 Wilkes re-injected himself into the political consciousness of the nation, for his cause attracted support all over the country, not just in London, and from a population that went beyond those entitled to vote. He surrendered to the legal authorities, but also he stood for Parliament and was returned for the county in which London was situated. The majority of the electorate in that constituency was made up of small businessmen and even some laborers, as near to a genuine democracy as eighteenth-century England could manage. Troops fired on a crowd gathered outside the prison where Wilkes was held and killed seven protesters. The fight to gain the right to take his seat in the Commons included repeated re-elections, rejection of the choice of the voters by the Commons, and finally admission to the chamber. Church bells rang in village churches all day when Wilkes achieved a legal victory in November 1769. This was a new kind of politics.

The Wilkes affair drew attention to the failure of the system of government always adequately to reflect the will of the people, and to the selfishness of the narrow political nation. He identified his own cause with that of British liberty and appealed directly for popular support outside Parliament. His insistence on the liberties of the subject was heard across the Atlantic as well, although Wilkes had little interest in America. From 1769 he introduced the new theme of parliamentary reform. George III and Bute had blundered onto the political scene, wreaking havoc as they went. Wilkes was the immediate beneficiary of the concern evoked by their incompetence, although in the long run it would be the Whigs who were rejuvenated and would find their cause in parliamentary reform.

In the midst of the Wilkes controversy Rockingham, Grenville, and Chatham combined to overthrow Grafton. George III, however, had learned from his mistakes and matured into a more able politician than his early years and intransigence on American issues might lead a casual observer to believe. Several times during his reign he took bold but calculated risks, escaped Houdini-like from what appeared to be intractable situations, and settled on unlikely candidates for prime minister who turned out to be excellent choices. The first of these occasions took place in 1770. Muttering as he sometimes did that he would abdicate if he did not get his way, the king selected Lord North (1732–92) as prime minister. As heir to an earldom, North could take a seat in the Commons. Though by no means a flamboyant orator, he was an effective debater. Like Newcastle, he knew how to operate the delicate patronage machine and understood finance. Yet, his jovial manner and loyalty to the king helped draw independent country gentlemen and incipient Tories to the support of the government. His blindness to the root problem of the crisis brewing in America was shared by the vast majority of the British people. However, he tried a new tack. He abandoned most of the customs duties imposed by previous governments, although the Cabinet insisted that he retain a single charge on tea as a reminder of Westminster's sovereignty. That exception had unexpected and fatal consequences.

The American Revolution

Britain's empire had been acquired in a haphazard way. Only a few territories, such as Gibraltar, were seized for military and strategic reasons. Unlike the Spanish possessions, the colonies were not producers of precious metals or continental in scale. A diversity of religions were practiced. No centralized system of administration or fiscal management existed. The phrase "British Empire" does not seem to have been used until the 1720s and 1730s and only gained real significance during the later half of the century. It took the Seven Years War and expanding trade to bring the colonial possessions into the center of political life. Though the economic value of the Atlantic trade was thought to be significant, imperial mastery did not easily accord with the image Englishmen held of themselves as members of a free society. Government policy towards North America at mid-century was described as one of "salutary neglect." Nearly everyone except the royal governors on the spot, who struggled with the issue, missed the growth in self-confidence and assertion of authority of the colonial assemblies. This was now a formidable problem because the population of the empire in America had quadrupled since 1700.

Lord North's Tea Act of 1773 reduced the duties on tea re-exported from Britain to the colonies but did not eliminate them. Bostonians proved ungrateful for this generosity and dumped a shipment into the harbor in protest. From the British point of view, the Boston Tea Party was the last straw. King and ministers believed a firm response was required to deal with such unruly and childish behavior. Coercive legislation was enacted. Paranoia reached a new level in the colonies, heightened by the granting of rights to Catholics in the newly absorbed French colony of Quebec. To the largely Protestant population on the seaboard this seemed like pandering to popery and a threat to their own liberties. The colonists gradually grasped that George III was on the side of Parliament.

Biography 3.1

James Aitken
1752–77

James Aitken was born in Edinburgh in 1752, the eighth of 12 children whose father died when he was seven. After a spell in an orphanage he was apprenticed as a house painter. His ambition to become an army officer reached beyond the social boundaries of the day. After working in London, he took to robbing stagecoaches for a living. A narrow escape from the law precipitated his emigration to America, where he spent two years. Having found neither fame nor fortune, he returned to England and alternated painting houses with stealing from them. Aitken experienced an epiphany in 1776 during the outbreak of the American Revolution. Since the war depended on the success of the Royal Navy, he decided to burn down the major dockyards that sustained Britain's war-making machine. He was little more successful at this than he was at crime or painting. As an arsonist, he was at best unlucky, and after setting a few warehouses alight he was tracked down by the Admiralty and arrested. A brief trial brought him to the scaffold.

Even men of modest means and ability were able to drift around Britain and the empire with remarkable fluidity during the eighteenth century. Aitken does not seem to have had a strong Scottish identity, and his war work on behalf of the Americans was motivated more by a desire for celebrity than republican principles. Although the British state had little in the way of a formal police force, they were able to find and arrest the nascent terrorist without undue difficulty. The government was particularly adept at infiltrating double agents into revolutionary organizations during the eighteenth and nineteenth centuries, snuffing out trouble while it was still brewing. The evidence needed to convict the firebrand was provided by a jail-house snitch paid by the authorities. Aitken was ultimately successful in achieving personal fame, but the law got their man.[10]

Insurrection broke out in Massachusetts in April 1775. The publication of Tom Paine's (1737–1809) stirring polemic, *Common Sense*, in January 1776 mounted a powerful case for independence that helped crystallize many minds. After much discussion and political wrangling a Declaration of Independence followed in July 1776.

At first, British war-making met with success. Canada stayed loyal. General Washington, the commander of the rebel army, had never shown much ability as a military tactician and was a political appointment in any case. He blundered badly in New York. Boston was already under control and Philadelphia, the seat of Congress, was occupied. Yet these advantages were lost at the critical battle of Saratoga in 1777. The French were encouraged enough by this performance to take the Americans seriously as allies. Money, troops, and ships were directed into what the European powers saw as a rematch after the humiliation of 1763.

Many Britons, such as James Aitken (Biography 3.1), sympathized with the rebel cause. The Whig opposition in Parliament harried Lord North unmercifully. The duke of Richmond sailed his yacht through the fleet flying the American flag. His sister bought a bust of George Washington and displayed it at her country house. Charles James Fox wore the buff and blue colors of the American military uniform in the House of Commons. Privy councilors resorted to duels. In 1779 a reform movement was established by a leading Yorkshire landowner, Christopher Wyvill (1740–1822), denouncing corruption and inefficiency in government. This sparked the foundation of other committees or associations. The parliamentary session of 1780 was the worst North suffered. On April 6 John Dunning made his historic motion that the "influence of the crown had increased, is increasing and ought to be diminished," which was carried by 233 votes to 218 (see Figure 3.1).

The Rockingham Whigs, though anxious to jump aboard Wyvill's reform band-wagon, sought only to reduce the crown's influence through "economical reform," that is, cleaning up the patronage morass. They were alarmed by the radical nature of the support for the Association Movement in London under the leadership of Major John Cartwright (1740–1824), who first publicly proposed the vote for all males over the age of 18. The climax of the 1780 session was reached during the Gordon Riots, which scared everybody. A Roman Catholic Relief Bill had been pro-posed by a leading Whig, Sir George Savile. It was intended to remove legislation that discriminated against papists, none of which had been enforced in recent years, but which formed an embarrassment to the enlightened. The son of a Scottish duke, Lord George Gordon (1751–93), headed a Protestant Association in London that provoked attacks on prominent Catholics and their churches. Anarchy stalked the city. Breweries were broken into and prisoners freed from jails while mayhem exploded during the course of a chaotic week. Only the intervention of the king and 10,000 troops managed to restore order.

Soon after the riots North tentatively offered Rockingham a coalition, but the Whig terms included recognition of American independence, the enactment of "economi-cal reform," and the dismissal of leading ministers, which proved too much for George III. In September North called an election that sustained his majority in the Commons,

Figure 3.1 A stout, smiling John Bull (the British equivalent of "Uncle Sam") directs a blast from his backside towards a poster of King George III tacked to a wall. On the left, the head of Prime Minister William Pitt the Younger exclaims, "That is Treason Johnny." Depiction of politicians and the royal family was often disrespectful and even obscene. "Treason!!!" by Richard Newton, 1798

but Lord Cornwallis's (1738–1805) surrender at Yorktown in October 1781 was an enormous setback. The king wanted to go on fighting, but North understood what had happened. Henry Conway's motion in favor of ending the war made on February 27, 1782 was carried 234 to 215. The war had to end. North resigned. The king drew up another declaration abdicating the crown, although he did not in the end commit political hari-kari. It was a bitter pill to be obliged to turn to Lord Rockingham to form an administration in which Charles James Fox took the lead in the Commons.

Aftershocks

Ironically, the American Revolution turned out to be as much a long-term success for the home country as it was for the colonies. The valuable sugar islands in the

West Indies were retained, and the archipelago soon returned to trading again with the Americans without the expense of defending them. The war sent France into headlong bankruptcy. Yet, for a moment, the British political elite had lost its grip. Neither the commanders on the ground not the strategic managers in London fought a good war. It was less incompetence than smugness and overconfidence that caused the trouble.

A number of ironies associated with the war rarely attract American attention. For example, Cornwallis surrendered at Yorktown because a crucial segment of the Royal Navy was dispatched from its American station to Gibraltar, which was being threatened by the French and the Spanish. This decision makes no sense if we adopt present-day perspectives; however, it is perfectly logical if we remember how vital the British considered the Mediterranean to be in strategic, imperial, and commercial terms.

Another irony was that a war Americans passionately believe to be about liberty was hardly that for a large portion of the colonial population. Tens of thousands of slaves responded to a call to the British colors fighting against the colonists for what they believed would be their freedom. Amerindians and immigrants from non-British homelands also sided with the imperial power. These marginalized peoples believed Britain would give them protection and justice.

The America War also produced an important constitutional change. Lord North asserted the doctrine of collective Cabinet responsibility. In 1778–9 the Commons attempted to censure several ministers for incompetent management of the hostilities. The prime minister refused to hear of it. If criticisms were to be made, all officials must share the blame as a unit. Thenceforward Cabinet solidarity became the norm.

Perhaps the most dramatic unanticipated consequence of the American Revolution was the transformation of the situation in Ireland. Support for the American cause came from **Ulster** Presbyterians, whose creed was in sympathy with the colonial spirit of independence, and personal links among the Scots-Irish were widespread due to emigration.[11] This broadened the Irish "patriot" movement beyond the boundaries of the landowning elite. The dispute with America opened the eyes of many Ascendancy politicians to constitutional issues and economic inequities imposed by British rule. "Patriots" began to protest against Englishmen holding Irish offices and discrimination against Irish trade, while agitating for budgetary control and more frequent elections. The Irish suffered a recession due to the disruption of trade with America. The North administration was torn between appeasing the Irish and keeping protection for home manufacturers. The Irish dissidents organized a boycott of English imports along the lines of the American one. As the war went wrong, the Westminster Parliament granted Ireland free trade within the empire.

Irish constitutional grievances proved harder to assuage. Volunteer militias composed mainly of "respectable" Protestants were established without government authorization. Some prosperous Catholics also joined. The aim was to defend against the threat of French invasion. The Volunteer movement became a political force that put pressure on the regime to address the economic and political grievances of the "patriots." In the Dublin Parliament Henry Grattan (1746–1820) and others launched an impassioned oratorical campaign. The Whig leadership in London coordinated with him, and once in office quickly granted Ireland legal and legislative independence.

Now Ireland was in a similar position to Scotland before the Union of 1707. It possessed an independent Parliament that could cause serious disruption of the state if it split with Westminster over key issues. For example, when George III's illness prompted another discussion of a regency in 1788–9, the Irish Parliament sided with the Whig opposition against the government over what powers should be accorded the Prince of Wales. The issue was only resolved by the king's recovery. In fact Ireland did not launch an independent foreign policy and the viceroys generally were able to govern satisfactorily. The Ascendancy continued to think of themselves as the rightful rulers of Ireland because they were "Englishmen." But "Grattan's Parliament" symbolized a tendency towards independence.

The Struggles of George III

Some viewed the Rockingham ministry of 1782 as having "stormed the closet" (the monarch's office), forcing the king to accept ministers he did not want. George III certainly believed he was again the victim of dictatorial aristocratic arrogance; that the Whigs were trying to reduce the king to a mere cog in the machinery of government. The Rockingham ministry, short-lived though it was, represented a landmark in constitutional history. The ministerial changes of 1782 involved a more extensive upheaval among officeholders than any since 1714, virtually replacing one administration with another drawn from the opposition. Not just the top echelon resigned. Substantial changes of personnel among the minor office holders running more deeply down the scale than anything since the reign of Queen Anne challenged the convention that placemen were permanent officials who served the king rather than a particular prime minister. From thenceforward, when administrations of different political allegiance changed it became customary for a clean sweep of officials to take place. Rockingham and Fox also came to power with what can be described as a legislative program. The "economical reform" measures of 1780 were finally enacted.

The new administration, however, only lasted a short time. It was terminated by the death of the marquess. A coalition of Rockingham Whigs and Chathamites was cobbled together by the unpopular earl of Shelburne (1737–1805). The personal hostility between the new prime minister and Charles James Fox made it wobbly, and it lasted little more than half a year before disintegrating. In an amazing specimen of cohabitation Fox and Lord North then formed a ministry that also lasted only a year. Many of the latter's supporters were appalled. On Fox and North shaking hands in March 1783, a parson wrote in his diary: "O North, how low art thou fallen."[12] George III was equally disgusted. The king could not control Parliament, but he could undermine ministries he hated. That he proceeded to do.

India provided George's deliverance. British involvement there in the early eighteenth century was largely limited to coastal commerce. In the 1740s the East India Company's relatively modest holdings were composed of trading posts at Bombay, Calcutta, and Madras. The equivalent French company became a serious challenger for business and territory. During the 1750s Robert Clive led successful military campaigns against the French and their allies among the native rulers. As a result the Company gained control over considerable amounts of land, most notably Bengal and other states inland from Calcutta along the Ganges Valley. The French were pushed out. Swallowing so much land meant that the East India Company had become a colonial power in its own right, with substantial administrative, judicial, and taxing responsibilities.

Growing humanitarian disquiet arose over the methods of rule used by the East India Company's agents and administrators, some of whom acquired enormous fortunes by what appeared to be questionable means. Far-sighted observers also wondered whether in time the British state would have to assume the financial and military responsibilities for territories so rapidly being devoured. Parliament passed legislation to impose some control. A new Supreme Council in Bengal, whose members were appointed by the government, squabbled with Warren Hastings (1732–1818), the administrator appointed by the Company to the newly created office of governor general. Legislation was proposed by Edmund Burke, who would later pursue Hastings in a prolonged Parliamentary inquiry, to take over the entire management of the East India Company's territories. George III and his friends succeeded in making the legislation look like a grab by Fox to engross the immense patronage and influence of the Company's operation in the East for the benefit of the Whig Party. The king seized his moment and let the word be sent out that any peer who voted for the bill would henceforth be considered his enemy. The Lords rejected it. George III then dismissed Fox and North and invited 24-year-old William Pitt, a younger son of the earl of Chatham with only two years' parliamentary experience, to take on the premiership. Few thought he could last in office for long.

Pitt the Younger

The appointment of Pitt was one of George III's boldest and most successful political moves. Many people held the king responsible for the loss of the American colonies. Wyvill's movement pressed for reforms in order to limit royal power. Some country gentlemen were persuaded that the monarchy was still too powerful, and radicals like Thomas Paine directly attacked the institution. Would the king be able to marshal enough support to uphold the youngster in power?

Pitt clung to office even though Fox commanded a majority of votes in the Commons. George handed out peerages to strengthen his minister in the upper house and win the support of men with control over elections in multiple boroughs. MPs were offered patronage and office. Country gentlemen were alienated by Fox's extreme language against the new government. Then the king appealed to the country in a general election, taking the high ground of protecting the integrity of government from attack by corrupt Whigs. Nearly 100 Foxites and about 65 other MPs who had supported the coalition were unseated, either beaten at the polls or forced by their patrons to withdraw. It is true that no government had lost an election since 1708, and patronage was lavishly used in this one. Nevertheless, it was the only election between 1710 and 1807 that can be regarded as a full-blown appeal to the nation. Many contests were fought over traditional family and local rivalries, but national politics dominated in a number of cases. The king triumphed. He and Pitt were sober and chaste men now seen as reliable compared to the wild man, Fox. Pitt would remain prime minister, with a brief break, for the rest of his life and almost to the end of George's active reign.

In the 1780s Pitt concentrated on modest economic and administrative reform. He is especially associated with efforts to reduce the National Debt, which is ironic considering the fact that it ballooned under his leadership in later years. His India Act of 1784 established a Board of Control in London appointed to determine overall British policy towards the subcontinent, but the Company's directors were allowed to continue to rule some territories and conduct commercial operations. Pitt's program was suddenly endangered by the regency crisis of 1788–9. George III became incapacitated by another more serious bout of his mental affliction, but hopes were held out for his recovery. The Whigs expected to be returned to office if the Prince of Wales was given power in his father's stead (Figure 3.2). In the best Hanoverian tradition the heir to the throne had gathered around him the opposition leaders. Pitt played for time and wanted restrictions placed on the powers of the regent. The king resolved the crisis by returning to his normal state, somewhat the worse for wear.

Pitt's long reign brought an end to the revolving-door ministries in the years immediately after the loss of the American War. Ironically, that period of instability strengthened the cohesion of the Whig Party and gave shape to a Pittite/royalist/ country conglomerate that came in time to be called the Tories. This conservative alliance lasted in office from 1783 to 1830. Although the prime minister sometimes called himself a Whig, imagining that he stood in the tradition of Walpole, Pelham, and Newcastle, his fundamental principles made him a very different man from Rockingham and Fox. Pitt and his followers were not so much dedicated to the Hanoverian succession, which was assured, but to deference to monarchy. Moderately progressive in some respects, he was happy to work with deep-dyed reactionaries. What gave the prime minister special stature, however, was his personal reputation for integrity and financial prudence. He was also cool and competent in the Commons where until 1789 he was the only senior minister. It is difficult to warm to such a glacial personality. He lacked human interest except for an astounding capacity for holding his liquor. Yet he could inspire devotion from his friends and detestation among his enemies. In the past he was probably overrated

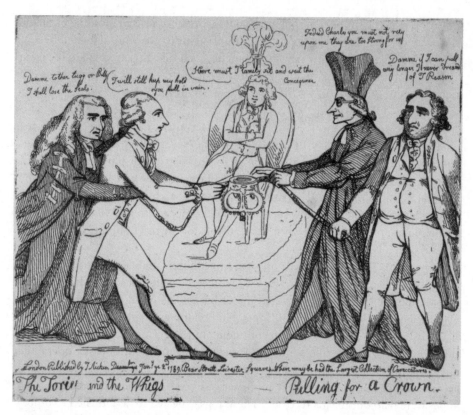

Figure 3.2   The cartoon shows George III's eldest son, the prince of Wales, seated on a throne in the background waiting for the result of a tug-of-war over the crown (his appointment as regent during his father's episode of madness, 1788–90). The Tories are represented by the **lord chancellor** Thurlow and prime minister William Pitt the Younger on the left and the Whigs by Edmund Burke (dressed as a Roman Catholic clergyman to mark his support for Catholic Emancipation) and Charles James Fox. "The Tories and Whigs Pulling for a Crown," 1789

as a statesman and today is sometimes criticized too much. He was the best that Britain had to throw against the French Revolution and Napoleon, and he proved up to the job.

Fox was prolix, emotional, sloppy, incoherent, and erratic, but he possessed great personal charisma. His brain was fertile and febrile. Debates became more polemical in the 1780s and party feeling was intense during the 1790 election. The Whigs continued their tradition of creating campaign war chests to fund major contests and help secure borough seats for the party. Without a great popular cause that would electrify the electorate, however, the Whigs could not gain traction against the implacable, almost pathological, hatred of the king of their principles and their leader.

The French Revolution

On July 14, 1789 a mob stormed the Bastille in Paris and what had begun as a serious but not critical dispute turned into one of the most influential and dangerous political events of modern times. Fox was in ecstasies: "How much the greatest event it is that ever happened in the world! & how much the best!" Pitt ignored the whole thing. Although Burke warned of danger ahead, many British people tended to agree with their prime minister. What could one expect from the French except folly and hand wringing? Yet Burke's genius as a writer and political analyst never shined brighter than in his great tolling of the bell, *Reflections on the Revolution in France*, published in November 1790 (see Biography 3.2). His message – that the revolution was destructive, contagious, bred tyranny and terror, and fundamentally threatened traditional values – turned out to be correct. "When ancient opinions and rules of life are taken away, the loss cannot possibly be estimated. From that point we have no compass to govern us; nor can we know distinctly to what port we steer."[13] Intoxicated by his own passionate prose, Burke depicted the old regime in France with lush romantic zeal, but he posed profound questions about radical and rapid change in government and society.

Though Burke's analysis was widely read and praised, it did not begin to reach the audience of his chief polemical opponent, Thomas Paine, who re-entered the lists with another slashing attack on the monarchy and praise for revolution. No book ever put the case against the eighteenth-century regime in Britain more vigorously than his *Rights of Man* (1791). It sold over 200,000 copies by the end of 1793. He gained no support from the legitimate political world, however. Fox called it "a libel upon the constitution."[14] Mary Wollstonecraft (1759–97; see Biography 4.1) also weighed in with the powerfully argued *Vindication of the Rights of Men* (1790), attacking the current frame of society and distribution of wealth. French politics began to invade Britain long before actual armies threatened its shores. Clubs and societies took sides. In Sheffield, a northern manufacturing center, the first Corresponding Society to agitate for reform was established in 1791 and other cities soon followed. Unlike earlier extra-parliamentary organizations with landed, professional, and commercial wealth to the fore, membership in these radical clubs consisted mainly of small men: artisans, shopkeepers, tradesmen, and the like. Dues for the London Corresponding Society cost only one penny a week. Further alarm was elicited when the more advanced Whigs founded the pro-reform Society of Friends of the People. On the other hand, "Church and King" clubs were started up, and conservative mobs, egged on by parsons and country gentlemen, attacked targets associated with radicalism and Dissent. The government clamped down in 1792. Pitt's "Terror" launched prosecutions against Paine, purveyors of radical literature, and genuine conspirators.

In April 1792 the French Legislative Assembly declared war on Austria. In November the radicalized National Convention made known its mission to export the Revolution. This led to a grave political crisis in Europe and in the highest reaches

Biography 3.2

Edmund Burke
1729–97

Edmund Burke's father was a successful Dublin attorney and Protestant. His mother came from an impoverished but well-bred Roman Catholic family. His sister was raised as a Catholic, although Edmund received his education at a Quaker school and the Protestant bastion of the Ascendancy, Trinity College. He moved to London in 1750 to attend law school but never practiced the profession. He made his way in life as a writer, editor, and politician in England.

In the 1760s he entered into a relationship with the marquess of Rockingham and became an MP, the chief ideologist of the Whig Party. On his patron's death in 1782 he transferred his allegiance to the fourth Earl Fitzwilliam (1748–1833), Rockingham's heir, and remained a Whig strategist until the French Revolution split the party.

Burke is one of the most complicated and interesting thinkers of his time, and the greatest Irishman of his generation. Although a Protestant, he despised the tyranny of the English in his home country. "I think," he wrote, "I can hardly overrate the malignity of the principles of Protestant ascendancy, as they affect Ireland."[15] He was sympathetic to the American cause, but condemned the French Revolution vehemently. Burke is difficult to categorize. He can be seen as a reactionary supporter of the *ancien régime*, yet his writing and career show him to have believed in commercial progress. He was against the slave trade and for religious toleration. To the Victorians he appeared to be in politics what Shakespeare was in the moral world.

Burke socialized with the intellectual elite; David Garrick, the actor, Oliver Goldsmith, the poet and playwright, Joshua Reynolds, the painter, and Samuel Johnson, the critic, were his intimate friends. Yet, he purchased a country house and set up as a landed gentleman, hoping for a peerage to pass to his beloved son, who died young. He was a great orator and writer, yet his rising to his feet in the Commons often served as the dinner bell, clearing the benches, and his prose could carry him in raptures to strange and contradictory conclusions. His obsessive drive to destroy Warren Hastings seems petty and vindictive. After two centuries the *Reflections* remains not just majestic in style but relevant to the present day.

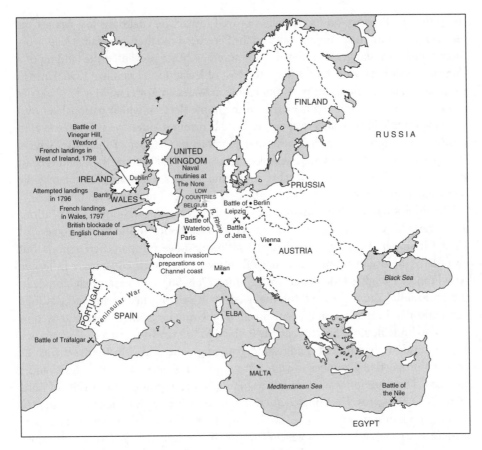

Map 3.1   Europe and the Wars of the French Revolution

of British politics. Fox continued to assert that no danger existed. Young Charles Grey (1764–1845), a leader of the Society of the Friends of the People, introduced reform proposals in the Commons, which Fox supported. Burke demurred and deserted the Whig Party, along with others who were frightened by the violence and demagoguery in Paris. Pitt invited the leading figures in this group, such as the third duke of Portland (1738–1809), to join the government. Whig magnates like the Earls Fitzwilliam and Spencer swung behind the ministry as a great national emergency unfolded. When revolutionary French forces "liberated" the Low Countries, traditionally seen as a region vital to Britain's economic and military security, Pitt was obliged to accept the necessity of war (see Map 3.1).

"The Napoleonic mobilization for national defence was undoubtedly the greatest 'national project' in Britain's experience," notes J. E. Cookson.[16] British war strategy was traditional: imperial conquest, mastery of the seas, and subsidies to Continental allies. This protected British commerce and the home islands but did not offer an opportunity to strangle the monster in its den. The first coalition that formed against the French lasted until 1797 but accomplished little. Each succeeding alliance failed to do the job. Reliance on foreign allies proved futile. The coalitions lost against the revolutionary extremists, they lost against the Directory, and they lost against Napoleon. Occasionally real danger threatened. Only severe weather prevented the landing of a French expeditionary force on the south coast of Ireland in December 1796. Early in the next year a French raiding party put ashore in Wales. In April and May 1797 a series of naval mutinies caused a grave crisis in the home fleet on which national survival depended. Incredibly, sailors' wages had not been raised since the mid-seventeenth century and shipboard conditions were deplorable. In October of that year General Bonaparte, then a coming man, assembled an army of 120,000 along the Channel coast where he stood waiting for favorable conditions to invade Britain. Fortunately, the government in Paris changed its mind and decided to send him to Egypt instead.

The situation in Ireland remained a cause for concern throughout the revolutionary decade. A group of liberal Dissenters and Catholics founded the Society of United Irishmen. Initially, their rhetoric was more powerful than their actions, but eventually the organization became a full-blown treasonous conspiracy in league with France. The gifted ideologue Wolfe Tone (1763–98), a Protestant passionate in the **nationalist** cause, became the main agent in seeking justice for the Catholic population and repudiation of British rule. The United Irishmen were outlawed in 1794, and Tone fled to France where he lobbied for an invasion force.

The London government made some grudging concessions to the Irish such as enabling propertied Catholics to vote, but no generous policy to address grievances emerged. The situation was made more volatile by the appointment in 1795 of Lord Fitzwilliam as viceroy. His bungled attempt to grant Catholic Emancipation and precipitate recall disappointed hopes and inflamed opinion. Sectarian rioting and gang warfare rose to a new level of violence. The ultra-Protestant Orange Order confronted angry Catholics. In 1798 small French forces made landings that triggered two extraordinarily vicious episodes of rebellion. The insurgents were crushed by British troops in the west and at Vinegar Hill in Wexford, providing a new list of martyrs that would inspire nationalists for another century of struggle. A younger son of the great Ascendancy figure, the duke of Leinster, became a rebel and was captured and died of his wounds before he could be executed. Tone committed suicide. These events undermined the confidence of the Scottish and English aristocracy in the Irish elite.

Pitt began to take the war seriously. He introduced an income tax. The trend of forcing the poor to bear much of the burden by increasing excise taxes was reversed. A graduated levy on all incomes over £60 meant that the rich paid at the highest rates, and ordinary working people were exempt entirely. Landed society and prosperous merchants picked up the financial burden of the increasingly expensive struggle against the enemy.

At sea the war went well. Despite the mutinies in 1797 Britain went on to achieve a succession of victories. The Channel fleet did superb work, holding station in often very adverse weather conditions. Other units captured islands in the Caribbean and destroyed the French Atlantic trade. When Bonaparte set off to Egypt, his conquests did him no good. Rear Admiral Sir Horatio Nelson (1758–1805) became his nemesis. In August 1798 in the Battle of the Nile the French fleet was destroyed at anchor.

The future dictator had to scurry back to France without his troops and spin the facts so grotesquely that only a coup d'état saved his reputation. Malta and Egypt now fell under British influence, completing the trio of British outposts in the Mediterranean at its mouth, middle, and far end.

Critical to naval success was the copper sheathing of ships' hulls. This made the British fleet faster than those of her enemies, because the sea life that attached itself to the wooden undersides of vessels, creating a drag that slowed them down, were repelled by the copper. The problem was how to attach the sheathing. Copper nails were too soft. Iron nails triggered a chemical reaction that destroyed the metal and the sheathing fell off. British technology triumphed with an innovative alloy to get around this problem. Thoughtful, hardworking, and highly intelligent naval officers and aristocratic administrators implemented the new system. Lord Spencer (1758–1834), who was in charge of the Navy, selected a series of brilliant officers for command, culminating in the appointment of the difficult genius, Nelson, to postings that turned out to be critical at each turn in the war.

A new alliance was formed with Austria, Prussia, and Russia in what became the War of the Second Coalition. Allies quickly fell by the wayside, however, leaving Britain alone to fight France. A temporarily pacific Bonaparte concluded the treaty of Amiens in 1802. Pitt was no longer in office when the accord was ratified. Excessive consumption of alcohol and his long years in office had taken their toll. The real problem, however, lay with the king. During the negotiations for the Union with Ireland in 1800, which will be more fully discussed in the next chapter, the Cabinet had agreed, without telling George, that Catholic Emancipation would follow. When the truth came out, the king was adamant against religious concessions, his special *bête noir*, and Pitt felt obliged to resign in February 1801. Henry Addington (1757–1844), speaker of the House of Commons, formed a new government. He was something of a novelty in that he lacked ministerial experience and was the son of a doctor, the first prime minister in the century after 1714 not connected with the peerage. He was, however, a king's man and anti-Catholic, which is what George wanted. Pitt had stood up to the king and lost. For the last time, a British monarch stared down a formidable politician and won.

Some of the cautious Whigs such as Spencer moved back into opposition and denounced the treaty as humiliating, but they were not yet ready to reunite with Fox. The latter's party gained seats in the 1802 election and even more in 1812. A group of heirs to Whig magnates were elected to the Commons in these years who would further liberalize its ideology over the next few decades, although the party was plagued by the lack of assertive and experienced leadership after Fox's death in 1806.

Duel to the Death

Bonaparte's explosive, overweening ambition, woven with an ideological thread of radicalism, made it impossible to stay at peace. Addington decided pre-emptively to declare war in May 1803 and blockaded French ports. More energy and vision was invested in the war effort than Pitt had been capable of for some time. Nonetheless the ex-premier was getting restless and wanted to be back in power. In April 1804 he went into active opposition, the ministry crumbled, and Pitt returned to office.

The military situation was now grave. During 1803 over 800,000 men, more than one in five of the male population of military age, were in armed service. Britain sent more soldiers to the West Indian campaign during this period than they had to suppress the North American rebels two decades earlier, and the war cost more lives. Of 89,000 white officers and men who served in the Caribbean between 1793 and 1801, over 45,000 died in battle or of disease, accompanied by an additional 19,000 sailors.[17] Government spending stood at 6 percent of GDP (gross domestic product) in 1793 and rose to the unprecedented level of 25 percent by 1815. Nothing like this had ever happened in Britain before. A great patriotic rallying against the French was energized by Napoleon's despotic behavior. The danger of a full-scale French invasion was now imminent. Plans were devised to evacuate the royal family and establish a temporary government headquarters well north of London in the remote countryside.

A third coalition was hauled into place in April 1805, but it malfunctioned just like the others. Then Admiral Nelson chased the French fleet across the Atlantic to the West Indies and back again before the enemy was finally engaged on October 21, 1805 off the Spanish coast at Cape Trafalgar. Although fatally shot by a sniper during the battle, Nelson, whose ego was matched in these years only by Napoleon's, produced the most brilliant and innovative performance of his career and achieved an epic victory. France was permanently denied the chance to invade Britain, which not only saved the nation but also in the long run put paid to Bonaparte's career. It also placed the Royal Navy in a position of dominance that was not to be overtaken until the 1940s. A great monument was erected in Nelson's honor in the center of London in a plaza called Trafalgar Square. He remains an object of national veneration. When a boy, the modern novelist William Golding was presented with a sliver of wood from the spot on the deck where the admiral died. It seemed so sacred that the only thing he could think to do was swallow it like the host at a Eucharist.

Pitt died in office on January 23, 1806. George III had little alternative but to turn to a coalition that included Addington and Fox and was led by William Grenville (1759–1834). It was known as "The Ministry of All the Talents." The general election of 1806 increased the support for the ministry and left Pitt's followers in disarray. Abolition of the slave trade was high on the ministry's agenda and found widespread support. Raising the property tax from 6.5 to 10 percent was less popular. Fox moved to bring an end to the war even on very unfavorable terms, but Napoleon was in no mood for peacemaking. Fox's death in September, only seven months after that of his arch-rival, was an irreparable loss in the House of Commons. The king managed to rid himself of an unwelcome ministry by demanding a pledge that they would not press him on any concessions to Roman Catholics. The Cabinet resigned in March 1807.

The duke of Portland became prime minister for a second time. He called another election that strengthened his position, the only time after the passage of the

Septennial Act when two appeals to the public were made so close together until the twentieth century. Though an able man, the duke was too old and ill to take firm command. A number of talented colleagues worked together to achieve progress in the war, including Spencer Perceval, George Canning (1770–1827), Lord Hawkesbury, and Viscount Castlereagh (1769–1822).

A fourth coalition with Russia and Prussia had been put together in October 1806 with minimal results. Russia drifted away as usual, and Prussia was annihilated at the battle of Jena. In May of that year Britain embargoed the coast of France and its empire. Napoleon countered in November with the Berlin Decrees, which initiated the Continental System, a commercial blockade between the British Isles and mainland Europe. The "All the Talents" ministry responded by prohibiting seaborne exchange between one French or French-ruled port and another and other restrictions on trade. Napoleon retaliated with the Milan Decrees aimed at further damaging British commerce. Smuggling remained widespread and both sides turned a blind eye to this profitable trade, but the British got the better of the economic war.

It was only in 1808 that Britain finally turned to a strategy that had the potential to bring down the tyrant: direct military action on the Continent. At first this was tentative and on a small scale. An expeditionary force was sent to Iberia to challenge the French invasion of Portugal. Even this step, which produced a quick victory, was not at first pursued energetically by the government, but ultimately a British army would penetrate France by this southern route. The campaign came to be led by the able Anglo-Irish general, Viscount Wellington (1769–1852), who eventually rose to the premiership in the 1820s.

A fifth coalition staggered into place, and it was defeated in battle by Napoleon as usual. The British mounted a disastrous attack on the Dutch coast in an attempt to take pressure off its Continental allies. Everything seemed to go wrong after that. A scandal involving the king's son, the duke of York, whose mistress was alleged to have sold commissions in the army that were in his gift as commander–in–chief, outraged public opinion and ardent young Whigs. The prime minister lay dying. Two members of the Cabinet, Lord Castlereagh and George Canning, fought a duel. The king turned with relief to the sober, frugal, and devout Spencer Perceval (1762–1812) to form a new government. The earl of Liverpool, formerly Lord Hawkesbury (1770–1828), calm, shrewd, and capable, was put in charge of the war effort. The unfortunate Perceval became the first and last prime minister to be assassinated, in May 1812, by a lunatic with a grievance against the government. Liverpool replaced him. He and Castlereagh, who became foreign secretary, were the key figures in the end game leading to Napoleon's fall.

The Americans, who were suspicious of the British, had territorial ambitions in Canada and were upset with British interference in Atlantic shipping. They declared war in 1812. This sideshow to the main event in Europe demonstrated that Britain was now gearing up for a gargantuan effort. A British army marched on Washington, set fire to the White House, and quickly concluded the affair. Fortunately for Lord Liverpool, Napoleon finally overreached himself with an invasion of Russia. Castlereagh negotiated a sixth coalition that grew larger by the week. Even small countries scented the blood of a wounded giant and joined the hunt. At the Battle of Nations near Leipzig in October 1813 Napoleon was driven west of the Rhine. The Allies under Wellington invaded France from the south.

Napoleon abdicated and was exiled to the island of Elba. As the Allies consulted at Vienna, the French emperor managed a brief comeback that was ended on June 18, 1815 by Wellington at Waterloo in Belgium. This time the warmonger was sent to live out the remainder of his life on a large rock in the middle of the South Atlantic which the British used as one of their supply stations on the route to India. He died there in 1821. The Bourbon monarchy in France was restored.

In October 1810 the king again slipped into a mental breakdown from which he never recovered, although he had a decade more to live. The Prince of Wales, eventually granted full powers as regent, considered bringing in the Whigs but decided against it. Always a fair-weather friend, he discovered that he shared his father's scruples over Catholic Emancipation, and felt that his oppositional courtiers had been insufficiently enthusiastic in supporting his expensive lifestyle.

George III was the last of a formidable trio of Hanoverians who had ruled Britain for almost a century. Unlike his predecessors, he came to the throne without maturity or good judgment, but he rectified this over time. He remained obdurate about constitutional changes but otherwise proved flexible. Like the first two Georges he grumbled and mumbled from time to time, held personal grudges against a few enemies, and asserted his powers where he could, but also like them he accepted that he must work within the constitutional restraints on royal power. Ironically, for a man pilloried by the Whigs for the assertion of royal influence, his willing agreement to accept a fixed annual income that quickly proved inadequate led to further erosion of monarchical authority. George III was cultivated, uxorious, well educated, a man of sincere faith, a patron of importance, and interested in art, music, theater, architecture, farming, and science. He had a good sense of humor. His remarkable book collection, donated to the British Museum, stands to this day at the core of the national library. In more respects than most of us he was a kind, generous, and good man. He admitted to John Adams, the first American ambassador to London after the Revolution, that he had opposed independence: "but the separation having been made, and having become inevitable, I have always said, as I say now, that I would be the first to meet the friendship of the United States as an independent power."[18]

The Fiscal-Military State and Victory

The strong fiscal-military state arose in the seventeenth and eighteenth centuries, but it produced most effective results in the nineteenth. Although it took a long time to defeat Napoleon, in the end he was crushed by British military power, which was the product partly of skilled commanders and excellent technology, and partly British finance. The latter not only paid for arming the nation but also funded enormous subsidies to keep allies in the fighting. The National Debt shot upwards during the Seven Years War and the American War, tripling in size between 1757 and 1783. The situation remained stable until resumption of hostilities in 1793. Then the Debt ballooned to extraordinary proportions, reaching a value of almost double the nation's gross national product. Yet, much of the expenditure on the war, or at least the interest on debt, was covered by the imposition of new taxes. Altogether the rate of taxation was 18 times higher in 1815 than in 1660. The ruling elite accepted strict fiscal discipline. When spending rose, taxes kept pace.

The revenue bureaucracy described in Chapter 2 continued to grow. By 1782 there were some 14,000 employees. Lord North ordered 15 reports from the Commissioners of Public Accounts, which were issued between 1780 and 1786. These helped Pitt and his successors slowly to improve the probity, uniformity, and efficiency of public service. The wars of the eighteenth century, and especially the long and exhausting struggle with France between 1793 and 1815, changed the nature of government itself. The British state had become a superpower. Aside from the Royal Navy, which assumed a position of unassailable mastery over the world's oceans after Trafalgar, it had at its command an army of unprecedented size and effectiveness. The recruits, whether poor Irishmen fleeing poverty, English criminals, or native **sepoys**, submitted to ruthless discipline and single-minded leadership. While a young colonel in India, Wellington showed what he was prepared to do. On the capture of Seringapatam in 1799, he reported that the men ran wild: "Scarcely a house in the town was left unplundered. … By the greatest exertion, by hanging, flogging, &c. &c., in the course of that day I restored order among the troops."[19] Masses of men died in Britain's imperial adventures, many of them not in battle but on interminable sea voyages in conditions little better than slave ships, and in rural swamps and urban stews where hygiene and comfort were unknown. Dr. Johnson wrote that they "languished in tents and ships, amidst dampness and putrifecation; pale, torpid, spiritless, and helpless; gasping and groaning, unpitied among men, made obdurate by long continuance of hopeless misery; and were, at last, [dumped] in pits, or heaved into the ocean, without notice and without remembrance."[20] Yet their sacrifice was not without effect. Their country survived its most dangerous exposure to conquest by a foreign power between 1066 and 1940.

Part II

The British Century

Chapter 4

A United Kingdom, 1815

At what point did Britain become a "modern" society with an industrialized economy, widely accepted Enlightenment values, a class structure, and well-developed sense of national identity? Some historians believe that the old regime survived well into the nineteenth century. They say that not until after the constitutional reforms of the 1820s and 1830s and the full development of railways and heavy industry can one declare a new world to have begun. They make the case for a "long" eighteenth century dating from 1688 to 1832. The divisions in this textbook do not follow that pattern. I do not discount the importance of 1832, which was a turning point. Other forces, however, that would push forward the political reforms were gathering momentum earlier. Indeed, these factors were critical in Britain's ability to marshal the resources necessary for military victory in 1815, to retain social stability in the face of the French Revolution, and to meld the archipelago into a United Kingdom that presided over a global empire.

Population

One of the biggest changes under way in Britain during the second half of the eighteenth century was a population explosion. By 1800 England and Wales numbered in excess of nine million, moving towards twice the size of a century earlier. Most of that growth took place after 1750. Scotland was near two million though not growing as fast, until right at the end of the century when it began to accelerate rapidly. Ireland succeeded in doubling its size, most of the expansion coming after the terrible famine of the 1740s. A diet of potatoes grew in importance during the century until it was the predominant food among the Catholic poor by the 1770s and 1780s.

The rate of growth was even more rapid than these numbers imply, for substantial emigration to the colonies also took place during this period. In the 15 years alone between the end of the Seven Years War and the War of Independence 125,000 people crossed the Atlantic from the British Isles. Despite an incoming flow from Ireland, Wales, and Scotland, England probably suffered a net loss of half a million to emigration during the eighteenth century. Contemporaries actually believed the population was shrinking, which was frightening to contemplate when constant warfare with an enemy estimated to be four or five times Britain's size confronted those who had to recruit troops and sailors. In reality the British rate of growth was roughly twice that of France.

Why did the population expand so rapidly in the second half of the eighteenth century? Prosperity helped, although this was not the cause in Ireland. Increased fertility, not reduced mortality, was the main engine of growth. In many but not all social groups the average age of marriage for women declined from a little under 26 to 24. More people relied exclusively on wages to live, which encouraged settling down at an earlier age than among those who had to build up resources to begin a business or to farm. Some historians claim the rise in real wages that had occurred earlier in the eighteenth century enabled people to marry younger and that they had more children because they could afford them. Others think they needed children to bring in extra income in order to survive.

Decline in death rates also contributed to population growth. The disappearance of the plague and introduction of smallpox vaccination helped. The key factors in reducing infant mortality were probably improved child-rearing practices and better-constructed housing. Pollution, especially of the water supply, and coal smoke in the air were severe problems in cities. Diet and health, however, improved intermittently but significantly over time.

The movement from the country to the city was also accelerating. In 1700 there were only seven towns with more than 10,000 people; by the end of the century it was nearly 50. In 1700 one in six English people lived in a town with more than 2,500 inhabitants. The proportion reached one in three in 1800. London numbered nearly one million inhabitants in 1800, although its share of the national population stood steady at about one person in 10. The slums spread but so did better paving and lighting of streets (gas lamps were first installed in 1807) and the creation of new squares and terraces (rows of houses) for the middling and upper orders. The aristocracy moved westward from along the river near the City to areas that remain fashionable today in the **West End**. Magnates built great urban palaces for themselves. The industrial centers in the middle and northern areas of the country such as Manchester and Glasgow also grew rapidly. Even Ireland became more urbanized by the end of the eighteenth century. Dublin rose to over 180,000.

An Industrial Revolution?

The concept of an "industrial revolution" arose in the later nineteenth century, and remained the foundation on which explanations of modern British exceptionalism have long been based. As with almost all historical interpretations, revisionists have challenged the validity and utility of this explanatory tool. A consensus exists that the economic growth in the eighteenth century was more modest than the term "revolution" conveys. The annual rate of expansion was no more than one percent per annum to 1780 and no more than two percent up to 1830. The great achievement of the British economy as distinct from its rivals lay in employing a lot of people in industry and relatively few in agriculture (exploiting the improved productivity of labor on farms), rather than reaching outstanding growth rates in industry taken as a whole.[1] Preliminary data from a recent study of male occupations shows that the movement from agricultural labor to manufacturing began well before 1700 and had risen to over 40 percent by 1750. In the most industrialized areas of Lancashire and Yorkshire the proportion had reached two-thirds of the population. These figures were achieved before the factory system took shape.[2] Manufacturing did not necessarily involve new techniques or an enlarged scale of operations. Small artisans and craftsmen continued to be important well into the nineteenth century. Generalizations are often difficult to make because of incomplete data, diversity within the manufacturing sector, and the challenge of establishing at what point lives and outlooks were changed sufficiently to speak of a new way of thinking and doing.

The revisionists have been helpful in redrawing the map of economic development. The role of agriculture in promoting growth is much better understood than it once was. We now see more clearly that innovation began before 1750 and many aspects of the economy and society were traditional long after big changes took place. The number of male workers engaged in manufacturing actually declined slightly between 1750 and 1815. A second, more rapid industrial transformation began after the Napoleonic wars came to an end.

Britain's relative gains in comparison to other countries were huge. Improvement in transportation, marketing, finance, and credit lifted the economy by increasing market integration and reducing transaction costs. Another recent finding of the male occupational study has revealed significant growth in employment in the "service sector" (transportation, retailing, wholesaling, clerical, and professional services) from the late eighteenth century onwards.[3] The emergence of large coal- and iron-based industries liberated the economy from old restraints. British coal output in 1700 was between 2.3 and 3 million tons. It produced five times as much coal as the rest of Europe by 1800. Output expanded to about 15 million tons in 1800 and 30.4 million by 1830.[4]

The Scottish experience is often forgotten in the debate about industrialization. In the middle decades of the eighteenth century its economy went into overdrive. After 1760 large and rapid increases in agricultural and commercial growth took place in tandem with a huge expansion in mineral production, construction of textile factories, and the rise of an innovative chemical industry. The Tennant works in Glasgow became the largest chemical factory in the world. Urbanization in Scotland was very rapid between 1750 and 1850 and resulted from its swift economic growth. Between 1785 and 1835 exports from Scotland rose ninefold.[5]

Agriculture

Fundamental to the growth of population and the birth of industrialization was an expanded food supply, a large body of surplus labor, and enlarged streams of capital. For a long time historians predicated the rise of the new British economy on an "agricultural revolution." In recent years the chronology of this development has been pushed back as more and more evidence showed that changes in farming practice appeared earlier than previously thought. No major technological breakthroughs in agriculture took place between 1750 and 1850. Some historians question whether the word "revolution" is appropriate to describe such a protracted process. While once the story was told in terms of famous innovators and the dispossession of the peasantry through abolition of customary rights and access to land, today historians point to increased productivity of labor as the key element of change. In addition, pools of capital were needed to fund improvements in infrastructure and other investments necessary to advance manufacturing capacity. In the eighteenth century no sector of the economy other than agriculture could produce surplus wealth on that scale. Britain is the only country in history that industrialized without external sources of financing.

A major breakthrough was achieved by enhancing soil fertility and intensifying cultivation. Continuous cropping of grains exhausted the nutrients in the soil rapidly. Innovative systems of rotation were gradually introduced. It dawned on farmers that certain plants such as clover returned vitality to the soil rather than taking it away and new crops such as turnips could provide fodder for animals, who in turn manured the fields. Selective breeding of livestock also improved output. Harvesting tools were perfected. New plowing techniques and threshing machines were introduced. A plentitude of horses helped release human labor for other tasks. Farms close to the rapidly growing cities made good profits as market gardens. Improved diet allowed workers to expend more energy. However, care has to be taken not to exaggerate the impact of change. Much of the agricultural research in the eighteenth century was amateur and the results contradictory in nature. Some innovations required high cost (marling, drainage, parliamentary enclosure) compared to alternative methods of improving output. Change came slowly.

Land had come to be seen by the elite as more than a means to status, an heirloom for the family, a source of military power, and the foundation of their notions of honor. Eighteenth-century aristocrats exploited their estates methodically. A Scot from a titled family proudly proclaimed that he supervised his farms like "a branch of trade."[6] Landowners and their agents forged the system of large units managed by entrepreneurial tenants that formed the basis of successful commercialized agriculture. New economies of scale in the use of labor became possible. Ending customary rights helped create an agricultural proletariat of laborers who could be more effectively controlled and managed or were freed to seek employment in manufacturing or transportation. This structure largely dominated the English scene by the eighteenth century, and in Scotland both Lowland lairds and Highland clan chiefs radically changed the structure of production as well. The Scottish nobility played a key role in the early dissemination of scientific innovation and best practices.

Landowners were also at the heart of another development, the widespread enclosing with fences or ditches of open fields and common lands. Most "enclosure" was completed by private agreement. Using acts of Parliament, however, made it easier to overcome local opposition, and this method became more common from the 1760s. Already in 1700, however, nearly two-thirds of England had been enclosed. The final surge was the tail end of a long process that served many social as well as economic functions. Parliamentary enclosure has received disproportionate attention because it left extensive records. It produced a further step in improvement rather than a sudden change. The romantic notion that a historic class of small owners, known as yeomen, was systematically eradicated by greedy magnates has now been shown to be incorrect. The number of owner-occupiers remained much the same in 1800 as it had in 1700. Yet, higher rates of productivity by individual workers did drive laborers from the countryside.

Had there been a speedy alteration in land tenure and enclosure, far more resistance to reforms would have been likely. Instead piecemeal change over long periods left the laborers like frogs in pots of water slowly being brought to a boil, unable to notice the temperature was rising until it was too late. T. M. Devine calls it "the silent revolution."[7] The process of consolidation of properties that took place with more rapidity in the Highlands between 1780 and 1830, most famously "the clearances" on the million-acre Sutherland estate, evoked strong protests at the time and much condemnation by later observers. In fact the small farms known as crofts had become economically unviable and most of the dispossessed tenants were absorbed into the labor force of the new large farms, worked in newly developed industries such as fishing and distilling, or emigrated to what was almost certainly a better life elsewhere. The interior regions were turned into vast sheep ranches, which required little labor to manage. The advent of cash rents, entry into market-driven production, and evictions destroyed traditional Gaelic culture and the clan system, which was psychologically traumatic and led to widespread bitterness. We now know that even in the Highlands this process had its origins earlier than previously thought and was an inevitable and irreversible cost of entering a larger economic system. It also happened by small stages until the nineteenth century. The enemies of landowners clung to this memory (neglecting the even worse consequences awaiting the crofters had things stayed as they were) and used it as a tool for demonization in the battle to destroy their quarry. Selective memory and myth making used for political purposes is sometimes more powerful than prosaic or unpalatable truth.

Eighteenth-century Ireland did not progress in step with the rest of Britain. Irish rents were always low in relation to the capital value of land and never provided an economic return; this as much as careless practice accounts for the small proportion ploughed back into estate improvements. Only the increased prevalence of potato cultivation made possible the demographic expansion that was founded on a dangerously narrow base.

After 1760, with a rising population demanding more food, the export of grain decreased and imports rose. However, England and Scotland, unlike Ireland, were able to increase national wealth through manufacturing and trade sufficiently to avoid starvation. Although some years of shortages occurred, by and large Britain was able to feed itself and even enact tariffs to inhibit the importation of grain. These measures seem to have made little difference to the supply of food, although eventually their existence would cause a political crisis in the 1840s.

The landed elite got rich, reaching unprecedented levels of wealth during the years of high prices between 1790 and 1815. As incomes rose and estates were consolidated, the large landowners had a greater propensity to save. They accumulated more capital than they could possibly spend on consumption, even after rebuilding large houses, looting the Italian art market, and having diamonds sown on their waistcoat buttons and inserted in ladies' tiaras. Some became among the richest private citizens who had ever lived. This was truly a case where the rich got richer, and yet the process ultimately benefited the whole of society, for without these massive accumulations of capital in a few hands it is hard to see industrialization proceeding with enough momentum to break through the barriers of the traditional economy to support the second phase of industrialization after 1815. Some of the money was invested directly in sinking coalmines, constructing harbors, developing urban property, and building better roads and canals. More was channeled through mortgages and family settlements into the wider market for capital that helped fuel industrialization directly. Devine calls the great nobles of eighteenth-century Scotland "economic revolutionaries."[8] David Spring and others have uncovered the determined progressive and entrepreneurial outlook of the British elite in the age of coal and iron.[9]

Transportation and Communication

Integration of the national economy was necessary for industrialization. Transportation by road in the eighteenth century was by packhorse, wagon, and horse-drawn vehicles. Heavy stagecoaches that stuck in muddy roads were replaced by lighter and speedier ones whizzing along turnpikes established by Parliament and maintained as business operations. Journey times decreased dramatically; long trips were cut in half. New services linked growing industrial centers to London and each other for the first time. The road and bridge engineers, Thomas Telford (1757–1834) and John McAdam (1756–1836), both Scots, enabled further continuous and successive reductions.

The turnpike mania was overtaken by a canal boom. Inland waterways had been improved in previous centuries by dredging and widening. A new era of artificial canals, most built by joint stock companies authorized by Parliament, began in 1755 with a channel designed to provide Liverpool with cheap coal. A great landed magnate, the third duke of Bridgewater, opened a canal to move coal from his mines to Manchester in 1761. Approximately 1,000 miles of navigable waterways were added to the national network in the succeeding three decades. Most of the major rivers of England and Lowland Scotland were linked by 1790, and Ireland also developed a canal system. The engineering of the new waterways was often spectacular. Tunnels plowed through inconveniently located hills and aqueducts carried boats across valleys. Canals even passed over and under each other in the way superhighway ramps do today. The system increased reliability, speed, and safety in moving heavy cargos such as grain and coal as well as manufactured goods and fertilizer. Fragile pottery could be transported in bulk. Cattle were taken to market without losing the weight that walking on the hoof would have caused. Map 4.1 shows how transportation improved in this period.

Wagons pulled by horses first ran on iron wheels from the 1730s and on iron rails from the 1760s. During the first decade of the nineteenth century stationary steam engines began to haul them up steep gradients. The railroads were much cheaper to construct than canals. The appearance of steam-powered ships and railway locomotives

(a) 1750 (stage-coach)

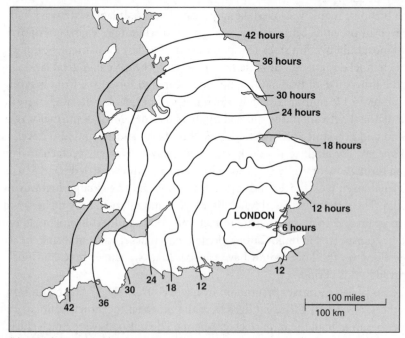

(b) 1821 (stage-coach)

Map 4.1   Improved Transportation, 1750–1821

in the early nineteenth century followed the improvements in engineering and mechanical technology discussed in the next section. Goods, ideas, information, and people could be moved from place to place easily. Something approaching a unified national market and culture, still characterized by regional specialization, had emerged.

Manufacturing

The first authentic factory, a water-powered silk yarn mill, was built between 1718 and 1721. In 1733 John Kay applied for a patent to protect his mechanical flying shuttle that constituted the first important technological breakthrough in the textile industry. Josiah Wedgwood's pottery factory was employing advanced management and production techniques by 1735. His approach to marketing was recognizably "modern" as well. However, innovative approaches to manufacturing remained slow in coming and largely confined to the cotton industry. Water power still greatly exceeded steam in 1800. Only the spinning process was fully mechanized before 1830. Handloom weavers continued to work at home into the 1840s (Figure 4.1).

Figure 4.1   London weavers at work. *The Fellow 'Prentices at Their Looms* by William Hogarth, 1747

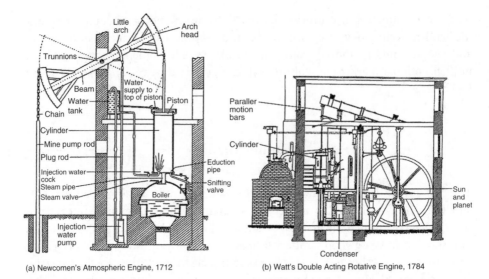

(a) Newcomen's Atmospheric Engine, 1712   (b) Watt's Double Acting Rotative Engine, 1784

Figure 4.2   The steam engines of Thomas Newcomen (1712) and James Watt (1784). Newcomen's "Atmospheric Engine" was first developed to pump water out of mines. Though stronger than animal power, it was inefficient. Power was transmitted to the beam only on the down stroke. Watt's "Double Acting Rotative Engine" with its separate condenser patented in 1769, tight-fitting metal parts thanks to the sword maker John Wilkinson, and a double action by the beam on both the up and down strokes was far more efficient, and, indeed, was the machine that made the modern world

Nevertheless, the number of patents registered between 1760 and 1785 was more than the total for the period 1617–1760. Cast iron increasingly replaced wood and stone. The process of puddling, which was patented by Henry Cort in 1783–4, was a critical innovation. Britain became the largest iron smelter and refiner in Europe.

Britain began producing more cotton than woolen cloth, overturning an ancient colossus from its central place in the British economy. Competition from high-quality, low-cost imports from India placed pressure on British manufacturers to invest in technological change.[10] Richard Arkwright's water frame and carding machinery, which he developed in the 1770s, made him a great fortune and reinforced the trend towards factory operations. More and more machinery was made out of iron and operated by steam. Factories offered the opportunity to achieve efficiencies of scale and management. Hiring women and children to tend the machinery allowed owners to pay low wages and enforce strict discipline. Other areas of innovation during the later eighteenth and early nineteenth centuries included: the production of non-ferrous metals, papermaking, chemicals, glass, food processing, and shipbuilding.

The great genius of the industrial revolution was a Scot working in England, James Watt (1736–1819). His invention of a separate condenser for the conservation of steam power, which made engines much more efficient, took place in 1765 and was patented four years later (Figure 4.2). His partner, Matthew Boulton (1728–1809), had a flair for publicity and marketing. It was he who delivered the epic words: "I sell,

Table 4.1   Per capita levels of industrialization, 1759–1860[11] (relative to the UK in 1900 = 100)

	1750	1800	1830	1860
United Kingdom	10	16	25	64
Habsburg Empire	7	7	8	11
France	9	9	12	20
German States/Germany	8	8	9	15
Russia	6	6	7	8
United States	4	9	14	21
China	8	6	6	4
India	7	6	6	3

Sir, what all the world desires to have – power."[12] At the beginning of the nineteenth century Britain was on its way to becoming the workshop of the world (see Table 4.1).

By the mid-1700s Britain ranked first in global trade. The shape of commerce changed radically over the course of the century. Traditional European customers and exporters faded away to be replaced by colonial and North American producers and consumers. Merchants accumulated capital that assisted in industrialization and provided the raw materials, ships, marketing, and insurance needed to export the expanding output of the factories, whose production surpassed what the home market could absorb. The Atlantic and Caribbean trade helped push the British economy forward, fed consumption, raised wages, and promoted social mobility. France also enjoyed a comparable business expansion but had three times the population. Per capita, Britain was far richer and by 1805 had taken control of the sea trade routes of the world.

Eric Williams famously argued that the profits from the slave trade were a key ingredient in providing the capital for industrialization, thus linking the evil of slavery with the emergence of modernity. The data that could prove the case are very difficult to come by or interpret, but recent research suggests that the profit from the commerce in human beings was not as large as Williams believed and could not have revolutionized the economy on its own. The fact that wealth derived from slavery had very little effect on the economic structures of other European powers heavily involved in the trade suggests a similar conclusion.[13]

Scottish merchants, especially in the tobacco trade, were more effective and skilled than their English rivals and undercut them on a grand scale. By 1758 Scottish tobacco imports were greater than those of London and all other English ports combined, much of it re-exported for sale in Europe. The Scots were also very good at smuggling. They became major players in the East India Company once Henry Dundas became president of its board in 1784, and they would later dominate the China trade. Commercial profits were invested in booming Scottish industrialization.

The banking system was unregulated and a weak spot in English though not Scottish finance. No national paper currency existed. Bank of England notes did not circulate widely outside London and until the 1790s were not available in denominations under the large sum of £10. Provincial banks grew in number and made up for the shortfall from the central institution, but they were fragile and frequently failed. A great inflow of foreign capital and financiers during the French wars at the end of the century, notably headed by the great Rothschild family, enabled London to replace Amsterdam as Europe's central capital market.

Causes and Consequences

The economy took time to gather its forces and much of this was done by intensifying traditional functions rather than through dramatic innovation. The fortunate geography and the rich resources of the archipelago gave Britain a leg up. Creative genius produced a bountiful supply of inventions and engineering marvels. The entrepreneurial spirit was also exceptional. The system of social mobility that allowed mercantile and industrial wealth to fund rises into the aristocratic hierarchy created a powerful incentive to succeed. Two of the most eminent prime ministers of the nineteenth century were the sons respectively of a cotton manufacturer (Peel) and a Liverpool merchant (Gladstone); another (Disraeli) was the grandson of a stockbroker. All three families purchased landed estates and gained peerages. The structure of landownership encouraged changes in agricultural production that in turn made it possible to feed a growing population, release labor for industry, provide capital to build infrastructure, and invest in mining and manufacturing. Britain was lucky not to be ravaged by conquering armies and to find colonies that produced raw materials and provided expanding markets for manufactured goods. The landed elite of England and Scotland mobilized resources to provide the fuel and infrastructure necessary to industrialize. The willingness of the aristocracy, merchants, and manufacturers to ally with each other to promote common interests was critical not only to economic growth but also to the whole process of modernization.

The power of the state was unleashed without any grand strategy but with massive effect. Although parts of the legal structure were too expensive, labyrinthine, and obscure, lawyers and judges played an important role not only in making the courts work for businessmen but also in directing the flow of credit, manipulating trusts, and advising landed magnates on the best management of their estates. The British political system was more flexible and friendly to commerce and manufacturing than any of its European rivals. The aristocratic leadership repeatedly demonstrated strategic thinking of a high order in waging war, and creating a system of trade within and outside the empire. While Parliament seemed to be running the nation recklessly into debt, in fact it was building a secure platform for economic, military, and political success.

Not everyone benefited from the growing economy. Regions such as the West Country and East Anglia that were once the centers of manufacturing sank into obscurity as the new factory system rose in areas close to coalfields and ports.

Surplus labor from the countryside moved into urban slums with diminished lives and standards of living. Highland Scots saw their culture decimated. We know, however, what would have happened to Britain if sustained population growth had continued without industrialization. Ireland provides an example of a poisonous demographic and economic mixture. Although Belfast flourished as an industrial center in the northeast corner of the island and some glassmaking and brewing developed on a large scale elsewhere, most of Ireland lacked the mineral resources, pools of credit, agricultural system, and political leadership to create a significant manufacturing base. Landowners were less attentive to the development of their estates. Full economic integration with the rest of Britain came too late. For a time, the potato allowed the population to expand, but when the crop failed a catastrophic disaster followed.

Continued population growth probably suppressed significant advances in the standard of living. National expenditure on poor relief tripled between the 1740s and the early 1780s. Recession and bad harvests added more to the misery. Game laws, the criminal code, and legal kidnapping to recruit sailors for the Navy made things worse. On the other hand, there is considerable evidence that the condition of housing and hygiene improved during the second half of the eighteenth century, and testimony from travelers contrasted the living conditions of English rural laborers favorably with the state of the European peasantry.

We can say with assurance that the middling orders not only expanded in numbers but also lived improved material lives. Only families on fixed incomes lost ground. Most members of the professions and businessmen tended to prosper. This advance, along with the radical shifts in the lives of manual laborers, has prompted intense scrutiny by historians who watch for shifting perceptions within society. Vertical lines of obligation and deference were fading, while some have discerned working people developing a collective self-consciousness based on a horizontal connection of economic interest we call "class."

--------------------   **The Language of Class**   --------------------

The old system of orders was remarkably resilient, continuing until the end of the eighteenth century to dominate contemporary thought and practice. Some prima facie evidence of heightened class-consciousness may be provided by the appearance of the terms "upper" and "lower" class in the mid-eighteenth century and "working class" and "capitalist" first recorded in 1789 and 1792 respectively. E. P. Thompson argued that "the final years of the 18th century saw a last desperate effort by the people to reimpose the older moral economy as against the economy of the free market" provoked by state repression and wartime hardship.[14]

That some, perhaps many, working people believed in a "moral economy" based on fair prices enforced against greedy businessmen with the paternalistic help of landed magistrates is true. The trouble with Thompson's argument is that hostility between different groups in society was a staple of early modern as well as modern history. Masters and men had been in conflict for centuries. However, little hard evidence exists of widespread underground revolutionary thinking among a working class who made connections about their plight from region to region and trade to trade.

A stronger case for class-consciousness can be made in the period after 1815. By then the patriotism evoked by the war had dissipated. Hard times provoked labor conflict. More and more members of the lower orders were drawn into the world of factories and urban squalor. The government was insensitive and harshly repressive. Yet even then much industrial conflict was confined to particular sectors and focused in specialized ways.

Women

Could the industrial revolution have created a new gender order? Was the modern system in which women were marginalized, subordinated, and immured in the private sphere of home and child rearing a product of the eighteenth century? Such a view was the prevailing orthodoxy until recently. Undoubtedly, society was patriarchal, but variations within regions and classes are largely ignored by the "separate spheres" thesis. Moreover, no economic change significantly altered the habits or structure of the middle- or upper-class family. Nor did working-class women seem ready to retreat into passivity. Recently, Amanda Vickery argued: "It is clear that the explanatory power given to the notion of the separation of the home and workplace is unwarranted." A closer look at the operation of early modern businesses raises doubts about the conviction that female enterprise decayed substantially between 1700 and 1850. Female participation in public affairs had always been episodic and remained so, but was no less vigorous when it happened. Male complaints about the proper female sphere might just as easily demonstrate a concern that more women were seen to be active outside the home rather than proof that they were so confined. The shrill response of those unsettled by change suggests expanding opportunities for females.[15]

Abject servility was certainly expected of kitchen maids, but also of junior male servants. As one ascended the social scale, the job of women managing the household, domestic though that was, involved a wide range of "working" skills and technical expertise. A prosperous merchant family might have two residences, a town house and a villa, large gardens, 10 or more male and female staff to hire, train, fire, and oversee, and business colleagues and clients to entertain. By the time one reached the land-owning class the scale of household management became prodigious. Three or more large residences were not uncommon. Women controlled budgets of hundreds of thousands of dollars in today's money and supervised staffs of dozens and even hundreds. One large mid-eighteenth-century country house consumed annually 7,934 gallons of milk, 3,405 pounds of butter, 16,666 eggs, 160 sheep, and 2,377 pounds of candles to support the life of the childless couple who owned it and their guests and servants.[16] Political entertaining and alliance building required great sophistication

THE TWO PATRIOTIC DUCHESS'S on their CANVASS.
Requesting the favour of an early Poll.

Figure 4.3   The duchess of Devonshire and the duchess of Portland, both ardent
supporters of the Whig cause, campaigned for their party leader in the Commons,
Charles James Fox, in the Westminster election of 1784 (where the franchise was held
by an unusually wide spectrum of society). The aristocratic ladies distributed kisses to
butchers, bakers, and candlestick makers and may even have slipped some of them
bribes, as is shown here. "The Two Patriotic Duchesses on Their Canvass" by Thomas
Rowlandson, 1784

and knowledge of public affairs. Heiresses who had inherited their estates and wid-
owed women with children who were minors (much more common then than today)
might take over the control of stables, leasing, building projects costing millions in
current dollars, appointment of clergymen, and the supervision of electoral influence.
Women selected candidates for Parliament and told them how to vote. Women were
also organizers of public concerts, charitable boards, and made social decisions that
could exclude or include both men and women from the circles to which they were
trying desperately to gain access. In Ireland women were members of secret societies;
they wore uniforms to advertise in public their support for the Volunteer movement.
In England and Scotland women were prominent in the campaign against the slave
trade and established independent political organizations to further the cause. Until
recently, the predominantly male historical profession simply did not pay attention to
the evidence of women in the public sphere. Now, as we begin seriously to look at the
subject, we can see a world formerly invisible come into view.

As usual, the most lavish documentation comes from the aristocracy. Recent studies of the extraordinary daughters of the second duke of Richmond and of Georgiana, duchess of Devonshire highlight the ways in which rank trumped gender in British society. Amanda Foreman argues that Georgiana should be credited with being one of the first people to refine political messages for mass communications. "She was an image-maker who understood the necessity of public relations, and she became adept at the manipulation of political symbols and the dissemination of party propaganda." Her work helped to foster a sense of collective identity among the Whigs in the late eighteenth century as well as recruit new blood into the party.[17] Women regularly canvassed and publicly supported the campaigns of family members and political associates (Figure 4.3). Judith Lewis recently discovered that over a quarter of the county elections in England, Scotland, and Ireland in the period 1790–1820 recorded women participating in the process.[18] Plenty of information exists relating to female authors, poets, playwrights, novelists, painters, and patronesses. Some voices were raised against patriarchy. Mary Wollstonecraft's *Vindication of the Rights of Women* (1792) was notable, but others made the case as well (see Biography 4.1). Writers advocated the right of women to education, free choice in marriage partners, and more equal relationships with men in the legal arena.

Women did suffer new forms of subordination as they entered the factory system and replaced male servants in prosperous households. Men were constantly thinking of new ways to assert patriarchy. But the married women who worked in factories contributed vital income to the family, which gave them leverage they could not sustain later in the nineteenth century when men's wages became sufficient to support the household without help from wives.

----------------   **An English Ireland**   ----------------

One of the great contributions of the industrial revolution was the way it integrated society through changes in transportation and communication. Migration of workers between countries helped meld the pot, as did the mixture of the Scottish and Irish elites into life at Westminster and military service. Pitt the Younger's promotion of many Irish and Scottish magnates to seats in the House of Lords pushed this further, although emulsification should not be exaggerated.

The Union with Scotland, accomplished in 1707, had become accepted broadly among the population by 1800 as a good idea. Ireland, on the other hand, remained only partially integrated. The English considered the mass of the populace unreliable at best and many members of the propertied orders, even among Protestants, were less cooperative than the London government would have liked. "Patriotic" aspirations were abroad amongst the Ascendancy. The fundamental injustices of the society were extreme. Ninety-five percent of the land belonged to some 5,000

Biography 4.1

Mary Wollstonecraft
1759–97

Mary Wollstonecraft was born into a prosperous merchant family, but her father squandered his inheritance and ended as a handkerchief weaver. She did receive some formal schooling but in her teenage years became an autodidact. Later she ran a school and served as a governess in Ireland. In the 1780s she began a literary life as a reviewer and author of books. Wollstonecraft became the common-law wife of the American commercial adventurer Gilbert Imlay, and had a daughter by him. He deserted her, and she twice attempted suicide. Later she married the philosopher William Godwin and died as a result of giving birth to their daughter, Mary. The latter grew up to marry the poet Shelley and author the celebrated story of the monster, *Frankenstein* (1818).

Mary Wollstonecraft is remembered best for her two great works, the *Vindication of the Rights of Men* of 1790 that answered Burke's denunciation of the French Revolution, and the *Vindication of the Rights of Women* of 1792, a celebrated and revolutionary manifesto for female equality, which became an immediate bestseller. Wollstonecraft visited Paris in 1792 and was critical of the Terror. She lived in the most advanced and radical intellectual circles in London during an era of dramatic change and knew Thomas Paine, William Blake, and William Wordsworth. She was an advocate of equality of the sexes and a new form of education that would transform society. In a posthumous work she asserted that women had strong sexual desires and that it was degrading and wrong to pretend otherwise. Her great achievement was to focus attention on the ways in which society imposed false distinctions of class, age, and gender that victimized human rights. She asked people to think in new ways and wrote of women that they were "confined in cages like the feathered race, they have nothing to do but to plume themselves, and stalk with mock majesty from perch to perch."[19]

Protestant landowners. For most of the century even wealthy and well-educated Catholics could not vote or serve as MPs. Another structural problem was the differing attitude of the English and Irish elites about winning the loyalty of the Catholic majority population. London pressed for concessions; in Dublin strict suppression was seen as the only viable strategy. Relief began in the 1770s, only because of English pressure. The franchise finally came in 1792–3.

Legislative independence was granted by the Whigs to the Irish Parliament in 1782, but even before the French wars Pitt came to believe that the reform was a fatal mistake. "We may keep the Parliament, but lose the people," he wrote privately in September 1784.[20] Irish MPs believed that in 1782 they had achieved a practical equivalent of home rule. However, although the legislature was now fully in the hands of the Ascendancy, the executive was not.

The pressures caused by the war brought Irish discontent to a head from 1793 onwards. Irish radicals became disillusioned by the "patriot" politicians who subordinated themselves to Pitt's regime in the emergency. The United Irishmen reflected the radicalization and disillusionment that the events of the 1790s brought to Irish society at much wider levels. Behind the French wars was the Revolution itself. The French attempt to land in Cork in 1796 and uprisings in 1798 brought things to a head. Pitt decided to abolish the Irish Parliament and create a United Kingdom of Great Britain and Ireland.

A minority of articulate Irish public opinion supported the Union of 1801, rather more opposed it, and the rest were apathetic. Outside Parliament in Dublin on the day of the vote the crowd was reported to be "very numerous but perfectly quiet, neither hissing or huzzaing."[21] The Irish Parliament, haunted by its insecurity and fearing its isolation, accepted the Union with reluctance as a safeguard to the Ascendancy's way of life. The deep divides in Irish society and the profound inequality in the distribution of political power remained unaltered. Ireland was granted 100 seats in the House of Commons and 28 seats in the Lords for Irish representative peers elected for life and four seats for bishops of the Irish established Church. Duties on all Irish products but grain were abolished and general United Kingdom expenses were to be shared by a ratio of 15 to 2. The Union preserved the inequitable distribution of land until the 1880s.

The Irish economy improved after the Union. State-sponsored education was established. Ireland also enjoyed more state intervention promoting public health and public works than in the rest of the United Kingdom. The machinery of British rule at Dublin Castle to some degree spared the Irish people the full force of home-grown Ascendancy oppression.

Scots, Wha Hae

The great cry of Scottish nationalism, "Scots, wha hae" ("Scots who have" … fought alongside national heroes such as Wallace and Bruce), from a patriotic song by Robert Burns written in 1793, is fitting in its ambiguity. It was a poem about pride and resistance to English rule. The Scottish national identity was complex: Scottish, British, and imperial. It became mythic during this period, assuming the cloak of Highland culture that had been despised as barbaric by Lowland Scots for centuries and was now dying or dead in any case. The Gaelic way of life had been largely destroyed by the military defeat of Jacobites and the economic revolution in land tenure that ended clanship.

Figure 4.4   A Highlander. *Col. The Honorable William Gordon* by Pompeo Batoni, 1765

Scottish participation in the expansion of empire during the second half of the eighteenth century created prosperity at home and provided employment to tens of thousands of ambitious Scots. A British imperial identity helped place the inhabitants of the archipelago in the context of a group of peoples each contributing to the whole rather than satellites following in England's wake.

Pitt the Elder had had the idea after the defeat of the Jacobites in 1745 of recruiting Highland regiments and turning their military ferocity on the French and other enemies. These kilted clansmen went on to serve in most battles around the world, culminating in courageous action at Waterloo. They became heroic figures seen as symbols of loyalty and bravery (Figure 4.4). A new vision of the Highlander was imprinted both in the Lowlands, where wearing the tartan began to be adopted as "Scottish," and in England, where a romantic glow enveloped the now safely de-fanged Stuarts and the heroes of the war against Napoleon. The poetry and novels of Sir Walter Scott (1771–1832) and the development of ideas that rugged landscapes were sublime led to a rage for tourism in the Highlands. Sir Walter also discovered the "honors of Scotland" – the old Stewart crown, sword, and scepter – locked up in a forgotten cupboard in Edinburgh Castle. These were paraded before George IV in 1822 on the first visit of a legitimate monarch to Scotland since 1651, where the king appeared in full Highland garb (and pink tights). He even proposed a toast to the clans.[22]

Much of this folderol was bogus, though the crown was real enough. Historians are offended or bemused by the "invention of tradition" and the false notion that somehow Highland dress and traditions were representative of Scottish society as a whole. But as so often happens, and this time in a positive way, myth becomes reality whatever scholars may have to say about it. To make Bonnie Prince Charlie a heroic figure presses the case rather far, but the acceptance of this new "Highland" identity by the Scots came at just the right moment. The economic and cultural momentum of England in 1815 threatened to swallow Scotland whole, making it simply "North Britain," as many English people actually called it. By embracing the Highland identity, the Scots could assert symbolically what was true in reality, that they had distinctive laws, educational system, religion, and culture. This new outward dress could hardly offend the English because of the loyal service of the clansmen in war, and did not threaten a restoration of absolute Catholic monarchs since the Stuart dynasty was extinct. Modern Americans who get a little weepy watching *Gone with the Wind* empathize with a tragic story, but their false nostalgia does not imply support for slavery. Stories of romance in former times pull at the heartstrings, especially if accompanied by emotive music such as "Dixie," or rather "Will ye no' come home again." Americans have turned the destruction of Indian culture into a mythic "Wild West" of independent living and enterprise. Slavery and the Civil War have become a redemptive story of reconciliation and freedom. Myths bind disparate cultures together into a single society. So when the Scots dress in the tartan they enter into a world of make-believe that asserts their distinctive identity while not disturbing their ability to be loyal Britons. The romantic nationalism that swept across Europe, where it did so much damage and became a curse for the world in the nineteenth and twentieth centuries, breathed gently on Scotland.

Englishness

For the past three centuries, what one historian calls "that nasty English habit of using the terms English and British interchangeably" has continued unabated.[23] The English still tend to use English and British interchangeably, while the Scots and Welsh define the words more consciously and conscientiously. (Americans are still inclined to speak of the queen of "England.") "I do not think there is a people more prejudiced in their own favor," a Continental visitor wrote about the English in the 1720s.[24] Edward Gibbon, an Englishman, of course, called his homeland "the sole great refuge of mankind."[25] Shakespeare's work was raised to supreme status at the core of English national pride in the eighteenth century. His vision of the homeland was of "This other Eden, … This precious stone set in the silver sea, … This blessed plot … this England."[26]

The English had much to be arrogant about. Success in war, a moderate religion, an expanding empire, a political system that was the envy of the world, and an economy that seemed destined to produce unending prosperity all reinforced self-satisfaction.

In so far as people define themselves by comparisons with others, the English had some right to feel that their way of life was in advance of that in Scotland, Wales, and Ireland. Dr. Johnson, in his famous dictionary, defined oats as: "A grain, which in England is generally given to horses, but in Scotland supports the people."[27] Anti-Scottish feeling, however, can be exaggerated. Johnson formed indelible friendships with a number of north Britons, and undertook a long and dangerous journey to learn about the country. More ugly was the vehement anti-Catholicism that led the English to despise the Irish.

The English were boisterous, aggressive, and proud of their liberty, beef, Church, and king. They thought of themselves as civilized, generous, and tolerant. They had little idea that their neighbors found them boorish, proud, and greedy. They saw themselves as committed to toleration and constitutionalism. In fact they embraced strong religious and political prejudices. They were bullies.

However, after accounting for human frailty, blind spots, and dubious characters, the English landed elite governed the nation in a liberal and open spirit. This was not a product of genetic superiority or moral ascendancy. It derived from historical experiences. They lacked the military and police resources that Continental states possessed to repress opposition from below. This taught them to wield authority cautiously. They had to practice the political arts in a competitive electoral arena and were obliged to win popular support to preserve their power. They associated love of liberty with the quality of honor. Out of selfish impulses the aristocracy had defined itself against the Crown, against the principles of absolutism, and against the maintenance of standing armies. At bottom, this was what Parliament, the landowners' assembly, stood for. Parliament, in turn, helped school the nation in liberal practices and a liberal spirit.[28] Alexander Pope addressed these ideas in his *Essay on Man* in 1734:

> How shall he keep what, sleeping or awake,
> A weaker may surprise, a stronger take?
> His safety must his liberties restrain;
> All join to guard what each desires to gain.
> Forc'd into virtue thus by self-defence
> Ev'n Kings learn'd justice and benevolence:
> Self-love forsook the path it first pursu'd,
> And found the private in the public good.

More than wealth, more than literacy, this concept trickled down to the lowest levels of English society. The belief in rights and liberty was at the core of England and made the nation distinctive, blind as many – but not all – were to slavery and the empire abroad. Handel set it to music in his most popular oratorio, *Judas Maccabaeus*, written in 1747 to commemorate the final victory over the absolutist Stuarts:

> 'Tis liberty, dear liberty alone.
> That gives fresh beauty to the sun;
> That bids all nature look more gay,
> And lovely life with pleasure steal away.

At a more humble level Thomas Turner, the shopkeeper in Sussex, wrote in his diary with pride of England being "this land of liberty and freedom."[29]

The Oak in the Flowerpot – A British Empire

One thing that bound the British together was the shared possession of an empire. English, Welsh, Irish, and Scots served in the armies and fleets that conquered and secured it. Aristocrats, merchants, sailors, and private soldiers acted together to bring it about (see Biography 4.2). Britain cannot be seen by itself without imperialism being included as part of the story. In the early eighteenth century the British

Biography 4.2

Henry Salt
1780–1827

Henry Salt was the son of a provincial surgeon. The young man had a wanderlust, and left England for the first time in a party accompanying Viscount Valentia on a tour of British possessions in India, Ceylon, and the Red Sea. He was latter appointed consul-general in Egypt where he spent the rest of his life. Salt developed a good relationship with the ruler, Mehmet Ali, and a passion for the recording and collection of Egyptian antiquities. His diplomatic appointment demonstrated how far it was possible for a man to rise in the new empire from comparatively humble origins, especially if he could gain the help of a patrician patron. "He ached to join the glamorous world of aristocrats and connoisseurs."[30]

Salt worked hard to pursue British influence in Egypt at the expense of the French. At the same time he opened ancient tombs, excavated historic sites, and sent home booty to the British Museum. He combined the pursuit of national interests with the quest for self-advancement. He spent too much money, however, in the search for art and prestige and was condemned as mercenary when he tried to sell his collections to the British government. Ironically, it was the French who finally paid him lavishly for some of his archeological discoveries. Salt was among the many Britons of the eighteenth and nineteenth centuries who looted the non-European world to benefit the culture and power of the homeland. They fanned out around the globe; their trajectories became the sinews of the empire.

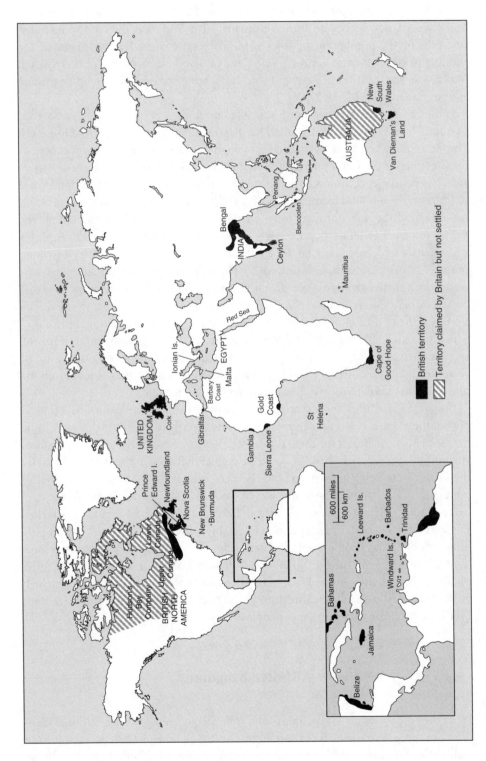

Map 4.2 The British Empire in 1815

ruled more than half a million white settlers as well as hundreds of thousands of free and enslaved non-whites on four continents. After Waterloo the empire included one-fifth of the population of the world. The war against France increased the number of colonies from 26 to 43. The Cape of Good Hope, Gold Coast, Trinidad, Malta, and vast swathes of Australia and India were annexed. The empire pushed west in Canada (see Map 4.2).

It used to be said that the British stumbled upon their empire in a "fit of absence of mind." Niall Ferguson, on the other hand, argues that "from the reign of Elizabeth I onwards, there had been a sustained campaign to take over the empires of others."[31] Debates rumble on about the impulse that created empire and the nature of British rule. It is no longer common to find historians arguing that a "second" empire arose in India on the rebound from the loss of the Thirteen Colonies. Expansion in North America and the subcontinent were on parallel tracks, moving in tandem. The degree to which ordinary Britons were aware of or even cared about the empire is still a matter of debate (see Chapter 8). Britain resembled, in C. W. Pasley's striking phrase, "an oak planted in a flower pot."[32] Three factors made world conquest conducted by a small island possible. The first was the fiscal-military state we have discussed earlier. The second was the cooperation of those who were being ruled. The third was the evolution of what Linda Colley calls a "precocious national ideology," which provided cohesion and induced belligerence.[33] Britain compensated for the large and dangerous nations that were her near neighbors by developing a kind of "Napoleon complex" that bred aggression elsewhere. The farther from home the more furious and determined British rule seemed to become.

Colley has identified and described the compromises and collusions that underpinned the empire. It was the sepoy armies made up largely of natives that won India for the British and held it for them until 1947. To a great extent the subcontinent was run and garrisoned by Indians. It could be argued that even at the height of empire the British were being allowed to hold their colonies at the discretion of the native populations. British military power was by no means always efficacious in the days before industrialization took full effect. Barbary pirates had regularly attacked English and Irish coastal villages and in the eighteenth century were still kidnapping hundreds of British people from merchant ships. Native Americans massacred huge numbers of settlers in the Carolinas, and Indian princes crushed British-led armies on the subcontinent as late as 1780.[34] Only the advent of mechanized weaponry such as steam battleships and machine guns gave Britain an insurmountable advantage over uncooperative non-European peoples.

A United Kingdom

What then of "Britons"? The people of the archipelago feeling as one? National identities are speculative stereotypes, useful but not to be taken as precise measures of reality. On the other hand, the establishment of the state known as the United

Kingdom of Great Britain and Ireland with a single king, Parliament, and flag was a fact in 1801. A mixture of farsighted leadership, homogenizing culture based on a shared language and expanded print media, joint efforts in war against a common enemy, and burgeoning commerce knitted at least three of the four nations together.

Colley's thesis about the sense of growing "Britishness" proposes an "invented nation" superimposed, if only for a while, onto much older alignments and loyalties in an archipelago that was culturally and ethnically diverse. Whether this was an English state turning itself into a British one or more of a shared enterprise is still open to debate. Britain was never a melting pot. Few would argue with Colley's judgment that a kind of "British" nationalism was forged by war. Though patriotic myths were contested by some, conflict with France brought Britons, whether they hailed from Wales or Scotland or England, into confrontation with an obviously hostile "other" and encouraged them to define themselves collectively against it. They saw themselves as Protestants struggling against the world's foremost Catholic power. They regarded the French as superstitious, militarist, decadent, and unfree.[35] English rights appealed to peoples throughout the archipelago and in the colonies. Colin Kidd argues that English liberties "embodied universal aspirations to freedom and self-government."[36] But was anglicization really briticization? The Ascendancy saw themselves as Englishmen in Ireland, which is different than being Britons. On the other hand, the Scots were wrapping themselves in bogus gaelicization. Nine out of 10 Welshmen still spoke Welsh.

The war undoubtedly stimulated a widespread increase in the popularity of and loyalty towards the monarchy, fostered by the government and George III. Military reviews, services of thanksgiving, and jubilees highlighted the ceremonial and unifying elements of the institution. The musty and rumpled air of the first two Georges was replaced by trumpets and ermine. At the same time the king was transformed by the French threat into the guardian of liberty. Royal ceremonies became affirmations of the constitution. As Marilyn Morris has pointed out: "Tradition, the first cousin of custom and the basis of common law, [turned out to be] as solid a doctrine as divine right."[37]

George III was too rigid in his views about America and the Catholics, but so were most of his subjects. The twin tragedies of his mental illness and inadequate sons made his personal life a kind of hell, yet he reached a level of popularity among his people that testified to his decency and his genuine love of country. After the debacle of the early years of his reign, he admitted he had made mistakes. He wrote: "That I have erred is undoubted, otherwise I would not be human, but … whenever I have failed it has been from the head not the heart."[38]

The United Kingdom of 1801, a British state, was fragmented, pluralistic, and yet amazingly durable. It could be holed in one place but, as with ocean liners that have multiple watertight compartments, still stay afloat. At the same time it could keep up speed and forge ahead aggressively. Success bred confidence and encouraged further expansion and national fervor. Yet this patriotism was to be centered increasingly on a weak, symbolic monarch and not on the conquest of Europe. The twentieth-century socialist George Orwell, no admirer of royalty, valued the monarchy's "function of acting as an escape-valve for dangerous emotions."[39]

Why There Was No Revolution

The French came within a hair's breadth of making a successful landing in Cork in 1796. Official opinion at the time held that Ireland could not have been saved.[40] Bloody rebellion followed in 1798. Harvest failures and rising food prices provoked serious rioting in England that peaked between 1794 and 1796. Inflation caused by rising food and other costs, driven up by the war, reduced real wages for skilled London workers by as much 15 percent. Mass protest meetings took place. Underground groups of revolutionaries organized in the big cities. Low pay in the Navy sparked mutinies, and some of the sailors spoke the language of revolution. For long periods the war was waged unsuccessfully and economic hardship was suffered by millions of people. Demands for parliamentary reform increased as the grip of the peerage over the election of MPs reached unprecedented levels. Pitt and his colleagues, no wilting lilies, became seriously alarmed. What saved Britain from revolution?

As the British people watched the events in France unfold – the Declaration of the Rights of Man, renunciation of feudal privileges, limited monarchy, abolition of titles, redistribution of noble lands to peasants, and the end of **tithes**-paying to clergy – one imagines that many of these reforms appeared attractive to the poor and the oppressed in Britain. The prominent political role of, and financial boost received by, the French bourgeoisie must have seemed alluring to middling people across the Channel. In fact the opposite occurred. The execution of Louis XVI and the institution of the Terror understandably shocked and horrified the landed elite in Britain, but bloody revolution did not win the approval of the masses either. They accepted their king, Church, and the aristocracy as their legitimate rulers. If anything, events in France reinforced established institutions in Britain. In part this was due to fear of change and scorn and loathing for Catholicism and the French. The rise out of the ashes of the Revolution of tyrannical and aggressive Bonapartism confirmed the suspicions of an already dubious British public.

We have noted above that the monarchy gained new luster during these years and George III became ever more popular even as he teetered on the brink of insanity. His suffering evoked sympathy, not revulsion. Moreover during the crucial years of the war and revolution the king had his wits about him and was far more effective and vigorous executive than Louis XVI. No power vacuum existed at the top of British politics. Although some of George's disreputable children were unpopular, most notably the Prince of Wales, others, such as the duke of Clarence (1765–1837 – the future William IV) and the duke of Sussex (1773–1843), earned more affection. The king's granddaughter and heir presumptive, Princess Charlotte (1796–1817), was well liked and did not die until after the war was over.

Although bad harvests and inflation inflicted hardships, the common people of Britain believed themselves to be well off economically and politically compared to their counterparts in other lands, especially the hated French. Famine had long ceased in Britain but continued in France into the nineteenth century. The innovative economy during the second half of the eighteenth century had the potential to create great tension between inherited mentality and rapidly expanding material progress, but the pace was slow enough, the people adaptable enough, and the state flexible enough so that this did not culminate in an explosion. Bumper harvests eventually brought food prices down. Life never became unsupportable.

The British were taxed nearly three times as heavily as the French in the 1780s. Yet war finance never produced a fundamental challenge to the social and political order. Parliamentary control over the choice of taxes created support for the fiscal system. The British aristocracy enjoyed no exemptions from direct taxation. The deeply unpopular method of tax farming used in France did not exist across the Channel. Moreover, the tax burden seemed "invisible" to most consumers. Above all, the British state found ways to tap the nation's wealth through loans that produced positive and not negative military, financial, and social results.

The sharp edge of poverty was also abated in Britain by working people clubbing together to provide mutual assistance in disasters, illness, and to cover costs of funerals. Parliament enacted legislation in 1793 to increase the protection of funds in such "friendly societies," as they were called. Parliament was also willing to intervene to protect wage structures. Judges sometimes acted in favor of workers against masters. In 1772, 10 men prosecuted by the Currier's Company in a labor dispute were found innocent by sympathetic juries, and they were able to bring actions against the company to claim damages for assault and false imprisonment. The Scottish courts were particularly noted for their willingness to check the unlimited authority of employers over men. Food rioters were usually treated with sympathy and leniency. Magistrates exerted pressure to satisfy popular feelings.[41] As the century progressed, the limits on what could be said in public debate (or depicted in satirical cartoons) grew wider and wider. The battle for the hearts and minds of the political nation in a volatile partisan era was fought out healthily in a rapidly expanding arena of open disputation inside and outside Parliament. If opponents stayed within the confines of the constitution, almost anything could be said.[42]

The propertied paid a substantial price to assist the destitute and showed a keen eye both in England and Scotland in understanding that the danger of social turmoil could be reduced by creating a kind of safety net below which the poor could not fall. Though the indigent were sometimes herded into communal buildings or workhouses, outdoor relief to the able-bodied poor had long existed. In 1795 reform-minded magistrates instituted what came to be called the Speenhamland system to help support the poor in a period of falling wages and rising bread prices. The example was widely followed.

The Union with Scotland held firm. It left national identity unmolested and opened up jobs, patronage, and economic opportunity. Even sword-wielding clansmen had integrated themselves into the British army and become key elements in military successes all over the world. In 1784 the government returned estates confiscated after 1745 in gratitude. Scottish elites were conservative and had become anti-French. A "United Scotsmen" organization paralleled the revolutionary United Irishmen and developed links with France, but it never attracted many members. The Scottish middling orders, like their counterparts in England, showed no signs of wavering. They felt that their interests were taken into account by Parliament.

The British elite had become so rich and powerful by 1815 that they were in serious danger of overplaying their hand. The disruptions between 1815 and 1832 were in part a response to this, but they never lost their nerve and were willing to make concessions. To focus on repression in understanding the failure of those opposed to the regime to spark a revolution is a serious mistake. The kindling simply would not burn, to say nothing of the logs. Some historians have attributed this to the influence of conservative religious movements, especially Methodism and the Evangelicals. These groups certainly encouraged loyalty to the monarchy and obedience to superiors. But it is hard to see how such comparatively small groups (the Methodists numbered about 57,000 at the time of Wesley's death in 1791) could have held a strong revolutionary movement at bay. The established Churches in Scotland and England were also profoundly anti-revolutionary in spirit. The Enlightenment had not seriously corroded either the spiritual or civil leadership of Britain. Nor had the loss of America inflicted lasting damage either on the regime's confidence or its beliefs. The celebrated French historian Elie Halévy was incorrect in his assessment of the role of Methodism as an antidote to the French Revolution, but he was right to say that England was "a country of voluntary obedience."[43] At the core of British stability was a genuine devotion at all social levels to the ideals for which they believed their country stood.

The Triumph of the Old Regime?

Jonathan Clark has reminded us that eighteenth-century Britain was more old-fashioned than we thought. He believes it was just another one of the European *ancien régimes*, each a little different but all patriarchal, deferential, and confessional states. Until the 1820s Britain "had three essential characteristics: it was Anglican, it was aristocratic, and it was monarchical."[44] This is a welcome reminder that religion still mattered mightily in the eighteenth century, the monarchy was intact, and the aristocracy continued to command taste, society, wealth, and the state. The growth of the fiscal-military apparatus consolidated central government power. If one looks anywhere in British life during the eighteenth century one finds noblemen in the midst of things: digging canals and coalmines, holding agricultural shows, overseeing the scientists of the **Royal Society**, commanding ships, commissioning portraits, presiding at trials, conducting embassies, exploring distant lands, governing colonies, setting new fashions, ordaining clergymen, concluding business deals, designing new buildings, leading mobs, planning revolutions, conducting archeological excavations, getting richer, happier, and more powerful as the century concluded.

Critics have not been feeble or absent in answering Clark. One of the most damaging challenges to his thesis is that it fails to account for a contrasting view of the state. Those who advocated "Throne and Altar" values were reacting against what in their view was the destructive and all-consuming ideology of the Enlightenment, secularism, egalitarianism, and what to them was an unhealthy obsession with progress. Even though some may have claimed Divine Right monarchy still existed, it was clear to all that had eyes to see, including the kings themselves, that they ruled by the will of Parliament not God. Moreover, though George III remained a significant political player, his role in executive decision making was much reduced from the 1780s onwards, partly due to dramatic growth of government business, especially in wartime, which made it impossible for anyone to maintain an overview of all that was going on, and the more immediate reason of his illness.[45]

Britain was neither an *ancien régime* nor a "class society," though evidence for both can be found. People were aware that traditional conceptions of society no longer fitted the changing landscape. The situation was too fluid for them to capture in a new conceptualization.[46] Like most of Europe, Britain was a profoundly unequal society in the eighteenth century, hierarchical and awash in poverty. Dominic Lieven calls the peerage "the richest, the most powerful … of all Europe's noble elites in 1815."[47] Yet it was also a place were the elite admitted newcomers with comparative ease, and tens of thousands of people were rising into the middle classes. Uniquely, England was free of famine and provided state-sponsored assistance to the indigent. The common law and trial by jury gave Britain a fundamentally respected legal system. The conception of individual freedom held and practiced by the common people was exceptional.[48] The established Church did not enjoy the dominance that it did in other *ancien régime* states. In spite of corruption the system of parliamentary elections created a completely different dynamic within the landed elite than anything to be found in France, Russia, Austria, or Germany. This made the aristocracy more politically alert and willing to foster economic and social interests that were not their own. From the 1780s the criticism of electoral corruption mounted and began to undermine the legitimacy of Parliament. The continued effectiveness of the system rested on the willingness of the elite to respond to external pressure. The abolition of the slave trade in 1807 is a notable example of a concession to opinion shaped in what historians call the "public sphere," a developing force that will be discussed more fully in the next chapter. Even deeply entrenched interests and moral obduracy could now be overborne by pressure from outside the ruling class. This willingness of the elite to interact with public opinion led to a heightened interest in the political process that reached deep into British society. Thus did the centrality of Parliament to national life, unique among the great states of Europe, remain viable.

Unusual dynamism in agriculture, commerce, and manufacturing had developed in Britain before 1700 and was changing Britain faster than anywhere else in Europe. In population growth, rapid urbanization, and the rise of a large middle class no other country matched the United Kingdom in 1815. The economy under-pinned a war-making capacity that proved spectacularly successful. It was evident already, as a master of nineteenth-century British history noted, that "neither the institutions, nor the ideas, that had been inherited from the eighteenth century would suffice."[49]

Chapter 5

Reform, 1816–41

Contents

Britain's triumph over France in 1815 was an unparalleled victory, but the government had seriously underestimated the consequences of high prices during wartime and the economic slowdown that came with peace. During the war manufacturing had flourished with the demands for uniforms and armaments. After 1815 that stimulus disappeared. Hundreds of thousands of soldiers and sailors were demobilized without immediate prospect of re-employment. Ordinary people became desperate. A revolutionary outbreak took place in northern England in June 1817, one of the few attempts at organized armed rebellion ever to occur in nineteenth-century Britain. Yet, the rising fizzled out and was easily suppressed. Another conspiracy in Glasgow imploded in 1820.

The old regime maintained its position in the tempestuous early years of peace by means of repression and reform. The "fiscal-military state" of the eighteenth century was dismantled. "Old corruption" was extinguished by the 1830s and replaced by an increasingly efficient and incorruptible central bureaucracy that was small in scale and lay lightly on the taxpayers' backs – "the minimal state." Tax revenues dropped by a quarter between 1816 and 1846 despite a nearly 50 percent rise in population. Many questions puzzle historians about this period. How close did Britain come to revolution? Why did the vibrant world of radical protest fail to jell into effective opposition to the old regime? Was the force used to repress radicalism excessive? Did reactionaries want to impose autocracy?

The Postwar Era

The radical leadership, notable among whom were Major Cartwright, William Cobbett (1763–1835), and Henry "Orator" Hunt (1773–1835), were by no means in agreement with each other. Much protest, such as that coming from "Luddite" machine breakers, was not directly connected with any organized political movement. They simply wanted better wages and feared unemployment brought about by mechanization and the introduction of new technology.

In 1816 a group of extreme radicals called "Spencians" after Thomas Spence (1750–1814) announced a meeting to be held at Spa Fields near London, to be addressed by Hunt, Cartwright, and Arthur Thistlewood (1770–1820). The crowd marched on the Tower of London looting en route. Another famous protest meeting was organized in Manchester at St. Peter's Fields on August 16, 1819, where perhaps as many as 100,000 people gathered to hear Hunt speak. Although warned by the London government not to interfere, the city fathers called on the peaceful crowd to disperse, and troops were ordered to charge when it failed to do so. Eleven people were killed and hundreds injured. "Peterloo," as the affray became known, quickly took on mythic stature. Few things are so damaging to a government as the murder of innocents by incompetents. Even more serious was the determined, though failed, Cato Street conspiracy led by Thistlewood in February 1820 to assassinate the entire Cabinet while they met for dinner at a private house in London. Radical journalism, though frequently suppressed, managed to keep an open discussion of the abuses and corruption of the system before the eyes of the public. The prime minister, Lord Liverpool, felt disaffection among the people was more serious than during the height of the French Revolution in the 1790s.[1]

Perhaps the oddest eruption of political discontent in the postwar years was the storm over George IV's (1762–1830, king from 1820) failed attempt to divorce his wife, Caroline of Brunswick (1768–1821). Enemies of the government, who ranged from great Whig peers to urban paupers, rallied to her cause. The brouhaha was explosive, yet did not actually endanger the structure of society since nobles were in sympathy with the middle class, and working men and women were found on both sides of the issue. The king took revenge on Caroline by locking the doors of Westminster Abbey during the coronation so that she could not wear her crown. Conveniently, she died a few months later. When reporting the death of Napoleon, which had occurred shortly before Caroline's, an aide said to the king, "I have the pleasure to tell your Majesty that your bitterest enemy is dead." The George replied, "No! is she, by God?," thinking he meant the queen.

Radicals were critical of the privileges and power of landed society that they saw as resting on unfair distribution of wealth and manipulation of the powers of the state. They denounced sinecures held by members of the elite or distributed to clients as patronage, and they criticized the unprogressive tax system. Tariffs on imported wheat known as the **Corn Laws** protected the agricultural incomes of landowners from market forces and foreign competition while keeping food expensive for the poor. The corrupt electoral system was increasingly seen as the means by which the landed elite sustained their advantages over the rest of society. As the radical critique unfolded, more and more members of the aristocracy realized reform was necessary.

The Tory government, however, turned first to repression. Henry Addington, now Viscount Sidmouth, was put in charge. The Coercion Acts of 1817, prompted by Spa Fields, and the Six Acts of 1819, a response to Peterloo, were the principal steps taken to suppress dissent. The former temporarily suspended **habeas corpus** for the first time in English history and made "seditious" meetings illegal. The Six Acts curtailed the radical press by imposing taxes that made newspapers and periodicals too expensive for ordinary people to buy and imposed other repressive measures. Spies employed by the government infiltrated radical groups.

The dictatorial policies were effective but provoked venomous criticism. The poet Percy Shelley (1792–1822) wrote in anger about a member of the government:

> I met Murder on the way –
> He had a mask like Castlereagh
> Very smooth he looked, yet grim;
> Seven blood-hounds followed him …
> He tossed them human hearts to chew
> Which from his wide cloak he drew.

The Whig grandees were horrified by the desecration of civil liberties. Viscount Althorp (1782–1845) and a group of young Whigs led the opposition to the repressive legislation. His friend, Viscount Ebrington, called the Six Acts "the most alarming attack ever made by Parliament upon the liberties and constitution of the country."[2] When one of the greatest Whig magnates, the fourth Earl Fitzwilliam, criticized the Peterloo massacre, he was summarily dismissed as a lord lieutenant in Yorkshire, which blew a chill through even conservative Whig circles. For the first time in the nineteenth century Whiggery began to coalesce around the idea of parliamentary reform.

By the standards of repressive regimes on the Continent the Six Acts were hardly draconian. Moreover, the national and local authorities took some positive steps. Despite protests from many taxpayers disbursement of poor relief almost doubled between 1803 and 1818. Some factory reform was enacted and expenditure budgeted for the employment of the laboring poor on public works. The old regime was saved, however, by returning economic prosperity and by the lack of unity within the radical movement itself.

The Economists

Lord Liverpool had many excellent qualities and often seemed more like a wise uncle than a tyrant. He confronted social unrest as he had the Napoleonic threat – with calm directness. He also managed to survive several grueling debates about national finance in Parliament that provoked as much heat, if less violence, than protests outside the chamber. The ministry bowed to commercial demands to reduce taxes. "Industrial Britain was favoured at the expense of agricultural Britain."[3]

The greatest parliamentary debate swirled around the currency. The convertability of paper into specie had been suspended during the war. "Bullionists" were anxious to restore the **gold standard** after the close of hostilities, which they believed would end wasteful speculation by financiers and put the country on a solid economic foundation. Among the supporters of this policy were the famous economic theorists David Ricardo (1772–1823) and Thomas Robert Malthus (1766–1834), leading government politicians such as William Huskisson (1766–1834), and many Whigs. Businessmen and bankers tended to oppose the change. Eventually, Parliament directed that the Bank of England begin the return to the gold standard in stages as of February 1820. Within months cash payments, by restoring the currency to its prewar value, had increased the value of the debts of landowners while benefiting those involved in international commerce, the reverse of what many had expected. Price deflation helped the workers. Despite the impact of the change on its own supporters in the countryside, the government stuck with its decision. Economic growth burgeoned and industrialization expanded rapidly.

Many senior politicians were persuaded to accept the tenets of free trade (laissez faire). Removing impediments to commerce made sense even to those who had not mastered the sometimes obscure writings of Ricardo, best known for his opposition to the Corn Laws and the first man to see economics as "a method of thinking rather than a body of concrete results."[4] He, along with Malthus and a coterie of followers, came to be called the "classical" economists. Malthus, an Anglican clergyman, published his *Essay on Population* in 1797. In it he argued that population would outstrip the food supply and lead to famine, disease, and death. He criticized the Poor Law, which offered only short-term help and would engender further suffering in the long term, discouraging prudential restraint among the populace, the only positive means of checking further growth.[5] Ricardo's masterwork, *On the Principles of Political Economy and Taxation* (1817), argued that wages must be kept at subsistence level or population pressure would raise the cost of labor which in turn would have a negative impact on profitability and the growth rate of the economy. By keeping wages low the maximum amount of capital could be invested in the expansion of manufacturing. This was a free pass for businessmen and farmers to ignore humanity and justice. Most members of the classical school felt that the economy could not escape from a closed and finite system that held back the expansion of a shared prosperity – hence the sobriquet, "the dismal science."

Liberal Toryism

The term "liberal" came into use during the postwar period. It implied a preference for low taxes and low public spending, for non-intervention in the operations of the workplace and the market, and for a minimal (meaning harsh) welfare system. Members of all political parties were influenced by or reacted against emergent economic theory and supported various elements of this program. Hence the term "liberal Toryism" has been used to describe the reforming era of the 1820s when Peel, Huskisson, Canning, and others introduced new measures. Some historians see "liberal" and "Tory" as contradictory terms, proof of the continued unfocused nature of parties.

The terms "Tory" and "Whig" continued to have ill-defined cores and lacy penumbras through which all sorts of political opinion could pass. Lord Liverpool sometimes referred to himself as a Whig, and Tory was used as a term of abuse by the Whigs and was only embraced wholeheartedly by the opponents of the Reform Bill in 1831. Some of the party's leaders preferred "Conservative." Yet, the government in these years self-consciously rallied to the call of "Church and King," assumed that the lower orders had to be beaten into submission, and venerated the memory of Pitt. The Whigs, though still divided about parliamentary reform, celebrated their devotion to religious emancipation, grumbled about royal influence, argued that the masses would be loyal if they were treated fairly, and remembered Fox with affection. The Whigs' broadening definition of "public opinion" grew to include larger and larger numbers of people. The Tories were much slower to accommodate themselves to this conception. London newspapers aligned with opposing camps and served as engines of partisanship. Each party also had a journal, the Tory *Quarterly*

Review and the Whig *Edinburgh Review,* whose readership consisted of much of the political nation. The magazines were edited by leading intellectuals and gave direction to the faithful. The terms "Whig" and "Tory" were unselfconsciously used in national and local elections. The historian John Phillips gathered voting statistics that demonstrate how the postwar political system cannot be understood without them.[6]

No one embodied "liberal Toryism" more than Sir Robert Peel, second baronet (1788–1850), who became home secretary in 1822. Norman Gash argues that he turned a ministry primarily oriented towards the preservation of law and order "into an instrument of social policy."[7] Peel was the first man whose family had made their wealth in the textile industry to enter the front rank of British politics. However, he had been educated in the traditional manner of the elite, owned a large landed estate, lived in a great country house, and embraced many old-fashioned values. Some Tory aristocrats disdained his parvenu origins, but such snobbery was hard to sustain successfully once the archpriest of old regime values, the duke of Wellington, allied himself with Peel and continued to support him through thick and thin in the struggles that arose later when they abandoned untenable conservative positions. Each recognized and respected the other's genius.

Peel drafted legislation that reduced the number of crimes punishable by death. He substituted transportation, whippings, solitary confinement, and the treadmill for lesser offenses. The number of executions dropped precipitously even though the population grew rapidly. He also commenced serious prison reform. He established a uniformed police force headquartered at "Scotland Yard." The officers on the beat became known as "Bobbies," immortalizing Sir Robert, although these agents of the state were long distrusted as an intrusive and repressive force.

Two fundamental problems continued to plague British society for which, successful as he was, Lord Liverpool had no answer: discrimination against Catholics, which kept Ireland stewing, and the antiquated, corrupt electoral system. The prime minister avoided addressing either issue before he was removed from the scene after suffering a stroke in February 1827.

Wellington

The king chose George Canning as his next prime minister, but the new leader died unexpectedly in August after only a few months in office. An experiment with the hapless Lord Goderich ended quickly. George IV then turned to a more durable alternative, the duke of Wellington.

Wellington was one of the most accomplished Britons in history, already a hero as a result of his victories over the French in Spain and at Waterloo. He was born in Ireland, made his career in India, and defeated Napoleon in Europe. He was also interested in politics and lived the remainder of his life after 1815 in England. His instincts were profoundly conservative, but his successes as a general and prime minister came when he combined acute observation with bold strokes. At his best he had an almost superhuman ability to rise above prejudice and convention to achieve what appeared to be impossible. At his worst he could be bigoted and authoritarian. His loyalty to the monarchy survived even George IV's weakness of character. He sat at dinner with the drunken king, who described to guests how it was he (actually safely in England at the time) who had won the battle of Waterloo, not the duke.

Soon after Wellington took office in 1828 a young Whig, Lord John Russell (1792–1878), successfully introduced a motion in the Commons to repeal the Test and Corporation Acts which barred Dissenters from holding public office. Extreme Tories voted for it even though they despised Nonconformists because they hoped Protestant prejudices could be used to reinforce efforts to block Catholic Emancipation, which would admit Roman Catholics to the right to vote and govern. Nevertheless, the foundations of the old regime could be felt to tremble, so fundamental was the idea of an Anglican settlement to traditional conceptions of government. What justification remained to hold down Catholics?

At the outset of Wellington's administration the king had insisted on the exclusion of Catholic Emancipation from the legislative agenda. He was not, however, another George III. When in July 1828 the nationalist Roman Catholic leader, Daniel O'Connell (1775–1847), was elected an MP for an Irish county, a crisis unfolded that Wellington correctly diagnosed as grave. O'Connell's repeated re-election after being technically unseated led the duke and Peel to act to salvage civil peace and national security. Weeping and pleading, George IV surrendered. Never again would the sovereign be able to halt the course of legislation if the Cabinet was united in its will to go forward and prepared to resign over the issue.

Catholic Emancipation was enacted in April 1829, although the law remained debarring "papists" from inheriting the throne. Moreover, the franchise was adjusted in Ireland so that only the most prosperous levels of society could vote, which liquidated most of the Catholic electorate. O'Connell, who was a social conservative, accepted this adjustment. Peel would never quite live down his 180-degree turn, perhaps because the "ultra" Tories could never quite bring themselves to pillory the duke for doing the same thing.

A revolution in France in the summer of 1830 was unsettling. Unrest in industrial towns and the countryside later in the year made property owners uneasy. Wellington issued an unnecessary and disastrous declaration against parliamentary reform in Parliament in November 1830, which sent the stock market plunging and precipitated a vote of no confidence in the newly elected Commons. He was obliged to resign and the Whig the second Earl Grey (1764–1845) was appointed prime minister. A significant number of ultra Tories swung over to his support in order to register their outrage at the passage of Catholic Emancipation. No leader who sought the confidence of the public could any longer deny the passage of reform and survive in office. Grey never lost sight of this fact in the ensuing political storm. Why this change in the importance of public opinion took place is critical to understanding the rest of the nineteenth century.

-------------------- **The Public Sphere** --------------------

The commercialization of culture and an increase in the active number of educated and affluent participants in it during the late seventeenth and throughout the eighteenth centuries created a new kind of cultural space, which has been christened "the public sphere," a network for communicating information and points of view that mediated the transition to modernity. Previously isolated individuals (largely prosperous men – women and the poor could only intermittently participate) came together to exchange ideas and criticism, which in turn shaped a new political consciousness. This communication could take the form of subscribing to the same periodicals or meeting face to face in a coffee-house or in one of the new voluntary groups such as the anti-slavery campaign. Tim Blanning observes: "the public acquired a collective weight far greater than the sum of its individual members." It was from the rapidly expanding public sphere that a new source of authority emerged to challenge the opinion makers of the old regime.[8]

Members of the elite had begun to pay serious attention to the emergence of "public opinion" during the second half of the eighteenth century. The importance of the Wilkes affair, for example, was much greater than it might have been earlier. The market for news expanded rapidly in the early nineteenth century, facilitated by less expensive newspaper production. It is likely that by 1820 the majority of British children attended school for some part of their childhood, and literacy was now widespread even among the poor. Many businesses and organizations subscribed to the press and almost anyone who could read had some sort of access to printed opinion and the discussion of it.[9] Increasingly, a consensus arose among politically conscious workers and members of the middle classes about the necessity for electoral reform. By 1830 a new settlement, as momentous as that of 1688–9, was in the making.

Marx argued that the Whigs acted as the representatives of the bourgeoisie, passing legislation vital to the latter even though the landed elite dominated the Commons. It is more accurate to say that the elite intended to incorporate the middle classes into the political nation where they were likely to stand beside the aristocracy in defense of property. Men such as the Birmingham banker Thomas Attwood (1783–1856) and the writer Thomas Babington Macaulay (1800–59) worked with the Whigs to achieve reform. The radical journalist William Cobbett (see Biography 5.1) was not a friend of the Whigs, but they also listened to him. The Whig grandees had grasped the point, as the editor of one Whig newspaper put it, that "without the middle classes they are not much."[10]

The conservative historian Jonathan Clark argues that it was not class conflict or economic change that triggered reform but the breakdown of the religious settlement – led by Dissenters who attacked the established Church and Catholics who desired emancipation. The Whig Party, resentful of their long exclusion from power, "Samson-like, was to pull down around their ears the late-eighteenth-century constitution."[13] Left-wing historians tend to make a different sort of mistake by

Biography 5.1

William Cobbett
1763–1835

William Cobbett, the radical journalist, was intensely English, romantic, visionary, and eccentric. He hated London, Jews, Scots, and Quakers, and the "parasitical" aristocracy. Yet, in many ways he was a reactionary, looking back to a golden age before urbanization and industrialization. High government taxation and excessive public spending were anathema to him. He believed in traditional social and personal values governed by a sense of moral responsibility. He was a champion of human dignity.

Cobbett was a self-educated ploughboy of great literary gifts. He was responsible for the development of "editorials" in journalism and began the regular publication of parliamentary debates later known as Hansard. He provided highly readable and penetrating critiques of the new industrial society in his widely read weekly publication the *Political Register* (1802–35), which argued that only parliamentary reform could bring amelioration for the poor. He spoke of the corrupt voters in the unreformed boroughs with withering contempt. "I can tell [them] … by the nasty, cunning, leering, designing look of the people; a look between that of a bad (for *some* are good) Methodist parson and that of a pickpocket."[11]

J. H. Plumb noted that the backward-looking, rustic strand in English radicalism which Cobbett embodied ran deeply through the political left in Britain. Plumb claimed that no one "can understand the development of liberalism and socialism in England, even the British Labour Party today, without understanding William Cobbett."[12]

accepting uncritically the case made by contemporary radicals against the old parliamentary system without taking into account the many ways during the eighteenth century, though progressively less so in the early nineteenth, it had proved responsive to pressure even from those not accorded a vote.

The unprecedented scale of the French Wars, however, had opened up new opportunities for venality and the exploitation of government power. Hereditary parliamentary families had been pre-eminent in the House of Commons, but many of them were untitled and even resentful of electoral interference by the peerage. As more of these families were gathered into the upper chamber and more seats became dominated by the House of Lords, the situation changed. In 1734 there were 75 sons of peers and Irish peers sitting in the lower house out of a total of 558 members

(13 percent). By 1810, in a chamber enlarged by the Irish Union to 658, there were 279 (42 percent) noble MPs.[14] One of the radical reformers not inaccurately claimed that the influence exercised by the Lords over the Commons meant there were "two hereditary houses of parliament instead of one."[15]

Many constituencies possessed tiny electorates who could be intimidated or bribed. The county electorates were also subject to aristocratic influence. The lack of a secret ballot made uncooperative voters vulnerable to retribution. The electoral system had also not kept up with the shifts in population and economic power brought on by industrialization. Great manufacturing cities in the north of England such as Manchester, Birmingham, and Leeds elected no MPs at all. In Wales the MPs were in thrall to a small handful of families. Due to lack of contests only 546 people in the whole principality voted in 1826 and none in 1830.

Lord Grey and the Reform Bill

At 66 Lord Grey came late to the premiership. Yet, W. D. Rubinstein argues that he was the greatest peacetime prime minister in British history.[16] His steadiness of judgment and courage in the midst of turmoil were incomparable. As a parliamentary orator, he had few equals in modern times, and, unlike his famous contemporary, Henry Brougham, Grey did not need the flagons of liquor that sometimes brought the former literally to his knees on the floor of the House of Lords in order to sustain a verbal tour de force.

Grey intended that in the composition of his Cabinet he would "show in these times of democracy and Jacobinism it is possible to find real capacity in the high Aristocracy."[17] It was packed with noblemen and included five past or future prime ministers. The ultra-Tory duke of Richmond and a few other conservatives, along with some former liberal Tories such as Goderich and Viscount Palmerston (1784– 1865), gave it the look of a coalition, but all the fundamental decisions were made by the Whig leadership on Whig principles. Grey chose Lord Althorp, one of the most progressive men in the party, as his chief lieutenant.

First the Whigs had to deal with unrest in the southern counties, during the later part of 1830, caused by economic and social ills in the countryside. The disaffection took its name from an imaginary leader, "Captain Swing." The response of home secretary Viscount Melbourne (1779–1848) was harsh not only because he was a property owner in the affected area but also because the Whigs wanted to demonstrate (especially to the king) that they were by no means wild-eyed radicals or incapable of carrying out the executive tasks of government with judgment and dispatch. Radicals stayed relatively silent during the "Swing" unrest both because the violence was sometimes extreme and because they did not wish to throw the Whigs off the course to change.

Although he was popularly believed to support reform, William IV (1765–1837, king from 1830) was instinctively a Tory, while his German wife, Queen Adelaide

(1792–1849), was a full-blown reactionary. Almost from the start William began to drag his feet, and it took much coaxing mixed judiciously with threats to nudge him forward. In this Grey was assisted by mounting waves of popular agitation and ultimately an explosive outpouring of protest that seemed to threaten the foundations of the state. Again and again the House of Lords rejected the Whig attempts to pass a bill. The debates in the Commons over the measure were among the longest and most acrimonious relating to any single piece of legislation in modern British history.

The conservative poet Winthrop Mackworth Praed ridiculed popular enthusiasm for the bill:

> It will conjure up wealth for the ledger and till;
> I wish I could only find out how it will! …
> It will bring health to sickness, and warmth to the cold,
> And wit to the foolish, and youth to the old; …
> It's to change, in a minute one guinea to ten,
> It's to marry out daughters to handsome young men.

A fierce general election was fought to gain ascendancy over the opposition in the Commons and to send a message to the Lords. Public debate reached a fever pitch.

The final crisis came in May 1832, when the House of Lords again looked ready to reject the Whig measure. William IV at first resisted the mass creation of peers to overwhelm opposition requested by the Whig government (who believed the threat alone would be sufficient to pass the bill). Eventually, Grey had to resign while William tried to put in place a jury-rigged Tory administration led by Wellington. This effort collapsed in the face of public fury.

Michael Brock argues that it is impossible to tell how close Britain came to revolution in May 1832. Whatever pressure had been assembled to push, had it turned violent, would have fallen through an opening door. "The struggle was certain to end in the reformers' favor before blood had been shed."[18] Moreover, the core of the anger in May 1832 was focused on obstruction to the passage of reform, not against the monarchy or aristocracy. In the end Wellington and William kept their heads and Grey provided the necessary staunchness and skill to avoid a catastrophe. The "Great" Reform Act was passed in June 1832.

The Reformed System

It is generally believed that the number of men entitled to vote in England and Wales grew from 435,000 in 1831 to 653,000 in 1833, an increase of about 49 percent, about one adult male in five. Radicals at the time and historians since claimed the struggle to pass the bill had been superficial, no more than play acting.[19] The ordinary working man got nothing (although the existing poor who possessed votes were allowed to keep the franchise). Politics went on much as they had before.

Figure 5.1   A collective portrait of the newly reformed House of Commons in 1833. The Speaker sits at the far end of the room with the government ministers on the "front bench" to his right, led by Viscount Althorp. The Tory leader, Sir Robert Peel, sits on the Opposition benches on the other side of the table in the center. Earl Grey and the duke of Wellington watch from outside the bar of the House. *The House of Commons* by Sir George Hayter, 1833

Lord Grey was always a moderate reformer: "I am indeed convinced," he reassured a fellow peer in 1831, "that the more the bill is considered, the less it will be found to prejudice the real interests of the aristocracy."[20] One of his recent biographers argues that 1832 opened "a new era of aristocratic revival" and "refreshed and revived that supremacy"[21] (Figure 5.1).

The Reform Act has also been seen as the inevitable triumph of liberalism over oligarchy and corruption. Both contemporaries and later historians argue that 1832 was a decisive turning point, the British equivalent of the taking of the Bastille. Macaulay believed that the Reform Act was as important as the Civil War of the seventeenth century, which had brought the Crown into harmony with Parliament. The events of 1832 were "the Revolution which brought the Parliament into harmony with the nation."[22]

Since the 1980s evidence from historians of many ideological perspectives has continued to accumulate, demonstrating the profound nature of change brought about by the Act. Clark argues that, along with the abolition of religious disabilities, the Reform Act constituted a precipitate collapse of the old order. John Phillips showed that 1832 helped create widespread partisan voting on a national scale and fostered the rise of national parties.[23] The number of MPs connected to titled families declined more dramatically after 1832 (see Table 5.1) than after subsequent extensions of the franchise in 1867 and 1884, despite a substantial increase in the rate of peerage creations over the course of the nineteenth century.

Table 5.1   Noble MPs in the House of Commons, 1810–90[24]

Year	MPs	% of Commons
1810	195	29.6
1820	249	37.8
1830	279	42.4
1840	175	26.5*
1850	179	27.2
1860	166	25.2
1870	140	21.2[†]
1880	141	21.6
1890	71	10.5[§]

All peers and close relatives in the male line elected MPs while the family was titled.
* After the First Reform Act of 1832. [†] After the Second Reform Act of 1867. § After the Third Reform Act of 1884.

The changes in Wales, Ireland, and Scotland were not as far-reaching as in England. Only about one in eight Scotsmen gained the franchise. In Wales the political control of the small elite was largely unimpaired. In Ireland the Act added many fewer voters to the rolls than in Scotland. In 1833 only about one in 20 adult males held the vote. Yet, the number of families who traditionally were represented in Parliament took a deeper plunge in Ireland than elsewhere in the United Kingdom. From controlling 83 percent of the Irish seats in the House of Commons in 1830, they dropped to 56 percent after 1832.

Although the electorate had been increased in size by less than 50 percent in 1832 the numbers of people actually voting increased by 500 percent thanks to the greater frequency of contested elections.[25] Rising incomes, intensified political engagement, and population growth led to further significant expansion in the electorate in the 1840s and 1850s.

The Reform Act made it virtually impossible for the monarch any longer to form a ministry purely on the basis of his or her own inclinations. The king and the House of Lords had been forced to concede a major alteration in the constitution against their will by a political party beholden to popular support both within and outside the traditional electorate. This fundamentally changed the relationship between the three elements in the constitution. The monarch retained great influence in the selection of individual Cabinet members and even prime ministers, but parties winning an endorsement from the electorate now presented an immovable object in the path of royal power.

Lord Althorp and the liberal wing of the Whig Party also understood that further reforms were likely to follow although the pace of change was hard to predict. The novelist R. S. Surtees noted: "Men that never thought of anything but their shops, now talk of their *politics* just as their fathers used to talk of their wives, their horses, or their watches."[26]

The Whig Revolution

The Whigs and their allies, including some radicals, won 479 seats and the Tories only 179 in the first election after reform. They did particularly well in Scotland and Ireland, which presaged a long-term trend. Althorp and his friends were determined to use the momentum to make government more progressive and efficient. What was critical to this process was the pressure of public opinion, now enhanced inside Parliament but also much aroused outside. Wellington forecast gloomily: "I cannot see what is to save Church, or property, or colonies, or union with Ireland, or eventually monarchy ... We shall be destroyed one after the other, very much in the order ... I have mentioned, by due course of law."[27]

Many politicians still saw Parliament's task as one of mere monitoring and regulation, not making improvements. Lord Liverpool once said: "by far the greater part of the miseries of which human nature complained were in all times and all countries beyond the control of human legislation."[28] Acceptance of classical economic theory encouraged the Whig leadership to slash spending. They embraced the "minimal state." Total government spending dropped from 23 percent of GNP (gross national product) in 1810 to 11 percent under the Whigs in 1840.

Yet, cutbacks were only part of the story. Although Whigs and Liberals (the largely middle-class political movement allied with the aristocratic Whigs) remained wary of the agency of the state, they came to accept the notion of "improvement," that the human mind could be developed by education, that progress was normal and natural. "An improvement party" within the aristocracy arose that looked to fashion legislation that went well beyond regulation.[29]

The Whig government of the 1830s was the first administration systematically and continuously to employ the process of collection of data and then develop recommendations based on the resulting research. The use of **royal commissions** was hugely influential in changing attitudes towards government. Exposure to the actual state of things, revelations about raw sewage, prisons, mines, disease, schools, and human suffering gradually shifted people's understanding about society, even if the resulting legislation was often a mere baby step in the direction of change. The business of government accelerated. Parliamentary sessions grew longer and more bills were enacted. The number of government employees rose. Inspectorates were established to follow up on regulatory legislation. The government often relied on local authorities (and local taxpayers) to take up the burden of providing expanded services, so the "minimal state" became like an iceberg that continued to present a low fiscal profile at the national level, but out of immediate sight local government responsibilities multiplied and proliferated.

In 1831 one of the first Whig reforms after gaining office established a new state-aided system of national schools in Ireland open to children of all denominations. However, rural unrest and widespread refusal to pay tithes, a tax collected from the Catholic population to support the Protestant state Church to which only a small minority of the population adhered, worried Lord Grey, who had no hesitation in coercing the Catholic peasantry into obedience by force. He was also willing, however, to enact Irish Church reform. In 1833 the top-heavy hierarchy of archbishops and bishops was drastically pruned, and new, less objectionable financial arrangements were instituted.

Legislation to abolish slavery in the British Empire was also introduced during the first session after the passage of the Reform Act. It has been argued that Britain only ended slavery in the Caribbean when it had ceased to be profitable. However, the fierce opposition to the measure by the West Indian lobby representing the planters suggests that slave owners were by no means ready to surrender their property or powers. Moreover, the sugar industry continued to be lucrative for some years after emancipation. Slavery was ended because the Whigs had been long committed to do so on humanitarian grounds. Once electoral reform was safe, they had no hesitation in forcing the king, who was pro-slavery, to acquiesce to emancipation.

Whig laissez-faire economic principles made the party reluctant to interfere in the relationship between workers and owners in the factories. Many aristocrats in both parties were, however, paternalists and deeply committed Evangelicals who could not avert their eyes from the evidence revealed by investigations into the condition of children in the textile towns. Lord Althorp reluctantly agreed to cooperate with the Evangelical Tory Lord Ashley (later seventh earl of Shaftesbury, 1801–85), who campaigned tenaciously to protect workers against abuse. A bill referred to as "Althorp's Act" ended employment of children under the age of nine and limited the hours of work by older children in most textile factories. The Act also required employed children under 13 to attend school at least two hours a day. A factory inspectorate was established to police the enforcement of these regulations. The new system was understaffed and initially ineffective but was gradually expanded. The system of state employees assigned to enforce regulations became a model for reformers in other areas such as education, mines, and the Poor Law. The Act began the slow process of blunting the sharp edge of capitalism through government intervention, which eventually would make modern industrialized society tolerable for the workers.

Another issue directly relating to the condition of the working poor and the unemployed was reform of the Poor Law. The cost of relief had more than tripled between the 1790s and 1830, which prompted complaints from landowners and middle-class taxpayers. A commission was appointed in 1832 whose report in 1834 was deeply influenced by classical economic theory. **Outdoor relief** was to be ended for employable men and women. An obnoxious principle, euphemistically called "less eligibility," required involuntary confinement in a workhouse where family members were separated from each other and hard labor was performed. These conditions were designed to drive away all but the most desperate from seeking assistance. The New Poor Law stripped magistrates of their discretionary charitable powers. Parishes were grouped into unions to be run by boards of guardians elected by the ratepayers with a system of plural voting to give the largest landowners more influence. A permanent Poor Law Commission headquartered in London was responsible to Parliament. The new centralized system appeared to run counter to laissez-faire principles since it enhanced state intervention on a big scale, but by giving control of expenditure to the ratepayers the reform actually localized power.

The measure was deeply flawed. The commission of inquiry did not grasp the nature of cyclical unemployment in the new industrial economy. By abolishing the traditional paternalism of the landed elite, the social contract that had provided stability to English society for generations was put in danger. Anti-Poor Law riots took place in industrial areas, and poor houses were called "Althorp's Bastilles."

The vast majority of Poor Law recipients, however, were never required to submit to confinement. Moreover, the number of able-bodied receiving public assistance fell due to the spread of friendly societies, a form of self-insurance, and the general rise in the standard of living (see below). The full severity of the Act was also undermined from within by the progressive aristocratic party itself. Lord Althorp deliberately blocked the appointment to the new Poor Law Commission of the key figure in shaping the original report, Edwin Chadwick (1800–90), a man of good intentions and no imagination, a white-hot advocate of the "scientific" management of humanity. Britain continued for some time as the only European state to fund out of taxpayers' money a basic safety net below which no one could fall.

Other parts of the United Kingdom approached the problem of poverty in different ways. The New Poor Law met much resistance in Wales, where a historic regional antipathy to interference by the central government continued to survive. In Scotland a strongly Presbyterian view existed that social problems arose from moral failings and could only be solved by personal responsibility assisted by charity. The trouble was that industry and mining had created a new social order and economic problems. Eventually, a Scottish Poor Law in 1845 replaced control by the Kirk with parochial boards under a Central Board of Supervision, which introduced bureaucratic, legal assessments of relief. No Irish Poor Law existed, and the legislation when enacted in 1838 proved totally inadequate to the crisis of the potato famine of the 1840s discussed in the next chapter.

Melbourne's Reforms

In the summer of 1834 Lord Althorp resigned in protest over renewed coercion in Ireland, which prompted Grey to retire as well. The king chose Lord Melbourne as prime minister. The latter has long held the reputation as not only a cautious Whig but also a lazy one who lacked ambition to achieve progressive advances. In fact, he was a highly intelligent and skilful politician. He slithered frictionlessly through the morass of Westminster with every intention of enacting further necessary reforms.

His willingness to make concessions on Irish coercion in order to retain the activist Althorp as leader of the House of Commons was a sign of his intentions.

Before Melbourne could get seriously under way Althorp's father died, which raised him to the House of Lords as third Earl Spencer. The king chose the opportunity to toss Melbourne out of office on the dubious grounds that no suitable candidate could be found to replace Althorp. This is the last time a British monarch engineered the dismissal of one government and the installation of another formed by the opposition party. It ended badly. The Whigs won the ensuing election, and William IV was obliged to recall Melbourne.

The first step of the new government was to enact a long-planned corollary to the 1832 changes in the electoral system. The Municipal Corporations Act of 1835, another product of a commission report, uprooted the old system of local government in towns. Closed oligarchies that had managed the affairs of cities and boroughs for centuries were swept away. A more uniform system was put in place, although the relatively narrow basis of the new franchise assisted conservative elements to retain control in many towns.

The flow of commissions and reports continued, among them ones on sanitary conditions and public health. To appease Dissenters in 1836 a system for the civil registration of births, marriages, and deaths removed the Anglican clergy from their privileged but anomalous position as civil bureaucrats. Clergy from all faiths were permitted to conduct marriages. London University, the only English home of higher education for Nonconformists, was granted a charter. After 1837 the death penalty was abolished for all crimes except murder and treason, which reduced hangings to a very small number. Legislation transferred authority for prisons from local magistrates to an inspectorate with the intention of standardizing conditions throughout the country. The legal system was overhauled and made fairer. The Municipal Corporations Act of 1835 required new borough councils to establish police forces.[30] In Ireland the government imposed an activist and interventionist system, with positive initiatives in education, railways, police, coastal fisheries, and land reclamation. Reductions in the stamp duty on various forms of print journalism began to lower the cost of newspapers, which increased demand. The subsequent expansion of both the national and provincial press created a genuine democracy of knowledge that made further extension of the franchise likely. In 1840 the first adhesive postage stamps were issued, and a price revolution radically reduced the cost of mailing a letter, another democratization of life.

Young Queen Victoria

King William IV expired in June 1837 without a direct heir, his legitimate children having died in infancy. Though in failing health for some time, he clung to life so that his niece, Princess Victoria (1819–1901), daughter of a deceased younger

Figure 5.2   The duke of Wellington raises his coronet near left, and Viscount Melbourne, the prime minister, holds up a sword just beside the Queen. Detail from *The Coronation of Queen Victoria* by Sir George Hayter, 1838

brother, could succeed him without a regency. William rightly despised the girl's mother, a German princess of remarkably poor judgment, who was likely to rule while Victoria was a minor.

Victoria, who was barely 18, emerged from a somewhat difficult upbringing remarkably self-assured. She spent her entire adult life as queen, ruling into the twentieth century. She stood at the center of politics: formidable, difficult, and helpful. Despite her idiosyncrasies, biases, and the mismanagement of the lives of her own children, she possessed a sharp intelligence and benign outlook (Figure 5.2).

The inexperienced Victoria was fortunate to be tutored in her job as queen by Lord Melbourne, who fell a little in love with her. He gave her good advice and training, easing the transition from girlhood to marriage in 1840 with Prince Albert of Saxe-Coburg-Gotha (1819–61). Due largely to the influence of Melbourne and Albert she was Whiggish in her sentiments during the first half of her reign. The German Albert, who was often underestimated during his own lifetime and by some historians later, was a devoted servant of his adopted country and dedicated the influence of the monarchy to progressive goals. He was what today would be called a "policy wonk."

Feminist historians often regard Queen Victoria with ambivalence. On the one hand, she took the initiative in proposing marriage to her husband, was forceful in argument, could rebuke her prime ministers, and became in her later years immensely popular. Although she enjoyed sex immensely, the queen hated child bearing and babies: "I think much more of our being a cow or dog at such moments." On the other hand, she protested against "this mad wicked folly of 'Women's rights' with all its attendant horrors."[31]

Radicals and Chartists

Lord Melbourne and Queen Victoria represented elements with deep roots in British history that nevertheless continued to adapt successfully to changing circumstances. A long radical tradition also existed but struggled with only partial success during the nineteenth century to achieve change in the face of inequality and suffering among the people. Why was this the case? The answer, of course, must take into account the reforms enacted by both Tory and Whig administrations. The example of the French Revolution was also important. Ultimately, however, continuity was preserved in British society by forces greater than whatever politicians or fear of violent revolution could have achieved. One of the contributors to stability was a radical tradition that presupposed problems confronting society were political in origin and not the result of economic inequality.

Socialism began in Britain in a different and less radical way than on the Continent. A wealthy cotton manufacturer, Robert Owen (1771–1858), was one of the first persons to use the term. He was deeply concerned with improving factory conditions and sponsored cooperative industrial communities in Scotland and the USA. Owen expressed unease about the values inherent in modern capitalism but, like many critics in nineteenth-century Britain, he respected "the old aristocracy of birth" more than he did the new capitalists.[32]

More long-lasting influence on the left came from the "philosophical radicals." They were middle-class intellectuals, businessmen, and bureaucrats. Most were influenced by Jeremy Bentham's (1748–1832) "Utilitarianism," the maximization of pleasure and the minimization of pain. Many were willing to work with the Whigs, though they looked down their noses at shuffling and timid aristocratic reforms. To Bentham everything, including the human spirit, could be reduced to a mechanistic system and put in a box.[33] Chadwick is the most overrated of the group, John Stuart Mill (1806–73) by far the most interesting and formidable.

It is easy to exaggerate the influence of the Utilitarians. Historians used to present the development of Victorian government as the unfolding of Bentham's thought into action and still too easily slip into the habit of drawing lines connecting dots that were in actuality quite independent in origin. The historians Oliver MacDonagh and George Kitson Clark did much to temper these views. As they pointed out, a great many of the reforms and changes were what the latter explained as "the result of empirical actions and hard-bought experience of a number of officials, many of whom had probably never heard of Bentham, but on whom public demands had imposed novel and very difficult tasks."[34]

Unlike the predominantly middle-class radicals discussed above, the "Chartist" movement of the 1830s and 1840s led to what Boyd Hilton has called "the supreme crisis of authority ... almost the only time in history England experienced what could legitimately be called class conflict."[35] Chartism became the first well-organized mass movement in the history of British radicalism. It took its name from a document, the "People's Charter" (1838), which demanded universal male suffrage, annual parliaments, equal electoral districts, abolition of property qualifications for MPs, the secret ballot, and payment of MPs. The Chartists also hoped for a cheap and honest free press, a unified working class, repeal of the Irish Act of Union, and other goals. Remarkably, no demand was made for the abolition of the House of Lords. The Charter was based on the assumption that Parliament was the key to the solution of the problems of poverty and injustice. One leader, Bronterre O'Brien (1805–65), an Irish lawyer, declared: "Knaves will tell you that it is because you have no property, you are unrepresented. I tell you on the contrary, it is because you are unrepresented that you have no property ..."[36]

There was no gloomier year in the whole nineteenth century than 1842. Prolonged business difficulties and four years of harvest dearth made England, in Asa Briggs's words, "unhappy and afraid, a country of conflict and despair." Movements of protest and revolt spread. The novelist and resident of Manchester, Elizabeth Gaskell (1810–65), argued that the depression in trade of 1839–42 had a huge impact in industrial cities like hers. "Whole families went through a gradual starvation. They only wanted a Dante to record their sufferings. And yet even his words would fall short of the awful truth."[37]

The original Chartists eschewed violence and used traditional tactics including protest rallies and petitions to fight their battles, but those who were willing to employ general strikes and contemplate revolutionary force such as Fergus O'Connor (1796–1855) were also attracted to the movement. Even more radical activists such as O'Brien believed armed rebellion was appropriate. The movement incorporated both "physical force" men and "moral force" moderates.

In February 1839 a National Chartist Convention was held in London. The moderates were in control. A giant petition signed by over one million supporters was dragged to Parliament in a cart, where it was introduced by Thomas Attwood but was rejected by the Commons 235 to 46. Disappointment and some strikes and rioting ensued, but the army easily suppressed the few instances of serious violence. A second petition was presented in 1842 signed by over three million people, which was rejected again. More rioting took place with a general strike affecting 23 counties. Again the police and military authorities dealt with problems quickly and decisively. The government used arrests, show trials, and transportation to Australia to suppress the movement. A final phase in 1847–8 also met with failure.

---------------------------- **The Economy** ----------------------------

The impact of the revolutionary technology on social and political relationships remained slow paced, but an estimated annual growth rate of 3.5 percent between 1815 and 1861 was extraordinary by contemporary European standards. During the first half of the century, the factory system was confined to a few sectors of production. Much so-called industrial activity long remained small in scale, but agriculture's proportionate contribution to the British economy fell. By 1871 more people were working as domestic servants than farm laborers. Only Ireland remained predominantly agricultural.

Ever more creative inventors and engineers branched out from canal building and textile machinery to transform heavy industry and transportation. Isambard Kingdom Brunel (1806–59) built a spectacular series of tunnels, suspension bridges, railway structures, and iron ships. Coal production rose from about 15 million tons a year in 1800 to 100 million in 1865 and 200 million by 1897. In the 1870s total British iron output was equal to that of Europe and the USA combined. Manchester became the shock city of the world. From a distance, Mrs. Gaskell reported, "a deep-lead-colorded cloud [hung] over the horizon." The streets were thronged with workers desperately engaged "in the struggle for bread" amid a massive array of factories.[38] The introduction of J. B. Neilson's (1792–1865) hot blast technique in 1828, which used preheated air under pressure coupled with exploitation of a plentiful form of ironstone first discovered in 1801, gave the west of Scotland a technological edge. Scottish production of pig iron rose 20 times between 1825 and 1840.

Britain was building up a huge lead over other countries. Exports and imports grew exponentially. By 1850 the old system of mercantilist restrictions on trade had been fully swept away. Large markets abroad eager for British goods allowed industrialization to progress without a serious check. Even before the French Revolution, London had taken the place of Amsterdam as the world's leading financial center. The great investment banks such as Rothschild's and Baring's enabled Britain to dominate international trade. Insurance for shipping and fire became big business at Lloyd's of London. Britain became not just the "workshop of the world" but also the "clearing house of the world."[39]

Those workers who did not keep pace with the march of industrialization such as the Shaw family (see Biography 5.2) began to suffer even more than those immured in the factories. In large measure the weaving of cotton cloth continued to be done by hand until the 1840s.[41] Domestic workers were already badly off even before mechanization expanded. One observer noted as early as 1812 that the stocking weavers of Nottingham were in such miserable condition that their situation was "a disgrace to a civilized country."[42] Increasingly they were treated as a reserve workforce, and, when demand declined, they were the first to be laid off. They had to work longer hours for lower compensation as their living standards spiraled downwards into extreme poverty. Changing technology crushed them.

Biography 5.2

Benjamin Shaw
1772–1841

Four out of five Victorians were members of families who survived by manual labor. The family into which Ben Shaw was born supported itself by his father's clock-making, while mother and children wove cloth on hand looms at home. They also farmed a smallholding. The Shaws moved to Lancashire to work in a water-powered woolen mill. It is often forgotten that men made up only a relatively small part of the first wave of textile workers in factories where women and children constituted a majority of the industrial proletariat. Illness, death, industrial accident, and irregular work broke up the family. By 1798 the teenage Ben was left alone serving out his mechanic's apprenticeship, with his family living 20 miles distant. Ben married his sweetheart Betty with no money and a baby on the way. He eventually commanded good wages in a rapidly growing textile town while Betty wove cloth. Eight of their offspring survived to adulthood and all of these conceived children in their turn out of wedlock or before marriage. The family was repeatedly stricken by illness and disease. Sons and daughters went to work in the mills early; several died as children or young adults. A chronic thrombosis in his leg kept Ben out of work for long periods, until he had it amputated. Recurrent poverty and uncertainty plagued his life. In 1826 Betty was becoming increasingly sick with consumption (TB); she died two years later. None of the children helped Ben very much as he became increasingly ill and aged. He had invested socially and materially in his family, but circumstances made it hard for them to return this in kind. He did, however, have enough energy and education to write an autobiography before he died.[40]

The Making of the Working Class

The term "class," based on income, rapidly replaced "rank," based on birth and status, as the principal social descriptor in the unequal industrial society of the early nineteenth century. Historians want to know how far "class" generated cultures, identities, value systems, and ideologies that shaped the nature of social and political conflict. Did class consciousness turn into class hostility and, if so, when?

Mention has already been made in Chapter 4 of E. P. Thompson's argument that a new form of working-class consciousness emerged between 1815 and 1830.[43] His bold thesis launched a seminal discussion. Other historians, such as Harold Perkin, coming from a non-Marxist perspective, also argued that a distinctive working class was formed before 1830. The new industrial system grew "like a vortex within the old, and gradually pulling into its orbit of production and demand circle after circle of producers and consumers." "The alienation between employers and employed, and between both and the landed aristocracy, was inherent in industrialism."[44]

The emergence of a new collective self-consciousness among the working class has been challenged. The evidence for genuinely revolutionary activity on a mass scale does not exist and can only be conjectured. Many countervailing factors such as sectarian religion, ethnicity, regionalism, gender, and income fragmented class solidarity. As the economy became more complex the proliferation of different kinds of employment, the small size of many businesses, and elaborate hierarchies in the workplace hindered the growth of class-consciousness. Servants, agricultural laborers, and construction workers did not share the same outlook on life as factory hands. The gap in status and wages between skilled and unskilled workers was huge. In the 1860s an engine driver might make 35 shillings a week, and a road worker 14 shillings. Families like Ben Shaw's moved in and out of different groups according to their employment history and life cycles. Only a small number of men became involved in trade union activity. The unions were based on local associations of skilled males, and did not branch out significantly to achieve national scope until late in the century.

Class politics associated with socialist movements came very late. Increasingly, historians see the final third of the century as the period in which coherent and consolidated classes in the national sense were finally created. Theodore Hoppen dates it even later than that. Only in the early twentieth century in Lancashire did the politics of class come to predominate over more traditional factors.[45]

Evidence has accumulated that a working-class consciousness, if it existed, did not take a political or ideological form. In the 1815–32 period, political radicalism was most active among skilled workers and artisans, not the proletariat. The strongest protests and pro-reform movements were in the provincial cities such as Bristol where factories had not yet appeared. Local studies show little sign of the politics of class among enfranchised laboring men. Until 1886 religion was overwhelmingly the main determinant of voting behavior, with the Liberals aligned with Nonconformity and Conservatives with the Church of England. What one rarely encounters in working-class protests from Luddism to Chartism is any serious questioning of capitalist ownership of the means of production. Working-class protests focused on wages and conditions of labor. Rural unrest did not prompt demands for the expropriation of land.[46]

One of E. P. Thompson's greatest insights was that "the making of the working class is a fact of cultural, as much as of economic, history. It was not the spontaneous generation of the factory system."[47] The perception of culture as a mediating sphere between social position and political consciousness has attracted more and more interest among historians of the "linguistic" or "cultural turn." Nothing, they argue, can be known independently of language. Scholars interested in the analysis of language as a method of inquiry see texts as statements by people in a particular context that can be decoded and interpreted in the same way and perhaps with even greater validity than more traditional forms of evidence. Culture means ideas, values, language, social habits, and institutions, which give people a sense of identity and purpose. Social identities were formed through contemporary discourses about experiencing urban life as related to competing identities such as gender, politics, occupation, and nationality. In these ways people presented themselves and understood their world.

Most historians have read the "cultural" work of their colleagues with interest but remain unconvinced that class as an economic category is not the most realistic and effective form of analysis both for contemporaries and ourselves. As Richard Price has noted: "The language of class is always unstable." He argues that after the term "working class" emerged for a time and was used during the Chartist era, it retreated and the vocabulary of ranks and orders revived.[48] Perhaps more potent than any class divide in the nineteenth century became the gulf between those who sought and those who achieved "respectability," a desire in different forms shared by both middle- and working-class populations. Geoffrey Best argues that it represented "the sharpest of all lines of social division."[49]

The Middle Classes

The term "middle class" came into use early in the nineteenth century. As with the manual laborers, we can now see how fragmented middling people were by religion, party politics, occupation, moral values, and relations with the landed elite. They embraced "respectability" but were separated by gigantic gaps in income. One term simply cannot encompass a textile millionaire like Peel's father, on the one hand, and an Anglican curate poor as a church mouse, on the other. The division between the professional and business communities remained deep.

An often forgotten ascending social group of the nineteenth century was that of tenant farmers. Those who managed substantial tenancies could live like minor country gentlemen, yet they were really rural entrepreneurs who identified politically with the landed elite. Some even managed to acquire land themselves, though farmers without landlords did not fit easily into the social structure. "Monsters … one can't tell how to class them," complained a member of the gentry in one of George Eliot's novels.[50] Tenant farmers formed almost half the electorate until 1867, which helped sustain the power of the aristocracy.

A man who rose from a modest background to considerable prosperity and status wrote in 1839 that the means to social mobility were "in the power of every young man himself and they are neither many in number nor irksome in practice. They consist in the undeviating exercise of Honesty and Sobriety carried out by an unceasing diligence in and attention to that worldly Calling in which he is engaged."[51] Such typically unimaginative musings of the self-made concealed the fact that although the middle classes expanded rapidly during the Victorian period, already perhaps more than a million and a half people at mid-century, most recruits were from prosperous backgrounds in the first place. It remained difficult for someone not born with access to capital or education – or both – to move up. Few factory owners came from among the ranks of manual laborers.[52]

The Standard of Living

For a long time optimists and pessimists have debated the extent to which conditions became worse for the laboring masses and whether they ever received the rewards they deserved for the sacrifices the early stages of industrialization seemed to require. The catalogue of inhumane treatment inflicted by the factory system is a long one. Mines were even worse. Recurrent economic booms and busts made employment insecure and life frightening for people living from week to week on inadequate wages. Crowded living conditions in slums were unpleasant and unhealthy.

Accurate assessment is difficult. We cannot easily calculate the psychological costs and benefits of moving from village to city and the changing nature of labor. How does one measure the loss of clean air balanced against freedom from living under the authority of the gentry? Housing in the countryside was often very bad, and agricultural wages were at the bottom of the scale among all workers. On the other hand, the spread of disease in the cities was appalling. When factory and mine reform did take place, it did so at the speed of an arthritic snail. Yet, by the 1870s bodily deformities were far less evident among factory workers, workrooms were better ventilated and lighted, and hours reduced. Can one balance the negative effect of lost wages due to unemployment, sickness, union dues, and other variables, against positive additions such as overtime, free coal, subsidized housing, charity, and embezzlement? After the Corn Laws were repealed in 1846 and the price of wheat fell, people spent as much money on food as before, but they purchased white bread rather than darker loaves made from lesser grains. No net financial gain was registered in the statistics on wages, but quality of life improved. Optimists and pessimists in the standard of living debate used to pass like ships in the night. Different measures produced different results, and little progress was made in coming to a consensus. More recently the arguments have become less heated and have produced more light.

The British population was rising very fast during the nineteenth century, doubling between 1811 and 1861, and for the standard of living to keep up the economy would have had to grow at least as fast or faster. Progress came in bursts, however, not in a continuous line. There were periods when the population increase exceeded economic expansion. Some laborers experienced considerable advances, especially among skilled workers, but until the population explosion slowed down considerably, which it only began to do in the later part of the nineteenth century, it was not possible for all segments of the working classes to enjoy a significant rise in their standard of living.

Charles Feinstein is now the widely accepted authority on the financial condition of the working poor. He has found that real earnings did little more than crawl forward from the 1770s to 1830s, made some better progress in the latter decade but fell back in the depression of 1838–42. It was not until the mid-1840s that real earnings grew steadily. More substantial gains did not come until the 1860s. Moreover the number of dependents supported by each wage earner rose and reduced the standard of living of the average family by about 10 percent. The overall gain was only 10–15 percent between 1778–82 and 1853–7. The real advances came after 1873 as hours of work, prices, and the number of dependents all began to fall, while living conditions in cities – both in housing and in sewerage – began to improve. Only rents failed to go down, but housing quality was rising. Use of steam-powered machinery became more universal, which increased productivity. The share of wages in the sum of profits plus wages rose from 52 percent in 1870–4 to 62 percent in 1890–4, which is remarkable. Increasingly, workers were able to force wages up above price rises in boom years and then hold the line in periods of depression. That made the upward trend continuous. Friendly societies and the Co-operative Store movement allowed members, who were the owners, to accumulate modest savings, acquire credit, and gain cheaper food. The proportion of the population totally unprotected from financial adversity except by the Poor Law dropped to no more than one in 10 by 1900.[53]

An Age of Equipoise?

The economic crisis of 1847 and 1848 briefly gave Chartism a renewed life, but in the latter year "the storm which swept away half the Governments of Europe passed harmlessly over the islands."[54] In Paris the second of three bloody convulsions in less than 80 years took place while ministers were hanged from lampposts in Vienna and mobs foregathered outside the royal palace in Berlin. The Pope fled a revolutionary government in Rome. In London the latest version of the Charter petition was taken to Parliament in a taxi. Some disruption in the industrial north of the country took place, but the aristocracy and the middle classes stood together to protect the 1832 constitution. Further disturbances took place as the century progressed, but none of them were genuinely threatening in character. The British had no violent revolution.

The Great Exhibition of 1851 in London that celebrated the productive power of industry was conceived of and enjoyed by the elite but also visited and embraced by many working families. Over six million visitors came from all over the country to help celebrate a genuinely shared achievement which could not have occurred without the capable political leadership of the aristocracy, the creativity of middle-class entrepreneurs, and the sweat and blood of the workers.

W. L. Burn famously called the mid-Victorian period an "age of equipoise."[55] Many historians, however, no longer accept this concept of a placid "middle" period. There is also debate about what kept British society stable in these years. Some historians believe it rested on the triumph of middle-class values. Others argue that the middle classes were not culturally secure and remained deferential to aristocratic leadership. It is also possible a merger of the landed and business elites facilitated the peaceful transition to modernity. The realism and opportunism of the aristocracy also helped. Gareth Stedman Jones suggests that workers wrapped themselves in the language of constitutionalism because they feared not only the tyranny of the market but also the tyranny of the state. When the state turned in a reformist direction, their radical hostility evaporated. Patrick Joyce argues that the paternalism inherent in the organization of the new textile factories tended to keep workers more directly under the thumb of their employers and undermined their capacity to express class autonomy and solidarity.[56]

Undoubtedly, greater prosperity and rising living standards helped prevent dangerous social unrest. Lord Shaftesbury reported to Lord John Russell from Manchester in 1851 that "Chartism is dead in these parts; the Ten Hours Factory Act and cheap provisions have slain it outright."[57] The rise of stable trades unions after the 1850s provided a mechanism for effective negotiation between owners and workers. The best estimate is that the average full-time hours worked per week fell from 65 to 56 between 1856 and 1873. The nine-hour day and half-holiday on Saturday emerged as a standard. A key to social equilibrium was that the national unemployment rate exceeded 10 percent only in two years, 1879 and 1886, and only in one four-year stretch did it average above 7.5 percent. In general the levels were low, averaging around 4 percent or so between 1855 and 1894.[58] Upsurges in patriotic fervor during foreign and imperial conflicts helped unify the nation.

British workers were still committed to religious values and most children were conditioned by their experiences in Sunday schools. Three-quarters of working-class children aged five to 15 attended them in the mid-nineteenth century and numbers continued to rise. Michael Thompson argues that:

> Family and neighborhood ties, upbringing, inherited cultures, and group loyalties proved more persistent and resilient than technologies, which might change overnight. These social forces were sufficiently powerful to smooth the impact of new working and living conditions, and to ease the passage towards large-town society without disastrous dislocation. A fruitful tension, and accommodation, between social continuity and conservatism, and economic innovation and discontinuity, was an underlying theme of the Victorian period.[59]

Imperial Britain, 1842–84

Contents

No other country in the world could match Britain's commercial, industrial, and imperial power in the nineteenth century. Its literature, science, Parliament, queen, men's clubs, railways, navy, legal system, schools, and aristocracy were admired around the world. It was seen to set the standard for "modernity."[1] Those who could afford it, whether in Rome, Berlin, or New York, sent to Britain for hair lotion, hunting garb, shot guns, nursemaids, horses, and tennis balls. Russian aristocrats even mailed their laundry to London to be cleaned and ironed properly. Exiled revolutionaries from Berlin to Budapest made their way to the British capital along with princes, publishers, lumber merchants, and law students from India. The German theorist Karl Marx studied quietly at the British Museum, writing the books that would convulse the world in the twentieth century. A huge swath of the planet directly or indirectly came under British control. **Football** and the English language sallied forth and conquered the world.

Britain's increasing political, economic, and cultural dominance as Victoria's reign progressed created huge challenges for the political leadership. The preconditions for stability and continuity had, however, been established in 1832. As Benjamin Disraeli, one of the key figures in the search for the means to manage so much success, said of the Reform Act, it "set men a-thinking," and "it enlarged the horizon of political experience; … it created and prepared a popular intelligence to which one can appeal."[2] Radicals, Chartists, Irish nationalists, and others dissatisfied with the status quo decided to work within the parliamentary system, which gave Britain the chance to maintain its balance in the avalanche of modernization and imperialism.

A Conservative Government

The general election of 1841 gave the Conservatives a substantial majority over the Whigs in the House of Commons. Much of the credit for the victory goes to Sir Robert Peel, who became prime minister. The key to his strategy was the "Tamworth Manifesto" (1834) in which he pledged that there would be no going back on electoral reform. Peel promised to continue to be forward-looking and to correct abuses. More and more property owners and businessmen also began to rally to the Conservative cause, broadly defending the established order, distrustful of tinkering with tradition, willing to prune abuses but not overthrow them. The historian Robert Blake characterized their response to reform as "opting to bend rather than to break."[3] Peel could embrace surprisingly creative solutions to practical problems. He was flexible, ruthless, pragmatic, and creative. He had the courage to reverse course. This opened him to harrowing criticism of his personal integrity by erstwhile supporters and his opponents and would provide political drama of the highest order before his premiership was over.

Peel made a number of fiscal and economic reforms including reorganization of the Bank of England. He removed duties on 600 articles and reduced them on another 500, but he won the 1841 election in part by implicitly promising to defend the **Corn Laws**. He came to see, however, that they must be abandoned and that he might have to sacrifice himself to ensure that this be accomplished. He moved tentatively at first, laying the groundwork for the economic revolution ahead by finding alternative sources of government revenue. In 1842 he enacted the first ever peacetime income tax. It was set at a very modest rate, paid only by those with incomes over £150 a year (which exempted the working classes), and was presented as a temporary measure. In fact there is evidence that Peel saw taxing the wealthy business elite from which he sprang as a means to reconcile class antagonism.[4]

The Repeal of the Corn Laws

Peel's motives for repeal of the Corn Laws remain open to debate, but intellectual conviction was undoubtedly one of them. By the 1840s Ricardo's ideas had been superseded. Economists were more ready to accept that wages could rise while prices came down, and that economic growth would raise the demand for labor and wages at the same time. Peel was concerned about Britain's ability to feed itself in wartime, but he recognized population expansion had made it impossible to do so from home sources alone.

Peel also had to take into account pressure from the Anti-Corn Law League that grew out of a movement begun by manufacturers. Leaders such as the radical MP and Quaker mill owner John Bright (1811–89) and Richard Cobden (1804–65), a Manchester merchant and calico-printer, shaped the League into a great national movement. Many of the organizational techniques adopted by them prefigured modern political campaigns. Peel could not but fear that he would lose the next election to the Whig-Liberals (see below), who supported repeal, unless he could appease the League.

Unlike the Chartists, the Anti-Corn Law Leaguers were predominantly middle class, and saw themselves as a counterweight to the workers' movement. They believed free trade would promote long-term economic expansion for industry and commerce. Foreign producers of wheat would gain enhanced incomes, which they were likely to spend on British-manufactured goods. Wages would go up and the cost of food go down, a double benefit to the workers, which would reduce working-class unrest. Cobden and Bright cast the battle very much in class terms, seeing it as a struggle between businessmen and the landed elite. Radicals attacked the aristocracy in ferocious terms. Peel understood the danger and responded to it as guardian of the established order. Many of the Whig grandees such as Earl Fitzwilliam (see Biography 6.1) also saw trouble ahead and swung into line behind Peel for this reason.

The Tory gentry fiercely opposed any reduction in agricultural protection. In the end only 112 out of 368 Tory MPs supported Peel in the crucial vote for repeal. The miraculous passage through the House of Lords in 1846 was due in part to Whig support motivated by a combination of Evangelical charity, belief in laissez-faire

Biography 6.1

Charles William Wentworth Fitzwilliam, fifth Earl Fitzwilliam
1786–1857

Earl Fitzwilliam was the temporal and spiritual heir of the marquess of Rockingham. His father inherited Burke's papers, which Fitzwilliam edited and published. He owned well over 100,000 acres, which included massive coal seams and what would become a huge industrial complex of mines, blast furnaces, and chemical works that made the family one of the richest in Britain. Throughout his life he was actively engaged in the management of the family business concerns. At the same time his aristocratic hauteur was notorious.

Fitzwilliam was highly intelligent, erudite, and a deeply committed Evangelical. While he was a zealous upholder of aristocratic privilege, he jumped fully clothed into a river to save an unknown urchin from drowning and played cricket with his servants in his shirtsleeves. He campaigned for 20 years to achieve repeal of agricultural protection and bluntly told an unsympathetic House of Lords: "He blushed for the order to which he belonged when he thought of the Corn Laws and the arguments by which it sought to maintain them." He reminded the aristocracy that "we stand … upon a noble eminence … Let us beware how we teach men to scan too minutely the value of *our* claims, and the reasonableness of their favour."[5] At the heart of his political creed was a Whiggish sense of the need for improvement and understanding that the landed elite could not survive if it looked only after its own interest. He wrote at the time of Peterloo: "It is of the utmost importance to conciliate the lower orders and to show that we are as jealous of the rights of the subject, when violated in *their* case, as we should be in our own."[6] However, it was not fear of revolution that led him to embrace reform. His reading of classical economics convinced him that the Corn Laws had to be abolished if the economy was to grow and prosper. Repeal, Martin Daunton reminds us, should not be seen as "a sign of surrender to the industrial middle class," but "a mark of [the elite's] ability to opt for economic adaptability." It was their willingness both to adapt to the times and pursue the national interest that led David Spring to call the nineteenth-century British aristocracy "a highly successful class – possibly unmatched in modern history."[7]

economics, and a sense of self-preservation. The duke of Wellington, though personally opposed to ending protection, stayed loyal to Peel, and he managed to scrape together the votes of enough Tory peers to carry the day for the government.

Agriculture remained profitable and productive during the era of "high farming" after 1846 based on new techniques for feeding animals, improved drainage, and lots of fertilizer. This helped sustain the aristocracy's economic and political dominance. Legislation in the 1850s allowed landowners to charge the costs of improvements to estates held in trusts. Peel, along with many of his contemporaries, however, put too much faith in innovative farming, which required very expensive investment that never paid the expected dividends.

The short-term consequence of Peel's reform was to destroy the existing Conservative Party. A group of young Tory grandees with their sidekick, the non-aristocratic but able Benjamin Disraeli (1804–81), developed a romantic new political vision emphasizing paternalistic links between the landed elite and the people opposed to the individualism and materialism of financiers, merchants, and industrialists. They attacked Peel with gusto. Many anti-Catholic Tories also feared and despised Peel's efforts to treat the Irish with generosity and tolerance. They could not stop repeal but they sought revenge.

Tory free traders such as the young William Gladstone (1809–98) and others, who became known as "Peelites," left the party. Most drifted across the aisle in Parliament to be gradually absorbed into and eventually to lead the Whig–Liberal alliance. Gladstone would become the high priest of the laissez-faire "minimal" state. The Conservatives lost the ability to command a majority in the Commons for a generation and did not win a full-fledged electoral victory again until 1874. Peel was defeated by his vengeful former followers in conjunction with the Whigs and Liberals on a piece of Irish legislation on the day the Corn Law repeal was carried in the Lords. He resigned without calling a general election in June 1846, soon after a dreadful calamity had overtaken Ireland.

───────────────   **The Condition of Ireland**   ───────────────

Both Melbourne and Peel made fair-minded and serious attempts to reform abuses and improve conditions in Ireland during the 1830s and early 1840s. Everything positive, however, was swept away by a horrendous famine that broke out in 1845, which took the Irish situation from bad to catastrophic. A fungal disease attacked the potato crop in 1845 and greatly reduced output. In 1846 three-quarters was lost. The 1847 yield was better but little was planted as the people had eaten their seed potatoes. Perhaps one million people died (most from diseases due to weakened immune systems rather than direct starvation), and one and a half million emigrated in the immediate aftermath. Over 2.1 million people left Ireland between 1845 and 1855, more than half going to the United States. By 1851 the population was down to 6.6 million and in 1891 to 4.7 million.

The situation was very complicated. Most of the effects attributed to the catastrophe – large-scale emigration, altered farming structures, new economic policies, and demographic decline – were already under way before the potato blight struck. In the pre-Famine Irish countryside, big estates rented out land to substantial farmers. Some of these operated like their equivalents in England, using hired laborers to work in the fields, while others sublet the property to smallholders. The mass of the population were landless laborers who lived in small cabins. The sustained fall in agricultural prices after 1815 led some farmers to turn from tillage to cattle and sheep, which held their value better. Land clearance of small cultivators increased often through eviction. Employment opportunities failed to expand to meet demand. Modern industrial production did not flourish in Ireland except in the North, where coal was imported from Scotland to fuel factories. The linen mills and shipyards of Belfast were the only serious industrialized sites on the island. Lack of capital and lack of mineral resources held Ireland back.

Considering the attitudes of the time, much was done to help the starving during the Famine. Peel acted expeditiously in response to the disaster and purchased supplies of American corn to feed the starving. After he left office the Whigs established public works and soup kitchens. By 1847 three million people were getting daily rations, mostly without charge. Farm consolidation and encouragement of emigration were sensible responses. The Irish Poor Law Extension Act of 1847, however, forbade giving relief to anyone with more than a quarter acre of land. The legislation was aimed at reshaping the Irish masses into a wage labor force similar to that existing in England by driving them into desperate poverty. This was more than active cruelty; it was murder. The Whig administration and the civil servants responsible for government policy in Ireland during these years deliberately followed a policy of restructuring the Irish economy by letting thousands of helpless people starve.

Most English politicians believed, with chilling indifference bred by a dangerous mixture of ideology and theology, that God was teaching the indolent Irish a moral lesson for their own good. Combined with laissez-faire economics, this created in many minds an almost religious belief in letting market forces work. The British were also influenced by cultural stereotypes about the laziness and improvidence of the potato-eating poor in Ireland. The otherwise admirable and sympathetic Scottish wife of an Anglo-Irish landed gentleman wrote of the potato failure in September 1846, "may be 'tis so best, for the cheapness of this low description of food encouraged idleness, pauper marriages and dirty habits … What a revolution for good will this failure of cheap food cause."[8] A dreadful failure of imagination and human sympathy pervaded the archipelago.

The memories of bitterness and loss among both Catholics who stayed and those who went into exile metastasized over time until it was virtually impossible for many Irish people to see Protestant Britain other than as innately evil. This view of the past produced a sense of fear among the Protestant "British" minority in the North. The normal process of political dialogue that advances the prosperity and stability of nations became impossible in Ireland (Figure 6.1).

Figure 6.1   Potato Famine Memorial, Dublin, by Rowan Gillespie, 1997

Ireland emerged as a recognizable nation in the nineteenth century with native leaders and an increasing impulse to be free. Many factors contributed to the heightened feeling among the population of their unique status as a people. Daniel O'Connell, the greatest Irishman of his age, was one catalyst. Born into an ancient minor chief's family, he was highly conscious of his lineage and status as a landowner. His decision to stand for Parliament in 1828 precipitated the passage of Catholic Emancipation. He founded the Catholic Association and harnessed peaceful mass protest to national politics in the cause of repealing the Act of Union of 1801. "There is a moral electricity," he said, "in the continuous expression of public opinion concentrated on a single point."[9] However, he opposed violence and had no agenda of social reform; he unleashed forces beyond his control.

The Young Ireland Movement was founded in the 1840s by those impatient with O'Connell's moderation. A number of its leaders were Protestants. They called for a spiritual, though secular, rebirth of Ireland through nationhood. It was William Smith O'Brien's (1803–64) abortive rising in 1848 that rejuvenated and organized this revolutionary spirit. The Famine "dissolved society" in the eyes of the ardent nationalists, and it came to justify any extreme method they chose to use to achieve independence.

The Gaelic language was increasingly abandoned. Many of the emigrants leaving Ireland came from the Irish-speaking regions, further weakening the culture. By 1890, 39 percent of all living people born in Ireland were exiles. Not all crossed the Atlantic or went to Australia. Many moved to Manchester, Liverpool, Glasgow, and London. There was also much seasonal migration to Britain for harvests as the cost of steamship fares and railways dropped dramatically. Ireland simply did not have the resources or jobs to support millions of surplus people.

The Whig-Liberals

Lord John Russell was called by the queen to form a government after Peel's resignation in June 1846. The Cabinet contained a cascade of marquesses and earls from old families, yet by responding to public opinion through a judicious series of reforms they held together the ministry effectively for six years. Some magnates had begun referring to themselves as "Liberal" in 1833, but the nomenclature remained binomial during this period. The "Whig" cousinhood of grandees continued to fill many of the top places until 1886. Middle-class Liberals and radicals, who were often hard to distinguish, made up the foot soldiers among a larger and larger portion of the party's MPs and local politicians. Voters who supported the Whigs included many middle- and working-class Nonconformists. The Peelites (without their leader, who died after a fall from a horse in 1850) increasingly acted with the Liberals, but they declined to join Russell's Cabinet. In addition, a substantial number of Irish Catholic nationalist MPs gave Liberal governments their tacit support. The fragility of this conglomeration gradually became more evident until it splintered in the 1880s, but between 1846 and 1886 the Whig-Liberal Party retained a significant degree of unity and ideological integrity. Voting patterns in the Commons largely matched the party labels people espoused. The notion of the "independent MP" in a kind of golden age of consensus and bipartisanship is a serious misreading of how the political system operated. Only the Peelites continued to dither, although they usually voted with the Liberals.

Russell's government was, except in Ireland, more humanitarian, more flexible and less dogmatically laissez faire than Peel's. The Whig-Liberals supported several factory acts that increased the number of trades covered, created the 10-hour day for most industrial workers, and expanded the inspectorate. Public health measures were also adopted. A rash of mining disasters prompted the government to establish a new inspectorate in 1850 and increase the number of offenses to which penalties were attached. The ministry continued to expand the role of government in funding public education.[10] Whigs believed strongly in the march of the mind. Francis Jeffrey, editor of the Whig oracle the *Edinburgh Review*, spoke of knowledge as a force "which tends to liberalize and make intelligent the mass of our population."[11] To keep spending low, much Liberal legislation was made permissive rather than compulsory and devolved on local institutions. Yet the state was steadily taking more responsibility.

The Conservative Alternative

An internal dispute between Russell and Lord Palmerston led to the defeat of the ministry in the House of Commons early in 1852. The queen sent for the former Whig Edward Stanley, now fourteenth earl of Derby (1799–1868), to see if the Tories could govern with only a minority of MPs. Derby descended from one of the most ancient and richest families in England. As he matured, more conservative impulses predominated in his thinking, but he was not a reactionary. His government was the first to enact a Chartist demand, abolishing the property requirement for MPs, and he also presided over the admission of Jews to Parliament in 1858. In many ways he remained a Whig at heart and passed to the modern Conservative Party, of which he was an important progenitor, a reduced rigidity.

Derby's chief assistant and leader of the Commons was one of the most unusual characters in Victorian politics, Benjamin Disraeli. He was a best-selling novelist who dressed extravagantly and looked even odder. His prosperous father had converted from Judaism to Anglicanism, but the son's name and looks constantly reminded everyone of his origins, of which he made no secret. The passion with which he resisted the repeal of the Corn Laws led to association with a number of Tory aristocrats, who quickly appreciated his skills as a debater and political strategist. The departure of the Peelites meant the Tory Party was virtually leaderless in the Commons. Disraeli was left like a young lieutenant after a great battle in which all other superior officers were killed or wounded.[12] This unique situation gave Disraeli his chance, which he seized with alacrity and skill. Derby was in charge of the government, but increasingly Disraeli was to the earl as Peel had been to Wellington and vice versa.

In 1852 the Conservatives accepted the political realities and abandoned their opposition to free trade. More and more businessmen were moving to support the party, and a renewed onslaught on protection would drive them back into the Liberal camp. In any case, Derby did not have the votes to pass legislation without the support of free traders. His government was soon defeated on the Budget and forced to resign. During the debate Disraeli and Gladstone squared off against each other in personal combat for the first time, the beginning of the most famous of all political duels of the Victorian age.

The Aberdeen Coalition

A general election was called and the Conservatives did quite well, in part due to a growing number of victories in English constituencies, which the Whig-Liberals only countered through success in Scotland and Ireland. If the Peelites had returned to the fold, Derby could have formed a new government. However, 40 or so of the free trade Conservatives now joined the Whig-Liberal administration on a permanent basis.

A coalition Cabinet was formed under the leadership of the Scottish Peelite, the fourth earl of Aberdeen (1784–1860).

Queen Victoria, who despised Palmerston's assertive policies, managed to block his appointment as foreign secretary, although the Irish peer did come into the government as home secretary. Perhaps most importantly, Gladstone became chancellor of the exchequer. His 1853 Budget was typical of his masterful competence in financial matters and tight-fisted resistance to unnecessary expenditure.

Palmerston proved not only a skilled home secretary but a surprisingly energetic innovator. He made vaccination compulsory, proposed the first legislation to reduce air pollution, abolished the transportation of prisoners to outposts in the empire, established the first juvenile reform schools, prohibited employers from paying their workers in kind instead of cash, and removed loopholes in previous factory acts. The Northcote–Trevelyan Report issued in 1854 (though it did not become fully operational until 1870) laid the foundations in the long term for an independent civil service chosen by merit through competitive examinations. This reform has often been seen as a nail in the coffin for the domination of landed society over government, but there is evidence that Gladstone and Palmerston supported it in order to forestall and circumvent criticism by radicals of aristocratic privilege. Many country gentlemen and younger sons among the peerage continued to have advantages of education and upbringing that enabled them to dominate the foreign service, where the merit system was less restrictive, and even enter the regular bureaucracy. Senior positions were still filled by the pre-1870 intake for many more decades. The incompetent and the time-servers were, however, eliminated.[13]

In spite of some successful reforms and able Cabinet members, Aberdeen's government is best remembered for stumbling into a conflict fought over issues that confused the public. The outbreak of the Crimean War in 1854 involved a dispute about who controlled the keys to the Church of the Holy Sepulcher in Jerusalem. The big question, however, was the role of Russia in the Balkans and Mediterranean. Castlereagh and his successors had withdrawn Britain from the commanding position it held in Europe after the Congress of Vienna and pursued a largely pragmatic foreign policy that kept Britain out of trouble while protecting her economic interests. The Mediterranean, however, continued to be central to British foreign policy. Even though they cooperated with Russia in helping to free Greece from Ottoman rule in 1827, successive governments feared Tsarist intrusion into the sea that was now regarded as a British "lake." While foreign secretary between 1846 and 1852, Lord Palmerston famously supported a British subject living in Athens who sought compensation from the Greek government for damage to his property. Despite the fact that "Don Pacifico's" claim to citizenship rested tenuously on his birth at Gibraltar, Palmerston unfurled the full panoply of the British state in the man's defense and sent the Royal Navy to the rescue.

The contrast between military operations led by Wellington and Nelson against Napoleon and the muddling mismanagement of the mid-century commanders who fought in alliance with France and the Ottomans against Russia was striking,

Map 6.1   The Eastern Mediterranean in the Mid-Nineteenth Century

neatly encapsulated in Alfred Tennyson's popular poem about a particularly shocking piece of incompetence:

> "Forward the Light Brigade!
> Charge the guns!" he said.
> Into the valley of Death
> Rode the six hundred.
> "Forward the Light Brigade!"
> Was there a man dismay'd?
> Not tho' the soldier knew
> Some one had blunder'd.

Most of the fighting took place on the Crimean Peninsula that juts into the Black Sea, a place remote from Moscow and St. Petersburg (see Map 6.1). The allies were woefully unprepared for long-range warfare on enemy soil. The army and navy had been starved of funds for decades. Lack of supplies and medical care led to scenes of unnecessary suffering being reported back by telegraph to London newspapers. Florence Nightingale (1820–1910) gained fame in undertaking a bold advance for women in the organization of nursing services for the troops.

Gradually, the allied forces gained ascendancy. The British military system proved resilient and efficient once its inadequacies had been revealed. The Russian army and navy were even more backward and poorly organized than those of their enemies. A formal peace was reached in 1856 through which Britain achieved its goal of blocking Russian penetration into the Mediterranean, but little else. The British public became hostile to further adventures on the Continent, and the failure to intervene a few years later in the unifications of Italy and Germany was in part due to the unpleasantness in the Crimea.

Palmerston

Lord Aberdeen's government lost a vote of confidence in the Commons in early 1855 and was replaced by one led by Palmerston, whose stint at the home office had left his hands clean of responsibility for the war. This old-fashioned Anglo-Irish aristocrat, who had first held high office in 1809, turned out to be the most popular premier of his time. He cloaked his fierce ambition with bonhomie. His survival skills were remarkable in a political world radically different than the one he had entered almost half a century earlier. The franchise was wider, the electorate more and more influenced by the industrial economy, and newspapers with mass readership required adept management. The prime minister navigated these challenges effortlessly. He won a general election overwhelmingly in 1857 that was a referendum on his personal leadership. Although he withdrew briefly from office in 1858 after a minor defeat in the Commons, when Lord Derby stepped in for a short time, Palmerston soon regained power and died at the helm 10 years after he became prime minister, beloved by many supporters among both the middle and working classes.

One of the chief challenges the Whig-Liberals faced in the early 1860s was how to respond to the American Civil War. A glut of finished textiles probably led to the increased unemployment in the industrial cities of the north of England. The distress was attributed to interruption of cotton supplies caused by the conflict. Many Britons were torn between their economic interest and a horror of slavery. War with the North over a series of incidents relating to blockade running and diplomatic immunity was narrowly avoided.

Palmerston died at 81 in October 1865. A general election shortly before the prime minister's death had given the Whig-Liberals a slightly larger majority in the Commons. The queen sent for Russell, whose government introduced a new version of parliamentary reform that would extend the franchise to more urban skilled workers without a radical change in the political system. Some Palmerstonian Liberals known as "the Cave of Adullam" (a biblical reference to their spirit of discontent) opposed extension of democracy. Whig aristocrats objected to the disfranchisement of their remaining pocket boroughs. Combined with the Tories, these forces were sufficient to bring down the ministry in mid-June 1866. Lord Derby was called for a third time to the premiership.

The Second Reform Act

The Second Reform Act of 1867 was a surprising outcome of a government led by Derby and Disraeli. Conservatives, however, had long been dissatisfied with the 1832 Act. In particular they felt that boroughs, more likely to vote for Whigs or Liberals, were overrepresented at the expense of rural county seats where their party could predominate. After a false start in 1858, the Tories tried again. The bill took on a life of its own in the Commons, ending up far more extensive than originally planned. Viscount Cranborne (1830–1903) and other strong conservatives resigned from the Cabinet. What Derby referred to as the "leap in the dark" was passed because the Tories were desperate to win elections and humiliate the Liberals.

One of Disraeli's greatest insights was that many workingmen would vote Conservative if given the franchise, motivated by their religious, job-related, and nationalistic feelings. Even though the Tory Party became the political home for most of the aristocracy as the second half of the nineteenth century progressed, it was never to be without a broad popular base.

The actual number of new voters is hard to determine due to disqualifications in meeting residence requirements, but about one adult male in three was now enfranchised in England, Wales, and Scotland, and one in six in Ireland. The composition of the electorate became broader and more diverse in the 1870s and 1880s and included many inhabitants of slum tenements.[14] In the House of Lords the practice of voting by proxy, which allowed peers to spend their days shooting and hunting in the countryside while their party leaders cast long lists of automatic votes left to them by the absentees, finally came to an end. An effort was made to improve the image of the Lords in other respects. The disgraceful scenes in which it was reported insane peers were brought from their asylums accompanied by their keepers to vote in crucial divisions were ended.[15] If they wanted to block reform, their lordships now had to take the trouble to appear in person and preferably sane.

Gladstone

Although the 1867 Reform Act contained advantages for the Tories, the Liberals won the first general election after its passage in 1868 (387 seats to 271). The victory placed Gladstone, whose leadership had superseded Russell's, at the head of a new

Liberal ministry, which would do much to transform Victorian Britain. His large majority in the Commons gave him the ability to launch a program of reform comparable in scope only to the Whig legislation of the 1830s. Although old-line aristocrats were heavily represented in the Cabinet, it also included John Bright, one of the first Nonconformists to hold a senior position in the British government in modern times. A number of former businessmen were also appointed.

William Ewart Gladstone was one of the most remarkable men of the nineteenth century. His father was a successful Liverpool merchant who had gained a baronetcy and purchased a large landed estate in his native Scotland. The son was sent to Oxford and hustled into the House of Commons at an early age. Gladstone married into the Whig aristocracy. To him the landed elite was the natural ruling class. His supporters called him the G.O.M. (Grand Old Man); he evoked extreme hostility from his opponents, who preferred "God's Only Mistake."

Gladstone was an undoubtedly sincere man who was capable of great self-delusion and self-deception. His private life proved particularly titillating to both contemporaries and posterity. He spent many nights roaming London's less salubrious streets trying to convince prostitutes to turn to Christ. Almost certainly, his work was virtuous, but explosive inner forces were clearly hard to tame. When the Oxford University Press published his diaries in 1968 it had to design a special piece of type shaped like a whip to mark where he indicated bouts of self-flagellation with the symbol.

The monarchy, in Gladstone's view, was inextricably connected to his beloved Anglican church. His difficult relationship with Queen Victoria offers something of the fascination of watching a horror movie. Her hatred became pathological; he continued to offer loyalty with the resignation of a martyr. The general public never realized these revered national icons were at total loggerheads, and that the prime minister filled the queen with loathing.

Gladstone came to be known as the "people's William." There was something in Gladstone's make-up that was radical. He was no social leveler, yet his voice became increasingly democratic even if his heart still lay with the monarchy, the Church, and the aristocracy. He possessed oratorical skills of a high order, capable of conveying messianic appeals in the style of William Jennings Bryan and Billy Graham. What is astonishing is that so many of his working-class followers admired him for his tight-fistedness with public money and support for low taxes. Most skilled workers, at any rate, defined the respectability to which they aspired as self-reliance. Until World War I the ideas of the pro-capitalist Samuel Smiles, author of *Self-Help* (1859), appealed strongly to many manual laborers.[16] Under Gladstone the Liberal Party increasingly became a workingman's party, while the level of spending by the central government continued to increase less rapidly than the growth of GNP. Gradually, however, Liberals became more activist in their orientation. Moral fervor, the restlessness of the Gladstonian mind, and the human suffering resulting from full-scale industrialization shifted the orientation of his party to a more collectivist mode of operation where the state intervened on behalf of the mass of the people.

Gladstone more than many men of his age grasped that the state of Ireland was central to British politics and that creative and thoroughgoing reforms in religion, land tenure, and government were necessary if the United Kingdom was to survive intact. This was due not just to rural violence in Ireland, and the terrorist attacks in England by the nationalist Fenian Brotherhood, but also increasingly because Irish MPs held the balance of power between the two major parties in the House of Commons. In 1868 Gladstone rose above his own devout adhesion to the Anglican Church and introduced legislation to overthrow its established sister institution in Ireland.

Liberals realized that the educational system was inequitable and ultimately dangerous in a society extending the vote to a wider and wider range of citizens and where more and more jobs required a basic level of literacy and numeracy to perform efficiently. England was falling behind not only Scotland but also some Continental countries in literacy rates. Early attempts to address the problem foundered on the difficulty of denominationalism. Gladstone shrewdly appointed a Nonconformist Cabinet minister, W. E. Forster (1818–96), to chair the committee preparing an educational reform bill. Forster's Act of 1870 established a system of schools for children under 13 funded by local taxes. Modest fees could be charged, but these were waived for the very poor. The legislation was permissive rather than compulsory. Only in 1891 did compulsion become general and fees were abolished. Religious teaching was limited to the extent that Nonconformists could tolerate, although large numbers of Dissenters remained disgruntled by an underlying favoritism to the established Church. Secondary schools and universities remained private and largely accessible only to middle- and upper-class families in England. Scottish universities, however, were more effective engines of social mobility. Up to 23 percent of Scottish university students in the 1860s were the sons of manual workers, a figure not achieved in England for another century.[17]

The Liberals also reformed the army and judiciary, and enacted labor union legislation. Pubs were subjected to somewhat stricter regulation. Finally, in 1872 voters were allowed to cast their ballots in secret. However, in spite of the remarkable record of legislative achievement, tensions were building up inside the Liberal movement. Dissenters called for English and Welsh Church disestablishment, and populist agitators demanded that foreign and imperial policy should be shaped by cost-conscious considerations rather than assessment of national interest. The Irish nationalists aimed at self-rule.

Disraeli

Disraeli had briefly held the premiership in 1868 before the Conservative electoral defeat. In 1872 he shaped a set of policies sometimes termed "One Nation Toryism" that focused the party's thinking on imperialism and social reform. The 1874 Conservative victory in the general election seemed to confirm his good political sense. For a time both parties struggled with an internal contradiction. Disraeli wanted to enact legislation aimed at helping the workingman, although his party relied on the support of the middle classes and much of landed society. The Liberals, led by Whig grandees and laissez-faire businessmen, were equally reluctant to be social activists but had to offer an increasingly radical program to appeal to working-class voters. It took some time for these internal contradictions to work themselves out. Over the next few decades both Tory and Liberal administrations began tentatively to protect trade unions, clear slums, regulate food quality, reduce pollution, and make ships more seaworthy. The Education Act of 1876 compelled parents of children aged five to 10 to send them to school and obliged local authorities to pay the necessary fees for the very poor.

Much of what Disraeli accomplished was merely a continuation of a trend with bipartisan antecedents over the previous half-century. Moreover, after the initial surge, energy for reform dried up during the last years of his ministry. Yet, the Conservatives were to prosper for decades on the capital of their quasi-mythical social conscience, "Tory Democracy." Some historians see Disraeli as putting the needs of his party before personal ambition, while others view him as blocking reunion with the Peelites so that he could have the lead. Some see him teaching the landed elite to adapt to change. Some see no clear policy at all.

Disraeli became preoccupied by foreign affairs and the empire. In late 1875 he purchased the shares in the Suez Canal (opened 1869) owned by the ruler of Egypt. The coup was seen as a triumph of secret negotiation and imperial supremacy. The sea-lane to India, the most vital imperial trade route, cut the distance back and forth to the subcontinent by more than half. Now it was close to being fully under British control. In 1876 Disraeli persuaded Parliament to raise Queen Victoria to the rank of empress of India.

The slow-motion collapse of the Ottoman Empire continued to be a preoccupation for the British, both because of their increasing level of interest in Egypt and other parts of the Middle East still under Turkish control and because of their nagging fear that the Russians would find a way to penetrate into the Mediterranean. In addition, the Liberal Party and Gladstone in particular were concerned about the fate of Christians living in the Balkans where Ottoman authority was under challenge. After his defeat in 1874 Gladstone had retired to his country house to write pamphlets on religious topics. The marquess of Hartington (1833–1908), a kind of retro Palmerston without as much ambition, took over the leadership of the party. However, a series of atrocities in Bulgaria committed by Turkish mercenaries triggered the G.O.M.'s return to the national stage. Disraeli was more concerned about the Russian threat, which made it appear that he was unfeeling about the fate of the Christians. The crisis deepened when Russia declared war on the Ottomans in 1877. In 1878 an international Congress met in Berlin where Disraeli and Salisbury (formerly Cranborne, now succeeded as third marquess) claimed to have achieved a great diplomatic triumph. Russian penetration of the Balkans was checked and Britain was granted control over the large island of Cyprus, which gave the empire another major outpost in the Eastern Mediterranean close to the center of things in the Middle East.

Gladstone now worked himself up into a frenzy over Disraeli's handling of the Eastern Question and Ottoman misrule. He chose to stand for the Scottish county of Midlothian, where Edinburgh is situated, during the next general election. There he launched a new style of campaigning, a whistle-stop tour where he spoke from the platform of a special train. His speeches were reported by telegraph to the London papers and thereby to a national audience. In 1880 the Liberals triumphed over the Conservatives by a convincing 353 seats to 238.[18] Lord Hartington was obliged to defer to the obvious agent of victory, Gladstone, as prime minister.

Gladstone Again

The G.O.M. turned his attention to electoral reform. Between 1883 and 1885 several pieces of legislation, collectively known as the Third Reform Act, altered the electoral landscape yet again. First, corrupt and illegal practices were addressed, which led to reduction in electoral expenses. The next stage was to standardize the franchise between rural and urban areas. Most workingmen in boroughs had received the vote in 1867 but laborers in the counties had not. Finally, in 1885 parliamentary constituencies of similar size were established. The redistribution of seats meant that the big cities and especially London were now granted the number of MPs commensurate with their size, although Scotland and Ireland remained overrepresented.

It is estimated that the electorate in England and Wales rose by 67 percent while in Scotland the increase was at least 80 percent. It was in Ireland, however, that the most dramatic change occurred, with the electoral roll going up by 229 percent. About two-thirds of adult males in England and Wales could now vote, about three-fifths of Scotsmen, and one-half of all Irishmen. However, the residency requirement of one year remained in place, which eliminated a substantial number of transient voters in any given election.[19] Domestic servants and paupers were still excluded, and women were not included until after 1918. Up to half a million university alumni and owners of multiple properties were able to exercise several votes in different constituencies.

A majority of historians agree that the 1880s witnessed a major political shift. A democratic polity was formed. José Harris writes:

> by 1900 close to two-thirds of electors were of working-class origin. Within this new culture, mass organization and class, group and ethnic interests began to press upon and transform the traditional concerns of high politics. Protestantism gave way to pluralism and ultimately to the "secularization" of political life; and the mere fact of citizenship increasingly challenged property, moral character, education, and economic independence as the basis of civil rights.[20]

David Cannadine argues: "Until the 1880s, the lower house of Parliament was essentially a landowners' club."[21] This is misleading. The traditional elements in the

Commons had been in steep decline since 1832. By 1874 only 40 percent of MPs were landed gentry or had peerage connections while 45 percent were merchants, manufacturers, bankers, and lawyers; but the Third Reform Act reduced representation of the old elite even further. In 1890 about a third of the Commons was composed of MPs from the traditional ruling class and by 1915 no more than 20 percent.[22]

The Cabinet, however, remained aristocratic. Young patricians of ability and ambition continued to enter the Commons at an earlier age than self-made businessmen, lawyers, or labor leaders all of whom had to establish a career outside Parliament first before becoming MPs. This gave the sons of peers and greater gentry a huge advantage in terms of accumulating years of party and government service. The need to find grandees of ability to rule India and Ireland and to represent ministries in the House of Lords meant that prime ministers had to promote junior nobles at a faster rate than ordinary men.

Imperial Expansion

British culture and civilization continued to draw power and inspiration from a global span. The seas grew ever more important as a highway to wealth, knowledge, and empire. New territories were acquired in every sector of the globe from the Caribbean to the Pacific. Key strategic outposts such as Singapore (1819), Aden (1839), and Hong Kong (1842) were acquired. On the East and West coasts of Africa operations against the slave trade led to further acquisitions. During the 1820s and 1830s most of Australia was subsumed under the British flag. The first colonists arrived in New Zealand in 1840. In the 1870s Pacific islands such as Fiji (1874) were taken over. British rule also expanded rapidly in India. From a comparatively small base in the later eighteenth century, virtually all of the subcontinent came directly or indirectly under the authority of the East India Company and then later the Crown. The population of British India grew from 40 million in 1815 to 303 million in 1911. A final surge of acquisitiveness brought a substantial portion of the whole African continent into the empire in the 1880s and 1890s. By 1910 Britain's holdings were three times the size of the French and 10 times the size of Germany's. The empire encompassed a quarter of the globe's land area and a fifth of its population, with additional regions and peoples held under more informal sway, and it was not even yet at its full extent (Map 6.2).

The British empire was much more complex than was once understood not only in its fragmentary nature – with protectorates, spheres of influence, treaty ports, coaling stations, dependencies, Crown colonies, white settler colonies, informal empire, and the uniquely diverse India – but also in its economic functions. Much of it was less under the control of London than appeared superficially. Barren rocks, naval stations, canals, cable routes, and shared territories added to the confusion. The number of white settlers varied from region to region. In West Africa, the indigenous population remained dominant in agricultural production, while in East Africa

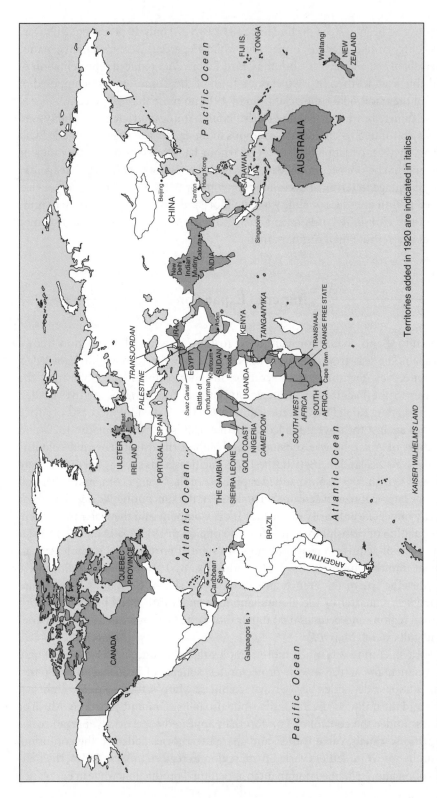

Map 6.2 The British Empire in the Early Twentieth Century

whites moved in to run plantations and take over land, accompanied by a large immigrant Indian community that dominated trade. Settlement of the empire was by no means a matter of only white British people going out to the colonies. Massive migrations of peoples of various ethnic groups and colors moved laterally within the system from one colony to another.

We have already noted that the empire required the cooperation and collusion of native peoples for British rule to work. The oak in the flowerpot did not have enough troops and ships adequately to garrison and guard all of its possessions. In Uganda in the 1890s Britain administered a colony of three million people with 25 officials. Often the existing chiefs, emirs, princes, and kings in places such as Sarawak, Tonga, Egypt, and India provided most of the troops and the structure of government. The system worked because the British could be ruthless, and the Royal Navy was very powerful. New technologies made it possible for fewer soldiers to control larger territories. The Maxim gun was introduced in the 1880s, which could fire 11 bullets per second. In 1898 at the battle of Omdurman the British suffered 48 dead, the Sudanese rebels 11,000.

An Imperial Vision?

The growth of a "new" or "second" empire after the loss of the American colonies is a somewhat misleading concept. Expansion had been taking place long before 1790. It may be that a new paternalistic and moralistic imperial vision was made possible by "liberating" French territories after the defeat of Napoleon, but the process of acquisition was so diverse and piecemeal that it is difficult to construct an overarching explanatory theory that suits all circumstances.

The famous historians of Victorian empire, John Gallagher and Ronald Robinson, characterized the nineteenth century as a period of "the imperialism of Free Trade." They played down what they saw as superficial changes in British expansion and argued for a basic continuum across the century where Britain sought to protect its economic interests in competition with other states by indirect means wherever possible and by direct annexation when circumstances required. This process was dictated by local conditions, not London.[23]

Peter Cain and Anthony Hopkins argue that the driving force in the expansion of empire were the "gentlemanly capitalists," a coalition of interests including those of banking and trading sectors, service industries, and the professional classes from the City of London. Other historians say industrialists should be added to the mix.[24] Yet the empire did not recapture the position of importance in Britain's economic life that it held before 1776.[25] Imperialism was an important but not dominant part of British international economic experience.

Advances in technology and the use of the anti-malarial drug quinine made it possible for the empire to expand more rapidly and further than before, although military setbacks still occurred. Humanitarian feelings prompted expansion to assist in the suppression of the slave trade and end practices such as head-hunting. Missionaries, most famously the Scot, David Livingstone (1813–73), explored unknown regions. Learned societies sponsored journeys of exploration to ever more remote spots. Finding outlets for emigration was a concern never far from the minds of British statesmen worried about a Malthusian catastrophe. Some politicians saw imperialism as a means of softening class divisions at home by promoting feelings of patriotic fervor and racial supremacy among workers.

The most convincing reason for expansion, however, is that once an empire had been acquired, the government was reluctant to stop. In part this was due to fear that retreat or withdrawal might be read as weakness and evoke both external threats from rivals and internal rebellions by subject peoples. As Charles Maier suggests, empires emerge out of what social scientists call "path dependency, that is, clinging to choices made early on whose reversal seems unthinkable. The imperial project is sustained, not because its advocates always press it further, but because even the hesitant can see no 'responsible' way to liquidate it."[26]

The empire contained many ambiguities, chief among them the fact that it embraced the racial superiority and dictatorial authority necessary to rule a vast imperium while at the same time British national identity was increasingly based on a belief in political and economic liberalism antithetical to oppression. Some contemporaries feared that imperialism could erode liberties at home, encourage autocratic forms of government, and embroil Britain in expensive wars with other European powers. It corrupted and coarsened the culture by its encouragement of an arrogant assumption of racial superiority. The dissonance between being believers in liberty and freedom, on the one hand, and ruling an empire, on the other, was a poisonous element of imperial rule.

Informal Empire

As we have noted, British imperialism was not confined to colonies under direct rule from London. Indeed, one of the most valuable elements was what has come to be called the "informal empire," an analytical concept first put forward by Gallagher and Robinson. Britain helped secure the independence of the Latin American countries from Spain and Portugal, after they had been invaded by Napoleon and fell under French rule. As the nineteenth century progressed, export of textiles to South America was followed by the development of railways, banking, oil, engineering, mining, weapons sales, and insurance, especially in Argentina and Brazil.

Some historians believe the concept of informal empire exaggerates the government's willingness to intervene overseas before 1880. Others argue that British capitalism created structural distortions in Latin American economies and that London's interference in political affairs there forestalled autonomous development. Little evidence exists, however, to prove that excessive profits or long-term bargaining advantages were gained. There was often a gulf between businessmen and the Foreign Office, with the latter reluctant to interfere. A new generation of Latin American historians has emphasized the complexity of the interplay between foreign business-men and domestic elites and the mutually beneficial results. The point of informal empire in South America was to keep markets open, not to take over or oppress the countries.[27]

China was also drawn into entanglement with a rapidly expanding British empire. Trade for tea, silk, and porcelain drained the East India Company of gold and silver. The latter organization equalized exchanges by sending Indian cotton and opium to Canton. Forty percent of the total value of Indian exports came from the sale of addictive drugs. Beijing's resistance to the importation of opium dragged it into the sights of British naval guns. London disgracefully supported the drug merchants in the "Opium War" of 1839–42. China was "punished" again in 1856–60 for attempt-ing to throw off British interference and further concessions were extracted. Until the 1880s British business dominated the China coast.

India

India was the premier British imperial possession in population, economic value, and grandeur. The East India Company's commercial monopoly there ended in 1813, but it continued to play a major role in the political administration and mili-tary security of the subcontinent. The Board of Control, whose president was usu-ally a member of the Cabinet, exercised an overview, and the government was represented by a governor general in Calcutta. The British reduced costs through indirect rule. About 40 percent of the territory was still governed by local princes and kings tied to Britain by treaties and increasingly subservient to the will of the Calcutta administration.

The small size of the British administrative footprint was amazing. In the later nineteenth century between 200 and 300 million Indians were overseen by about 2,000 Europeans. Only one solider in five was British. Resentment sometimes built up to explosive levels, most notably during the deadly rebellion of 1857, termed the Great Indian Mutiny. At least 100,000 Indian soldiers were in active revolt or deserted. Europeans were massacred in horrific circumstances, and the British imposed equally horrific and unjust punishments. Most of the country, however, remained quiet and took no advantage of British weakness in the crisis.

Aside from the princes whose wealth and thrones remained untouched, many educated Indians were brought into government service, at first in subordinate positions, but from 1863 their responsibilities increased. For most ordinary Indians the only contact they had with government officials were with fellow countrymen. Some historians argue that consciousness of racial difference and of racial superiority began to permeate British culture to a far greater extent than earlier.[28] This contention will require far more documentation than it has so far attracted to be convincing.

The British interfered with the traditional culture of India in a variety of ways, which caused a good deal of ill feeling, including the introduction of Christian missionaries, capitalist agriculture, and ending practices such as infanticide, child brothels, and sati, the burning alive of Hindu widows on the funeral pyres of their husbands. Some historians had tried to downplay the existence of the latter practice, but this is hard to do. In the province of Bengal alone 7,941 women died by fire between 1813 and 1825.[29] There was cultural arrogance in interfering with religious tradition. Previous British rulers had been reluctant to act; the Evangelicals of the nineteenth century were not. One has to judge whether the horror and suffering that was ended justified the exercise of cultural dominance. Many Indians were relieved to see such practices stop.

Evangelicals such as Macaulay saw an opportunity to turn Indians into "Brown Englishmen," ultimately "lifting" them to such a level that they could achieve freedom. When independence came, he said, "it will be the proudest day in English history."[30] On the other hand, many British administrators saw the value of leaving alone as much as possible native culture, religion, education, and structures of authority.

After the Mutiny it was decided to abolish the East India Company for good and achieve a firmer grip. A new Cabinet position was created: secretary of state for India. The title of the governor general was changed to viceroy to indicate high rank and direct representation of the monarch. Until 1947 viceroys were almost always selected from the titled aristocracy and given large discretionary powers. In 1853 the British began to build railways and within less than 50 years more than 24,000 miles of track had been laid. The system became the largest railway network in the world and remains to this day one of India's most precious national assets (see Biography 6.2).

The darkest aspect of British rule in India, as in Ireland, was indifference to famines. Unlike in Ireland, the colonial authorities were not only responsible for letting people starve, but also they helped cause the problem in the first place. As usual, when the Victorians were caught at their most heartless, classical economics lurked in the background. A combination of weather events and unwise administration resulted in mass starvation twice during the second half of the nineteenth century and would do so again in the twentieth. The British had encouraged Indian farmers to shift away from traditional crops, which provided a diversity of food sources that helped protect against unfavorable conditions and generally guaranteed subsistence, to market-oriented crops. The latter could be sold to provide the means to buy food but made villagers vulnerable to weather patterns and the fluctuation of world prices. When the monsoon rains failed to arrive between 1876 and 1879 and again in 1896 to 1902, catastrophe unfolded. Those officials who were moved by humanity and paternalist values protested in vain against the harsh policies of viceroys and their advisors who believed that, painful as the losses were, weeding out the weak was healthy for Indian society as a whole.

Biography 6.2

George Everest
1790–1866

The Great Indian Arc of the Meridian was begun in 1800, the longest measurement of the earth's surface ever to have been attempted. The 1,600-mile trigonometrical survey required accuracy to the inch and took almost half a century to finish. The struggle to drag an instrument weighing half a ton across fever-ridden landscapes, over hills, floods, and swamps, was begun by William Lambton and completed in 1843 by George Everest, whose life's work it became, within sight of the great mountain to which his name was given. Platforms 90 feet high had to be constructed every 20 miles and the heavy theodolite winched up to the top to make the necessary measurements. Two relays of 12 men carried the instrument in turns between sightings. Several catastrophic accidents claimed lives and equipment. Long chains used for triangulation had to be calibrated for temperature shifts because even minute contractions or expansions could throw the calculations off by miles over long distances. Employees were eaten by tigers as they hacked through a jungle filled with ferocious spike thorns, boa constrictors, and bird-sized spiders. The operation cost £6,000 a year, a sum that could support a nobleman in some splendor in England, and up to 15 deaths per annum among the staff. Here embryonic imperialism flexed its muscles as the British imposed their mastery on a vast subcontinent through technology and maps. The imperious Everest made nature and the Indian people bow to his will as he located the positions of towns and forts. Routes for roads, irrigation canals, armies, telegraph lines, and railways could now be laid out. Everest was not a pleasant man, but his drive and professionalism helped tighten Britain's grasp on the greatest of its imperial prizes.[31]

The extent of the tragedy is hard to establish, but it is likely that between six and ten million Indians perished from starvation and related diseases in the 1870s and possibly as many as 20 million between 1896 and 1902.[32] To be sure, comparable numbers died in China and Brazil where indigenous governments ruled. Many of the deaths were from diseases such as cholera and the plague, for which no medicines then existed. For the richest and most powerful state in the world to let such suffering go largely unrelieved, especially after the lesson of the Irish famine, was shameful (Figure 6.2).

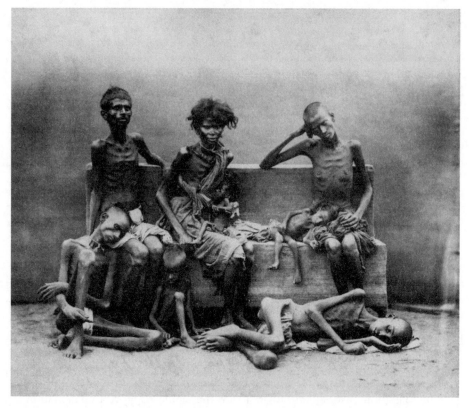

Figure 6.2   "Those who have got to this stage rarely recover." Famine victims in India, 1877

Colonies of Settlement

Though the Thirteen Colonies were lost in the 1780s, the British retained a vast empire in Canada, and soon acquired another in Australia. Between 1787 and 1853 almost 150,000 prisoners were "transported" to Australia. With the arrival of mounting numbers of European sheep the economy took off. Voluntary emigration to Australia grew rapidly in the 1820s and 1830s (Figure 6.3). The gold rush in 1851 attracted even larger numbers.

Although deference to British rule was strengthened by the emigration of American **Loyalists** to Canada during the War of Independence, danger lurked for a variety of reasons. The substantial French population in Quebec was not naturally sympathetic to the Crown. Voluntary union with or invasion by the United States were possibilities. London governments, however, understood that the mistakes made in the 1770s should not be repeated. The Whigs, who had been sympathetic to the colonists' cause in those years, put into practice a benign approach when they gained power in the 1830s. Unrest in 1837 prompted Melbourne to send Lord Durham (1792–1840) to investigate.

Figure 6.3   Emigrants. *The Last of England* by Ford Madox Brown, 1864

The Durham Report of 1839 paved the way for the unification of the two Canadas and provided a template for development of the empire of white settlement. The establishment of governments responsible to indigenous elected legislatures created internal autonomy and even allowed for tariffs to be levied against British goods. Britain continued to enjoy, however, the benefits of special trade and strategic advantages while offloading most of the cost of protecting both on the colonists. Similar constitutional arrangements were made for the Australian states and New Zealand in the 1850s. A further step was taken in 1867 with the establishment of the "Dominion" of Canada, which constituted self-government under the nominal supervision of the monarch and her viceroy. The latter office was held by British peers and royalty until after World War II (the Stanley of ice hockey's championship Cup was one of the earls of Derby). It was not until 1931, however, with the Statute of Westminster that Canada gained control over foreign policy. Dominion status was subsequently granted to the white-controlled colonies of Australia, New Zealand, and South Africa.

One of the most striking characteristics of the colonies of white settlement was their brutal treatment of aboriginal populations. Rarely were rights to land or cultural traditions respected, and active genocide was practiced by the white emigrant population in Australia. The treaty of Waitangi (1840) in New Zealand, however, promoted a less ruthless division of land among the British and natives than took place elsewhere. For the most part the indigenous peoples were robbed and degraded.

The Empire Strikes Back

Empire was not simply something done by one country to another, but a two-way system affecting politics and social, institutional, material, religious, and intellectual aspects of life. A "new imperial history" has emerged, bringing attention to the possession of the empire as a fundamental part of British culture and national identity affecting matters at home as much as in the colonies, and to the role of race, class, and gender in the making and ruling of empire.[33] Bernard Porter, on the other hand, suggests that the British were "absent-minded imperialists."[34] He argues that evidence for popular interest in empire is thin.

How conscious were the British of empire and to what degree did it shape their identity? Andrew Thompson has argued that the straitjacket of a tight ideological or interpretative framework simply does not do justice to the immense complexity of nineteenth-century imperial history. Virtually everybody was affected, but unequally and in different ways.[35] Moreover, imperial history is freighted with exceptional moral questions that can easily distort our views and that in the past have precipitated polemical writing rather than hard analysis.

Politically, empire was a constant factor in government decision making and very much on the minds of aristocratic governors and prime ministers. More than in the eighteenth century, there was a recognition among the ruling class that the imperial role brought responsibilities for the welfare of subject peoples and, at least theoretically, a day could be foreseen when they would be capable to independent development. Many people came to perceive the empire as a progressive force bringing moral uplift and modernization. Capitalism and free trade would help civilize the world. Progress was defined in terms of British values.

Backwash from the colonies impinged on gender roles and reshaped understanding of nature, science, and sexuality. India's impact on Britain can be traced in terms of religion, the economy, class structure, aesthetic concepts, literary styles, patterns of consumption, knowledge of botany, geography, zoology, political philosophy, kashmiri shawls, curry, and the position of women in the public sphere. New academic disciplines such as anthropology and tropical medicine appeared. Vocabulary such as "shampoo" and "khaki" entered everyday speech. New consumables such as rubber, palm oil, and New Zealand lamb changed people's lives. Robert Baden-Powell (1857–1941) introduced his admiration for aspects of African tribal culture into the heart of the Boy Scout movement.[36] Advances for both men and women in gaining the franchise in Australia, New Zealand, and Canada put pressure on the British government to reform. The empire enabled the Scots, Welsh, and English to find a common identity as British. The development of global electronic communications led to greater understanding of weather patterns and the beginning of forecasting. Imperialism was, as Edward Said pointed out, "inexorably integrative."[37]

Millions of people were aware of the importance of the colonies of settlement either because they were thinking about emigrating there or had relatives or friends who had done so, sending back information, money, and even returning for visits. The value of Canada and Australia to Britain was obvious to even the most geographically challenged persons among the urban poor. After 1850, increasing public interest was evoked by imperial heroes.

Porter largely neglects the huge surge of interest and information deriving from the anti-slavery agitation that stretched from the eighteenth century deep into the nineteenth. T. M. Devine argues that imperialism was "one of the truly seminal developments in Scottish history. So intense was Scottish engagement with empire that it had an impact on almost every nook and cranny of Scottish life over [the eighteenth and nineteenth] centuries: economy, identity, politics, intellectual activity, popular culture, consumerism, religion, demographic trends and much else."[38] The "cotton famine" during the American Civil War, which heavily impinged on industrial workers until other sources of supply could be brought in from the colonies, had a large impact. Visiting colonial sports teams attracted much attention. Stamp collecting, attendance at exhibitions, popular songs, adventure stories, political lobbying groups, emigration, and trade union contacts all spread knowledge and interest. In 1911 a two-and-a-half-hour documentary film of King George V's Durbar (enthronement) in Delhi and the royal tour of India was shown all over Britain. It was a major hit, and took in more than £150,000 in receipts.[39] The British knew they were a great power because of their empire.

Did It Pay?

Britain remained the premier maritime power of the world throughout the nineteenth century. The great naval base at Portsmouth was without parallel anywhere. Miles of docks lined the rivers in London, Liverpool, and Glasgow. Yet, it is difficult to establish whether the costs outweighed the benefits of imperialism in purely financial terms. How does one separate out the expense of maintaining the Royal Navy from what would have been spent even without the empire? Britain lived by trade and the protection of sea-lanes around the world was vital to national prosperity whether territories were ruled by Queen Victoria or by someone else. The investments in infrastructure were heavy, but the economic benefits of safe harbors, railways to bring products to the docks, or communication systems to speed business were great. Who would have paid for these if the British had not? The empire cut the price of food for the poor, but it also forced down domestic agricultural prices, which led to low wages for farm workers. The conquest of Africa (except in the south) brought little return, but then most new colonies cost very little to administer.

Calculations on the costs of military defense suggest that the empire was retained on the cheap. Between 1870 and 1913 the United Kingdom spent approximately 3 percent of national income on defense compared to 5–6 percent post-1945. This level of expenditure was in line with, or actually lower than, European great power norms.[40] A steep increase in arms spending came only in the years immediately before World War I.

Would Britain's economy have been more innovative and dynamic without the captive markets of the empire? Patrick O'Brien argues that after about 1846 Britain could have brought an end to empire with impunity and reaped a "decolonialization dividend" in the form of a 25 percent tax cut, which could have been spent encouraging further industrial production of consumer goods for the home market.[41] Other historians argue that the industrial development of Britain clearly benefited from large export earnings. Overseas emigration helped balance population growth, and opened up new markets for the imagination. Many colonies offered good opportunities for safe and profitable investment. In the period 1856 to 1914 around two-fifths (39 percent) of British overseas capital went to the empire.[42]

It is argued that the empire brought little economic benefit to the masses. The jobs it created, except in the military, were taken by members of the middle and upper classes. The return on capital investment went to the rich. Avner Offer, however, points out that British investment overseas made food cheaper for manual workers at a time when more than half of working-class expenditure was on food. This was a substantial benefit. The direct contribution of empire to Britain was not negligible, but in its absence British average incomes would still have been ahead of such contemporary front-rank economies as France and Germany.[43]

The establishment of overseas English-speaking dominions was by far the largest permanent advantage created for Britain by the empire. The former colony of the United States was also linked to the old homeland by strong ties of kinship, language, and commerce.[44] These societies were among the richest in the world, and made enormous financial contributions to Britain's prosperity. Twice in the twentieth century they rallied to the mother country's defense, helping to ensure its survival and future success.

Queen Victoria's Diamond Jubilee of 1897 demonstrated the pride that Britain felt in empire at what might appear the zenith of its power, but at this moment Rudyard Kipling (1865–1936) was prompted to write his poem "Recessional," a somber warning about the transience of power.[45] Intimations of trouble ahead came with the rise of the Congress Party (1885) in India, dedicated to the achievement of independence. Ireland was not the only place where nationalism took on new strength. The British responded by swathing themselves in more and more symbolic grandeur to overawe the Indians. King George V initiated the idea of moving the seat of government from Calcutta on the coast to the interior Delhi, the former capital of the Mughal emperors, and announced the decision at his Durbar there in 1911. In 1912 Sir Herbert Baker and Sir Edwin Lutyens were given the commission to design the layout of the new city and its principal buildings. The scale was terrific, comparable only to the ceremonial center of Washington (Figure 6.4).

Figure 6.4   Viceroy's House, New Delhi, India by Sir Edwin Lutyens, 1913–31

Lutyens combined a Western classical style with Indian images and motifs to achieve a cultural blend unprecedented in modern architecture.[46] As it turned out, the completion of construction in the 1930s left only a decade or so for British occupation.

Orientalism and Ornamentalism

The literary critic Edward Said pointed out that Western historians tended to assume that the imperialized world was merely a stage on which the European empires acted out their roles, with both positive and negative results, on supine native populations who were mere responders and not at the center of their own creative cultures. Westerners believed that "the Oriental is irrational, depraved (fallen), childlike; … the European is rational, virtuous, mature, 'normal.'" Thus could the African or Asian be "othered," which "invited" Europeans to take the initiative and assume control over "inferior" peoples.[47] Said and his followers, however, fell into the error of confusing modernization with Westernization. He also failed to understand that Westerners were often anxious and doubtful about their own role in the face of what they saw as powerful civilizations worthy of respect. It is not helpful to stereotype either the colonized or the imperialists.

Empire was not just about race and "otherness." David Cannadine argues that status and class were based on a presumption that colonial societies were, in the eyes of the imperial elite, in many ways the same as society at home. Empire reinforced traditional hierarchy in Britain, and helped to counter the forces of transformation engendered by the industrial revolution. Hierarchy cut across race. Not all foreigners were seen as savages. Cannadine's thesis has encountered much criticism, but it is undoubtedly true that the possession of a vast empire made Britain appear to be the dominant civilization of the nineteenth century.[48] The public face of that empire was composed of the queen and her aristocratic viceroys. The traditional elements of British society continued to lead what was at the same time an aggressively modern state.

The Challenge of Democracy

Lords Palmerston and Derby, among others, demonstrated the aristocracy's continued ability to adapt to changing circumstances. Middle-class leaders such as Peel, Disraeli, and Gladstone, who were closely allied with the old elite, were equally adept at balancing reform and caution in meeting the dual challenges of more democracy and burgeoning empire. It helped that many manual workers supported the "minimal" state and gradual change. The relationship between the rulers and the ruled cannot be described as a partnership, but the paradigm of responsiveness from above and willingness to compromise from below continued for the rest of the century. Industry and empire made Britons feel strong and prosperous, which diluted the pain suffered by the poor among whom revolutionary sentiments might have kindled into flame but did not.

Chapter 7

New Century, 1885–1913

Britain, unlike most other European states, proved to be infertile soil for revolution or authoritarian rule because extreme ideologies did not easily interlock with the social, economic, and political culture of the archipelago. Ireland was the exception. The accelerating pace of change in industry and military technology was, however, a worrisome development in the eyes of the ruling class. Progress exploded with possibilities, and many people were increasingly impatient with the delaying tactics deployed by those who had an interest in maintaining traditional authority and the status quo. In the new century the old elite faced a tidal wave of demands for change and the threat of another great Continental conflict. As in the days of Trafalgar and Waterloo, so again in 1914 the British state found it immensely costly to prepare for a massive land war while also maintaining global naval supremacy. What made the situation even more alarming was the fear that the British economy had already reached its peak and was in decline.

Home Rule

In 1841 almost one in three citizens of the United Kingdom lived in Ireland. Sixty years later barely one in ten did so. This change in both absolute and relative size, however, was not reflected in its position of importance in British politics, which intensified over the course of the century. Questions relating to the Irish Church, education, landownership, and disaffection dominated discussions in London as much as Dublin. The problem was compounded by British ignorance and prejudice. Disraeli never set foot on the island and Gladstone spent a couple of weeks there, once. Queen Victoria visited four times in a reign of over 60 years.

The unjust distribution of land led to rural unrest, involving "Whiteboys" and "Ribbonmen," who burst on the scene carrying out cattle-maiming, assaults on estate managers, burning of buildings, occasional assassinations, and even uprisings that had to be suppressed with troops. Coercive legislation giving the government special powers was imposed from time to time. Protestant vigilantes and **Orangemen** tried to intimidate Catholics. Irish nationalism rooted in separate religion remained powerful. By 1834, 80 percent of the population was Catholic, and that church was growing in vigor and influence over more than spiritual affairs. To the Irish masses England seemed the center of urbanism, unbelief, and cruelty. Fenianism was formally constituted as the secret society of the Irish Republican Brotherhood in 1858. Their central belief was that England was a satanic power oppressing a virtuous Ireland. Violent attacks were carried on English soil in 1867 with bombs and assassinations in London and Manchester. Further terrorism took place in the 1880s undertaken by even more extreme splinter groups.

A Tenant League laid down demands which became the core of the Irish farmers' case for decades to come, the so-called "three Fs": fair rent, fixity of tenure (protection from eviction), and free sale (the ability of tenants to "sell" an "interest" in their holdings upon giving these up to successors). Gladstone's first Land Act of 1870, which granted legal recognition of certain limited demands while at the same time operating ineffectively, actually encouraged the spread of rural resentments. A "land war" arose in the late 1870s.

In 1874 the Home Rule Party in favor of a restored Dublin Parliament and self-governance won more than half the Irish seats in the House of Commons. In 1878 their leader was Charles Stuart Parnell (1846–91), a Protestant from the landlord class, whose political gifts were remarkable. Parnell came to stand second only to O'Connell as the tribune of the Irish people. In the 1880s Irish tenant farmers unable to pay their rents were evicted, which evoked increasing hostility. In 1881 the Liberal government introduced against Gladstone's personal opposition a Coercion Bill, which suspended habeas corpus in Ireland and gave increased powers to the viceroy's administration. Parnell masterfully manipulated parliamentary procedure, forcing one debate to last 41 hours straight, though the Bill did eventually pass. Gladstone attempted to win support from the Irish by giving tenant farmers the "three Fs." A Land Court reduced the rents of about two-thirds of all tenanted property by an average of 22 percent. Returning prosperity and falling rents brought a lull in agitation. Then in 1882 the chief secretary, Lord Frederick Cavendish (1836–82), who was Lord Hartington's brother and married to Mrs. Gladstone's niece, was stabbed to death in Dublin by Irish terrorists. Aristocratic society and the British public in general were deeply shocked.

In June 1885 the Liberal government was defeated on a Budget vote in the Commons. The Irish Nationalists had switched sides, seeking an alliance with the Conservatives. Parnell was interested in Tory support for Home Rule, because that party was more likely to see it passed by the House of Lords. He held discussions with Conservative leaders, and urged Irish voters in Britain to cast their ballots for Tories in the upcoming election. Gladstone resigned and Lord Salisbury formed a minority government that lasted seven months, dependent on the goodwill of Irish MPs. The new prime minister proposed a land purchase scheme (Lord Ashbourne's Act of 1885) designed to place more farms in the hands of the peasantry. It evoked little interest among farmers in buying their holdings despite the availability of state funding. They intended to hold out for better terms. It was Wyndham's Act of 1903 that made an offer most of them could not refuse. In 1870 only 3 percent of farmers owned their farms; by 1914 three-quarters did so.

In an attempt to gain a majority in the Commons the Conservatives called a general election. The Liberals seemed divided. Joseph Chamberlain (1836–1914) and a party of supporters wanted major reforms. He had made his fortune as a manufacturer and was later an activist mayor of Birmingham, where he promoted municipal ownership of utility and transportation companies. He also favored provision of urban amenities funded by taxation. Without Gladstone's approval he publicly proposed a higher rate of taxation on large landed estates, which along with new local imposts would help fund housing and other improvements. He also sought free elementary education, contemplated disestablishment of the Church, universal male suffrage, salaries for MPs, and land redistribution. At the Whig end of the party's spectrum Lord Hartington and others were uncomfortable with what they perceived as a drift leftwards. Yet, they remained committed to a progressive agenda; they knew, as the political novelist Anthony Trollope's prime minister, the duke of Omnium, believed, that all was not "as it ought to be."[1] Gladstone tried to mediate, toning down Chamberlain's rhetoric and appeasing the grandees as best he could.

The results of the election were indecisive. The Liberals suffered due to Gladstone's failure to relieve a garrison surrounded by rebels in northern Africa at Khartoum, which led to a massacre and the "heroic" death of the commanding general, Charles "Chinese" Gordon (1833–85). Although they won a substantial majority of seats over the Conservatives, the votes of the 86 Irish Nationalist MPs held the balance of power. Salisbury thus failed to gain enough support in the Commons and had to resign. Gladstone came into office for a third time in early 1886.

Within the prime minister's mind a great change had been secretly taking place well before the election. The G.O.M. became convinced that Home Rule for Ireland, leaving only defense and foreign affairs in the hands of the London government, was essential for the future peace and security of the United Kingdom. Ireland had moved much closer to a genuine democratic polity, and Gladstone believed that in such circumstances it was impossible any longer to make a respectable moral argument to hold them in the Union against their will. Moreover self-government had been granted to white colonies such as Australia and Canada. He did not announce his change of heart during the 1885 election, but he may have authorized (the circumstances are still unclear) his son to fly a "kite" in an interview with journalists, suggesting that the Liberal leader had embraced a new approach to Irish affairs.

One of the old man's most serious vices was that he believed his instinct for "right-timing" was his greatest gift as a statesman.[2] Whether accidental or intended, the announcement of Gladstone's conversion to Home Rule shook British politics to the foundations. Parnell and the Irish nationalists now shifted their support fully to the Liberals, while, ominously, Lord Hartington and other Whig magnates declined to serve in the new Liberal Cabinet. Chamberlain and the radicals also balked. They suspected Gladstone was using Home Rule to avoid implementing social reforms. In addition, Chamberlain was an ardent imperialist, and he declared the empire would be in danger if Home Rule was enacted. The great Whig families such as Hartington's and those of Earl Fitzwilliam and the marquess of Lansdowne owned vast estates in Ireland aside from their English properties. They feared for their possessions and worried that land reform legislation might be extended to England. The G.O.M. went forward convinced that destiny decreed that he and only he could save the nation. The Liberal Party splintered apart (Figure 7.1).

Jonathan Parry believes the Liberal split was not inevitable but "sudden and dramatic," due largely to Gladstone's dictatorial manner.[3] Some historians regard Gladstone as ambitious and manipulative, a calculating politician more interested in blocking his rivals from replacing him as leader than caring about Ireland. Many working-class Liberals could be deflected from demanding social reforms by persuading them that they should give precedence to Ireland because important principles of civil and political liberty were at stake.[4] Gladstone may have felt Home Rule would salvage the role of the landed proprietors by ensuring stability and good government in Ireland. Yet, with all his complexity and capacity for self-delusion,

Figure 7.1   In the center group stand from left to right: Joseph Chamberlain, Charles Stewart Parnell, William Gladstone, Lord Randolph Churchill, and the marquess of Hartington. *The Lobby of the House of Commons* by Libero Prosperi, 1886

Gladstone had noble qualities as well. Some historians see his commitment to Home Rule as a heroic struggle for justice and freedom, a product of mature reflection, generosity of spirit, and honest conviction.

Unnoticed by most politicians, the Protestants in the northern counties of Ireland in Ulster were becoming alarmed by the prospect of a Parliament in Dublin dominated by Catholics. The ambitious son of the seventh duke of Marlborough, Lord Randolph Churchill (1849–94), visited the province and coined the phrase "Ulster will fight, and Ulster will be right." The provincial capital, Belfast, suffered severe sectarian riots. The Ulster Convention of 1892 symbolized the determination of the Ascendancy to retain its hold on the North. It represented a cross-class alliance between workers, landlords, and factory owners whose determination was underestimated by both Irish nationalists and British politicians. The narrow historical vision of the Ulster Protestants was to prove rigid and durable.

Lord Salisbury

On June 8, 1886, 93 Liberals voted with the Conservatives to defeat the Home Rule Bill in the Commons 343 to 313. Gladstone responded by calling a general election. He lost. Chamberlain and others stirred up anti-Catholicism, always a dependable source of prejudice: "Home Rule is Rome rule." The number of Liberal MPs dropped from 334 in 1885 to 190. The Liberal Unionists (the name adopted by anti-Home Rulers willing to vote with the Conservative Party) elected 79 MPs and the Irish Nationalists 85.[5] Now the anti-Home Rule forces numbered 395 in the Commons with a solid phalanx in the Lords as well. Gladstone was obliged to resign, and Lord Salisbury was appointed prime minister. Churchill became leader of the House of Commons and chancellor of the exchequer, but no Whigs or Liberal Unionists entered the Cabinet immediately.

The leadership of Salisbury, who succeeded Disraeli as head of the party in 1881, was a huge asset. Profoundly patrician yet alert to the modern world, he played the game of mass politics in order to shore up aristocratic rule, about the future of which he was pessimistic. He understood that to survive the great landowners would have to forge an alliance with all property holders, however modest their homes, against the forces of labor and socialism. Special efforts were made to reach out to the middle classes, "villa Toryism" as it became known. It was his achievement to use Home Rule for his lifelong political purpose: "to rally the possessing classes into a formidable party of resistance."[6] By 1870 he had become convinced that the Irish aristocracy had proved incompetent and unworthy and moved toward a position of throwing them overboard, like a captain cutting away damaged rigging that might endanger the ship. At the same time he aimed a policy of repression against the restive peasantry.

Salisbury first had to rid himself of Churchill, who proved uncontrollable. Gifted but unsteady and sometimes bizarre in his behavior (which was possibly caused by illness), Churchill became an advocate of "Tory Democracy," urging the landed class to look after the interests of the workers through state intervention on their behalf. His first Budget reduced income tax, cut military expenditure, and raised inheritance and luxury taxes. Many of his Cabinet colleagues found these measures hard to swallow. When the secretary for war, W. H. Smith (1825–91), refused to accept proposed army cuts, Churchill resigned, expecting to be recalled by a chastened Salisbury. The reverse occurred. Salisbury was relieved to see Lord Randolph go and found a sound replacement for him at the Treasury, who had the additional advantage of being a Liberal Unionist.

The Salisbury administration enacted a surprising amount of social legislation that benefited workers and urban dwellers. Government funding for universities increased and was more widely distributed. These reforms made it possible for Chamberlain and his followers to unite fully with the Conservatives, although he only joined the Cabinet after the 1895 election. Chamberlain pressed repeatedly in 1899 for an old-age pension scheme, but this would not come until the Liberals returned to power in 1906.

Gladstone Yet Again

In the 1892 election the Conservatives and Unionists won 314 and the Liberals 272 seats in the Commons. The 81 Irish nationalist votes cast in support of the Liberals put

Salisbury in a minority. Now 82 years of age, Gladstone was called to office for a fourth time. He remained strongly committed to Home Rule. The measure was carried in the Commons but defeated in the Lords 419 to 41. Gladstone wanted to dissolve Parliament and fight a campaign against the upper house on the issue of "whether the people of the U.K. are or are not to be a self-governing people," but not a single minister in the Cabinet supported him.[7] A majority of the electorate was in agreement with the Lords.

Old age and ill-health wearied the prime minister, and his fury at being unable to carry his colleagues with him on Home Rule and other matters led him to resign in March 1894. The queen declined to offer him the usual accolade of a title, nor did she consult him about his successor. The G.O.M. died in 1898.

Had the queen asked, Gladstone probably would have recommended the fifth Earl Spencer (1835–1910) as his successor. Victoria preferred the fifth earl of Rosebery (1847–1929), the foreign secretary, who, though a man of great intelligence, turned out to be too quixotic for the role. His ardent imperialism in a party filled with anti-imperialists and his lack of staying power weakened the Liberals. His government, however, did enact one significant piece of legislation. The "Death Duties Budget" of 1894 treated the taxation on the inheritance of landed estates in the same way as personal property. The rate was very modest to begin with, but the long-term danger to aristocratic wealth was serious.

Rosebery resigned after losing a vote in June 1895, and Salisbury became prime minister for a third time. The Tories called an election. Chamberlain and Hartington's Unionists became direct supporters of the Conservative leadership. The combined forces of two increasingly coordinated parties achieved a great victory, attaining a total number of MPs larger than the Liberals and Irish Nationalists together, a result duplicated again in 1900.

The Boer War

Joseph Chamberlain took the Colonial Office in the new government and was increasingly obsessed with issues of empire, especially South Africa. Originally a place of Dutch settlement, the situation there became very complex during the nineteenth century. Cape Town had been taken over by the British because of its strategic location on the pre-Suez route to India. The Dutch (Boer) settlers retreated inland and established several states including Transvaal and the Orange Free State. The discovery in 1867 of large diamond fields led to further British incursions on Boer territory. Into this mix was added the personality and vision of Cecil Rhodes (1853–1902), a British business mogul interested in promoting his own and his country's ascendancy over what was one of the greatest concentrations of gold and diamonds in the world. His influence came up against that of the Boer leader Paul Kruger (1825–1904), who began to import advanced armaments and open diplomatic lines to the Germans, Britain's chief economic rival at this time. Kruger's denial of voting rights to British immigrants coupled with irksome taxation supplied London with a pretext for intervention.

Rhodes, Cape prime minister since 1890, tried to organize a coup in favor of British rule in the Transvaal in 1895. Chamberlain probably gave guarded assent to the plan, assuming raiders would only cross the border following a "spontaneous" rising of the British-born population. The raid failed, and Chamberlain disassociated himself from what had happened. Sir Alfred Milner (1854–1925) was sent out as High Commissioner and worked to mobilize pro-British elements throughout South Africa. In the end Kruger declared war first. Salisbury was not enthusiastic but accepted the necessity of exerting control over the Boers.[8]

Most observers assumed that rich and powerful Britain would have little difficulty in winning the war. As it turned out, the two republics (with a combined white population smaller than London's) held the imperial armies at bay. The British generals were unimaginative and even incompetent. The Boers used guerrilla tactics suited to their home terrain. Britain staggered into a quagmire that lasted three years until May 1902, when a costly victory was finally achieved. The war was won by applying overwhelming force. A scandal arose over the high death toll among women and children held in "concentration camps." No premeditated murderous plan existed; the inhumane treatment was the result of criminal incompetence of the sort that held sway on the battlefield. A modern war was being fought by men trained and selected for command by traditional methods wholly inadequate to the time, place, and circumstances.

Balfour

In January 1901, when she died, Queen Victoria had been a fixture in the lives of most people since they could remember. "Every one [felt] as if she was their grandmother."[9] Her son, Edward VII (1841–1910), rather unexpectedly for a fat, self-indulgent, aging roué often mixed up with scandals, mistresses, gambling, and "fast" society people and plutocrats, turned out to be widely popular. Like his mother, he gave his name to an era, the "Edwardian" years, which were often seen as a golden age of peace and prosperity before the horrors of World War I arrived. He sustained royal influence in the field of foreign affairs. He also swept republican Paris off its feet with charm and obvious Francophilia in a decisive visit, moving the two countries toward warm cooperation as their mutual alarm over Germany increased.

In the summer of 1902 Lord Salisbury, the last prime minister to lead the nation from the benches of the House of Lords, resigned in favor of his nephew, Arthur Balfour (1848–1930). Like his uncle, Balfour was an intelligent aristocrat and played a long and distinguished role in public life. His personality, something of a mystery even today, remains the object of considerable fascination to historians. Unfortunately, his temperament was not suited to the responsibilities of the premiership, nor did circumstances favor his tenure.

Chamberlain's call for "imperial preference," a tariff barrier around the whole empire, which reversed the longstanding attachment of the nation to free trade, was proclaimed soon after the end of the Boer War. He hoped to tie the empire together so that Britain could remain a great power as it competed against emergent giants such as Russia and the United States. The tariff would produce fuller employment for the working classes while the revenues generated could be used for social reform such as old-age pensions.

Many Liberal Unionists, however, remained devoted to free trade and the Conservative coalition threatened to split apart. Critics argued that Chamberlain's policy would undermine the legacy of the repeal of the Corn Laws. "No tax on bread" became the cry of the free traders. Balfour handled the situation unskillfully and eventually both Chamberlain and Hartington, now eighth duke of Devonshire, resigned. Balfour made more sympathetic sounds about tariff reform but was not able to heal the rift in the party by the time of the 1906 election.

Balfour's government did have some successes. The Irish Land Purchase Act of 1903 provided additional funding for tenant acquisition of land in Ireland. Important reforms were made in the army, and Admiral Sir John Fisher (1841–1920) set in motion the modernization of the navy.

The Boer War forced the dismantling of the Gladstonian fiscal constitution. The massive commitment needed to gain victory could not be funded by "minimal" means. Furthermore the nature of military technology had changed and a new alliance was forged between the state and science. The giant battleships of the era demanded sophisticated systems of fire control; the state was heavily involved in the development of aircraft. The general feeling of insecurity and growing fears about an ambitious German naval program led to higher expenditure. New initiatives in social reform after 1906 piled a double burden on the backs of British taxpayers. Britain was developing a "welfare state" and a "warfare state" (see Chapter 9) simultaneously and had to forge new methods of paying for both.

The Dilemma of Poverty

Britain was not only an unequal society, but also a cruel one. The masses who lived in poverty were trapped in an unending series of humiliations and deprivation. Those who were in receipt of poor relief in 1885 numbered 768,938, 2.9 percent of the population of England and Wales. Four-fifths of the population were supported by manual labor and nearly 88 percent fell below the income tax threshold of £160 a year.

At the end of the nineteenth century agricultural labor still employed more people than any other occupation, and conditions for the rural poor remained bad. Life in the countryside stood unchanged in many ways. In remoter areas, people rarely traveled far from home. The stocks were used for punishment as late as the 1870s, and memories of the tales of earlier generations about witches and wizards were retold. Pitched battles between villages in which people were killed and maimed still took place.[10] An Agricultural Labourers' Union of the early 1870s was short-lived.

The fall in the price of grain and increasing mechanization undermined laborers' hopes for effective trade unionism. It was not until the founding of the Farm Labourers' Union in 1906 that more ambitious efforts were made to improve their condition.

Industrial workers also faced difficulties. Many jobs were unsafe. Mining was notorious both for accidents and occupational diseases. Construction, railways, chemical plants, and factories claimed many lives and limbs. A cycle of booms and busts made life insecure. Few opportunities for social mobility existed. It has been calculated that 70 percent of working-class income went on food and only 2 percent was discretionary. The diet of the poor was unhealthy and irregular, which led to marked differences in height between schoolchildren from different social backgrounds. Toward the close of the century the gap widened between the number of children born to white-collar and blue-collar families. The latter was 25 percent higher, widening to 42 percent between 1910 and 1924. The disparity was somewhat offset by higher mortality rates, but more mouths to feed acted as a drag on workers' finances.

Housing was deplorable and expensive. The mass of the poor lived in rented accommodation, moving frequently as family and occupation required. Furniture was simple; people slept in their clothes and rarely washed. Only at the end of the century did mass-produced furniture and linoleum make inroads on cleanliness and comfort. In 1861 in Scotland a third of all houses had a single room, another third, only two rooms. Indoor plumbing was a rarity. As late as 1911 two-thirds of working-class inhabitants of Manchester lived in houses without an indoor toilet connected to a sewage system.

Some improvements in the lives of the poor had been made. Note has already been taken of the passage of legislation to improve conditions and hours in the workplace. Dire poverty declined after 1850. More entertainment such as professional sports added color and enjoyment to working-class lives. Some municipal leaders had tackled housing problems on a local basis. Cheaper imports of wheat and meat from the 1870s onwards helped raise the living standards even of the very poor. The fall in the price of cotton made it possible for them to afford more comfortable clothing. Even the harsh Poor Law was gradually subjected to revision. An increasingly sophisticated public hospital system was established. Employers began to provide opportunities for a dignified retirement and old age. In 1859 a pension scheme was introduced for the civil service, which included not just elite administrators but workers in the Post Office, the single largest employer in the country. Private businesses followed.

Eric Hobsbawm and others famously argued that a well-paid and hence docile labor "aristocracy" of the skilled trades which embraced middle-class conceptions of respectability imposed conservatism upon working-class institutions, thereby concealing but not eliminating the underlying militancy of the proletariat. Marxists call this "false consciousness" since they assume such developments must be the result of social manipulation rather than self-generated assumptions about the inherent value of thrift, manners, and education.[11]

Henry Pelling pointed out that the evidence almost invariably suggests that it was the prosperous workers who were the more politically militant and radical, while the lower ranks displayed either apathy or conservatism.[12] Moreover, it was hard to identify exactly who the labor aristocrats were. It makes no sense, for example, to lump both miners and postmen into such a category. Skilled craftsmen formed only 10 percent or so of the labor force, but "respectable" members of self-help societies formed a much larger part of the laboring classes. Labor hierarchies varied between industries, some based on age, others on strength rather than skill. Moreover, the separation of skilled from less-skilled workers on the shop floor was not the product of a "divide and rule" policy designed by employers to create a submissive class. It arose out of the desire of some workers better positioned than others to gain economic advantage over their fellow workers, often against the will of and to the disadvantage of the employers.

Two major attempts to study poverty were made in the 1880s and 1890s in London by Charles Booth (1840–1916) and in York by Benjamin Seebohm Rowntree (1871–1954). The former found that about 30 percent of London's population fell into a category of "very poor," those who failed to earn enough to provide the minimum to sustain a family with basic necessities. While middle-class observers were inclined to attribute poverty to drink, laziness, and lack of thrift, Booth argued that irregular employment, illness, old age, and large families were more to blame. Rowntree perceived a cycle in working-class life in which living standards peaked twice: when men were young and strong and without children to raise, and again after the children left home but before their energy and strength began to fade. Youth and old age were the worst times. These were eye-opening discoveries. The amount of extreme poverty was a surprise and so was the dynamic of the cycle (Figure 7.2). The work of Booth and Rowntree obliged thinking persons living in comfort and prosperity to reconsider what obligations society might have to protect honest and hardworking people from suffering. The focus shifted away from concentration on the moral inadequacies of the poor and more toward the deleterious impact of the urban environment.[13]

Trade unionism played a role in helping the laboring poor. At first the movement was weak with no inspiring leaders. Most unions were small and restricted to skilled workers. The Trades Union Congress (TUC) was founded in 1868. By 1874 over a million workers both skilled and unskilled had joined. Yet, as late as 1891 only one among every seven workingmen were members. Though willing to adopt militant action, the main interest of the unions long lay in preserving craft restrictions and pay differentials. Although the Liberals enacted some legislation to foster the movement, it remained vulnerable to prosecutions and adverse legal rulings. The 1889 strike by benighted dock workers in London won considerable sympathy even from the middle classes, and after a month-long struggle achieved victory. Membership in the TUC increased to 4,000,000 by 1913. Unskilled and semi-skilled workers began to gain support. In a dispute between the Taff Vale Railway and its workers, the courts held that a trade union could be sued by employers or anybody else and its funds confiscated as damages. The Conservative Party seemed sympathetic to this

Figure 7.2   Poor people at a Welsh almshouse, *c.* 1890

decision, while the Liberals promised to reverse it, which they did after winning the general election in 1906.

The Labour Party

Socialism was the logical ideology for proletarians to adopt. Yet, most early socialists were not manual workers, and many workingmen remained loyal to the Liberal Party straight through to World War I. Extreme socialists were contemptuous of the often deeply religious trade unionists, and the leaders of the latter movement did not appreciate their condescension and were unwilling to embrace communist tactics or ideology. Henry Hyndman, who founded the first Marxist Social Democratic Party in the early 1880s, was out of touch with working-class attitudes. The more moderate William Morris (1834–96), the leader of the Socialist League, lived in a country house and designed wallpaper for the elite. The more successful and long-lasting Fabian Society, founded in 1884, was full of middle-class intellectuals such as the playwright George Bernard Shaw and the novelist H. G. Wells, who were no revolutionaries. They were gradualists dedicated to peaceful and democratic achievement of socialism and the empirical study of social problems.

Working-class candidates advocating the support of the laboring poor first entered the electoral lists in 1868. Only in 1893 did a genuine working-class socialist group, led by Keir Hardie, the ILP (Independent Labour Party), come into being (see Biography 7.1). Like the middle-class socialists they were committed to a gradualist strategy, seeking power through the existing political system and opposed to violent revolution. The ethical socialism of working-class leaders dovetailed with the strong Nonconformist tradition and values of the leaders. They sought to work with the trade unions, not look down their noses at them, although to the latter the ILP sometimes seemed intent on trying to highjack union funds for impracticable purposes remote from the immediate needs of workers. Gradually, however, the TUC became more militant and a convergence of feeling and strategy began to develop.

Biography 7.1

Keir Hardie
1856–1915

Keir Hardie was the illegitimate son of a farm servant and probably a miner. He grew up in Glasgow and the Scottish coalfields in Lanarkshire with little formal education and worked in the mines from age 11 as a "trapper" regulating ventilation machinery and then as a hewer on the coalface. He became a deeply committed Christian and lay preacher, took up journalism, and was a miners' trade union official. His political creed shifted in the 1880s from Gladstonian Liberalism to socialism. Hardie was never a Marxist but called openly for opposition to the capitalist order; he learned to live with the constitutional structure of Britain and work within it. In 1892 he was elected an MP but lost his seat to a Conservative after his criticism of the royal family backfired in 1894. Labour politicians came to treat the monarchy with caution, and few of its leaders have ever avowed republican sentiments openly since that time. Hardie's work as a journalist and politician laid the foundations for the modern Labour Party, which he helped to animate and direct toward a successful triumph over the Liberal alternative. He was committed to internationalist solidarity among workingmen and traveled the world to learn about labor conditions and build relationships between countries. Unlike most of his socialist colleagues in Europe, he courageously led anti-war demonstrations in August 1914. He also committed the Labour movement to granting Indian independence. He was a man of powerful integrity and a passionate voice for the victims of capitalism.[14]

In 1900 delegates representing the Fabians, trade unions, the ILP, and the Social Democratic Federation established a Labor Representation Committee (LRC) whose aim was a distinctive Labour group in Parliament. The secretary of the LRC was James Ramsay MacDonald (1866–1937), later Labour's first prime minister. They elected only two MPs in 1900. But the Labour movement found itself strong enough to enter into negotiations with the Liberal Party. A secret agreement was concluded that the leaders of each party would use influence during the forthcoming election to prevent the running of "wrecking candidates" whose entry would create a three-way race, handing the seat, on minority votes, to the Conservatives.[15] The name "Labour Party" was first used in 1906. A breakthrough came in that year with the election of 29 MPs, increased to 40 and 42 in the elections of 1910. Payment of MPs from 1911 enabled the Labour Party to put up a large number of candidates for the first time.

Liberal Triumph

L. T. Hobhouse (1864–1929) noted: "the task of Liberalism in the nineteenth century had been the achievement of political democracy; in the twentieth century it would be social democracy."[16] This required the party to abandon the doctrine of the free play of market forces and to intervene to reform capitalism on a moral basis. In 1906 the Scot, Sir Henry Campbell-Bannerman ("C-B") (1836–1908), led the party to a great victory with 400 seats to 157 for the Conservatives and Unionists, and was called upon to form a government. C-B provided low-key leadership, but a number of younger men such as Herbert Henry Asquith (1852–1928), David Lloyd George (1863–1945), and Winston Churchill (1874–1965), who had deserted the party of his father Lord Randolph, waited in the wings. The prime minister died in 1908 and was succeeded by Asquith, son of a Nonconformist woolen merchant, who had risen to be a star at the bar and married the daughter of a wealthy Scottish industrialist.

The Liberals argued that the state had a fundamental duty to intervene directly with reforms and to redistribute wealth by progressive taxation to improve social conditions. Irish Home Rule was downgraded as a priority. The first step was a scheme that conferred a weekly pension of five shillings on all British citizens aged 70 or over whose income fell below a set figure. About half a million people drew a pension on January 1, 1909. By 1911 the pension population rose to over one million. Lloyd George announced plans for a National Insurance Bill, based on compulsory contributions, which would embrace the sick, disabled, and unemployed. The health scheme covered all insured workers aged 16 to 70 earning £160 or less for medical treatment, unemployment due to illness, and long-term disability. Winston Churchill set up a national network of Labor Exchanges to help match people with jobs. In 1911 in another bill he proposed unemployment benefits administered through unions for men in trades subject to cyclical employment, mainly building and engineering.[17]

Other important social legislation made it compulsory to provide a half-holiday each week, prevented the sale of alcohol and tobacco to children, established separate juvenile courts, ended imprisonment for child offenders, allowed local authorities to provide free school meals for poor children, and established a centralized school medical inspection service. Housing, town planning, and the needs of the mentally deficient were addressed. After this spate of reforms the government's attention was deflected from social policy by other events, although miners' minimum wage legislation was enacted in 1912. The "minimal" state went up in smoke.

The welfare policies of the Liberal Party were motivated by the need to mollify unions and fend off the challenge of the Labour Party, but pure humanitarianism and considerations of "national efficiency" played a role. Interest groups such as charities with knowledge of particular problems, insurance companies and friendly societies, medical practitioners, and women's organizations also helped. Many employers were anxious to improve productivity, and state officials, who believed a happier, healthier, better-educated workforce would prove more efficient, also pushed for it.[18]

The impact of the Liberal social reforms was far-reaching. Costs for social legislation were shifted from local authorities to the broader shoulders of national government. At the same time the pattern of central taxation started to change from proportionally equal to progressive redistributive imposts in which the wealthy paid more. Super-taxes were imposed on rich people. A distinction was made from 1907 onwards between earned and unearned income, with the latter taxed at a higher rate.

Liberal Government

The Liberals confronted other important issues as well as social reform. They launched an attack on the veto powers of the House of Lords (see below), which had hitherto blocked Home Rule, and a new bill granting devolved powers to a Dublin legislature was introduced in 1912. The situation was made complicated by the emergence of extreme groups such as Sinn Fein (pronounced "shin fain") on the Nationalist side and a more radical stance among Ulster Protestants. The leader of the latter, Edward Carson (1854–1935), threatened armed resistance. The Conservative leader Andrew Bonar Law (1858–1923), who had succeeded Balfour, was a Presbyterian with Ulster connections and threw his support behind the Northern Irish Unionists.

Many Liberals, including Asquith, did not grasp that some separate arrangement would have to be made for Northern Ireland, and they let extremist initiatives develop without any adequate government response. Lloyd George and Churchill proposed to the Cabinet that the predominantly Protestant counties be allowed to opt out of Home Rule, but this was not adopted. The bill treated Ireland as a single entity.

The evidence does not survive for us to be certain about how close the United Kingdom came to civil war in 1914, but the readiness of otherwise sane and respectable people – from judges and generals to the advisors of the king – to embrace what was tantamount to treason was extraordinary. The Ulster Unionists organized a Volunteer Force of nearly 100,000 men, ready to fight, as one of them wrote, "for their religion, their liberty and all that was dear to them."[19] In March 1914, 57 officers from units stationed at the Curragh near Dublin resigned their commissions rather than take part in operations in Ulster. Senior military personnel were seething; the government feared the army might not act to suppress disturbances in Ireland. It was clear that only force could coerce the North into accepting Home Rule. The outbreak of World War I in August diverted attention and deferred a final settlement.

The Liberals moved too slowly on further franchise reform. Nor did they give priority to women's suffrage even though leading figures such as Campbell-Bannerman and Lloyd George favored it and legislation was introduced for its advancement. The press of other business to which Asquith gave greater favor prevented a full debate of the issue.

Labour unrest became more frequent in the years before 1914 as the struggle began to achieve a minimum wage. In the famous case of a miners' strike at Tonypandy in Wales, Winston Churchill, the home secretary, unfairly gained the long-lasting enmity of the Labour movement. His decisions actually reduced the amount of bloodshed (one dead, 500 wounded), but he was seen as being aggressively hostile to the workers.[20] At points the country appeared on the verge of anarchy.

Changes in the structure of world trade lay at the source of many industrial disputes. Foreign competition had intensified and most workers felt their wages and conditions of employment were deteriorating. However, many strikes were successful, with only one in seven ending in defeat for the union. By 1914 average real wages had caught up with the rising cost of living, though the miners continued to fall behind.

Despite the many reforms enacted by the Liberals between 1908 and 1914, a sense of unease and decline in party fortunes was palpable. Home Rule had split off the Whigs and Chamberlainites. The crisis of identity between old-style laissez-faire liberalism and new collectivist/welfare liberalism disturbed other supporters. Rosebery and C-B had been lackluster leaders and rivalry between Asquith and Lloyd George dissipated energy. The middle classes were moving toward the Tories, workers toward Labor, and the Liberals found no great issue that could rally their followers. Yet, the party survived for some time longer. Radical decline came only after World War I.

Reforms in Local Government

Vital aspects of British society were reformed during the later nineteenth and early twentieth centuries, including local government, the system of justice, and the House of Lords. All three directly affected the role of the landed elite in British society. Dominic Lieven writes that Britain had a local "administrative system that, by

European standards, was so weird as to hardly seem to exist in some respects."[21] The informal influence of the great proprietors was still enormous. In 1861, 18,669 dinners were prepared and served at Holkham Hall in Norfolk for family, guests, and employees. The great estates were big business. The lives of thousands of people were integrated into the support system of a single peer. Even on smaller gentry estates most villagers remained directly under the supervision of the owner of the manor house, from the vicar of the church whom he appointed to the miscreants he jailed or fined in his role as JP. Much urban property was also owned by the aristocracy, and they and oligarchies of businessmen retained extensive authority in towns and cities.

In 1888, Salisbury's administration took the surprising move of reforming local government in a democratic way. What appeared liberal reform, however, had the real object of legitimizing continued authority by the landed elite. Elected councils replaced the rule of the magistrates. The new authorities raised revenues through local rates, controlled their own police forces, and took responsibility for schools and local welfare. Aristocrats did well in the new local elections and many peers were chosen as council chairmen. Just before World War I, over half the councils were led by titled aristocrats and many more members of the landed elite served on them. Even as late as the 1930s old-line families could "mobilize a large and spontaneous deference vote" in local elections in rural counties.[22] However, the aristocracy lost the vice-like grip they had had over the localities, and gradually fewer councils were decisively controlled by them.

Borough and county police forces were established, the state penal system was massively expanded, a juvenile justice system was put in place, and the legal system overhauled. A growing apparatus with which to record, identify, measure, and classify criminal behavior emerged. Much of the change came gradually. Parliament often seemed to resemble a bather sticking her toe in the water to test the temperature, slowly gaining in confidence as more and more of the foot was immersed. For example, from the 1820s legislation designed with the juvenile criminal in mind was passed. Need for separate accommodation was recognized in 1824; reform schools were established in the 1850s; but the full principle of separation of adult and juvenile prisoners was not finalized until 1876.

A more centralized and professionalized police force evolved. Previously, the costs of prosecution fell on those who brought a case, which meant many people could not afford to do so. This changed in the nineteenth century and the increasing abolition of capital punishment for many petty crimes made people more willing to bring charges. Peel's police force had not been greeted with open arms. Gradually, however, people grew more supportive. The police were eventually successful in imposing order on even the darkest areas of the slums. By the end of the century they had become a central institution in British society. The level of criminality probably dropped. Abusive drinking declined and better methods of treating alcoholics arose. New methods of registration, surveillance, and fingerprinting helped solve more crimes.

Major changes in types and style of punishment took place in the nineteenth century. The end of transportation to Australia was a turning point. The fledgling colony was developing its own identity and wanted to distance itself from its penal beginnings. In Britain an increasing chorus of criticism from the 1830s led to a new system of penal servitude, which aimed to achieve a balance between punishment and reformation. Various experiments, some eccentric, some inhumane, were tried. Incarceration developed into a system of brutal and unremitting labor designed to exhaust and subdue the prisoner.[23]

House of Lords Reform

In the eyes of the Labour and Liberal parties a further constitutional change beyond expansion of the franchise was required if Britain was to become fully modern. The House of Lords stood like a great ogre guarding the bridge to progress. It must be reformed or better yet abolished. One peer likened the atmosphere of the House of Lords to "addressing dead men by torchlight."[24] Many a lord slumped back in his seat and dozed off in the dark corners of the chamber. The aristocracy remained patrician: only one in five peers created between 1833 and 1885 owned less than 3,000 acres, and a number of these men, such as Macaulay, had no heirs and so were in effect life peers only.

Cooperation between the houses deteriorated in the 1880s, and the Tory aristocracy successfully blocked measures passed in the Commons. Many conservative peers subscribed to a new concept of plebiscite democracy, asserting the Lords' right to hold up controversial legislation as a necessary brake on change until it had received explicit endorsement through a referendum of the electorate. The rejection of Home Rule could be seen in this light. In 1906, even after a definitive victory at the polls, the Liberals were thwarted by the House of Lords in reforming sectarian education. The Lords also successfully rejected the tighter regulation of pubs and drinking hours, a reform cherished by the temperance advocates, but on which the aristocracy and most workingmen stood shoulder to shoulder in opposition.

In 1909 the chancellor of the exchequer, Lloyd George, had trouble finding the money for the old age pensions while at the same time funding the upsurge in defense spending that placed extra demands on tax revenues. He claimed that a large deficit loomed and introduced the famous "People's Budget," raising income tax, adding levies on the sale of land, and imposing a progressive super-tax on the very rich. He was waging war on the landed aristocracy, and they responded in kind by voting down the new taxes. They overstepped an important boundary, however, by deliberately ignoring a convention of several centuries not to reject finance bills originating in the Commons. This was not guardianship but provocation. It is true that by modern standards the proposed increase was modest, but to contemporaries the rise was striking and presaged further tightening of the screw. Lloyd George and the Cabinet may well have set out to provoke a confrontation, when it came they embraced it. The Labour Party supported the Liberals. They would have preferred higher taxes and outright abolition of the Lords but were willing to go along with the removal of the veto power as a first step.

The constitutional crisis brought everything to a standstill. A general election was called over the issue in January 1910. An informal renewal of the Liberal–Labour electoral pact took place. The government was returned with a reduced majority of only two more seats than the Conservatives, which made them dependent on the Irish Nationalists, though in general they could count on the support of Labour.

Asquith went into the election without any promise from the king about the creation of peers, which would be necessary to enact reform. In the midst of the fray Edward VII died, and was succeeded by his son George V (1865–1936). After a dignified pause, Asquith went to the new king for a second dissolution and sought a royal guarantee, as Grey had done from William IV, that in the event of the Liberals winning another election and seeing their reform thrown out by the Lords, he would create sufficient Liberal peers to swamp the opposition there. George reluctantly agreed. The election was held in December 1910 on the issue of constitutional reform, which ended in a tie. Each major party won 272 seats (only Irish and Labour votes continued to give the government a majority in the Commons). The Parliament Bill was introduced and the government announced the threat of a peerage creation. The Conservative leadership ordered abstentions in the Lords, but a group of "diehards" disobeyed. The bishops and a small group of "Judas" peers carried the day for the Liberals, 131 to 114.

Henceforward the Lords could not stop money bills and could only delay other legislation for three sessions. As usual with British reforms, the 1911 Parliament Act did not accomplish what it ought to have done, abolition of the hereditary chamber of Parliament. At the same time, however, it demonstrated a willingness to reshape the constitution in such a way as to get enough done so that the situation was not intolerable to reasonable people while preserving the forms valued by traditionalists that anchored the state to a bedrock of stability. In any case, replacing the hereditary chamber with an elective one would have threatened the supremacy of the House of Commons. This problem has inhibited further radical reform of the Lords ever since.

Trade and Industry

Britain remained stable in part because the country continued to prosper. One can afford to tinker with political machinery when the economic engines turn over smoothly. Agriculture raised productivity and increased output. Abundant energy supplies and expanding sources of raw materials and markets in the colonies encouraged continued growth. Reorganization of manufacturing and new technology made industry more productive and efficient. Britain's social and legal institutions

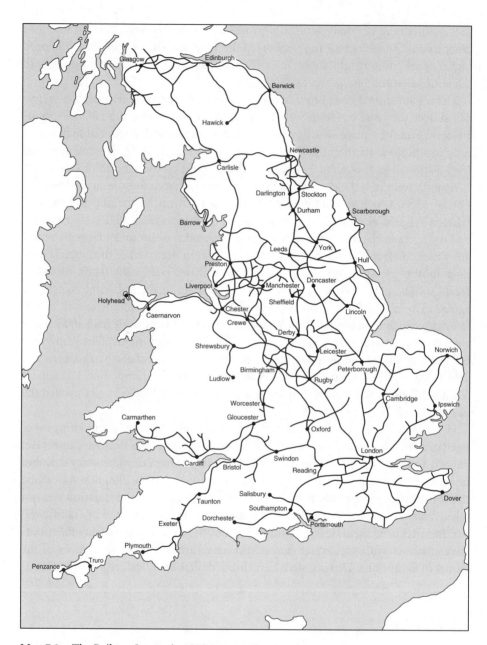

Map 7.1   The Railway System in 1852

also contributed to abundant availability of credit and a commercial culture that encouraged entrepreneurship, as did the law of bankruptcy, development of insurance, and the emergence of specialist bankers and brokers.

In 1881 41 percent of those with jobs in England and Wales were employed in manufacturing, mining, or transportation. The figure was 44 percent in Scotland.

Application of steam power in industry on a heroic scale did not come until surprisingly late: 300,000 horsepower in 1850, 977,000 in 1870, and 9,650,000 in 1907.[25] Around 1860 the United Kingdom reached its zenith in relative terms, producing 53 percent of the world's iron and 50 percent of its coal and lignite while representing 2 percent of the world's population. The nation generated 40 percent of the world's trade in manufactured goods. Great Britain's share of world trade also peaked at about one-quarter in the 1860s. Although net imports rose to ever greater heights leading up to 1900, exports of UK products did not keep pace. The negative balance of trade was £13 million in 1830 and £160 million by 1900. Net income from services and dividends from investments overseas rose dramatically, however, offsetting the losses. Toward the end of the century many of Britain's competitors began to construct protectionist barriers, while the UK stayed committed to a tariff-free economy.

New industries emerged in the second half of the century that were centered on chemicals and electricity. Electric light in houses remained rare, however, until the twentieth century. Unexpectedly, Lord Salisbury was one of the first private citizens to install the devices in his country house. The lights shorted out regularly, and the family was obliged to toss cushions up to the ceilings to extinguish the sparks.

British companies remained small in scale, a majority employing fewer than 20 workers. Hand labor was a vital part of most manufacturing operations. Large-scale factories were untypical and confined to a few regions. Family partnerships were the most common form of business organization. Legislation was enacted in 1856 allowing businesses to sell shares to raise capital without the purchasers assuming liability for debts or losses that might occur, but publicly owned companies accounted for less than 10 percent of important business organizations in 1885.

The largest industrial operations in the country were the big railway companies, which required thousands of men to construct and thousands more to operate. The first line to haul coal between Stockton and Darlington opened in 1825, and in 1830 passengers commenced travel between Liverpool and Manchester. Unlike on the Continent where governments were heavily involved, the British system was built by private enterprise. George Stephenson (1781–1848), and his son Robert (1850–94) were the heroic figures of the early railway age. The father was one of the few great businessmen to rise from truly humble origins. He began as a steam engine mechanic, who later developed the vision of a national network of railways (Map 7.1).

The rail system grew rapidly. By 1852 all the main lines between major cities had been laid down, and by 1870 most smaller towns had a station. The level of effort to design and lay track in an era before the steam shovel and dynamite was prodigious. Deep cuttings through hillsides and tunnels were made with picks and axes wielded by armies of workmen. Viaducts and bridges reached spectacular size (Figure 7.3).

Figure 7.3   The Forth Bridge carried trains over a two-mile wide crossing near Edinburgh, Scotland. Opened in 1890.

Many other developments in Victorian Britain can be at least in part attributed to the railways. Vacations at the seaside, national newspapers delivered everywhere in the country on the same morning, and the cheap and efficient postal service are examples. National time became important in order to coordinate train schedules. Professional sports teams traveled easily, and everyone could follow the results in newspapers. Rich people began to dress more simply and in dark colors due to the confinement and soot involved in train journeys. This democratized life to the extent that it became hard to discern by outward appearance who was a duke and who a bank clerk. New patterns of housing and the growth of suburbia became possible. "Englishmen are beginning to live on railways like Chinese on rivers, or Dutchmen on canals," noted the London *Times* in 1851. London became ever more the center of national life because many journeys from one part of the country to another could only be accomplished by passing through the capital from which the main rail lines fanned out like spokes in a wheel. Regional barriers were broken down. Market gardens and dairies could deliver fresh food everywhere. "The railway and the telegraph made all England into one extended city, or at least one urbanized region."[26]

The nature of retail business began to change. Thomas Lipton's first grocery store opened in Scotland in 1872, and the chain quickly spread across the whole island. Lipton developed modern business techniques such as heavy use of advertising and total control over tea processing, from ownership of plantations in Ceylon to final retail sale. Although historians tend to emphasize the multiple chain and department stores as the cutting edge of modernity and mass consumption, by far the largest part of retailing remained in the hands of small shopkeepers who did, of course, sell goods to which mass production techniques had been applied. These products were branded and marketed by large companies. The proto-department store arose in the 1850s and 1860s and the first purpose-built one appeared in London in 1877. By 1900 London boasted some of the most famous names in the world, such as Harrod's and Liberty's.

Financial Services

The City of London's financial and commercial businesses became the most dynamic and innovative part of the British economy after 1850, and by 1914 a huge proportion of the national income was supplied by returns on foreign investment filtered through this system.[27] Between 1850 and 1914 the United Kingdom provided much of the insurance, banking services, and warehousing of products to the whole planet. Nearly half of the steamship tonnage in the world was British in 1900. Wall Street did not overtake the City of London in productivity until after World War II. Industry relied heavily on the credit and marketing skills of British financial institutions to sell and distribute their products. The first Atlantic cable was laid in 1866 and telegraphic communication reached Cape Town in South Africa in 1879. Businessmen could communicate instantaneously with any city in the empire and buy raw materials or shares of stock in real time around the globe.

Some historians argue that Britain's strong record in services starved industrial expansion at home. The "gentlemanly capitalism" discerned by Cain and Hopkins excluded industrialists from a central role in the economy. By 1900 British overseas investments were more than twice as large as those of Germany and France and 24 times that of the United States. They rose to a quarter of net national wealth in 1890 and over a third in 1913. Surplus capital was invested in railways, public utilities, and government bonds more outside the empire than within.

Martin Daunton suggests that industry was not ignored nor opposed to the interest of finance. British banking provided a secure and stable platform for the economy. There is no evidence of a shortage of capital for industrial growth, nor were investors always passive coupon clippers. Daunton argues that the amount of active direct investment has been underestimated by historians. There was no massive shift from commerce into finance. The flow of income from overseas investments covered the deficit on the balance of trade so that Britain could purchase more food and enjoy a higher standard of living than it could otherwise afford.[28]

The situation may have been changing, however, just before World War I. It also may be that the availability of British capital abroad allowed borrowing countries to release their own capital for more remunerative investments while increasing the price of funds within Britain. Just before the war food prices failed to drop and the cost of local authority loans rose.

Economic Decline?

In 1900, the United Kingdom was the richest country in history. Yet, considerable concern and even pessimism about the economic future arose at the end of Victoria's reign. Both historians and contemporaries noticed signs of decay and decline. Much attention is given to identifying the peak and showing when signs of a faltering stride began to appear. It used to be fashionable to see this happening in the 1870s and 1880s during the "Great Depression," although now some observers place it as late as 1900. Others see the 1840s as the moment when a break began to occur. Absolute growth in national income did, of course, continue throughout the rest of the century but data suggest that the peak growth of real industrial output occurred somewhere between 1830 and 1850, after which decline set in.[29] Moreover, other countries such as France were competitive in per capita growth rates.

All this was relative, of course, and measured largely in comparison with only two serious competitors, Germany and the United States. One obvious problem was the size of domestic markets. Despite rapid population growth Britain began to fall behind its potential rivals in numbers of people. In 1871 the United Kingdom was just a little behind, but by 1910 it had only 45 million people compared to Germany's 65 million and America's 92 million.

A widespread interpretation of decline points the finger at a snobbish distinction made in Britain between theoretical and technical knowledge, which contributed in the long term to England's failure in continuing to produce inventive entrepreneurs. The British were said to have not invested enough in education while Germany was supposed to have had a higher-quality secondary school system in general and technical schools in particular. The classic explanation of decline was summarized by A. J. P. Taylor: "The simplest answer, which remains true to the present day, was the **public schools**. They taught the classics when they should have been teaching the sciences."[30] This view, that "gentlemanly" culture was privileged over science and technology, is echoed in the interpretation of decline by Martin Wiener. Bourgeois energy and entrepreneurship, it is argued, were enervated by aping the values and lifestyle of landed society. Not enough capital was reinvested in business as money went overseas or was ploughed into the purchase of landed estates. This supposedly drained away talent from the world of commercial industry. "Businessmen increasingly shunned the role of industrial entrepreneur for the more socially rewarding role of gentleman (landed, if possible). Hence premodern values were entrenched in the new society. The upshot was a dampening of industrial energies, the most striking single consequence of the gentrification of the English middle class."[31]

The Wiener thesis is odd in many respects. First, it posits that the most entrepreneurial and acquisitive aristocracy in Europe, noted for digging mines, constructing harbors, managing railroads, promoting resorts, and investing heavily in the stock market, somehow destroyed the dynamism of businessmen. Landed proprietors had been reading Adam Smith from the year he first published. Nor can one argue successfully that businessmen rising into the elite led to the "embourgeoisment" of the

Figure 7.4   Belfast City Hall, built between 1888 and 1906

aristocracy. As we noted earlier, the nobility had largely risen from the world of business and had never rejected the idea that making money through capital investment
and commerce was a good thing.

Many entrepreneurs never aspired to high rank, purchased no more than a subur-
ban villa, and eschewed the world of London politics and parties. We have no reliable
statistics to tell us whether the proportion of businessmen buying land declined during the nineteenth century. We do know that the number of very rich men grew
steadily, and since land was finite, probably fewer found it easy to buy estates, especially big ones. W. D. Rubinstein has shown that attendance by the children of businessmen at public schools did not produce a "hemorrhage of talent" from business
life.[32] The portion of the commercial elite that did become fully "gentrified" were the
London financiers and bankers whose entrepreneurial performance continued to
outdistance even New York's Wall Street well into the twentieth century.

Some historians argue that Britain lacked a confident urban bourgeoisie so that
the great industrial cities lost their leadership and civic culture became weak. In fact
the reverse was true. A powerful municipal elite emerged, of which the Chamberlain
family, Joseph and his sons Austen and Neville who later reached the highest places
in national politics as well, were the premier but by no means the sole examples.
Civic leaders founded universities, libraries, zoos, and museums, opened parks,
established orchestras, cleared slums, and built vast city halls (Figure 7.4). The
research of Richard Trainor has revealed a self-confident plutocracy that was comfortable in its dealings with the landed elite. The continued political role of aristocrats in industrial regions depended on a good working relationship with businessmen
and the professional middle class.[33] Pat Thane suggests that we need "to think in

terms of a negotiated relationship among the major social groups, resulting in a more or less satisfactory accommodation between them based on largely shared values. Landowners played the more prominent political roles, but with middle class consent and responsive to their needs. It was consent rather than subordination since the middle classes had nothing obvious to lose from the arrangement."[34]

The British tradition of small family firms restricted the ability to compete with large-scale amalgamations and cartels in Germany and the USA that achieved greater economies of scale and could raise larger amounts of capital for research and expansion. The British relied too heavily on a few staple industries such as iron and steel, shipbuilding, textiles, and exporting coal at the expense of newer technologies such as chemicals, man-made fibers, and automobiles. The British were slow to adopt speedier and more efficient mechanical devices used in business such as the telephone, typewriter, and adding machines. New coal-cutting technologies for mines arrived late in Britain and were imported from America where they had been in use for decades. American industry moved to standardized and interchangeable parts more quickly. It may be that the organization of the workforce was inefficient and trade unionism more widespread in Britain.

Mention has already been made that France, Germany, Russia, Austria, and the USA were sheltering their key industries behind protective duties. Britain's success had relied on free trade, and with that change in the stance of competitors it became entwined in what has been called the "hegemon's dilemma."[35] Should she use tariffs herself to force fairer trade, pursue an active imperial trade policy within the confines of the empire, or continue with the system that had served so well in the past and to which so many were attached by more than mere economic values?

One argument made by contemporaries, viewed skeptically by modern historians but characteristic of the time, was the perception in the Edwardian period that decline was due to the failure of the British "race" to breed properly. Although a significant eugenicist lobby developed in Britain, it was overborne by "environmentalism," which encouraged better provision for public health and preventative medicine rather than the use of sterilization of "inferior" types. It would be Germany that turned to the latter sort of thinking in the 1930s.

Dynamic Britain

The focus on "decline" leads us to think in terms of responsibility for failure and to conclusions that may be misleading or false. In fact Britain was the first country to industrialize and it was no one's "fault" when other, larger countries gained access to coal- and steam-powered technology and made use of it effectively. Britain's share of the world's industrial production inevitably declined during the later nineteenth century. What is striking is how strongly the country still performed against the emerging giants. Moreover, in terms of productivity, that is relative economic power per capita, Britain remained highly competitive and dynamic.

Table 7.1 Percentage of shares of different countries in total world manufacturing output, 1830–1913[36]

	1830	1860	1880	1900	1913
UK	9.5	19.9	22.9	18.5	13.6
Germany	3.5	4.9	8.5	13.2	14.8
France	5.2	7.9	7.8	6.8	6.1
Russia	5.6	7.0	7.6	8.8	8.2
United States	2.4	7.2	14.7	23.6	32.0
India	17.6	8.6	2.8	1.7	1.4
China	29.8	19.7	12.5	6.2	3.6

Table 7.2 Comparative GDP per capita and per worker hour, 1913 (UK = 100)[38]

	GDP per head	GDP per worker hour
United Kingdom	100	100
France	69	67
Germany	76	82
United States	105	120

We now know that any slowing down in the British economy after 1899 was probably due to cyclical retardation. In 1914 the balance of payments was extremely strong. Britain was the world's largest creditor. London was the world's financial center. The widening gap between exports and imports was reversed in the early twentieth century. In 1913 the United Kingdom's proportional share of world export trade in manufactures stood at 29.9 percent, Germany 26.5 percent, and the USA 12.6 percent. Compared to the rest of the world Britain remained an economic superpower (Tables 7.1 and 7.2).

Britain continued to surpass Germany in per capita GDP and labor productivity until well after World War II. British workers also gained better hours and working conditions at the same time. In financial services British per capita productivity levels were still in advance of the USA in the 1930s.

Wiener's critics have found little evidence to sustain his claim of a broad cultural attack upon the entrepreneurial mores in late Victorian Britain. It was by far the most capitalist society in nineteenth-century Europe, not least in comparison to Germany, where the far right and far left were much more hostile to commercial values. Rubinstein notes: "Britain's high culture was, demonstrably, perhaps the least hostile to entrepreneurship and business life of any in Europe and perhaps the world; its intellectuals were the least alienated of those of any leading society."[37] There is also no hard evidence to support the assertion made by Wiener and Taylor that the public schools disparaged science. Elite institutions may have placed too much emphasis on sports, but the training in writing and thinking skills was of a high order. Some of Britain's greatest engineers and scientists in the twentieth century were educated at the leading public schools. It was to those institutions that the premier American high school, Phillips Exeter Academy, looked in the 1930s for advice on how to improve science teaching.[39] Moreover, the traditional training ground for Germany's elites remained the *gymnasiums* where study of classical literature held pride of place just as it did at Eton and Harrow. In many technical fields such as armaments Britain continued to keep pace with or outshine its rivals. It was Britain that produced the super-weapon of the Edwardian era, the Dreadnought battleship. It remained the equal or ahead of its chief Continental rivals in almost every major field of science except rocketry until after 1945.

Sliding toward War

Political stability in the midst of reform made Britain strong. So too did a growing economy and a great empire. This was reassuring in a period of increasing international tension. At the turn of the century Lord Salisbury helped reshape British foreign policy. Traditional suspicion and hostility toward France and Russia gradually gave way to alliances with both as Germany's bombastic leadership and economic ascent made it appear to be a threat to Britain in particular and Europe in general. The last serious clash with France took place on the Nile in southern Sudan in 1898 near Fashoda. The crisis almost led to war, but the French backed down and soon after the two countries signed an agreement on their respective spheres of colonial influence. From that time forward relations continued to improve. In 1904 an "Entente Cordiale" was concluded, one step away from a full alliance.

Like a medieval castle, Britain was dependent on external supplies of food. If an enemy could lay siege and cut the inflow, the island could be starved into submission. Only naval superiority protected the nation from both blackmail and direct attack. Until the 1890s no country or combination of countries seriously challenged Britain's control over the oceans of the world. For most of the nineteenth century the Royal Navy was probably as powerful as the next three or four navies in fighting power despite significant economies and cutbacks in expenditure. Then the German Admiral Tirpitz began the construction of a large high seas fleet. Russia, the USA, Japan, and France were also expanding their navies (Table 7.3).[40]

The Royal Navy could not be strong everywhere. British strategy was based on the idea of a decisive battle (another Trafalgar) whereby victory would allow the navy to continue to keep the sea-lanes open and the dominions protected from aggressors. Dividing up the fleet would make it impossible to win such a battle.

The older, wooden-hulled navy had not changed very much over time. Ships could be dry docked between wars and used for several generations. Crews could be pulled from commercial shipping as needed. The new advanced battleships were very complex machines that required constant professional training and maintenance

Table 7.3 Warship tonnage of the powers, 1880–1914 in 1,000s of tons[41]

	1880	1900	1914
UK	650	1,065	2,714
France	271	499	900
USA	169	333	985
Germany	88	285	1,305

underway at sea. The innovative design of the British Dreadnought battleship in 1905 made all other existing warships obsolete, creating an even playing field among great powers prepared to spend heavily. Since several other industrializing nations were growing faster than Britain and they were able to compete, new alliances and strategic plans were necessary. Britain turned to Japan in the Far East, to France in the Mediterranean, to Russia in the Baltic, and to the United States in North America to eliminate threats and thus enable most of its battleships to be concentrated in home waters. She needed the bulk of her firepower simply to match the German threat in the North Sea.

Germanophobia began to seep through the British government and elite. Both Edward VII and George V, though of German descent, were increasingly distrustful of Berlin. From 1905 onwards they lent strong support to officials who sought to prepare alliances against a German menace. The Anglo-Russian Convention of 1907 brought agreement over remaining colonial disputes. Military and naval collaboration with France tightened. British thinking moved closer and closer to the idea that support for France against Germany was right, natural, and necessary. More and more battleships were laid down. Fear of a Dreadnought "gap" caused near hysteria. Invasion scare literature sold like hot cakes.

Yet, Anglo-French military conferences took place with only a handful of ministers being informed. Asquith and Sir Edward Grey (1862–1933), the foreign secretary, kept even close colleagues in the dark about what were becoming substantial commitments. Asquith actually misled the Commons about the true nature of the negotiations. This was due to the fact that the Cabinet was split on the topic, but divisions failed to stop a movement toward France. The Whiggish Grey used the rhetoric of peace and conciliation, which made most Liberals feel secure in his leadership. Asquith denied to the Dominion prime ministers in 1911 that Britain was entangled with France: "Our hands are free."[42]

Grey turned out to be no more competent in foreign affairs than his brothers were at shooting big game (one was killed by a lion and another by a wild buffalo while on safari in Africa). He assumed in the summer of 1914 that rational negotiation would be able to find a solution to the central European imbroglio caused by the assassination of the Austrian heir to the throne, Archduke Franz Ferdinand, in July of that year. Grey suggested mediation and then a European-wide conference. Germany remained obdurately opposed. Initially, the Cabinet favored Britain staying out of the war, but a turning point came on August 2. Bonar Law, the leader of the opposition, promised patriotic support. The pro-war forces in the government could see that if the Liberal administration collapsed they could form a coalition with the opposition to support France. Many members of the Cabinet came to accept that the fleet had an obligation to defend the French channel coast, given the latter's agreement to confine their naval activity to the Mediterranean. On August 4, when Belgian neutrality was violated by a German invasion, the fateful decision was taken. Only two Liberal ministers resigned.[43]

Britain should have done a better job of clarifying its own position earlier, but it is unlikely that the knowledge that she would stand beside France came as a surprise to Germany, which most historians believe was bent on conflict. Kaiser Wilhelm II and his government thought war in 1914, especially with Russia, was a much better option than a conflict later when the great Euro-Asian empire had grown to full industrial and military strength.

Britain entered the war with by far the smallest army of any of its peers and no draft. Many soldiers were overseas on colonial assignment. No plans for a protracted land campaign had been prepared. The idea of economic mobilization did not exist. The stock of munitions was inadequate. The leaders had no real grasp of the horrifying abyss into which they led the young men of the nation. Two compensatory factors existed, however. The first was that many of the leaders of the other great states of Europe were equally blind to the likelihood of a prolonged and apocalyptic conflict. Secondly, Britain's economic resources and popular loyalty to the state were more than equal to the task ahead.

Stability and Continuity

In 1914 Britain was the dominant force on the world stage. A strong sense of accelerating progress was emerging. Between 1832 and 1911 Parliament had been reformed and modernized. The civil service was efficient and incorrupt. Scarcity receded out of the lives of most people. Per capita income rose from 25 percent above subsistence in 1870 to 150 percent in 1914. The big trouble ahead did not come from revolutionaries nor from nationalists in India or Ireland. The great engine of change in twentieth-century Britain came out of the mouths of German rifles and cannons. Even though the United Kingdom emerged victorious from World War I, and arguably reached the apex of its global power in the 1920s and 1930s, a second round with Germany exhausted Britain in an unprecedented way. The role of the old ruling class was greatly diminished after the first war, and the empire was lost after the second. Yet, even in the dangerous world of the twentieth century the lives of ordinary people continued to improve in material terms and attachment to the institutions of government remained strong.

Part III

Dividing the Kingdoms

Chapter 8

The United Kingdom, 1914

During the nineteenth century British science entered an era comparable in importance to the age of Newton. Not since the days of Shakespeare had writers and poets reached such a level of high achievement. The stability and continuity of British society, which has been the recurring theme of this work, provided a platform for unprecedented creativity and prosperity.

Not everything was rosy. The slums in the inner cities, rural poverty, exploitation of the industrial working class, imperial arrogance, and incompetent military performances in the Crimea and South Africa are only a few of the things that were wrong with the country.

Nowhere on the Continent, however, did the weight of the state ride more lightly on the backs of the people than in Britain. Nowhere was the individual freer. Britain's bureaucracy was smaller, the press less censored, voluntary organizations more extensive, the presence of militarism more absent, civil liberties stronger, and the homicide, suicide, divorce, and illegitimacy rates markedly lower than in most other European countries.[1] The rancid scourge of nationalism, which would consume the lives of millions in a few years' time, was largely benign in Britain. The Scots, Welsh, and English could live happily in their own skins and at the same time as "British" people. Most of the hundreds of millions of imperial subjects around the world were efficiently governed. Only Ireland was an openly bleeding wound.

Before tackling the transformation of Britain after 1914 we need, as we did earlier for 1714 and 1815, to reassess the culture, institutions, and identities that underpinned the state and society as it faced foreign enemies and then serious economic difficulties ahead.

Population

A tsunami of human life swept over the British Isles during the nineteenth century. In 1800 England and Wales stood at near 9 million, which doubled by 1850, and doubled again by 1911 to 36 million. The United Kingdom total rose from 16 million in 1800 to 45 million just before World War I. Growth would have been even more explosive had it not been reduced by emigration and the Famine in Ireland. Over six million Britons departed between 1871 and 1911, although a third of them eventually returned home. Migrants were disproportionately drawn from among younger people, the most likely to have children.

Britain was probably the first modern society to shift from a system of very high birth rates, early marriages, and large families – accompanied by a high death rate – to a pattern of slower population growth characterized by lower birth rates, higher marriage ages, and smaller families with lower death rates, especially among children. Economic improvement had a different effect than in the past. Then fertility increased; now it dropped. A more consumer-oriented culture had emerged. As incomes rose, so did the expectations of parents for their own enjoyment and their children's futures. The greater the expectations, the greater the worry about the cost of large families. Having no more than two or three children became respectable.

A slight decline in the death rate began in the 1860s. Infant mortality fell. Improved medical treatment and social welfare may have helped but probably the key reason was improved living standards and the weakening power of several infectious diseases. Rising real wages and per capita incomes resulted in the consumption of more and better food. A cleaner water supply and effective sewerage helped, as did improved education, and the availability of cheap cleaning products. Smaller family sizes created longer intervals between child bearing for women, which meant mothers were healthier and had more time and resources to rear fewer children.

Cities

The 1851 census recorded for the first time that more Britons were living in towns than in the countryside. In 1901 nearly four-fifths lived in boroughs or urban districts, an almost exact reversal of the situation in 1801. Urban growth was extraordinary. Manchester had 75,000 inhabitants in 1801, 303,000 at mid-century, and 1,035,000 in 1911. Glasgow was at 77,000 in 1801 and 1,000,000 in 1911. If the surrounding conurbation is counted, nearly 2 million of Scotland's 4.5 million inhabitants lived in that one metropolitan area. Mega-cities like these were rare and many of the famous industrial centers in Britain such as Leeds and Sheffield were in the half-million range, but they were often located close together, forming densely populated regions. Scotland was second only to England among urbanized countries in Europe. In 1900 one Scot in three lived in one of four towns: Glasgow, Edinburgh, Dundee, or Aberdeen. Greater London dwarfed all other cities. It stood at 2.24 million in 1841, 14 percent of the population of England and Wales, and it had reached 7.25 million in 1911, nearly one-fifth of the country's population. It would peak at nearly 9 million in 1939. The next largest city in Europe in 1911 was Paris at 2.9 million.

The expansion of the franchise in municipal elections that took place after 1869 seems to have contributed to more political action and higher levels of social spending. From the 1870s cities were able to borrow large sums on the London capital market to fund massive projects in water, sewage treatment, transportation, and other improvements. New bridges, tunnels, railway stations, tramways, embankments, docks, and water pipes were built. Parks, wide new thoroughfares, statues, slum clearance, libraries, art galleries, concert halls, and stadiums were built. London was being transformed into an imperial capital.

Progressively more efficient and affordable buses and trams made it possible for workers and members of the middle class to live outside city centers. Life in the suburbs became more accessible to everyone. The London subway system (called "the Tube") was launched in the 1860s. It was initially hobbled by smoky steam technology not well suited to subterranean locomotion, but it avoided surface congestion and provided inexpensive workmen's tickets. The employment of electric motors in the early twentieth century allowed tunneling deep under ground. The middle classes retreated farther into the countryside.

Women

In the workplace women's wages were only half the male rate even when work was similar. Textile mills apart, mechanization and factories did little to increase job opportunities for them. As a proportion of all women in England and Wales those in waged employment probably fell slowly during the second half of the century. As a proportion of the whole workforce the numbers stood at 34 percent in 1861 down to 31 percent in 1891. This was followed by an increase in the 1900s, probably reflecting the falling cost of living in the earlier period and rise in the latter. After the collapse of handicraft trades women were largely confined to domestic service, agricultural work, textiles, sewing, and washing until late in the nineteenth century. Some jobs came to be held almost exclusively by women such as elementary school teaching, typing, nursing, telephone operation, and the like. Formerly males had dominated the world of the business office, but with the advent of the typewriter that changed. Many of the new white-collar jobs were given to women as part of a deliberate strategy to cut costs because they could be paid less than men. Most formally employed women were single or widows. Married women augmented family budgets with part-time work of various kinds. Male-dominated trade unions prioritized rights for men, tried to ban female employment, and asserted that women should be primarily wives and mothers.

Separate Spheres

Mention was made in Chapter 4 of the notion of women being confined to the private sphere of home life while only men had access to the public sphere. This is an unhelpful characterization of relations between the genders. There was separation of responsibilities but these did not necessarily take place along a public/private line of demarcation. Women continued to be involved in family businesses, and the vibrancy of the political sphere in Victorian Britain was due to both men and women. The latter were engaged in the careers of their husbands, published partisan books and pamphlets, and joined organizations and campaigns dedicated to reform.

It is a misperception to think that upper- and middle-class women involved in charity were not engaged in the public sphere. They went into the streets of the slums of big cities and the homes of the poor and into jails and brothels. By 1891 perhaps half a million women worked, Theodore Hoppen notes, "continuously, and semi-professionally in voluntary activities."[2] Women continued to be actively engaged in running households, which often involved extensive management of finance and personnel. Victorian women were energetic: hiking, climbing, fishing, swimming, exploring, playing tennis and cricket, and touring the countryside on bicycles, though few had the financial resources to be as adventurous as Jane Digby (see Biography 8.1).

A darker side of women's existence in the nineteenth century was the large increase in the number of prostitutes. They became an important part of London life, a city of such complex disparities that the American writer Henry James, when visiting, called it a "strangley mingled monster."[4] Very little was done to help women who were forced by grim economic circumstances into this occupation despite the fact that many influential and powerful people knew about the situation. Prostitution was often thrust on women by necessity, though it was usually a phase between youth and marriage rather than a lifetime profession. Estimates of those in London ranged from 10,000 to 10 times that number.

Biography 8.1

Jane Digby
1807–81

Jane Digby was the daughter of one of the captains of Nelson's ships at the Battle of Trafalgar. Although an aristocrat, he was a penniless younger son who had to make his own fortune, which he did with prize money from the sale of captured ships. Jane was a great beauty and was married off at 17 to a much older widower, Lord Ellenborough, in 1824. She soon fell in love with the Austrian ambassador, by whom she had a child. This provoked one of the rare and quite spectacular divorces of the period. The word "cad" derives from a nickname given to her beau, Prince Schwarzenberg (later to suppress the revolution of 1848 in Vienna), who deserted her to pursue his political career untarnished. Jane then became the mistress of the king of Bavaria, married a German baron, divorced him, and remarried to a Greek count, whom she also disposed of as a husband. Her travels led her to Syria where she became infatuated with both the country and a Bedouin sheik, who became her last and most beloved spouse. Although she maintained a house in Damascus, she often traveled with her tribe, risking death in the constant raids and wars that Ottoman rulers did little to stifle. She died in Syria after having lived away from her homeland for over 50 years. Digby was one in a series of unconventional female adventurers, stretching from Lady Hester Stanhope (1776–1839) to Freya Stark (1893–1993), who regularly set out from London to explore the world.[3]

The Vote

Growing assertiveness by women challenged the traditional political system. Although female property owners (usually spinsters and widows) had exercised their right to vote in various local elections thanks to a court ruling in 1739, the first did not stand for office as a Poor Law guardian until 1875. Most men did not favor granting them the franchise on the national level. Women worked in the Chartist movement, but no demand for female suffrage came from its male leadership. Emancipation societies appeared in the 1830s, but it was Millicent Garrett Fawcett's (1847–1929) organization that gave the suffragettes their real start in 1867. John Stuart Mill was converted to feminism by Harriet Martineau and introduced a bill to grant women the vote during the debate over the Second Reform Act in that year. More than 70 MPs voted for it. The activist suffrage campaign began in earnest in 1903 when Emmeline Pankhurst (1858–1928) and her daughter Christabel (1881–1958) formed the Women's Social and Political Union (WSPU). They set out to provoke mass arrests through civil disobedience. The tempo picked up with attacks on public property, setting railway cars on fire, bombing Lloyd George's house, slashing old masters in museums, and culminating in a woman suicidally throwing herself under the oncoming hooves of the king's horse at the Derby in 1913. The leadership of the Pankhursts turned into implacable fanaticism in which men were presented as inherently wicked. They could not see when they had begun to hurt their own cause. Membership in the WSPU plummeted, and the war placed other issues at the head of the national agenda.

The fight for the vote stood on the shoulders of previous efforts to win women other rights. Early in the nineteenth century a wife had no legal identity distinct from her husband's in England. However, in 1839, after a long battle by Caroline Norton (1808–77), an act was passed which gave custody of children under seven in cases of separation to the mother, providing that she had not been found guilty of adultery.[5] The Women's Property Act of 1882 placed wives on an equal footing with unmarried women as regards earnings and property. More began to be done to protect women from abusive husbands.

Despite some new legislation in the 1850s, getting a divorce remained difficult, and a double standard continued to favor husbands over wives. The playing field was not to be made equal for men and women until 1923. Divorce remained comparatively rare until the mid-twentieth century and involved costs that most poor people could not afford. Members of the middle and upper classes suffered social ostracism for getting divorced until the 1960s, even if they were the innocent party.

Sexuality, Gender, and Family

Many Victorian marriages were characterized by mutual respect, trust, and love. It is difficult, of course, to discover the intimate details of relationships about which few records were created or survive. Speaking of a "typically Victorian" attitude toward sexuality is presumptuous and inevitably misleading. For example, how do we explain the decline in fertility during the period? One possibility was the use of artificial methods of birth control. There is little direct evidence, however, that couples used rubber contraceptive devices with any frequency until after World War I. The other method to reduce the number of births was coitus interruptus or simply reduced frequency of sexual intercourse, both methods, it is argued, relying on male self-control. In the navy withdrawal was known as "getting out at Fratton," the station stop before the dockyards at Portsmouth.[6] Undoubtedly, the high age of marriage suggests a culture of sexual abstinence. Hera Cook, however, argues that it was the women and not the men who exercised restraint or rather repression to slow the fertility rate. By the end of the nineteenth century, according to her, "many, if not most, women repudiated physical sexual desire."[7]

Contrary to the stereotypical view of Victorian attitudes toward sex, only in the later years of the century did repressiveness become vigorous. It was not until 1885 that male homosexual activity was specifically criminalized and police were given new powers to close down brothels. Warnings against masturbation for both boys and girls grew more alarmist. However, at the same time Dr. Havelock Ellis and other brave spirits began to combat sexual prejudice and ignorance for the first time. His great work, *Studies in the Psychology of Sex*, was published between 1897 and 1910.

By mid-century the acceptance of a more deliberate concept of childhood as a distinct period led to reforms in education and the treatment of children in the workplace and by the judicial system. After mid-century relatively few children worked full-time. Another development from the 1880s was an increasing recognition of the distinct state of adolescence as a way station between childhood and adulthood. However, few efforts were made to organize young people's leisure time, until the Boy Scout and Girl Guide movements arrived after 1908. An estimated 80 percent of children continued to attend Sunday schools, though decline seemed to be setting in by 1914.

Men's emotional involvement in child rearing declined as their role in transmitting skills was taken over by formal education. The father's place was to earn a living to support a family as fewer and fewer women and children worked. Children could now be seen as economically burdensome and emotionally problematic rather than a means of expressing identity. Many fathers withheld intimacy from fear of undermining their manhood and that of their sons; others responded by asserting their status through repressive behavior. Many men found the shifting definition of masculinity to be difficult. The impact of domesticity on the man's position was ambivalent. "He lost authority in the home to his wife, leading to a polarization between the breadwinner and the home-maker with very different interests and education."[8]

Unlike in many parts of Europe and in Scotland, most English people aspired to – and most gradually acquired – a single-family dwelling rather than an apartment. This development had powerful social consequences. It encouraged domestication of the family by emphasizing the concentration of activities inside the house where they were not shared with strangers.

Recreation

One of the most pervasive changes in nineteenth-century life resulted from more time and money becoming available for leisure. Industrialization and the mass migration to cities reshaped human activity in profound ways. Many pursuits were distinctive to particular social groups while others were shared across class lines. Active steps were taken by many busybodies and humanitarians to suppress pleasure. This entailed the banning of traditional recreations such as bull- and bear-baiting and cockfighting. Much money was expended by philanthropists and municipalities to provide libraries, parks, concerts, museums, and other amenities enjoyed by everyone. The YMCA (Young Men's Christian Association) was founded in 1844. Adult education courses proliferated, although the principal consumers were members of the lower middle class, not the proletariat.

Among the middle classes lawn tennis, bridge, rowing, and croquet became popular, while the aristocracy took up polo, stalking deer in the Scottish Highlands, and big game safaris in Africa. Laborers enjoyed membership in one of the 40,000 bands in the United Kingdom or in immensely popular choral societies. Workingmen loved angling, quoits, fishing, dog racing, pigeon fancying, gardening on urban allotments, handicrafts, stamp collecting, and cycling. More time and money were available for visits to the seaside and country.

Nineteenth-century Britain was a particularly fertile place for the organization of athletic activities. The British pioneered mountain climbing. Every major sport now part of international competition has a British origin except for basketball and skiing. The Wimbledon tennis tournament, the British Open, the America's Cup, the Derby, and the Royal Henley Regatta remain premier events in their categories even today. **Football** became the supreme entertainment for workingmen. Once businesses began to close early on Saturdays the sport gained a great boost. The first FA (Football Association) Cup took place in 1871. Horse racing, gambling, and cricket remained popular. The latter was the national game for the English (though not elsewhere in the isles), but it was full of ritual distinctions between professionals and amateurs and workers and the elite. Competition with Australia and other parts of the empire commenced in 1861 and became a major part of British sporting life.

Music halls were patronized by working-class and upper-class men, segregated by ticket prices. William Fox Talbot developed photography from 1834 onwards, which was initially a hobby confined to the well-to-do. The working class, however, could for the first time record family faces for a small fee. The Kodak Brownie (1900) made picture taking available to an ever broader constituency. Movies caught on quickly as the technology developed. By 1914 thousands of cinemas had been opened around the country.

The ancient pastime of drinking took place for many workingmen in pubs. These were thick on the ground in urban areas. By mid-century pubs were predominantly used by the laboring poor and artisans and were great social centers for both men and women. Many families spent up to a third of their income on alcohol. Prosperous people drank at home or in exclusive clubs.

Some see working-class leisure as part of a culture of consolation, which seems to me humorless and condescending. The notion that workers were fobbed off with bread and circuses as a means of social control denies dignity and independent judgment to the laboring classes. The philanthropic provision of parks could conceivably foster the happily non-threatening recreation of ball throwing or stick chasing by dogs. It could equally be used subversively to have a quickie in the rhododendrons with a girl- or boyfriend. Working-class leaders feared time and resources were being taken away from the Labour movement and union activity. They would have done well to remember that vegetable-raising competitions on allotments, seaside holidays, and pigeon racing were authentic and legitimate outlets for human creativity and the search for happiness.

Culture

Victorian intellectuals and those with elite educations were steeped in the history of ancient Greece and Rome and in the Bible. These are more and more remote subjects to us, which makes it hard to recapture the framework and inspiration of the Victorian cultural imagination. H. C. G. Matthew believed that "the *mentalité* of the Victorian is perhaps more foreign to the twentieth-century mind than any since the reformation."[9] Shared pleasures in culture between levels of society may have diminished, and distinctions were made between "highbrow" and "lowbrow" reading matter, entertainment, and creative expression.

The nineteenth century produced one of the great meditations on the importance of freedom: John Stuart Mill's *On Liberty* (1859). The thesis of his essay was "that the only purpose for which power can be rightfully exercised over any member of a civilized community, against his will, is to prevent harm to others."[10] Without individual freedom to think and to act, a society was not free. Mill helped moderate the thinking of the classical economists, and, ironically, he gave his approval and helped bring the Liberal Party to accept a move toward collectivism.

In the nineteenth century British literature enjoyed a golden age. At first a reaction set in against the Enlightenment and Utilitarianism. William Wordsworth (1770–1850), Samuel Taylor Coleridge (1772–1834), and Robert Southey (1774–1843) reaffirmed traditional sanctities. The Romantic movement embraced "excited passion," whether it be wild yet tender sex or artistic originality. The poet, the sixth Lord Byron (1788–1824), exemplified the Romantic spirit. He wrote in 1821: "it is now the time to act."[11] Romantics could be liberal like Byron, Shelley, and John Keats (1795–1821) or conservative as Wordsworth, Coleridge, and Southey became. William Blake was a radical. Byron embraced the national aspirations of the Italians and Greeks while Southey recoiled from the materialism and industrialization of modern capitalism. In fiction the delicate Gothic novels of the later eighteenth century

Figure 8.1   *The Fighting Temeraire* by J. M. W. Turner, 1838. HMS *Temeraire* sailed directly behind Nelson's flagship *Victory* at the Battle of Trafalgar in 1805. Turner pictures her being pulled by a modern steam tug to be dismantled and the pieces sold off

turned into the rip-snorting, sword-swinging yarns of Sir Walter Scott. Although Scott was a deep Tory, Byron, the Liberal, could write of him: "Wonderful man! I long to get drunk with him."[12] Supreme among literary figures of the era, however, was the shrewd though retiring gentry lady, Jane Austen (1775–1817), who wrote arguably the greatest British novel, *Pride and Prejudice* (1813). Though not as inventive as Charles Dickens (1812–70), whose explosive genius resembled a fireworks display, no novelist has exceeded Austen's ability to penetrate character.

Early in the century taste in architecture, art, and literature was set by aristocratic patronage. England's greatest painter, J. M. W. Turner (1775–1851), developed his romantic style with the support of the third earl of Egremont (1751–1837) (Figure 8.1). The best commission a nineteenth-century architect could get was to design a great country house. The bourgeoisie still followed in the wake of the patrician leadership whether in the selection of furniture and china or the sorts of novels that they purchased.

Later in the century great writers and artists were often able to support themselves independently as public museums began to collect paintings, and a market for creative work of all kinds grew broad with expanded literacy and prosperity. Writers became less romantic and more earnest and progressive and wished to portray an accurate picture of ordinary people's lives, warts and all. The "Condition of England" discussion of the 1840s and 1850s was partly shaped in the novels of Elizabeth Gaskell (*Mary Barton*, 1848, and *North and South*, 1854), Charles Dickens (*Hard Times*, 1854), and Disraeli (*Sybil*, 1845). Female writers became more prominent. The Brontë sisters (Charlotte, Emily, and Anne) not only published great works in the 1840s and 1850s but openly addressed issues such as madness and sexuality. George Eliot (Mary Ann Evans) also produced serious novels that presented images from the lower reaches of life, although her masterpiece, *Middlemarch* (1872), was set among the middle classes.

No falling off from literary standards established in the middle of the century took place. Late nineteenth- and early twentieth-century writers such as Thomas Hardy (1840–1928), Henry James (1843–1916), and Joseph Conrad (1857–1924) produced fiction of the highest quality. The "Irish Revival" consisted of a superb set of poets, dramatists, and novelists including William Butler Yeats (1865–1939), Oscar Wilde (1854–1900), James Joyce (1882–1941), and George Bernard Shaw (1856–1950).

W. S. Gilbert (1836–1911) and Arthur Sullivan (1842–1900) became a national institution with the creation of their operettas. One of the greatest music festivals in the world, the Promenade Concerts, was founded in 1895. The composers Edward Elgar (1857–1934), Hubert Parry (1848–1918), and Ralph Vaughan Williams (1872–1958) raised the level of musical accomplishment well above what had been achieved in the mid-nineteenth century. The latter, despite his Welsh-sounding name, was born in Gloucestershire, and was told by his teacher, Parry, to compose "like an Englishman and a democrat," which he proceeded to do.[13]

The Victorians opened up whole new areas of scholarship in Assyriology, the pre-history of Britain, and biblical archeology, and they grappled with the problems exposed by French Egyptology and German classical studies. They decided, as they filled museums with artifacts and libraries with treatises, what was to be prized and what demoted or discarded.

Victorian and Edwardian culture had a strong transatlantic character. Henry James and the painter John Singer Sargent are the most famous Americans to take up residence in Britain, but literary discourse flowed back and forth along with the increased shipping traffic between Liverpool and New York. The Rhodes scholarships brought an increasingly distinguished line of Americans to study at Oxford from 1902 onwards. Joseph Chamberlain, Lord Curzon, and Lord Randolph Churchill were only a few of the many peers and leading figures in politics and society to marry American brides. Some American families such as the Astors transplanted themselves wholesale to Britain. American inventions such as the telephone, sewing machine, and typewriter transformed British life. Time and management experts and Hollywood were soon to follow.

What is most striking about the arts in the Victorian period is their close interconnection with public taste, whether it was the poetry of Lord Tennyson, the Gothic grandeur of A. W. N. Pugin's buildings, or the animals portrayed by Edwin Landseer. The upper and middle classes understood and approved of the literature, paintings, and buildings of their time. The isolation between artist and the general public of the twentieth century had not yet opened up.

--- **Religious Conflict** ---

Politics was not the only area fraught with division and change in the Victorian era. Religion grew in strength during the nineteenth century and produced several important new fissures in British society. Demands by Nonconformists for disestablishment of the state Churches in Wales and England caused much debate and political maneuvering. High Church and Low Church branches of the Church of England continued to cohabitate with many "Broad Church" followers, who lived somewhere in the middle. Harmony was disrupted by the aggressive Oxford Movement, also known as Tractarianism, that sought to reinforce traditional Anglicanism by extending the reach of High Church theology. Many feared the Tractarians were threatening Protestantism and trying to push toward reunion with Rome. These fears were strengthened by the adherence in 1845 of John Henry Newman (1801–90) and some others to the Roman Catholic Church, but no mass conversions followed. For the most part the clergy found the big tent of Anglicanism tolerable and they became more tolerant.

In Scotland the established Kirk faced a severe test known as the "Great Disruption," and it shattered under the impact in 1843. About one-third of **Church of Scotland** ministers, led by Thomas Chalmers (see Biography 8.2), wanted individual churches to be independent of central authority and in particular to have the right to choose their own ministers without interference by a patron. In addition the Evangelical wing were worried about the failure of the established Kirk to serve the needs and retain the loyalty of the expanding urban working classes produced by industrialization. It was also a movement of those who felt threatened by secular modernity.[14] Some 40 percent of the Kirk membership withdrew into the new Church. This "Free" Kirk built more than 700 church buildings and 500 schools in four years. Scotland remained more overtly and intensely religious than England.

Religious belief was undermined to some degree by the spread of the ideas of the Enlightenment. Modern science could also be interpreted as a challenge to the literal truth of the Bible. Many intellectuals and educated people began to experience a crisis of faith. "Doubt" arrived in the universities. George Eliot thought Evangelicals preyed on those with human failings: "they really look on the rest of mankind as a doomed carcass which is to nourish them for heaven."[15] Despite the dynamism of religion in the nineteenth century, fewer and fewer people held religion at the center of their lives. Movements to improve the condition of the people came increasingly from trade unions and government legislation and not from demands for spiritual reformation. Matthew Arnold's (1822–88) somber poem "Dover Beach" suggested the mood in 1867. The world, he wrote, seems,

> To lie before us like a land of dreams,
> So various, so beautiful, so new,
> Hath really neither joy, nor love, nor light,
> Nor certitude, nor peace, nor help for pain:

And we are here as on a darkling plain
Swept with confused alarms of struggle and flight,
Where ignorant armies clash by night.

Biography 8.2

Thomas Chalmers
1780–1847

Thomas Chalmers was, T. M. Devine argues, possibly "the most influential Scot of the nineteenth century." He served both as the official leader of the established Kirk in 1832, and then led the massive withdrawal of clergy and parishioners from the Church in the Great Disruption of 1843 that split Scotland nearly in half. He was a fiery preacher, who had experienced an intense Evangelical conversion in 1811 and put his ideas famously into practice in the great commercial and industrial city of Glasgow, which he believed contained "a profligate, profane and heathen population."[16] Chalmers embraced the ideas of classical economics and raised them to a spiritual plane. He took the view that poverty was due to personal moral failure and believed "the salvation of a single individual more important than the rescue of a whole empire from pauperism."[17] He hoped to build a "godly commonwealth" by combining preaching, schooling, systematic visitation, and voluntary poor relief to mold the community in God's image. The experiment failed, but, sadly, Chalmers and others believed it to have been a success. His work gave legitimacy to the rejection of state intervention and was hostile to attempts by organized labor to raise wages by industrial action. An estimated 100,000 mourners attended his funeral in Edinburgh in 1847, a stunning example of how powerful a mixture Evangelical Liberalism could be and how strongly even working-class Scots were under the grip of that ideology.

Science and Technology

Scholars at British universities began to take the lead in science, displaying a mania for collecting specimens and classifying the results. This process ranged from analyzing rocks and birds to unlocking the secrets of matter down to the mechanism of the atom. The Royal Institution (1799) in London offered public lectures by men such as the polymath Sir Humphrey Davy on chemistry and Michael Faraday, whose experiments in electricity in the 1830s and 1840s were revolutionary. In the late 1830s James Joule formulated the First Law of Thermodynamics. Significant advances in medicine took place. Invasive surgery became more successful with the introduction of anesthesia from the 1840s and antisepsis in the 1870s. Not all research was successful. Phrenology, the study of human character by means of analyzing the shape of the head, did not go into serious decline until after 1850, when spiritualism emerged to replace it.

The most controversial scientific work of the time has remained a central thread in our culture ever since. Despite the work of Hutton and others, the orthodox view that the Earth was created at the start of biblical history held the field until the publication of Charles Lyell's *Principles of Geology* (1830–3), which made educated people aware of the vastness of time. The voyage of his student, Charles Darwin (1809–82), on the *Beagle* (1831–6), especially his visit to the Galapagos Islands, led the latter to embrace the ideas of evolution, and by 1838 he had formulated a theory of natural selection. The traditional assumption is that publication of Darwin's *On the Origin of Species* (1859) opened up a large chasm between God and Nature and led to a "crisis of faith." Recent research has revised this view. Intellectuals who jettisoned religious belief in the 1850s did so as a result of a revolt against orthodox religion and not because of philosophical and scientific developments. Society had become more tolerant of agnosticism. For the most part Darwin's book was absorbed painlessly, often interpreted in an optimistic way deemed compatible with Christian belief. Many churchmen greeted the appearance of the *Origin* with enthusiasm. As Boyd Hilton points out, most mid-Victorians accepted the "savagely malevolent" doctrine of Darwin's theory of the random development of life leading nowhere (Figure 8.2). They saw it as confirming their optimistic view of progress that humans would improve and get "finer and fitter," "better and more beautiful," and that society would move onwards and upwards.[18]

The Victorian period was an age of energy, struggle, and competition, and thus it was easy enough for the influential social commentator and philosopher Herbert Spencer (1820–1903) to extend the "laws" of evolution to all spheres of existence, which tied nicely into the conception of "progress." Spencer saw laissez-faire capitalism as a form of the evolutionary process. He felt efforts to relieve poverty interfered with the natural process of separating the unfit from the fit, and it was he who introduced the phrase "survival of the fittest." "Social Darwinism," which seemed to justify everything from racist imperialism to hereditary privilege, popped out of this turgid brew. Fear of the multiplication of the unfit aroused worry and the "science" of eugenics.

The term "scientist" was coined in 1833 at Cambridge, and that university became a powerful center for theoretical research. Although Lord Kelvin and J. J. Thomson pioneered rigorous laboratory training at the University of Glasgow from the 1840s, it was at Cambridge in the 1850s that the teaching of science became an established part of the curriculum and a central part of modern academic life. The Cavendish laboratory was founded in 1874 (Figure 8.3), where the Scottish laird, James Clerk Maxwell, the English peer, the third Lord Rayleigh (the first Englishman to win the

Figure 8.2 The great biologist Charles Darwin published a book on earthworms in 1881, which prompted this caricature (Darwin is in the middle of the picture). The cartoon satirizes the theory of evolution. The process proceeds counterclockwise from a worm embedded in "chaos" at lower left to the modern English gentleman tipping his hat to the scientist. "Man is but a Worm," *Punch*, 1882

Nobel Prize for physics), J. J. Thomson, who moved from Glasgow, and later the New Zealander Ernest Rutherford laid the groundwork for advances in physics comparable to Newton's achievements. The late nineteenth century was a unique moment in the history of medicine. Discoveries of germs and microbes laid the foundations for revolutionary progress. For the first time, hospitals became major agencies for the cure and prevention of disease.

The changeover from sail to steam in shipping took place in the late nineteenth century. A son of the Irish third earl of Rosse (himself a well-respected astronomer), Charles Parsons (1854–1931), invented the steam turbine which made ships faster and more efficient. Liners could now cross the Atlantic in five or six days.

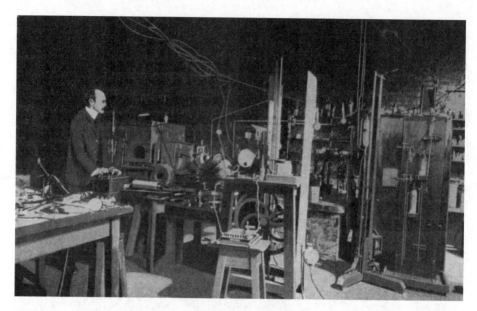

Figure 8.3   In 1897 J. J. Thomson discovered the electron, subsequently recognized as the first particle of physics and the basis of chemical bonding, electronics, and computing, in the Cavendish Laboratory at Cambridge University. Jet propulsion was first developed in the lab, and in 1953 Watson and Crick discovered DNA. The Cavendish Laboratory, Cambridge University

Oil provided a cleaner and lighter alternative to coal as fuel and increased the steaming range of ships. The first powered air flight in Britain took place in 1908. Guglielmo Marconi, rejected in his native Italy, established his company in Britain in 1900 and transmitted the first wireless message across the Atlantic the next year. The velocipede appeared in the 1860s, which developed into a recognizably modern bicycle in the 1880s. These extended the distance over which laborers could travel to work.

Eric Hobsbawm called science and technology in the nineteenth century "the muses of the bourgeoisie."[19] This view typifies the notion that the Victorian era was a time of triumph for the middle classes and excludes the traditional elite, who had welcomed and financed the railways and gave a lead in many fields beyond politics. The most productive single laboratory in the history of modern science, the Cavendish at Cambridge, was endowed by the seventh duke of Devonshire (1808–91). The eighth duke, along with Lord Rosebery and Balfour, coordinated the foundation of Imperial College in London in 1907, which became Britain's equivalent of M.I.T in America. No cultural aversion to science or industry afflicted the landed elite, who were equally interested in sponsoring agricultural research and business innovation. In fact one of Britain's strengths was the understanding of the late Victorian and Edwardian ruling class of the importance of science and industry. Innovation and continuity were not mutually exclusive.

The United Kingdom

Convergence of cultures and identities within Britain continued during the nineteenth century, although diversity flourished as well. Religion and history were vital elements of identity. Perhaps few lived quite so much in the past as Irish Catholics and Irish Protestants, but most people had a care for historic struggles to achieve liberty and victory over evil oppressors. Waterloo and Trafalgar were living memories and transcended the division between England, Wales, and Scotland. The British also thought of themselves as part of a progressive, technologically superior, modern and increasingly democratic society, and the owners of a vast empire. The intensification of Irish nationalism led to a greater sense of unity across St. George's Channel in Britain.

Movement of people and information around the island homogenized people, diminished tensions, and made Britain to some degree multicultural. Railways evaporated the distance between cities throughout the kingdom. Economic integration proceeded rapidly. In Britain and Northern Ireland urbanization and the growth of a consumer society was a shared experience.

Monarchs began to make more frequent and regular appearances all over the island. Victoria and Albert's decision to embrace the myth of Highland Scottishness led them to build a mock medieval castle at Balmoral, and they took to kilts and tartans with a vengeance. In 1873 she became the first British monarch to partake of the sacrament in a Presbyterian church in Scotland in defiance of the Archbishop of Canterbury.[20] Protestantism and anti-Catholicism bound the British together. The Irish felt ever more alien and alienated. The English language became dominant, however, even there. Scots Gaelic had almost disappeared and a significant decline in the number of Welsh speakers set in during the 1890s. Catholicism in Ireland, Presbyterianism in Scotland, and Protestantism in England and Wales each in their own way provided insurmountable barriers to the spread of communism among working people. The intense individualism of Nonconformity was particularly important in this regard.

The Scots and Irish played a disproportionate role in the expansion of the "British" – never the "English" – empire, which created a common imperial identity. A substantial proportion of the British troops deployed to hold and protect the colonies were Irish, the enlisted ranks full of Catholics and among the commanders Protestants. Political integration was strong in 1914. Leading politicians were drawn from all parts of the archipelago. Parties had separate national organizations but were genuinely British even if their strengths and weakness were regional in character. In World War I national cohesion was put to the supreme test, and a collective will to win emerged and was sustained under extreme conditions. Rising anti-German feeling before the war, much heightened during it, provided a new "other" to replace the French as the great national enemy.

Music came to evoke "British" emotions in an anthem written by Sir Edward Elgar in 1902: "Land of Hope and Glory." At King Edward VII's suggestion, he fitted his new "Pomp and Circumstance March No. 1," composed for the queen's jubilee in 1897, to the words written by Arthur Benson. In August 1914 it was sung spontaneously by the crowds gathered in front of Buckingham Palace after the announcement of the outbreak of war:

> Land of Hope and Glory,
> Mother of the Free,
> How shall we extol thee,
> Who are born of thee?
> Wider still and wider
> Shall thy bounds be set;
> God, who made thee mighty,
> Make thee mightier yet.

Overlapping Identities

Powerful local loyalties, however, demonstrated signs of intensifying separateness. Regions within the larger countries remained distinctive. Most obvious was the different economic, social, and religious organization of Ireland. Ulster was an increasingly prosperous but embattled place. Working-class Protestants became **Unionist** voters. The split between north and south Wales made it difficult to sustain a single Welsh identity, and attention has already been drawn to the distinctiveness of the north and south in England. London was almost a nation within itself. Scotland had long experienced the split between Lowland and Highland, but this became more marked with the industrialization of the south.

New forms of expressing localism and rivalry emerged in the later part of the nineteenth century such as professional football, county cricket, the military reserve system, local school boards, and county councils. In discussions over Home Rule in 1911 some Liberal ministers advocated a larger scheme of devolution. Winston Churchill proposed a separation between the imperial parliament and local assemblies. He wanted the United Kingdom to be divided into 10 or 12 provinces each with its own legislative and administrative body.[21] Britain was the only major power in Europe not to institute conscription during the nineteenth century. While in other countries this mechanism was used to homogenize regional variations and instill nationalist feelings, the continued distinctiveness of Wales, Scotland, and Ireland may in part have survived due to the absence of a draft.

Multiple identities are often perceived as ranked in importance from the largest entity to the smallest, but in fact the smaller ones may have more significance in everyday life. We better understand now about constructed identities and how these can be invented or imagined in origin and unconstructed at a later time. We all have "situational" identities that overlap and present multiple "selves": religion, class, ethnic group, region, and even institution. Women may experience national identity differently from men. Multiple identities were more common over time. Scots could be Scots and British and citizens of the United Kingdom coexisting with each other. Most Scots and Welsh felt comfortable in being both members of their nation and British.

England

In many ways England's is the hardest national identity in the archipelago to define and describe. An anonymous author in *Fraser's Magazine* in 1832 asked: "The People of England – Who Are They?"[22] The soldier poet Rupert Brooke (1887–1915) famously identified his likely grave in some foreign field that could be located almost anywhere on the planet as a place that would be "forever England." It continued to be common for both the British and foreigners to use "England" and "Britain" interchangeably.

In population England became ever more dominant. It consisted of 54 percent of the United Kingdom population in 1801, 74 percent in 1901, and even more after the Irish separation in 1922. In 1901 Scotland stood at only 13 percent (4.5 million to 32.5 million). On the other hand, Wales quintupled during the century: its population, once only a third as big as Scotland's, was half the size in 1911.

Englishness was less about ethnicity and more about ideas shared by the British people as a whole. Chris Williams argues that it is difficult to think of a British trait that is not also an English one: the sovereignty of Parliament, the English language, the monarchy, political stability, the avoidance of violent revolution, freedom of speech, religion, and trade, a claim to historic liberty, and a confidence in progress. Attachment to the ceremonies and liturgy of the Church of England as embodied in the Book of Common Prayer (1549, one of the most important of all documents in the nation's history) continued to shape language, culture, and identity. Yet, there was no English nationalism. People did not fly the flag of St. George (red cross on a white field) as they did the cross of St. Andrew (white cross on a blue field) in Scotland.[23]

Clearly forces existed to keep England separated from the other parts of Britain. Individual Reform Acts were passed for Scotland and Ireland in 1832 and 1867. The Welsh and Scots were more intensely religious than the English. The Poor Laws for the three kingdoms differed. One of the most distinctive characteristics of the English was among their least attractive traits: arrogance about their neighbors and almost everybody else. Many English people saw Wales as "backward." Prejudice against Scotland declined, but remained. Undisguised racism colored the English perception of Ireland. As for the rest of the world, well, as King George V was supposed to have said: "abroad is bloody."

Wales

Wales was smaller than Scotland and longer in England's thrall without the separate legal institutions and church, which provided bulwarks against engulfment. But it had one great advantage over Scotland, a living language spoken by the masses. In 1840 perhaps more than two-thirds of the population spoke Welsh, although around half of these also understood English. In 1901 about half the people could converse in Welsh whereas only 5 percent of Scots spoke Gaelic and 14 percent of the Irish. The proportion declined but in absolute terms more people spoke Welsh in 1911 than ever before or since (nearly one million).

Unlike the Scots and Irish, the Welsh did not have to emigrate in large numbers. The nineteenth century witnessed heavy industrialization of the south. Iron and coal were kings. Towns mushroomed. Industrialization provided jobs for all and did not drive Welsh speakers from the country. A resurgence of national feeling grew, fueled by religion. Between 1750 and 1850 Wales transformed itself into a Nonconformist country. The Anglican Church had become disconnected from Welsh culture. Enormous pressure grew for the disestablishment of the official Church, which became a political rallying point for the nation. The Anglicized landed elite was left isolated by this movement. Although their alienation from the people has been exaggerated, the majority of large landowners in Wales lost their ability to lead in their communities and began to sell their estates.[24]

Aside from the language the great pillars of Welsh identity became rugby, Sabbatarianism, temperance, education, Liberalism, choral singing, and a partly revived, partly invented new set of cultural rituals embodied in the "*eisteddfodau.*" As with the "Highland" Scottish identity, these "invented" assemblies that evolved during the nineteenth century at first constituted a fabricated past, but over time they became authentic expressions of national feeling. The gatherings included prizes for essays written in Welsh, evening concerts, patriotic speeches, competitions for crafts and trades, and poetry reading. The great national hymn, "*Hen Wlad Fy Nhadau*" (Land of my Fathers) was written in 1856 and soon took on a patina of ancient origin.

Scotland

Edinburgh continued to look and feel like a capital city, and a "foreign" one at that to English eyes.[25] The Court of Session and the established Kirk had their headquarters there. The great processional route, from the spectacularly sited Castle with its kilted soldiers, past the St. Giles' Kirk where the uniquely Scottish Order of the Thistle had its chapel, down to the Royal Palace of Holyrood, was used for public ceremonies. In the heart of the city new buildings arose such as the National Gallery and the memorial tower to Sir Walter Scott. Institutions such as the High School, the Royal Scottish Academy, the office of the Lyon King of Arms, the National Library, the National Register House, the Bank of Scotland, and a large number of other organizations gave shape to a Scottish nation. The management of Scottish legislation stayed largely under the supervision of the lord advocate after 1832. In 1885 a Scottish Office with a separate secretary of state was established. There was a growing tendency for Scottish MPs to meet separately to settle Scottish business, submitting the results for largely formal ratification to the full House of Commons, a kind of informal domestic parliament. Meanwhile Glasgow became "the second city of the empire," an industrial giant with an impressive new ensemble of civic buildings at its center. The overwhelming presence of the state in education meant that publicly funded schools did not develop the same social stigma that they had in England.

The ferment arising from the disruption of the Kirk, the selection of the Oxford and Cambridge curriculum as the standard for entry into the civil service, and insensitive drafting of legislation affecting the courts in Scotland may have contributed to an intensification of Scottish national feeling in the later nineteenth century. Chairs in Scottish history were established in universities, the cult of Robert Burns took on a new dimension, the holding of Highland games proliferated, and in 1881 the Lowland army regiments, which had no connection with the Highlands, were stuffed into "trews," trousers made out of tartan. A Scottish Home Rule Association was established in 1886.

Patriots rallied to the side of the national football teams as they battled England. A crowd of 102,000 gathered at Hampden Park in 1903 to watch the first such match. Scotland voted Liberal in every general election between 1832 and 1918, with the exception of 1900. "Liberal values represented Scottish values."[26] Religion continued to be a predominant force among the laboring classes in Scotland. It was hard for radical socialism to colonize the working class because this feeling was so intense.

Scotland experienced much greater emigration than England and Wales or most other European countries. Perhaps two million Scots left for overseas and somewhat less than half that for other parts of the United Kingdom out of a total population that stood at 3.36 million in 1871. From the 1850s Scotland may have lost almost a third of its natural population increase. Most of the departures came from the industrialized southern region, prompted by a wage structure that made Scottish goods cheap but kept living standards low. The growing manpower needs due to industrial expansion could only be met by immigrants from Ireland, who formed over 7 percent of the Scottish population in 1851. Up to half of Scottish university students left their homeland for employment in England or overseas in the later nineteenth century.[27]

The landed elite stood in a unique position among the aristocracies of the archipelago. Scotland had the highest concentration of landownership in Europe. In 1873 580 people owned three-fourths of the country. This situation made them targets of criticism, and poverty in the Highlands where ordinary people were most vulnerable to the power of landowners exacerbated the problem. Too many people lived on land that could barely support them after the potato crop failed partially in the 1830s and completely in the 1840s. Mass exodus was the only permanent solution. Perhaps a third of the population of the Western Highlands migrated in the 1840s and 1850s. "Clearances" of tenants, sometimes conducted humanely and sometimes brutally, continued. The powerful place that the Highlands had assumed in the national psyche gave these evictions a much higher profile than their relative importance deserved. A fresh outbreak of trouble in the 1880s led to fierce resistance. The farmers watched the success of the Irish "land war" and asserted a similar kind of historic right to the occupation of land now owned by others. In the Crofters Act of 1886 they gained substantial reductions in rent and virtually inalienable rights of hereditary occupation as well. The poorest inhabitants, who had no land, were ignored and got nothing. The population of the Highlands shrank further during the twentieth century.

The Monarchy

The survival of key traditional elements in British life helped sustain a United Kingdom, except in Southern Ireland. Some historians have seen the retention of the monarchy as a useful mechanism by which means the elite could hoodwink the poor into submission, sustained by invented traditions that had no authenticity. William Kuhn's study of the nineteenth-century institution tells a more complicated story. Important ceremonies supporting the monarchy were religious acts divorced from crass political calculation. The coronation, a genuine sacred ritual, had been continuously in use for almost a thousand years.

Kuhn argues that on the eve of the twentieth century "the monarchy appeared to be allied and not opposed to Britain's democratic system."[28] It was the Liberals, including Gladstone and Lloyd George, who played a critical role in fending off republicanism and celebrating the importance of the Crown. The monarchy continued to function at the center of British life in three important ways: as the mechanism that enabled the constitution to operate flexibly, as the center of nationalist emotion absorbing and transforming loyalty to Britain in relatively benign ways, and as the only universally connecting link holding the empire together.

The absence of a written constitution meant the continued importance of the Crown in the day-to-day affairs of government. The journalist Walter Bagehot (1826–77) published his celebrated *English Constitution* in 1867, observing that the monarch had "the right to be consulted, the right to encourage, the right to warn," which aptly describes the situation in 1999 but not 1899.[29] Queen Victoria played an important role in making appointments to religious, military, and political offices, regulating dissolutions of Parliament, and reviewing legislation. In the end she had to give in when a prime minister had the backing of a majority in the Commons and was determined to resign if he did not get his way. But the queen was a master of delaying tactics that wore her opponents down over time, although as the volume of government business grew the aging monarch could no longer keep up. Her successors on the throne in the twentieth century tended to concentrate on foreign, military, and imperial affairs.

The social and cultural leadership of the monarchy remained powerful. Victoria had done much to make theater-going respectable among the middle class, influenced taste in architecture, painting, and sculpture, set a fashion for travel to the romantic parts of Scotland and Ireland, and broadened interest in Indian culture.

Biography 8.3

Sarah Forbes Bonetta
c. 1842–80

On July 5, 1850, while on duty on the Africa station at Dahomey, Lt. Commander Forbes was offered "a captive girl" among other gifts by a Dahoman ruler. She was the daughter of an enemy chief. Her parents had been decapitated, and she was a prisoner. Concerned that if he rejected the "gift" she would face death, Forbes brought her back to England.

She was baptized Sarah Forbes Bonetta (*Bonetta* was the name of Forbes's warship). Later she called herself "Ina," which may have been related to her African name. Queen Victoria agreed to be her godmother, paid for her education, and placed her with a couple in Brighton on the south coast. It was there that she met James Davies, a wealthy black businessman and merchant whom she married in 1862. "There was a grand field-day in the fashionable world of Brighton," ran one press account of the wedding. "A coloured lady – Miss Ina Sarah Forbes Bonetta was led to the altar by a coloured gentleman, Mr. James Davis [*sic*]. She was escorted by a bevy of dark beauties and he was honoured by the attendance of coloured grooms."

Bonetta was relatively wealthy and surviving photographs show her in the fashionable clothes of a Victorian lady. However, the year she arrived in Britain she was painted in "native wear" against an "African" backdrop. Her life is a reminder of the diverse origins of many Victorian Britons and the complexity of the social and racial divides and unities.[30]

During the Crimean War she established and personally helped to design a medal for exceptional bravery, the Victoria Cross, which remains to this day the most prestigious award in Britain. Her lack of racial prejudice was admirable, and she took an interest in the personal lives of darker-skinned subjects of her empire, such as Sarah Forbes Bonetta (see Biography 8.3).

Until recently, when the work of anthropologists has enriched historians' perspectives, it was common to dismiss the importance of the monarchy as its direct political power waned. Now more attention is being paid to the indirect role the institution played in the national psyche. It is more fully understood that myth and emotion are vital aspects of societal life. The monarchy appealed to the heart and the imagination. It gave the state an inner cohesion tighter than might have developed otherwise. Rather than impeding modernity, it made change acceptable and reassuring.

David Cannadine emphasizes the importance of the monarchy as the unifying, magnetic force of the empire which also ordered the imperial hierarchy at home and overseas. "The British empire was a royal empire." Statues of monarchs proliferated around the world; heads of kings and queens were printed billions of times on stamps and coins. "You are the big potato," Field Marshal Smuts, a famous Boer leader who later transferred his loyalty to the British, once informed George V's wife, Queen Mary (1867–1953), "the other queens are small potatoes."[31]

The Aristocracy

Looking back from the vantage point of the 1930s, the patrician politician Harold Nicolson contended that aristocratic life was constricted during the nineteenth century as the peerage was increasingly obliged to bow to "what people thought." He noted despairingly: "the smoke of factory chimneys drifted darkly across the sun-drenched lawns of privilege."[32] Parliamentary reform and the abolition of the Lords' veto diminished aristocratic power. Yet in 1914 and even later, aristocrats remained influential in Parliament and the Cabinet. Andrew Adonis writes: "The persistence of the landed aristocracy as the principal economic, social and political elite in Britain until the First World War is now taken for granted by historians."[33] The landed aristocracy was resilient, adaptable, rich, and still in charge of acceptance and exclusion in the upper reaches of society. Even when straining every nerve, the Liberal Party barely succeeded in winning enough popular support from the electorate to limit the powers of the hereditary house of Parliament in 1910. Every earl of Derby between 1840 and 1940 and all but one of the marquesses of Salisbury in the twentieth century sat in the Cabinet. Greys and Cavendishes abounded. Virtually all the leading figures in British politics until 1906 were believers in the aristocratic principle. Many members of the elite embraced Evangelical religion during the nineteenth century. The values of Christian earnestness, gentleness, dutifulness, and compassion were taught to patrician children. The new self-restraint and respectability of the aristocracy rendered it an increasingly difficult target for attack by populists and democrats and encouraged noblemen to be "useful" as administrators and officials. Though significant changes led to decay, the grip of the aristocracy on power was pried loose one finger at a time.

Compared with the German and Russian elites, the author of a study of nineteenth-century European aristocracies calls the British patriciate "an active, forward-looking ruling class."[34] In 1883, 82 percent of dukes and 55 percent of earls were elected to the Commons before inheriting their titles.[35] They remained self-confident and continued to believe in their right to govern. They set the rules in sports from elite polo to plebeian boxing, established styles in dress, and were important patrons of the arts and education. The extension of the vote to the masses had not produced a cataclysm, and many aristocrats took satisfaction in the responsibilities still conferred on them by the democratic electorate.

Above all, the landed elite remained rich. In the late 1870s, one-quarter of the land in England and Wales was owned by 710 individuals.[36] Large estates still underpinned great prestige. The earls of Derby were referred to as the "kings of Lancashire" (a heavily industrialized and urban county) well into the twentieth century. Lord Byron, whose financial resources fell at the lowest level of the peerage range, enjoyed an income equal to that of the President of the United States.[37] The dukes of Westminster, Northumberland, Sutherland, Bedford, and Portland were richer than the greatest British industrialists and even the wealthiest American millionaire, W. H. Vanderbilt, as late as 1885.[38] Most of the peerage had sources of income that derived from and ballooned with the expansion of industry, either through direct ownership of enterprises such as coal mines, docks, railways, and urban property or indirectly from stocks and shares. Practicality and prudence were among their more characteristic behaviors.

The aristocracy also remained wedded well into the twentieth century to the preservation of property through the fearsome act of will known as primogeniture, leaving all the family property to the eldest male heir at the expense of younger sons and all daughters, however deeply loved. Even quite rich middle-class families were indifferent to holding together the mass of their wealth at its maximum amount but instead divided assets more equally between children.

Historians have long assumed that the Great Agricultural Depression of the last three decades of the nineteenth century did serious damage not only to aristocratic finances but also to their ability to lead. Cheap imports of wheat from North America and Russia and beef and mutton from Australia and New Zealand drove down agricultural prices. Recent research, however, has shown that the fall in prices began not in 1873 but in the 1860s and became less severe in 1887. In a longer context the period 1873–96 fails to stand out in any general economic sense.[39] The agricultural market had begun to change from the 1850s as rising living standards encouraged a shift toward a more varied diet, away from wheat toward meat and dairy products. The majority of the great landowners' agricultural income was no longer reliant purely on grain production, where the prices dropped lowest during the depression. Those who had not done so now shifted to mixed or pastoral farming, which was less affected by falling prices. Market gardening, fruit, and dairy products shored up incomes. Gross farm output actually increased almost everywhere in Britain during the "Great" Depression. Most of the wealthy aristocrats had long since diversified their assets. One estimate suggests that about 40 percent of the great landowners' income came from non-agricultural sources in the 1880s and 1890s. The wealth of the magnates continued to rise between 1850 and 1914.[40] In the later nineteenth century land values fell almost by half from what they had been in the 1840s, but for most aristocrats this was irrelevant since the sale of land was not part of their approach to life. Most held on to what they had in order to sustain the honor of their lineage and not because the market was depressed. Big sales did not occur in England before 1918. As with the Liberal Party, it was World War I that changed everything.

——————   ## The Transformation of Traditional Society   ——————

It is difficult to escape from the "Whig" interpretation of the nineteenth century as a bourgeois triumph and an aristocratic defeat, although some historians have argued for a merger of the two. Landed influence was endangered by the continued decline in the proportion of the labor force working in agriculture, which fell to 9 percent by 1911. The productivity rate per man hour was very high, but the evaporating population in the countryside diminished the prestige and the number of people directly subject to aristocratic influence. The proportion of national wealth derived from agriculture fell from 53 percent in 1850 to 19 percent in 1913.

Some anecdotal evidence suggests a loss of energy and determination among the elite in the years before the war. A gradual decline in aristocratic values of honor, reflected in the disappearance of dueling and acceptance of a wider range of marriage partners, constitutes evidence of this. In a nod to democracy, King Edward VII instituted the prestigious Order of Merit in 1902 that carried no title with it. The elite's ability to command seats in the House of Commons continued to diminish. Gathering together under the single banner of Conservatism left fewer constituencies available, and made the aristocracy appear to be acting in a more obviously self-interested manner. The Irish Ascendancy was battered and in full retreat except in Ulster. Many aristocrats sold their estates and moved to England. In Wales landowners began to sell, and the Welsh countryside increasingly was owned by small farmers. Episodes of hostility, especially during the Crofters' War of the 1880s, broke out in Scotland.

Another sign of the diminution of aristocratic authority appeared with the further expansion and advancement of the middle classes. The latter, broadly defined (not counting farmers), formed about a fifth of the English and Welsh population during the mid-nineteenth century, 17 percent in Scotland, and 15 percent in Ireland. As with the working class, the middle class took on a more unified and distinctive character in the final third of the century. Common patterns of assertive bourgeois public culture developed in urban Britain. The largely localized or provincial middle-class identities became more homogenous from the 1880s and a national culture, which characterized the bourgeoisie in the twentieth century, emerged in education, accent, residence, patterns of consumption, and leisure, although not in source of income. Some lived off unearned wealth, some off profits, some off fees, and some off salaries from jobs of varying status. Incomes ranged from modestly paid teachers to millionaires. The traditional professions of law, higher officials, military officers, and clergy continued to be prestigious and carefully regulated, but in general they were less remunerative than they had been for the top players in the eighteenth and early nineteenth centuries. It became virtually impossible for an admiral or judge to found a great landed family once prize money and a lucrative legal fee structure were reformed. Aristocrats, gentry, and members of the middle classes mixed socially. Members of the professions sought to enhance their status by establishing regulatory institutions. New categories such as engineers, architects, actors, musicians, accountants, and even journalists increased in number and some became elaborately structured.

The lesser gentry were the worst-hit category of landowners in the late-century agricultural depression. Many sank to become tenant farmers while others moved into the professions and business. In Hungary, Prussia, and France the middling and lower elites were enraged by declining incomes and status and often turned on their own societies to embrace extreme conservatism or fascism as a means of regaining lost ground. The British gentry, on the other hand, found outlets for their energy and preservation of status. They entered the colonial civil service, managed coffee and rubber plantations, and became officers in the army, and they remained loyal to the constitution. The dispossessed Irish Ascendancy avowed themselves imperialists, and in the words of an Anglo-Irish writer: "flung themselves" into the cult of empire with "bacchante abandon."[41]

Into the Fray

This chapter has assessed the state of British society and culture at the end of a long period of progress and on the eve of devastating war and economic crisis. After 1914 the Union of the four nations was never to be more severely tested, and it began to disintegrate while the ruling elite that had presided over several centuries of military success and economic growth was showing serious signs of wear and tear. Victory in World Wars I and II and success in surmounting the economic crisis of the interwar years suggests that Britain's dynamism and conservatism (with a small "c") gave it the means to survive and prosper during the second half of the twentieth century. Its position as a global power, however, was to diminish.

Chapter 9

War and Peace and War, 1915–39

The Great War (1914–18) was one of the most important events in twentieth-century British history.[1] It is impossible to convey in words the immensity of the tragedy. The economic hardships of the 1920s and 1930s and World War II that began in 1939 added further pain and horror. Many countries succumbed to the rule of violent and murderous dictators between 1917 and 1939. Britain survived the first half of the century intact. The role of government and state institutions was modified after 1945 but retained the outward forms of their pre-1914 guise. The nation's sinews and liberal outlook proved exceptionally strong.

The Conduct of War

Britons supported the war with a greater commitment than might have been expected considering the rather confused way the government became involved in the conflict. The German invasion of neutral Belgium, even when the exaggerated propaganda of barbaric mistreatment of the civilian population is discounted, aroused anger and resolve against which pacifist forces made no headway. Even in southern Ireland hundreds of thousands of men volunteered to fight. As the death toll mounted and civilian privations deepened, morale sank in every country engaged in the conflict. In Britain, however, the consensus that the war was just and necessary never broke down, even after the introduction of conscription.

The expeditionary force sent in August 1914 to northern France was miniscule (seven divisions compared to the French 74). As the massive and superbly organized German military machine swept down on the Allied forces, the British and French armies staggered under the blow. Yet the onslaught slowed as attacking troops were transferred to the Eastern Front to meet an unexpectedly vigorous Russian advance. Along the Marne River, north of Paris, the German juggernaut lost traction. Trench warfare, in which millions of men suffered and perished, descended on the unfortunate youth of Western Europe. The industrialization of death had developed during the later nineteenth century. Machine guns used in conjunction with barbed wire, which entangled advancing soldiers in its coils, hosed down victims with bullets fired by a few men at the rate of hundreds per minute. The defense had gained an insurmountable advantage over the offence. The armies that arrayed against each other during the fall and early winter of 1914 between Switzerland and the English Channel (see Map 9.1) remained largely frozen in place until the summer of 1918, and the "no man's land" between them became a morgue, made more dreadful by the employment of ever more advanced technologies meant to break the deadlock: poison gas, massed artillery barrages, bombs dropped from aircraft, flame-throwers, and tanks.

The generals on both sides, most notably the Scottish field marshal Douglas Haig (1861–1928), have been condemned as "donkeys leading heroes." They were accused of ordering armies of men to their deaths in attacks doomed to failure.[2] In fact, no solution existed on the Western Front other than a contest of attrition, although cavalry units were held in reserve to gallop on toward Berlin after the elusive big "breakthrough."

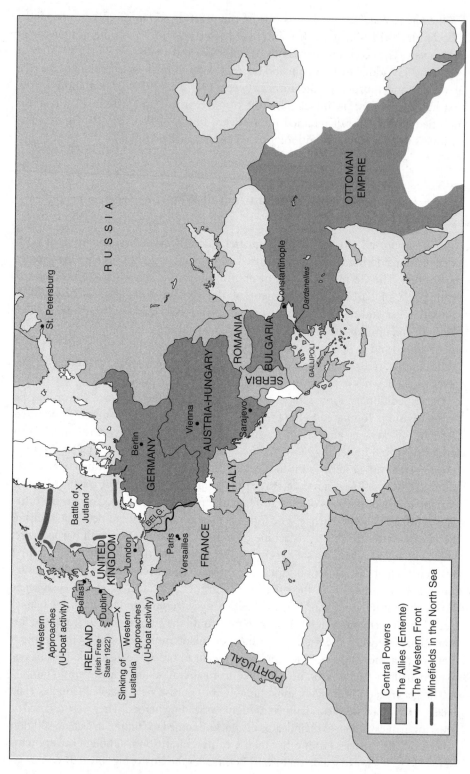

Map 9.1 World War I, 1914–1918

Harrowing stories of suffering fill the memoirs of those who fought. The poet Robert Graves remembered an officer lying wounded in no man's land between the trenches after an attack. Three men were killed in attempts to return him to his own lines. He waved back those who tried to save him, "saying that he was riddled through and not worth rescuing; he sent his apologies to the company for making such a noise." When darkness fell his dead body was recovered hit in 17 places. "I found that he had forced his knuckles into his mouth to stop himself crying out and attracting any more men to their death."[3]

Alternative strategies were attempted. Winston Churchill urged the British and French to capture the Ottoman capital at Constantinople and create a secure supply route to sustain the wobbling Russians by forcing the strait of the Dardanelles. The plan offered a genuine chance for a strategic breakthrough, but it was badly planned and led and met skillfully deployed resistance. The opportunity was lost. In 1917 the Germans gambled on unrestricted submarine warfare (sinking without warning ships of any nationality entering British waters) in the hope of starving Britain into submission. Berlin realized such a plan would entail American entry into the conflict but calculated that it would take at least a year for US forces to be trained and cross the Atlantic in any numbers, long enough to strangle the island enemy.

Asquith and Lloyd George

The law requiring elections every five years was suspended for the duration, as was implementation of Home Rule in Ireland. In May 1915 a coalition was formed in which the Liberals and Conservatives (and one Labour minister) shared power. In a series of speeches Lloyd George presented himself as the hammer of the Germans and articulated the goals of the war better than the prime minister, Asquith. He argued for the traditional values of honor, duty, patriotism, and sacrifice in order to achieve a better and more humane nation in the wake of victory and to destroy Prussian militarism. The Conservative leader Andrew Bonar Law worked closely with Lloyd George, although many Tories remained wary of the former radical who had attacked the House of Lords and wanted land reform. Asquith, disheartened by the death of his eldest son in battle and entangled in an overwrought relationship with a woman who was not his wife, performed poorly in parliamentary debates and drank too much. Matters came to a head in December 1915 when he attempted to remake the Cabinet. He resigned in the expectation of a restructuring of the government, but in the end his rival, the Welsh wizard, emerged as prime minister with Conservative support. Asquith never held office again. A permanent and bitter split arose among the Liberals. The ferocious dynamism of Lloyd George smashed his party to win the war and to gain the top political post. He did much to improve British fighting capability but no more than the generals could he find an escape from attrition on the Western Front. By August 1918 the last enemy advance had been broken and an exhausted Germany moved toward total collapse. An armistice was signed on November 11, 1918.

Why Britain Won

The Allied victory was achieved partly by the enemy squandering opportunities to win, partly by the steadfastness of the long-suffering French army, and partly by the arrival of American troops on the Western Front in 1918. In a war of attrition, however, resources and the will to win were critical. The wealth and the industrial base Britain had built up during the nineteenth century sustained the Allies through four desperate years of battle, and the country's deeply rooted social and political structure held together while Russia, Austria-Hungary, and Germany crumbled.

Germany imported about 25 percent of its food in 1914, the United Kingdom about 60 percent. Yet, it was the British naval blockade of Germany, exacerbated by an ill-managed agricultural and distribution system, that gradually tightened the noose with dire results for the populations of the Central Powers. German morale reached breaking point. Meanwhile Britain continued to acquire from the USA and the empire the resources unavailable at home needed to operate her munitions and war industries and to feed her people.[4]

The war at sea was at times a desperate one. German submarines wreaked havoc. In the end, the development of a convoy system for cargo ships and improved tracking and destruction of U-boats by the Royal Navy saved Britain. German surface ships made only one attempt to break the embargo, in a battle off the Danish coast at Jutland on May 31, 1916. Although the fleet did not perform brilliantly, by driving the Germans back into port, from which they never emerged again during the war, Britain retained mastery of the seas for another generation.

The Allies had a considerable lead over the Central Powers in wealth. The British empire spent more money on the war than any of its adversaries: by 1919, $23 billion, compared to the USA's $17 billion and Germany's $19 billion. Altogether the Allies spent $57.7 billion to the Central Powers' $24.7 billion. The British state proved efficient in mobilizing manpower for the military without crippling industrial production and in organizing a massive output of armaments.[5] German finances faltered. The highly efficient British tax system, on the other hand, was restructured in a new, progressive revenue stream. The government was able to secure loans, especially from America, on easier terms than its counterparts in the rest of Europe. At the outbreak of war the National Debt was 28 percent of net GNP in Britain compared to 44 percent in France and 87 percent in Germany.[6] Money was a critical component of victory, as it had been in the eighteenth century and during the Napoleonic wars.

The government became far more active in managing the economy. Ministries multiplied like rabbits. A leading authority on the war, Hew Strachan, explains that the British "tackled the integration of science, technology and tactics with greater success than the Germans … The link between tactical experience and factory production was a continuous loop, involving fresh blueprints and the rejigging of machine-tools and plant, as well as feeding munitions into the battle."[7] New inventions included a hardened manganese steel helmet that reduced head wounds by

75 percent and hydrophones that could locate U-boats. The British established the world's first independent air force in April 1918. The intelligence service also performed at a high level.

The empire was a critical component of victory. The vast majority of the Indian and Irish peoples remained loyal or at least did not actively rebel. Although nationalists were restive, the number of British troops in the subcontinent was reduced to the derisory level of 16,000 assigned to hold sway over the 300 million people. In 1914 almost 100 million of the world's 270 million Muslims were governed by the British. A jihad declared by their spiritual leader, the Caliph in Constantinople, had no significant impact. One and a half million Indians performed military service of whom 62,000 died, including some sent to the Western Front, and the New Delhi treasury supplied cash and loans. Ten thousand black Jamaicans volunteered, and King George V personally intervened to override racist objections among the generals to their serving in active combat.[8]

The white empire contributed 1,307,000 troops to the war. Over a quarter of all eligible Canadians enlisted in the army and nearly 40 percent of Australians and New Zealanders. By 1918 one-third of the British army's munitions were made in Canada. Jan Smuts, the former Boer general, was brought to London to join the War Cabinet. It has been estimated that British casualties might have been 30 percent higher without the participation of colonial troops.[9]

The Russian autocracy collapsed in the middle of the war and the German, Austrian, and Ottoman rulers and elites were swept out of office by a tide of revolution at the end. The Italian state survived, but the old political structure disintegrated in the early 1920s and was replaced by a fascist dictatorship. France surmounted the crisis of war but the guts had been ripped out of the Third Republic. When the Nazis arrived in 1940, the system shattered under the strain in one of the most rapid and dramatic military defeats of a great power in modern history. On the other hand, despite Britain's grossly unequal social and economic system no fatal signs of stress emerged. The opposition Labour Party endorsed the war by a large majority.

The Price of War

The number of Britons killed in the war was 723,000, not including those who died from their wounds and injuries later. Thirty percent of those aged 20 to 24 in 1914 were killed. More than 300,000 children were left fatherless. Casualties were distributed unevenly. Junior officers died at a higher rate than private soldiers. Nearly half of all the Irish peers and their sons who served in the military were killed or wounded, one of the most devastating outcomes suffered by any aristocracy during the war.[10] The Scots suffered more severe casualties than the English, who were worse off than the Irish or Indian troops in terms of fatalities. It may be that the reputation for courage and even ferocity of the Highland regiments led commanders more frequently to put them in the forefront of battle. Although soldiers from the dominions did not see as much of the fiercest fighting on the Western Front, the young men of Australia and New Zealand died in appalling numbers during the failed assault at Gallipoli in Turkey in 1915.

Dark shadows of horror, loneliness, and sorrow hovered over many of the survivors. It was hard to be as optimistic about the future and the perfectibility of human nature in 1919 as it had been in 1913. The writer George Orwell reflected: "Progress had finally ended in the biggest massacre in history."[11] A future Conservative Cabinet minister, who lost a majority of his friends in the trenches, reflected at the end of the war: "These last four years have so inured me to death that I can no longer feel it very deeply."[12]

Soldiers and civilians experienced different wars. Even if the troops tried to convey the horrors of the Western Front in letters home or while visiting on leave, it was hard for their families to grasp the depth of the suffering. A number of soldiers felt alienation and inability to share their feelings except with comrades. The poets of protest, who were usually officers from privileged backgrounds, included Siegfried Sassoon, who wrote:

> You smug-faced crowds with kindling eye
> Who cheer when soldier lads march by,
> Sneak home and pray you'll never know
> The hell where youth and laughter go.[13]

Losses were not confined to the battlefield. The war played havoc with the British economy. Britain ceased to be the richest nation in the world. The United States still had a smaller population than the British empire, but its economy was now bigger. As the cost of the war rose, the capital once used to finance trade was diverted to military expenditures. Payment of interest on the debt went from 10 percent of the gross income of the government in 1914 to 25 percent in 1920. International trade and finance, at which Britain had excelled before 1914, was severely disrupted. The invisible income vital to national prosperity vanished. Factories that had once produced goods for export concentrated on making munitions, and many countries had to go elsewhere to purchase manufactured goods. The USA and Japan, who were able to continue making non-military items, stepped into markets in South America and elsewhere that traditionally had been British preserves.

Savage cuts were imposed on government spending after 1918, but the repayment of the war debt and increased provision of social services meant the 1922 Budget remained five times the size of the one in 1914.[14] Before the war someone with an income of £10,000 paid 8.1 percent of their income in taxes, but by 1918 this was 42.6 percent, and, if unearned, over 50 percent. Death duties rose to 40 percent on estates worth over £2 million.[15]

The negative economic consequences of the war can be exaggerated. The City of London recovered after 1918 and remained one of the key financial centers of the world. An economic boom was fuelled by restocking, rebuilding the merchant fleet, and consumer demand. European competitors had sustained heavy damage that took time to restore and Britain surged ahead. The boom stalled, however, in the spring of 1920. Excess productive capacity and more mechanization eliminated jobs. Low growth and unemployment set in. Hours of work had been reduced (the eight-hour day became common) after the war without comparable cuts in wages, which made British goods uncompetitive in world markets.

In the past many British workers had emigrated overseas when their industry or trade suffered serious setbacks. That option was less easy to accomplish now, especially after the USA imposed immigration restrictions from 1924. In any case unemployment was now a global problem, so movement from one continent to another was no solution. The British unemployment rate was somewhat higher in the 1920s than in comparable countries but significantly lower during the world depression of 1929–33. Britain did not see the dramatic collapse of the labor market that occurred in the USA, Germany, and elsewhere. The image of the majority of British men being out of work for years at a time is misleading. Older, unskilled workers suffered this fate more than others. The majority of people unemployed were so for relatively short periods.[16]

Poverty continued. Perhaps a fifth of the population still lived in abject conditions with the caveat that more help was available to them from government-funded social services than prior to 1914. Those without jobs suffered both the loss of the psychological support of a work environment and a sense of inadequacy in failing to provide for their families. There was no money for medical or dental care. One woman told a social investigator: "Teeth is just a misery."[17]

Education was not much improved after the war. The school-leaving age was raised to 14 along with greater provision of opportunities for publicly funded secondary education. However, as the economy slumped much of this more generous social legislation was cut back. After 1920 students were increasingly subjected to testing at age 11 as a means of separating out those qualified to go on to secondary schools. The use of "eleven plus" testing led to tracking in elementary schools, and secondary education remained out of reach for the vast majority of children, although Scotland continued to enjoy a more egalitarian system.

Gains from the War

Many soldiers returned to civilian life without significant difficulties and remembered the war as a time of comradeship, adventure, and heroism. The notion that the conflict had been a meaningless slaughter of innocents was by no means universal. Most Britons took pride in their nation's victory. The archipelago had not been invaded or occupied, and suffered little physical damage from the few German incursions by sea and air. Germany, which had seemed Britain's most dangerous European commercial rival in 1914, lay prostrate and humiliated, stripped of its empire, merchant marine, navy, and dignity.

Once the Americans radically scaled back their military forces and adopted an isolationist foreign policy, Britain resumed its position as the only great power in the world with a global reach. The physical size of the empire reached a new peak with the addition of the former provinces of the Ottoman empire in the Middle East, including Iraq, Trans-Jordan, and Palestine placed under British control by the League of Nations. German colonies in eastern and southern Africa were also absorbed. Britain possessed nearly half of all the battleships in the world in 1919. The Royal Navy continued to out-build the US fleet in numbers and tonnage during the 1920s. **HMS** *Argus*, brought into service in October 1918, was the world's first flush-decked aircraft carrier.

In 1924 the cost of living was 75 percent higher than in 1914, but wages had nearly doubled. The standard of living for employed workers was at least 10 percent higher than before the war.[18] For the majority of people who had jobs, material life continued to improve. The cost of living index fell by more than a third between 1920 and 1938, and during the 1930s prices fell faster than wages with the result that real earnings rose perhaps by as much as a fifth. Households where women and children obtained well-paid work for the first time witnessed a transformation in living standards. The proportion of income spent on food by working-class families dropped from 60 percent in 1914 to 35 percent in 1938. Much of the extra money was spent on more fuel and light, clothing, household goods, tobacco, newspapers, leisure and entertainment, but more savings were also accrued. Agricultural workers benefited from the establishment of a minimum wage for the first time. Wage differentials flattened to the advantage of the lower paid. Working conditions continued to become safer. Paid holidays were made mandatory. Spending on social services rose from £101 million in 1913 to £596 million in 1938.[19]

About four million new houses were built between 1919 and 1939, of which about a quarter were in the public sector, thus partially fulfilling a promise made by Lloyd George to help returning heroes. The middle class shifted away from renting to ownership, which was made possible by cheaper methods of construction and financing. A portion of the skilled working class also came within range of purchasing a home.

Near full political democracy was enacted by the "Fourth Reform Act" in 1918 when the size of the electorate trebled. Three-quarters of the voters were now working class. Women over 30 who were householders or the wives of householders also got the vote. They were allowed to stand as MPs, and a Sex Discrimination Act of 1918 opened up jury service, the magistracy, and the legal profession to women. Unrestricted suffrage was achieved in 1928. Discrimination against women in the job market continued. Most earned substantially less than men, even when doing comparable work. Nonetheless, the adoption of a war economy created new roles for women and enlarged their sense of what they could desire and achieve. Women were more easily able to participate in athletic activities. Raised hemlines, slacks, shorts, and less tent-like bathing suits helped liberate the female body. Working-class girls became active cyclists and hikers. Middle-class women played bowls and competitive tennis in a really serious way for the first time.

Unfortunately, many wartime jobs that had opened to women disappeared in 1919. By 1921 the proportion of women in employment was lower than in 1911.

Women who retained employment after the war stayed in or retired to domestic service and office work. They tended to replace men in unskilled or semi-skilled jobs while males advanced to better-paid and more skilled positions in industry.

In 1923 an Act relieved a wife of having to prove cruelty, desertion or another "cause" in addition to adultery as grounds for divorce, and further reforms followed. Women's control over their property was confirmed on the same terms as men in 1926. On the other hand, men of all classes continued to expect women to do the housework unaided, even if the man was unemployed and the woman had a job outside the home. A satisfactory contraceptive diaphragm was invented in 1919, which became more reliable in 1932 when a contraceptive jelly was developed to go with it. Dr. Marie Stopes made such devices respectable in her book *Married Love* (1918 and many later editions). Still, progress was slow. Birth control was more easily available to middle- and upper-class women. Abortion remained illegal.

Continuity and Change

The successful leadership of the aristocracy in the upper reaches of politics and the military during the war reinforced the existing social system even as power became more diffused with the advent of a genuinely democratic franchise. No further reforms were imposed on the House of Lords, and leadership roles in the army, empire, and politics continued to be filled by peers. Perhaps a quarter of the agricultural land in England was sold off in the years immediately after the war. However, most of the large landowning families survived and even prospered. It was the lesser gentry who crumbled under the weight of increased taxation. In 1980, about half of great landowners in England that held big estates in 1880 retained all or a substantial area of the principal family property. In Scotland in the 1970s and 1980s one-third of land was still held in 121 estates larger than 20,000 acres while 10 percent of the nation belonged to 13 individuals, many of them members of the ancient titled elite.[20] When natural attrition is taken into account, this is a remarkable rate of survival.

However, the decline in the value of agricultural land meant that the aristocracy and greater gentry were proportionately less rich compared to rising commercial wealth. Influence in rural areas no longer commanded much weight in elections. Men with business backgrounds flowed into the leadership of the Conservative Party while middle-class intellectuals and union leaders formed the core of the Labour movement. The social elite and the political elite that had previously been one and the same began to detach from each other. Fewer and fewer successful businessmen purchased large estates, and only the oldest and grandest titled dynasties continued to practice primogeniture as the century progressed.[21]

Harold Perkin's argument that the class-based character of British society diminished after 1914 and that professional values emphasizing merit and trained expertise became more important than traditional forms of property in segregating society does not come to grips with the fact that property and wealth continued to be held by a very small portion of the population.[22] It is true, however, that many members of the middle classes did well out of the war. The governments of the interwar period tried to relieve taxation on the "productive" classes, to ensure that the bourgeoisie remained prosperous.

The war led to a revolution in the relationship between parties. The Liberals, already divided by the Home Rule controversy, went into an irremediable decline. The division between Asquithites and Georgites was never healed. By 1931 the party gained less than 7 percent of the vote.[23] Conservatives were frightened by the large expansion in working-class voters after 1918. This made them anxious to cling to the coalition government. However, the removal of 80 anti-Unionst MPs after the independence of Ireland (see below), the addition of a number of safe seats in the 1918 electoral reform act, and the tendency of Liberal and Labour candidates in three-way races to divide the anti-Conservative vote gave the latter an unexpected advantage. So too did the fact that until 1945 more members of the working class voted Conservative than Labour and a majority of women consistently cast ballots for the Tories. Labour became a broad-based mass party for the first time and an effective opposition to Tory rule. From less than 7 percent of the vote in 1910 its share rose to 30 percent in 1922 and 37 percent in 1929.

Victory in the war encouraged British patriotism. George V replaced the Germanic Saxe-Coburg-Gotha with Windsor as the dynastic name for the royal family. Playing "God Save the King" at the start of public events became standard practice. Loyalty to the monarchy, Parliament, and the idea of the United Kingdom (except in Ireland) surmounted the challenges of the economic and social suffering of the interwar years. The Germans took the place of the French and Catholics, whose "otherness" had been so helpful in binding the kingdoms together in the past. The Cenotaph war memorial in central London, the tomb of the Unknown Warrior in Westminster Abbey, and the annual Remembrance Day on November 11 were potent reminders of the new enemy.

The war reconfigured relationships between the kingdoms. Scottish men had been underrepresented in the prewar electorate, but after the reform of 1918, they gained a greater voice in national affairs. The opening of a National War Memorial in 1927 suggested that Scotland was beginning to see its identity in a different and freestanding way, while the London government established a "Scottish Office" in Edinburgh. The biggest change in the composition of the United Kingdom, however, took place in Ireland. The removal from politics of the Irish question and Nationalist MPs from the House of Commons left the remaining parts of the islands more "British."

Ireland

The Nationalist movement in prewar Ireland had continued to grow. The outbreak of World War I persuaded men committed to the use of force, such as the Irish Republican Brotherhood, that conditions were ripe for revolt. They feared that

Britain would emerge from the war stronger, and sought German assistance. The rebels who seized public buildings in central Dublin on Easter Monday 1916 expected to fail but intended to make a patriotic sacrifice, imposing an obligation on future generations to repay it by completing the campaign for full independence.

No more than 1,500 persons participated in the 1916 "Rising." Some 450 people were killed including 116 British soldiers and 16 policemen. The British military command insisted on executing 15 of the leaders by firing squad, which won sympathy for what had previously been regarded by much of the population as counterproductive behavior. Catholic opinion was permanently alienated, although it is hard to see how Asquith could have acted otherwise in the middle of such a great emergency as the war. Mass imprisonment of the surviving rebels and dissemination of the details of the rebellion also contributed to increased popular support for the Nationalist cause.

In the general election at the end of the war the Nationalist party Sinn Fein won all of the seats in the south of Ireland, pushing aside constitutional Nationalist candidates. They refused to swear oaths to the Crown as MPs, and met in Dublin under their own auspices as an Irish Parliament (the *Dail Eireann*, pronounced "doil erin"). This body declared Ireland a Republic in early 1919 with Eamon De Valera (1882–1975) as "president." With a slap in the face to Protestants, independence was declared exclusively in the name of "the ancient Irish people."[24]

The British government did not recognize the Republic and sent ex-soldiers (known as "Black and Tans" from their uniform colors) to Ireland to reinforce the existing police force. Meanwhile the IRA (Irish Republican Army) was formed to resist the oppressing power. Ireland plunged into a guerrilla war between 1919 and 1921. The Black and Tans ran amuck, and the IRA retaliated in kind. The rule of law disintegrated in parts of the south.

The declaration of a Catholic Republic provoked Ulster separatists, whose loyalty to Britain had been proved by massive casualties sustained on the Western Front, to implement "partition" of the six northern Protestant counties from the south. The Republicans failed to acknowledge the idea that a distinctive Protestant culture in the north, now three centuries old, had any legitimacy or even real existence.

The British Parliament enacted a new Home Rule Act, which became law in December 1920. This established two Parliaments, one in Dublin and one in Belfast. Anti-Catholic riots in the north deepened the distrust between the two religious communities. Sinn Fein treated the first election for the Dublin Parliament as if it were one for the *Dail* and won 124 of the 128 seats. The Irish government initiated negotiations for a settlement of the civil war at a point when the Nationalists feared they were on the brink of defeat. A truce was declared. A conference of leaders from both sides (see Michael Collins in Biography 9.1) met in London. A treaty emerged. Britain recognized the *Dail* as the Parliament of southern Ireland, a dominion (the status held by Canada and Australia) to be known as the Free State. The Irish government would acknowledge allegiance to the king, and the Royal Navy retained four bases in the south. Ulster was to continue as a separate entity defined by a boundary commission established to set the borders.

Biography 9.1

Michael Collins
1890–1922

Michael Collins was raised on a farm in County Cork. At 16 he moved to London where he held a variety of jobs in financial institutions. He lived mainly among the Irish community in the capital and became a radical Nationalist. In 1909 he was sworn into the clandestine Irish Republican Brotherhood. He moved back to Dublin in 1916 and participated in the Easter Rising in a minor capacity. He was imprisoned in Wales with other rebels and at age 26 emerged in the detention camp as a major leader. In 1918 he became minister of finance and then director of intelligence of the Irish Republic in their war for independence. His successful military efforts and attractive personal style made him a heroic figure. Collins could be ruthless, but he had a strong practical streak. The Irish "president" Eamon de Valera was jealous and distrustful.

   After the truce of July 11, 1921 Collins was sent to London to negotiate with the British. His willingness to accept a compromise, under the threat of immediate all-out war by the British, was endorsed by the *Dail* and the electorate: "What's good enough for Mick is good enough for me," the saying went. De Valera rejected the Treaty, and Collins was killed in an ambush in August 1922 by anti-Treaty forces. The hero of the revolution perished at the hands of his own countrymen.[25]

A majority of southern Irish people supported the Treaty, and it was ratified by the *Dail*. Power was handed over to what was for all practical purposes an independent Ireland in January 1922.

   A second civil war broke out between pro- and anti-Treaty forces that lasted until May 1923. The endgame in Ireland, both in the north and in the south, was fought over whether to take the oath of allegiance to the Crown. The supporters of the Treaty won. The boundary commission failed to take any action, and the existing borders that guaranteed a Protestant majority in the north became fixed with unhappy results in the long term. In Ulster sectarian interests dominated the government of the province. The borders of electoral districts were gerrymandered. Periodic outbursts of anti-Catholic rioting by working-class Protestants intimidated the Nationalist community and helped to keep the IRA alive. Unfortunately, the terrorists developed a kind of fantasy view of the Ulster situation based on a belief that a unified republic would emerge if they bombed their way to its formation. In the later 1930s the IRA sought ties with Nazi Germany and triggered over 100 explosions in British cities in 1939.

Irish people continued to emigrate to Britain in large numbers. In World War II, although the south remained neutral, 30,000 Irishmen enlisted in the British army and many more went to work in factories in England and Scotland. In 1936 the *Dail* removed the symbolic existence of the Crown from all internal matters, and a new constitution in 1937 changed the name of the Free State to the Gaelic "Eire." In 1948 it became a Republic, cutting the last link with the United Kingdom. In 1949 Ireland left the **Commonwealth**.

Political Instability

Lloyd George prepared to fight the December 1918 election (the first since 1910) in alliance with the Tories, opposed by the Asquithite Liberals and the Labour Party. An arrangement was made by which the prime minister's supporters and Conservatives were issued "coupons" that guaranteed no candidate from one party would oppose someone from the other. Many Conservatives remembered Lloyd George as a dangerous radical, but they also understood that he had emerged from the war as a leader on a heroic scale who had the power, popularity, and commitment to stem the Bolshevik tide that had consumed Russia and might triumph in Germany. Since the Conservatives widely outnumbered the Liberals in the coalition, the former felt safe in continuing the arrangement.

The postwar economic boom led 48 percent of the electorate to support coalition candidates while only 22 percent voted Labour. Lloyd George achieved one of the greatest parliamentary majorities in modern history with 478 MPs to the opposition's 85 (with MPs from other smaller parties also lending support to the government). Sinn Fein's refusal to participate in the Westminster Parliament made the prime minister's position even more dominant.

The Versailles Peace Conference preoccupied Lloyd George during the first half of 1919. He, along with the French premier Georges Clemenceau and the American President Woodrow Wilson, dictated terms to the defeated nations. Though Lloyd George recognized that the draconian peace treaty desired by the French was too punishing, he was distrustful of Wilson's idealism. The British prime minister was confronted by massive war debts, and his own electorate and the dominions demanded compensation and retribution. He pointed out, not unreasonably, that, "somebody had to pay. If Germany could not pay, it meant the British taxpayer had to pay. Those who ought to pay were those who caused the loss."[26] In the end heavy reparations were imposed on Germany. Today these are thought to have been not as severe as was once assumed. The economist John Maynard Keynes (1883–1946), however, resigned from the British delegation in protest at the harshness of the terms and published a prediction of doom in his *The Economic Consequences of the Peace*

(1919). Machiavelli's advice not to wound if you did not intend to kill was ignored. Germany was humiliated but not destroyed.

On the domestic front, Lloyd George did not accomplish a great deal as postwar prime minister. He built some public housing for returning veterans and extended insurance against unemployment to virtually the entire working class, a policy that retarded the shift of workers from declining to rising industries but helped the country to survive the coming economic crisis without revolution. The prime minister suffered a series of blows in 1922, including an outcry over the sale of titles, "softness" toward the independence movement in India, and disgruntlement over foreign policy. The right wing of the Conservative Party was unsettled by these issues, and also by the premier's resistance to tariffs and occasional radical rhetoric, although moderates wanted to continue the coalition as a means of keeping the Labour Party out of office. Lloyd George's untrustworthiness ultimately led to a Tory decision to leave the coalition. The prime minister resigned on October 19, 1922. The king sent for Bonar Law to form a single-party government for the first time since 1916. This was an unusual step, since Austen Chamberlain (1863–1937) was the official Conservative leader. In the end he refused to join Bonar Law's Cabinet, but the latter was able to put together a government that commanded a majority of votes in the Commons, so it did not matter.

Bonar Law drew heavily on the aristocracy for leadership. This was the last Cabinet to include a duke. Lord Curzon (1859–1925), whose family had been settled in Derbyshire since the eleventh century, became foreign secretary, the seventeenth earl of Derby was secretary of war, the fourth marquess of Salisbury lord president of the council, and another great landowner, the future earl of Halifax, began the rise that would lead him close to gaining the premiership in 1940.

The government survived a general election in November 1922 that gave them a majority of seats even over the combined forces of the Labour and Liberal parties. It gained some relief in repayments of loans to the United States but failed to achieve more moderate arrangements over German reparations. Early in 1923, however, Bonar Law was obliged by illness to resign. It was generally assumed that the experienced and able Curzon was to be his successor. The king decided to pass over the peer, who sat in the House of Lords where the principal opposition Labour Party had no representation (thus making direct parliamentary debate impossible), and chose the businessman Stanley Baldwin (1867–1947) as the next prime minister.

Baldwin presented himself to the world as a pipe-smoking, down-to-earth country squire interested in raising pigs. He harked on the time-honored verities of the simple rural life. Beneath his jovial smile and twinkling eyes Baldwin quite understood that Britain was predominantly urban. His money had been made in the steel industry. He decided to introduce a high tariff barrier to reduce unemployment, but because Bonar Law had promised that the Tories would not go forward with such a policy without a referendum or general election, the latter had to be called four years earlier than was required by law. Baldwin took the risk both because he was gravely concerned about unemployment and because it was a way to reunite the party. Austen Chamberlain and the other coalitionists were pro-tariff.

The Liberals and Labourites campaigned on the traditional platform of tariffs being a tax on food, a theme that temporarily brought the fragmented Liberal Party together again. In the event the Tories lost 87 seats but remained the largest single party. However, the combined forces of Liberals and Labour controlled almost 100 more seats than the government. This ensured that tariff reform could not be enacted.

The three-way split in the House of Commons (Tories 258, Liberals 159, and Labour 191) created a "hung" Parliament. When it met in January 1924, the Conservatives were defeated in a vote of "no confidence," and Baldwin resigned. The king sent for the leader of the next largest party, Ramsay MacDonald, who thus became the first Labour prime minister. The situation was tense because George V despised social-ism, but the king soon found his new Labour ministers were men with whom he felt comfortable. MacDonald himself had an affinity for aristocratic company and even the more radical working-class leaders made some accommodation to the mon-arch's obsession about archaic court dress. Soon harmony reigned at Buckingham Palace, but Labour did not have enough votes to rule single-handed.

MacDonald, the illegitimate son of a Scottish servant girl and possibly a farm laborer, grew up in poverty but was never a manual worker himself and never associ-ated with a trade union. He was an idealistic social democrat. His right-hand man and chancellor of the exchequer, Philip Snowden (1864–1937), was also never a union man, and like MacDonald he was a strong believer in change at a gradual pace. Eight out of 20 members of the Cabinet were upper or upper-middle class. One of MacDonald's achievements was to make Labour appear non-threatening, a legitimate party of government.

Snowden made little progress in reducing unemployment. The government was soon brought down when the Liberals and Tories combined to vote no confidence, prompted by an inept handling of the legal prosecution of a communist journalist. MacDonald asked the king for a general election. During the electoral campaign the Tories argued Labour was soft on communism. Both diplomatic recognition of the Soviet Union and the legal debacle seemed evidence of that. Four days before the vote a newspaper published a story alleging that Russian leaders were plotting to influence Labour policies and promote revolution. The "Zinoviev letter," now known to have been a forgery, xenophobia, and "red scare" paranoia that MacDonald could not counter effectively led to a Conservative victory.

Although winning support from only 48 percent of the electorate, the Tories gained 419 seats. Liberal representation shrank to 40 while Labour held 151. Baldwin was recalled as prime minister, joined by Winston Churchill as chancellor of the exchequer. The latter had drifted back into the Conservative orbit largely in response to the Russian Revolution and his desire to avoid going down with the sinking Liberal ship.

Baldwin's conciliatory approach did not satisfy many high Tories, but it helped Britain sustain a rational debate about politics and presented the Conservative Party to the mass of voters as an acceptable alternative to Labour. At the same time the government faced nearly intractable economic problems. Protecting British industry with tariffs had been ruled out by the electorate. In 1925 Churchill tried to strengthen the City of London by bringing back the **gold standard**, a symbol of secure finance. Many officials and economists opposed him on the ground that setting the value of the pound too high would price British goods out of many export markets and lead to unemployment. Keynes attacked the decision. Churchill admitted later that it was the "biggest blunder of my life."[27]

The General Strike

The consequences for manufacturing of Churchill's policies may not have been as severe as some have argued or, at least, not the fault of the chancellor. The traditional staple industries of shipbuilding, textiles, iron and steel, and engineering were suffering a sustained decline. The coal industry had lost its export markets during the war and was gradually becoming obsolescent. Over time oil, gas, and electricity replaced coal in powering ships and trains and heating homes. The onset of problems in the textile industry was due to Indian and Japanese competition, which predated the restoration of the gold standard. Exports to Germany and the USA dropped due to economic crises in those countries, which reduced imports, and the decline in food prices made it less possible for primary producers of imported food such as Argentina, Canada, India, and Australia to trade with Britain. British exports in 1931–2 fell to half what they had been in 1913.[28]

The unemployment rate rose to almost 18 percent in June 1921. Thenceforward it stayed above 10 percent, reaching a peak of over 22 percent during the Great Depression in 1932. Matters were even worse than these statistics indicated because official counts did not include agricultural laborers, the self-employed, and married women. Moreover, if a larger number of types of jobs had been open to women more would have been in the labor market. In addition, there were many men disabled during the war, such as amputees, who lived on pensions or were forced into marginal employment. Thus, a substantial portion of the working population was in distress.

Because many industries were concentrated in particular regions unemployment in parts of the country reached catastrophic proportions. By 1932 almost half the workers in iron and steel and two-thirds in shipbuilding were out of work. In 1935 nearly three-quarters of the coal miners in parts of South Wales had no job. Half a million people left the principality between 1921 and 1938, nearly one-fifth of the population, and the birth rate also dropped dramatically.[29] Due to its reliance on the failing textile and shipbuilding industries, Ulster became the poorest part of the United Kingdom. Levels of unemployment remained much lower in London and the south of England.

In the 1920s the coal industry was still the largest single employer in the country, the only one with more than a million workers. Miners evoked particular sympathy from their peers and even from members of the middle classes. Mining not only involved hard work in unpleasant circumstances, but also it was dangerous despite greater regulation imposed by the government and improved technology employed by owners. In Wales 439 miners died in one accident in 1913 and 266 at another in 1934. In 1925, 73 boys under the age of 16 were killed in Britain's coalmines and a further 15,241 injured.[30]

The **TUC**, representing all the unions, decided to support the miners against maltreatment by the pit owners and the government. The first truly mass strike in British history began at midnight on May 3, 1926. No other event in the twentieth century divided the country more deeply along class lines. Although by no means all workers participated in the strike, most large businesses, the trains, buses, newspapers, and transportation of goods ceased to function. The government proclaimed a state of national emergency. Middle-class civilians and the military were used to maintain essential services. University students drove buses.

The **BBC** continued to operate in support of the state. The army and navy remained loyal, and 250,000 special constables were recruited to keep order. Violent clashes between strikers and the police took place but never ignited into a revolutionary situation. The leadership of the TUC and the Labour party were anxious to find a peaceful solution. A vague promise to address abuses was rapidly worked out and the strike was called off on May 12. Radicals led a continued "second" General Strike that lasted until May 21, which was neither as widespread nor as threatening as the initial event. In the end only the miners remained out of work, and had to submit to lower wages in December when their lockout finally ended. A Trade Disputes and Trade Union Act was passed in 1927 that constricted union action in strikes.

Why Was There No Revolution?

Some British trade unions became politicized. The example of the Russian Revolution in 1917 impelled radicals forward. Wales and Scotland were more liable to labor conflict than England and Northern Ireland. The most serious outbreak of class conflict in the immediate postwar period exploded in Glasgow, "Red Clydeside," in 1919 when workers had to be kept under control by troops backed by tanks. Yet, efforts to spread the agitation beyond Glasgow failed. The government confidently arrested radical leaders and crushed the unrest. Despite suffering on a massive scale and the deep-seated alienation of some parts of the working class, the British state remained stable. Why?

Victory in the war had legitimized the existing regime and allowed the monarchy and Parliament to appeal across class boundaries to patriotic feelings in order to retain loyalty. The Bolshevik Revolution and the General Strike drove home to the property-owning classes that political stability was critical, and much of the government's approach to the economy thenceforward kept this principle to the fore. Baldwin's government made significant strides in the tradition of "Tory democracy," even a mild form of "Tory socialism." Neville Chamberlain (1869–1940), Joseph's younger son and Austen's younger brother, was responsible for much of this legislation. Pensions were improved and extended to more people. The old Poor Law was abolished in 1930 and relief responsibilities shifted to county and borough councils, although a "means" test was applied to those who claimed benefits after 26 weeks, a deeply humiliating process for people out of work due to forces beyond their control.

An underlying conservatism within the working class itself was reflected both in the ballot box and in more abstract attitudes toward the family, religion, the king, and the constitution. Richard Hoggart described the working-class world in which he grew up and that existed for much of the first half of the twentieth century: "Life is not seen as a climb, nor work as the main interest in it … 'keen types' are mistrusted … Horizons are likely to be limited … The 'real' things are the human and companionable things – home and family affection, friendship and being able to 'enjoy y'self': 'money's not the 'real thing', they say." George Orwell observed: "To the ordinary working man, the sort you would meet in any pub on Saturday night, Socialism does not mean much more than better wages and shorter hours and nobody bossing you about."[31]

Most Britons made the fundamental assumption that revolutionary violence was wrong. In the eighteenth and nineteenth centuries, at any rate, riots were a British tradition, but in the twentieth century "revolution" seemed an alien concept associated with "foreign" places such as France or Ireland. Sectarian prejudices led significant numbers of working-class voters to support the Conservative Party, especially in Scotland where the divide between Catholic and Protestant worsened in the years of unemployment. The geographical isolation of unemployment and the fact that prolonged joblessness afflicted older workers more than younger ones helped reduce the danger of a conflagration. Manual laborers remained divided by skill, age, gender, ethnicity, religion, and location and types of work, even though universal elementary education after 1870 helped diminish some of these differentials and opportunities for mobility had increased.

The TUC leaders in 1926, notably Walter Citrine (1887–1983) and Ernest Bevin (1881–1951), were not interested in revolution. They felt an obligation to help the miners, not overthrow property or government. They were formidable men who were able to block those more radical than themselves from gaining significant headway in exploiting the crisis for larger purposes. The existence of the Labour Party allowed workers' grievances and a socialist agenda to be debated in the central institutions of the state. The Labour Party officially rebuffed all efforts by the Communists to affiliate with it.

New forms of cheap entertainment may have helped to ease tensions caused by unemployment. The availability of low-priced, mass-produced consumer items exploded. Chain stores such as Marks and Spencer, Boots, and Woolworths expanded dramatically. This in turn stimulated the packaging and advertising industries and newspaper sales. In 1900 one adult in six read a daily newspaper; by 1920 one in two did so. New installment plans made it easier for ordinary people to purchase larger ticket items such as furniture. At the same time many outward signs of class distinction disappeared. Cheap, mass-produced clothing, which could include plastic

Biography 9.2

William Morris
1877–1963

William Morris was the son of a farmer. At 16 he was apprenticed to a bicycle maker and began his own cycle repair business in Oxford with capital of £4. He had no formal training as an engineer but was soon manufacturing motorcycles. He also ran a garage that rented cars. After a collision while at the wheel of one of Morris's hired vehicles, an undergraduate at the university, the earl of Macclesfield, agreed to provide £4,000 in capital so that the young entrepreneur could begin manufacturing automobiles. These became noted for their reliability and low price, and by 1923 Morris Motors was producing 20,000 a year. Sales were enhanced by aggressive advertising; purchases offered through installment plans and a nationwide system of dealers. By the late 1920s Morris supplied one-third of all cars made in Britain. Later, the company would produce two of the classic models of the post-1945 era: the Morris Minor and the Morris Mini.

Morris hated socialism and did everything in his power to block unions from penetrating his factories. Although created Viscount Nuffield in 1938, he lived simply and gave away his money. As a life-long hypochondriac, it is not surprising that he donated millions of pounds to hospitals and medical research. He was also exceptionally generous to Oxford, both town and university. He died possessed of £3 million, having given £30 million to charity. Morris's story was not quite a rags-to-riches one, but his career was an example of the continuous stream of innovative entrepreneurs who contributed to British economic growth during the interwar years.[33]

accessories that simulated leather in handbags and other items, made much of the population seem similar in outward appearance. Cigarettes got cheaper. In 1948 four-fifths of men and two-fifths of women smoked. Huge crowds attended soccer matches, and cricket enjoyed a golden age between the wars. These developments undoubtedly made life brighter and easier to bear for the poor. Orwell argued: "It is quite likely that fish-and-chips, art-silk stockings, tinned salmon, cut-price chocolate…, the movies, the radio, strong tea, and the **Football Pools** have between them averted revolution."[32] Britain had as yet, however, no tea bags or sliced bread.

Unlike in Russia or Germany, the middle class was large and robust with rising incomes. Middling Britain was self-confident and ready to fight to stay on top. The number of students attending private schools increased. More and more families were able to purchase cars thanks to the efforts of William Morris (see Biography 9.2).

In 1931 one in five of every households had at least one live-in servant and many more employed daily help for cooking and cleaning.[34]

Perhaps the single most crucial explanation for Britain's stability was economic. A good majority of working-class people were in work during the 1920s and 1930s and enjoyed a rising standard of living as real wages rose and hours declined. The miners were the only major group to experience a fall in real wages in the 1920s.[35] Manufacturing and marketing of automobiles, and new electrical products such as vacuum cleaners, refrigerators, stoves, and radios, stimulated much industrial production. In 1920 only one house in 17 was wired for electricity, while in 1939 it was two out of three. Rearmament from the mid-1930s created a surge in production, particularly in the aircraft industry. New materials such as rayon, rubber tires, synthetic dyes, pharmaceuticals, and fertilizers stimulated the chemical industry. Contractors expanded and proliferated to build houses and public buildings. Improved efficiency in industrial production and output per head, always a strength of the British economy, continued to rise unabated to unprecedented levels.

The Second Labour Administration

By law an election had to be held by 1929. The Tories suffered a huge setback, the Liberals continued to flounder, while Labour did better than ever before. The latter won 288 seats to the Conservatives' 260. Although he was 48 seats short of a majority, MacDonald again became prime minister. The Liberals with 59 seats had to support the new government if it was to survive. On October 29, 1929 the New York stock market collapsed. The immediate effect of the crisis was more severe on the Continent than in Britain, but American markets were important to British exports. In many parts of the world demand declined or disappeared. Unemployment grew.

The economist Keynes argued in his *Treatise on Money* (1930) that because wages were too high the economy had become uncompetitive. Mass unemployment was the result. To kick-start the economy public investment was needed. By this means Britain would also gain a modernized infrastructure such as limited access highways, large bridges, and the like. The government did build some bypasses around congested towns and constructed more public housing, but neither the Labour nor Tory parties embraced a Keynesian solution to Britain's economic woes. In folk memory "pump-priming" was thought to have pulled the United States out of the depression, but in practice success was limited. As in the USA, economic regeneration in Britain was stimulated more by rearmament in the face of oncoming war.

The most vigorous advocate of public spending in the Labour Party was the renegade aristocrat, Sir Oswald Mosley, sixth baronet. He left the government and in 1930–1 formed the New Party, supported by a number of radical MPs. Mosley's incipient fascism and megalomania, however, quickly drove away most of his respectable followers. He proceeded to found a fascist party and became pro-Nazi.[36] No other prominent British politician chose this political path.

The depression would not go away. Even Liberals began to rethink their position on tariffs. The depth and length of the economic slowdown was unprecedented in peacetime. The international banking system began to disintegrate and in August 1932 leading financiers in the City became convinced that the British economic system was near collapse. Confidence in the currency crumpled. A committee established to examine national expenditure advised increasing taxes and cutting government spending even further by reducing unemployment benefits, which it was hoped would make British goods cheaper and stimulate exports. MacDonald and Snowden accepted these conclusions but most Labour MPs were unwilling to go along with them. The Cabinet was deadlocked. The prime minister began meetings with the Liberal and Conservative leadership to discuss further budget revisions in an atmosphere of crisis.

The idea of an emergency National government seems first to have arisen during a conversation between the Liberal leader, Sir Herbert Samuel (1870–1963), and King George V in late August. The latter was meeting with party leaders after MacDonald informed him that the Labour government might have to resign. Baldwin agreed to serve under MacDonald in a coalition formed to save the nation from economic collapse. The monarch worked to shape a consensus. He trusted MacDonald and the politicians trusted the king.

The Labour government irrevocably broke down over the decision to cut unemployment benefits by 10 percent. MacDonald told them that in that case they were dismissed and that he would head a temporary emergency Cabinet with a few of his colleagues such as Snowden. He had moved to the right politically, and the king offered him a means to retain power and shift his stance. Most Labour supporters were then – and remained so later – bitter about this "betrayal" by their leader. The pressure from financial institutions and international forces was so great, however, that it is hard to see what else could have been done. The National government served the interests of the Conservatives and the capitalists, as did the New Deal in the United States. This was preferable, however, to the alternatives adopted by most other European states, China, and Japan. France, whose less industrialized economy was more modestly affected by the collapse of international trade, was the only democracy other than Britain and the USA to survive the immediate catastrophe, and it did so at a cost of political contortions that later proved fatal.

The National Government

Only a handful of Labour MPs followed MacDonald into the coalition in late August 1931. Some Liberals joined it, but the bulk of support came from the Conservatives. Taxes were increased, unemployment benefits cut by 10 percent, and public employees had their salaries slashed. Sailors in the Royal Navy rose in protest both because they were already paid very little and because officers were not as badly affected by the cuts. The "mutiny" in the heart of one of the world's most admired and powerful institutions shook confidence in Britain around the world. A majority of the gold in the Bank of England was withdrawn by overseas creditors, which led the government to abandon the gold standard. The value of the pound slumped, which helped British exports. The most severe wage cuts were moderated, and gradually confidence returned. Overall, joblessness began to fall after 1933 along with an upswing in economic growth, although unemployment in the declining industries remained an insoluble problem for the rest of the 1930s.

In October 1931, after the immediate crisis was over, an election was held to confirm the recent changes in government. The Liberals and Conservatives agreed to differ on the issue of tariffs, while MacDonald prevaricated. Snowden called the Labour Party electoral manifesto presented by his old friends, "Bolshevism run mad."[37] Labour tried to present the National government as a creature of the capitalist financiers and against the interests of the working class. Many voters, however, were persuaded by MacDonald's leadership to desert Labour and support the government. Over 60 percent of the voters cast ballots for coalition MPs, the most overwhelming popular victory achieved by a government in modern times. In the Commons the prime minister could count on 554 votes to Labour's 52. The Communist Party and Mosley's fascists hardly registered an electoral tremor. A majority of Britons sought consensus and compromise.

The National government finally introduced sweeping tariff protection. Food, however, remained exempt. An accord was reached with the dominions in 1932 to charge lower rates on trade within the empire. Other steps were taken to stimulate the economy that grew at a solid 4 percent per year in the mid-1930s. Over time the retirements of Labour and Liberal members of the Cabinet made the government Tory in all but name. Baldwin and MacDonald switched places in 1935. The former was confident enough to call an election a year earlier than the law required. Labour improved its position from 1931 but the Tories sustained their large majority of MPs.

In 1936 the nation was unexpectedly thrown into turmoil by the sex life of George V's heir. The old king died in January, not long after an enormously successful Silver Jubilee. He was succeeded by the glamorous but self-centered, frivolous, and still unmarried Prince of Wales who reigned as Edward VIII (1894–1972). The new king's mistress was a divorced American woman, Wallis Simpson. The government, leaders of the dominions, and the Church were adamant that marriage to her was unacceptable. Almost certainly Baldwin was also appalled by Edward's irresponsibility and selfishness. In what amounted to a coup, the monarch was hustled out of the country. His forced abdication, and the succession of his younger brother, who seemed equally but for different reasons unsuited to the throne, was thought by many to endanger the monarchy. The new king, George VI (1895–1952), stammered, was subject to uncontrollable rages, and possessed at best average intelligence. In fact no serious damage occurred. He turned out to be a model king. He was happily married to a successful consort with two attractive children. Indeed, the matriarchy of his wife, Queen Elizabeth (later the Queen Mother – 1900–2002), and his daughter Queen Elizabeth II stood at the center of national life for the next 70 years: both of them shrewd, dutiful, and durable.

Baldwin retired soon after George VI's coronation in May 1937 and was replaced by Neville Chamberlain. Though a master of domestic policy with genuinely progressive ideas, Chamberlain had little experience in foreign affairs, which became the dominant issue of his brief premiership. His lack of skill in this area was compounded by reliance on behind-the-scenes advisors, who turned out to be even more unwise than the prime minister himself. Chamberlain was both intelligent and decent. In the late 1930s he was the wrong man in the wrong place at the wrong time.

Changes in Society

The war formed a vast chasm between Victorian culture on the one hand and postwar life on the other. Partly this was due to the rise of Bolshevism, Freudianism, anthropology, and new science, all of which threatened traditional assumptions about religion and society. Discussion of sexuality became more frequent and open, though British inhibitions in this area remained a strong counter-current. The public authority of religion declined, although Church membership in absolute terms continued to grow until 1927. By the 1930s less than 10 percent of the English were going to church on Sunday and Sunday school attendance dropped dramatically. Dissent shrank much faster than Anglicanism. This was one of the reasons for the evaporation of the Liberal Party. The Welsh, Scots, and Irish perpetuated religious faith longer, although the Anglican Church in Wales was finally disestablished in 1919. The reunion of the established Kirk and the United Free Church in Scotland in 1929 helped to sustain the influence of organized religion. The majority of British people continued to baptize their children and conducted their marriages and funerals in churches. Christian opposition to divorce, homosexuality, artificial birth control, drink, pornography, and relaxed social practices gradually detached it from the everyday world of a majority of people.

The crime rate rose during the first half of the century, but the size of prison populations fell. Prison regimes became less harsh. The emotionally disturbed were more likely to be sent to places where they could receive treatment not punishment. Unlike the eighteenth and the nineteenth centuries, when violence and unruliness were characteristic of British society, the culture became more respectful of authority. Violent crime, outside dysfunctional families, was extremely rare.

The long demographic expansion begun in the eighteenth century came to an end in the second decade of the twentieth century. The rate of increase in population between the wars was about a third of that experienced in the previous century. Birth rates dropped by almost half in just a few decades. The death rate also fell but at a slower pace. Life expectancy increased. In 1900 a British woman aged 20 could expect to live for another 46 years; by 1930 she could expect another 60 years of life. Half the British people now lived in cities of over 50,000 inhabitants. The south continued to expand while population fell in the old industrial areas of the midlands and north.[38]

The Age of Anxiety

Much of popular culture was aimed at simple entertainment. The film industry, however, did address social issues and because so many movies were imported from Hollywood, exposure to egalitarian and materialistic American culture became widespread for the first time. British directors and actors achieved great success in California. Charles Laughton, Charlie Chaplin, Laurence Olivier, Cary Grant, Bob Hope, Deborah Kerr, Vivien Leigh, and David Niven were among the most famous. Radio, on the other hand, remained intensely British. Broadcasting began in 1922. Control over the new medium was given to the British Broadcasting Corporation (BBC), a public company independent of government control financed by users' fees with no advertising. The first director-general, Sir John Reith (1889–1971), a Scot of amazing drive and willpower, set a didactic tone. The Corporation resisted many concessions to ordinary tastes and was challenged by offshore commercial rivals, especially in the area of popular music. The news broadcasts became increasingly well reported and drew larger and larger audiences as anxieties about a coming war loomed. Edward VIII gave his farewell address to the nation live on the air, and Chamberlain announced the outbreak of war in September 1939. The Scot John Logie Baird produced the first television picture, and the first regular TV service was opened by the BBC in 1936, though this was on a very small scale and ended with the outbreak of war.

Britain was still a highly literary culture in the 1920s and 1930s and cheap paperback editions, most famously Allen Lane's "Penguins," made everything from murder mysteries to Shakespeare available at low prices. "Modernism" became a dominant intellectual movement reflecting the feeling that traditional culture had been disrupted and society dehumanized by the war. Noel Annan observes: "The artist's duty was to express his consciousness of living in an insane society."[39] T. S. Eliot's poem *The Waste Land* (1922) depicted the bleakness of material life and his despair at a Godless modern world. In "Sweeney Agonistes," he wrote: "Birth, and copulation, and death, / That's all the facts when you come to brass tacks."[40] Music became experimental and atonal and paintings and sculpture were deformed or abstract. High praise was reserved for the stream-of-consciousness novels of the Irishman James Joyce and the introspective work of Virginia Woolf. The edgy and contemptuous D. H. Lawrence, a miner's son, raged.

Not all writers rejected the past. The traditionalists P. G. Wodehouse and Evelyn Waugh wrote some of the funniest novels in the English language during these years.

Thomas Hardy, A. E. Housman, and E. M. Forster produced work of the highest quality. Perhaps the greatest English writer to emerge in the interwar years was George Orwell (the pen name of Eric Blair, 1903–50), whose early novels were not very interesting, but whose passion and intelligence were poured into reportage on poverty and politics delivered in a spare, pungent style. In music Gustav Holst, Ralph Vaughan Williams, and Edward Elgar composed melodically. The "Blooms-bury" circle that embraced the "Modernist" aesthetic in the 1920s and 1930s included Virginia Woolf and Keynes, who rejected conventional moral codes but were less radical than they thought themselves to be.

The Empire

King George V's Christmas radio broadcasts, begun in 1932, were relayed to all parts of the empire and demonstrated that the personal bond felt by white Australians, Canadians, New Zealanders, and South Africans for the mother country was still strong. In economic terms the empire became more important to Britain after World War I than it had been before. In the 1920s over a third of British exports went to the colonies and dominions, and by 1934 nearly half, much higher than before 1914.[41] The dominion governments won full recognition of their sovereignty in the Statute of Westminster in 1931. The monarch continued to be the connecting link to the homeland, and the establishment of the Commonwealth in 1926 laid the groundwork for a transition from empire. The royal visit to Canada in June 1939 was a huge event. Well over a million people came to see the king and queen in Montreal alone, more than had stood outside Buckingham Place on coronation night.[42]

The war stimulated a wave of nationalist feeling across the globe, which began to endanger the moral and practical underpinnings of imperialism. Critics such as Orwell began to land solid blows on British self-regard as a colonial power. His famous essays about shooting an elephant and a hanging, based on his experience as a policeman in Burma, opened up new routes to undermine the confidence of British rulers. He was particularly effective in turning the ideals evoked to encourage the Allies to win the war against the hypocrisy of continued oppression. He also made people think about the ways that imperialism might be endangering liberal values at home. You can only hold a subject people under your power, he noted, "by methods which make a nonsense of any claim for the superiority of western civilization." "When the white man turns tyrant it is his own freedom that he destroys."[43]

Labour and Conservative leaders sought to retain India's loyalty by making politi-cal concessions, most notably embodied in the Government of India Act of 1919. Mohandas K. Gandhi (1869–1948) now headed the independence movement. He embraced a non-violent approach, which almost always led to violence (by the police) and his incarceration in jail. The British aim was to create a "diarchy" (joint rule) with some power delegated to native-dominated legislative councils, although the princes and governors retained considerable authority. A plan for dominion status was laid out. The massacre of 379 people in Amritsar in 1919 (an additional 1,000 or so were injured) on the orders of General R. E. H. Dyer, which many British politicians considered to have been justified by the chaotic circumstances that provoked it, was nonetheless condemned by the government, who recalled and punished Dyer. The 1935 Government of India Act made further concessions. The nationalists were unappeased. The Labour Party became increasingly anti-imperialist.

The Warfare State

Mention has been made earlier of a tendency to see Britain in "decline" from the mid-nineteenth century onward. "Declinism" has been particularly influential as an explanatory tool in the period 1920 to 1970, but a new and powerful assault on this paradigm has been launched by David Edgerton, whose work on the twentieth-century "warfare state" is of similar importance to John Brewer's on the eighteenth-century fiscal-military state.

Edgerton's analysis shows that Britain's strength at sea, in the air, and later with nuclear weapons was far greater than "declinists" allow. The UK was a potent, imperialist, and technologically advanced state. It was no accident that it won both world wars. Victory would not have been possible without the American alliance, but until the mid-1940s Britain was a powerful global empire, and even in 1945 it ranked third in the world after the USA and USSR in military technology, research, and firepower.[44]

A closer and closer relationship between the government, industry, and scientists developed in the years after 1918: the state created a new research-oriented science integrated with the armed forces. In the 1920s Britain had the highest warlike expenditure in the world in absolute terms, and this stood even higher if one included the defense budgets of Canada, Australia, and South Africa. Its relative position slipped vis-à-vis Germany in the early 1930s, but this was due to Hitler's increased spending rather than British cuts. Between 1922 and 1940 Britain launched eight aircraft carriers to the USA's seven and Germany's one (never completed). Japan matched British carriers in total numbers by 1940, but once the war began it lacked the economic strength to keep up with replacing ships lost in battle. The British kept building (Figure 9.1). In terms of overall tonnage of warships launched between 1928 and 1941, the Royal Navy achieved one million tons, the USA 700,000, and Japan 600,000. In 1940 Britain had the greatest aircraft production of any power.[45]

Funded by the Air Ministry in the mid-1930s, Robert Watson-Watt, a Scottish descendant of the James Watt of steam power, developed a radio method of locating aircraft that became the first ground-based radar system. Later, Taffy Bowen, a Welsh physicist, developed radar that could be installed in fighter cockpits. Frank Whittle began to experiment with jet engines as early as 1930. Among European powers Britain stood alone in its capacity to develop and produce critical systems such as

Figure 9.1   HMS *Ark Royal*, 1939

immensely complicated aircraft carriers with their integration of naval architecture, specialized aircraft, weapons, pilot training, and escort vessels. The **RAF** defeated the German air force in part because of a high-powered engine developed by R. J. Mitchell, fitted most famously into "Spitfires," that made the British planes faster and more maneuverable than the equivalent enemy aircraft.

Appeasement

During the 1930s the British government was obliged increasingly to address the problem of its relations with aggressive and expansionist states. Japan's takeover of Manchuria (1931) and then China, Italy's invasion of Ethiopia (1935), and Germany's determination to reverse the diktat of Versailles once Hitler attained power (1933) threatened British interests and world peace. The specter of large-scale atrocities and the spread of totalitarian government made a world already blighted by the economic depression seem darker. The League of Nations proved incapable of imposing effective sanctions and the great powers, including Britain, did little to stand up to aggressors. Baldwin and Chamberlain have long been criticized for formulating a policy called "appeasement" in response to the challenge of the dictators. Yet, when looked at from the UK's perspective, it was not an unreasonable position to take.

The British people were horrified by the prospect of another war. For a time anyone who suggested that the country prepare for such a conflict and use force to restrain Hitler and Mussolini was accused of warmongering. The Labour Party opposed the idea of war. Nor did many people of any political persuasion grasp the depravity of the Nazi regime. Chamberlain (and the Labour leaders) was committed to building a better Britain. He wanted extra money for hospitals and schools, and was jealous of defense spending. Among the political elite Hitler was considered a vulgar upstart, but, as the leader of a great state, they assumed he would be governed by the constraints of convention.

Many people felt the Versailles treaty had been too harsh on Germany. The United States had withdrawn into isolationism, while France fell into a defensive crouch that left it little power to deliver an offensive punch. Many Conservatives saw Hitler as a barrier standing between the West and communist Russia. Even mad dogs have their uses as guardians, and maybe a war between the totalitarian states would so weaken them that further danger would be eliminated. Finally, as victors in World War I, Britons lacked an understanding of the depths of anger and openness to radical ideas among those who had suffered defeat.

Revisionists such as John Charmley and Maurice Cowling suggest that Britain could have found a means to negotiate a peaceful settlement with Germany and thus avoid the loss of power and stature the UK suffered after the war. Churchill is singled out for blame for urging resistance to Hitler.[46] In fact, the former wrote to his wife as early as 1935: "If the Great War were resumed … it will be the end of the world."[47] He understood that in all probability the empire would be lost, and yet he believed that honor and basic human decency demanded that the sacrifice be made. Churchill thought the German leader was an amoral tyrant with ambitions of global conquest. Even if a temporary peace had been concluded, no genuine independence could have been possible and, in the long term, only slavery or collaboration in monstrous crimes. Hitler was bent on developing nuclear weapons, which, had there been a delay in challenging his hegemony over Europe, could have led to holocausts of unimaginable magnitude.

Britain let the 1936 remilitarization of the Rhineland pass. It feebly protested against the absorption of Austria in March 1938. Britons remained bystanders as German bombers demolished Spanish cities. Chamberlain became seriously concerned when Hitler threatened to go to war if the German-speaking borderlands (Sudetenland) with Czechoslovakia were not granted self-determination. The prime minister flew to Germany to meet the dictator several times in a series of conferences in which France and Italy (but not the Czechs) were also involved. At a meeting in Munich on September 29, 1938, Hitler achieved his aim of bringing down Czechoslovakia without going to war with France and Britain. His promises not to absorb the entire state were soon disregarded. Though Chamberlain flew home proclaiming peace with honor, as Churchill warned: "We are in the presence of a disaster of the first magnitude."[48] The mass of British people heaved a sigh of relief and the king (who was an appeaser) made the most ill-judged decision of his reign by appearing on the balcony of Buckingham Palace with the prime minister beside him.

Figure 9.2   Number 10 Downing Street has been the official residence of British prime ministers since the eighteenth century. Chamberlain leaves No. 10 after making a broadcast declaring war on Germany. With him was an aide who later became the fourteenth earl of Home, prime minister in his own right in 1963

The government did, however, begin to ramp up military preparedness at a new radical pace. On February 22, 1939 the Cabinet made the unprecedented decision to authorize aircraft production "to the limit," that is, as many as could be produced without regard to cost.[49] The foreign secretary, Lord Halifax, who had been a key figure in managing appeasement, now began to shift gears. Hitler contemptuously brushed aside the Munich agreement, and it became impossible for anyone but the desperate and the blind not to see what had happened. After the Germans began to press Poland for territorial concessions, the prime minister declared Britain would go to war if Hitler invaded.

In the summer of 1939 Britain and France sent diplomats to Moscow to investigate a possible alliance with the Soviets to contain German aggression. In fact it was Hitler who pulled off a coup by signing a pact with the Communists. Stalin had no reason to trust the capitalists of the West. They could do little to help him in a war with Germany, and he may even have deluded himself into believing he was buying Russia a long-term delay in the final reckoning with Hitler while gaining control over half of Poland and the Baltic states, which a secret provision in the treaty promised him.

Early in September Hitler ordered the invasion of Poland. Two days later Chamberlain told the British people, the majority of whom supported the decision, that war had been declared (Figure 9.2). France (which had acted in concert) and Britain then faced a military prospect of immense difficulty. Poland was being raped and dismembered by both Germany and Russia. The only way to help was to invade Germany, a strategy for which the Allies were unprepared. The British dominions immediately offered their support, but no other friends appeared. Ireland remained neutral.

As in 1914, no invitation went out to the opposition party to help manage the war. A purely Conservative government took up the task in 1939. A small War Cabinet was formed that included Halifax and Winston Churchill, who was called back to office as first lord of the admiralty after years in the political wilderness due to his disagreements with Baldwin and Chamberlain over making concessions to India and appeasement. Until April 1940 relatively little happened on the Western side of Europe while Poland, the Baltic states, and Finland fought for their survival. The period was called the "Phony War." Hitler "had "missed the bus," according to Chamberlain. Then all hell broke loose.

Chapter 10

The Warfare and Welfare
State, 1940–79

The years between 1940 and 1979 represent some of the most dramatic peaks and valleys in British history. It is hard to exaggerate the danger the nation faced in the late summer and early fall of 1940. Therefore no moment was more glorious than **VE Day** in 1945. The Labour administration of the late 1940s implemented reforms more important than any since those of the Whigs of the 1830s. Britain was still a global power in 1939; by 1970 the empire had disappeared. The 1970s were the most tortuous peacetime years of the modern era. At no moment were the peoples of Scotland, Wales, England, and Northern Ireland more united than in 1945, yet in 1979 Ulster was in the midst of a civil war, while demands for home rule and even independence were growing in Scotland, and Welshmen bent on separate recognition of their culture employed hunger strikes and bombs to threaten the London government.

The Battle of Britain

Defense spending rose from £254 million in 1938 to over £3 billion in 1940. Total government expenditure went from 16 percent of GDP in 1938 to 62 percent in 1944. The German onslaught, when it came, was a series of hammer blows. Norway was occupied in April 1940. In early May Hitler invaded the Netherlands and Belgium. The seizure of the latter gave the Germans a means to outflank French defensive positions and placed the small British army directly in the path of the oncoming blitzkrieg, a deluge of tanks and planes that swept all before it. The French army surrendered quickly while the British were routed and retreated to the Channel coast.

The catastrophe was so extreme, rapid, and unexpected that all normal conduct and conditions were cast aside. A group of Conservatives led by the fourth marquess of Salisbury applied pressure on Chamberlain to resign.[1] The prime minister tried to reach out to the opposition, but the Labour Party refused to serve under him. Many people wanted Lord Halifax to take over. He was less tainted by appeasement than Chamberlain, but he still hankered after negotiations with the enemy. Had he been willing to serve (his peerage could have been abolished and a seat found for him in the Commons), the king, who was a close friend and admirer, would have appointed him. Halifax understood, however, that he was not qualified for war leadership and that Churchill was the man of the hour. Like many others, George VI considered Churchill a wild man (and almost an enemy, as an impetuous defender of Edward VIII in 1936), but he had no option but to offer him the premiership. A final hurdle was overcome when Churchill outmaneuvered Halifax within the Cabinet on the issue of pursuing negotiations.[2] The war was to be fought to the finish. Churchill understood and persuaded both the political elite and the British people to accept that the only possible course was to pursue victory as the sole surviving custodians of freedom and democracy in Europe. This was a remarkable moment, because it was impossible to see how the enemy could be defeated.

The army huddled on the beaches in northern France in total disarray, and a hostile invasion seemed likely.

Winston Churchill was 65 in May 1940. Had he died a year earlier his career would have been considered remarkable but a failure. He had written some interesting books, but his role in the Gallipoli disaster was held against him. His judgment about the gold standard had been a mistake. He was distrusted by many politicians because he had switched parties, twice. His policy on India was considered reactionary. Many felt he was a warmonger. He was an aristocrat of the old school, who inherited a landed estate in Ireland. He had little faith in egalitarian democracy, believed white people were superior to blacks, and would have preferred a nation ruled by a Whiggish aristocracy subject to public scrutiny. He loved luxury. He drank too much. He was a romantic eccentric. But Churchill was too large a man to pigeonhole. He was a brave soldier, a daring adventurer, a talented painter, an impulsive rebel, a master of oratory, an implacable enemy, and a creative genius from whom ideas and strategies flowed with the force of water from a fire hose. He had a large heart, great though badly informed sympathy for the poor, and a passionate, almost maniacal hatred of tyranny. He dressed in an outmoded frock coat and top hat on formal occasions, but also he adopted a famous zipper-fronted overall without necktie that was brashly modern. Most British people, including the leaders of the Labour Party, disliked his politics but understood clearly that he was a warrior who offered their best chance for survival.

Churchill's speeches in 1940, broadcast while he chomped on an outsized cigar, are among the most famous in the English language. They were old-fashioned and elevated to an almost fantastic degree, literally Shakespearean. Even in the darkest days of World War I they would have seemed overblown, but in the months of May through September 1940 they were attuned to the magnitude of events and touched the deepest chords of feeling in the English-speaking world.[3]

The army gathered on the beaches at Dunkirk was able to evacuate due to an error made by Hitler. The men came home, but their artillery, tanks, and transport lay abandoned in northern France. If the Germans had invaded immediately, the British would have had soldiers armed only with rifles and some hand grenades to offer resistance. Had Hitler's forces gained a beachhead it is likely that they would have swept all before them. Urgent discussions began about relocating the royal family and where to send the fleet if the home island fell. Gold reserves were sent abroad for safekeeping. People who were likely to be placed in concentration camps persuaded their doctors to give them poison to commit suicide. The church bells were silenced so that their ringing could be used to signal the beginning of the invasion. In mid-September the imminence of the attack seemed so serious that Churchill obsessively telephoned the Admiralty to check on weather conditions in the Channel. All Hitler needed was mastery over 20 miles of open water while his invasion force was at sea (Map 10.1).

The struggle in the skies above southern England and over the Channel in the summer and early fall of 1940 was epic and decisive. The British commander, Hugh Dowding, was exceptionally able and cool-headed. Radar, aircraft powered by Merlin

Map 10.1   Europe and North Africa in World War II, 1939–1945

engines, and a sufficient number of trained pilots integrated into a single operating system gained a defensive ascendancy. Heavy German bombing (the Blitz) conducted against London failed to destroy the city. Churchill called this moment "the Battle of Britain" (Figure 10.1). "Upon this battle," he told the people,

> depends the survival of Christian civilization. Upon it depends our own British life, and the long continuity of our institutions and our Empire. The whole fury and might of the enemy must very soon be turned on us. Hitler knows that he will have to break us in this island or lose the war. If we can stand up to him, all Europe may be free and the life of the world may move forward into broad, sunlit uplands. But if we fail, then the whole world, including the United States, including all that we have known and cared for, will sink into the abyss of a new Dark Age made more sinister, and perhaps more protracted, by the lights of a perverted science. Let us therefore brace ourselves to our duties, and so bear ourselves that, if the British Empire and its Commonwealth last for a thousand years, men will still say, "This was their finest hour."[4]

Figure 10.1   "Winston Churchill at War," by Sam Wells, *The Herald*, Melbourne, Australia 1941

The nation rallied. An American living near London reported a dramatic shift in both spirit and action in September 1940: "From all the grumbling and inefficiency that went on at the beginning of the war, the change over to grim determination is incredible."[5] Of course, panic, defeatism, strikes, looting, black marketeering, and other human failings tend to be erased by dewy-eyed accounts of heroic defiance against Hitler. In fact, for some, national unity "was provisional, conditional, and potentially fragile."[6] In places and at certain times disaffection and cynicism met the prime minister's broadcasts and royal visits to bombed sites. When Churchill announced to a crowd on a visit to south London that, "We can take it," a voice shouted back, "What do you mean 'we', you fat bastard!"[7] There is ample evidence, however, to show that strikes rarely disrupted production for long, and that people accepted their subjection to bombing with far more calmness than prewar estimates anticipated. In the summer and fall of 1940 something like a surge of national adrenaline occurred.

German submarines played havoc with merchant shipping, and Britain was brought close to starvation. Increased agricultural production helped. As in World War I, the British succeeded in keeping imports flowing despite U-boat action and distributed the food efficiently and fairly. President Roosevelt loaned destroyers and sent American planes and warships into the Atlantic to help protect convoys. He also persuaded a still isolationist Congress, where many grumbled about unpaid loans from the last war, to institute a "Lend-Lease" program to provide war material on a massive scale.[8] Although this plan made a significant contribution to victory, Britain continued to pay cash for much of what crossed the Atlantic and was stripped of virtually all its financial holdings in America to meet the bills. Canada supplied proportionately more to Britain than the USA. The UK ceased to be an exporting country. "We threw good housekeeping to the winds," Keynes remarked. "But we saved ourselves, and helped save the world."[9]

Hitler was convinced that air superiority was vital to launch an invasion, and when he was unable to achieve it, he turned on Russia instead. Leaving Britain undefeated to his rear, however, repeated the error made by Napoleon in 1812. Churchill, a lifelong anti-communist, had long understood that though Stalin was a human monster little different in kind than Hitler, a two-front war offered Britain a chance not just of survival but of victory. As he famously said: "If Hitler invaded Hell [I] would at least make a favourable reference to the Devil."[10] Then, on December 7, 1941, Japan attacked Pearl Harbor and British installations in the Far East. The Americans were now allies in the Pacific, and a few days later Hitler declared war on the United States. At that moment Churchill knew Britain would win. The arsenal of democracy could now spew out an endless supply of weaponry and ship enough soldiers to Europe to bring down the Nazi regime. In November 1942 the battle of Stalingrad halted Hitler's advance in Russia and blocked his access to vital oil supplies, while at the same time Sir Bernard Montgomery defeated General Rommel in North Africa, for the first time decisively defeating a German army on the battlefield.

A Strategy for Victory

Churchill raced to Washington within days of Pearl Harbor. He and Roosevelt agreed, despite the Japanese attack, that Germany was the most dangerous enemy. The decision to fight first to victory in Europe and pursue a holding action in the Pacific was the single most important Allied decision of the war. Making the North Atlantic comparatively safe for convoys was achieved by 1943, which allowed North American supplies and troops to flow uninterruptedly to Britain.

In the first years of the war the partnership between Roosevelt and Churchill was fruitful. Later a triumvirate was formed when they began meeting with Stalin. Churchill came to be treated as a junior partner both because British economic strength was ebbing and because the Russian and American leaders knew that by the end of the war only their countries would be superpowers.

D-Day finally came on June 6, 1944. The American Dwight Eisenhower was placed in overall command, but even as late as this in the war British and

Canadian troops outnumbered US forces on the beaches in Normandy (83,000 to 73,000) and the RAF and Royal Navy provided the majority of the air and marine support. By August 25 Paris was liberated, and the massive Allied armies swung north toward the German frontier. By then the USA provided a majority of the air and land forces engaged in the final battle. The Rhine was crossed in March 1945. The German Eastern Front collapsed as millions of Soviet troops flowed toward Berlin wreaking savage retribution. Hitler committed suicide, and Germany surrendered on May 8. British, American, and Commonwealth troops were in the process of transferring to the Pacific for the invasion of Japan when the atomic bombs at Hiroshima and Nagasaki brought that conflict to a close on September 2.

Why Britain Won

As in World War I, the German leadership contributed greatly to their own demise through strategic and tactical blunders. In 1938 the UK was still ahead of Germany in per capita levels of industrialization. Industrial productivity achieved extraordinarily high levels during the war. In 1940 the total value of British armaments production grew quickly, exceeding that of Germany in 1941. The Germans caught up in 1942, but even in 1943 Britain was spending $11.1 billion on arms production compared to Germany's $13.8 billion and Russia's $13.9 billion, a remarkable performance considering the island's smaller population. Britain produced over 15,000 aircraft in 1940 compared to Germany's 10,200 and the USA's 12,800. Once the US war machine was in full operation its industrial capacity outstripped every other state by a wide margin, but Britain kept ahead of Germany in producing planes through 1943. Only in its death throes of 1944, when they concentrated on making smaller and cheaper defensive fighters, did German output briefly exceed Britain's.[11]

Better than any of the major combatants Britain waged "total war" by managing its human, technological, and industrial resources in a comprehensive and efficient way. A command economy was established. Young women were drafted into war work, and the Women's Land Army replaced male labor in agriculture. Women moved into engineering and munitions production at levels never approached in Germany, which did not conscript females for war work. Four-fifths of the total addition to the labor force between 1939 and 1943 consisted of women who had not previously been employed. Nearly half a million women served in uniformed branches of the armed services.[12]

The empire provided Britain with soldiers, food, and weapons. London could call on the resources of territories covering a quarter of the globe with 500,000,000 inhabitants. Even India, where nationalist agitation against British rule had gone furthest and the time had passed when British military power could hold it easily against its will, remained loyal and helped win victory. Canada's navy was a key to success in the Battle of the Atlantic. While the Germans, Japanese, and Italians all suffered crippling shortages of vital materials and fuel, Britain got what it needed from the colonies.

The aerial bombardment of Germany remains controversial. The debate is largely academic because no democratically elected leader could have failed to respond to German bombing of Britain in kind and stayed in office. The air campaign caused far less damage than the proportion of resources of men and material devoted to it appears to justify. It did not break the will of the German people. However, the bombing was a key element in sustaining civilian morale in Britain. It also forced the Germans to divert resources and planes to defend against it that could otherwise have been deployed in Russia and during the Allied invasion in 1944. It was also essential to convince Stalin that something was being done to weaken Germany after the United States and Britain failed to invade the Continent in 1942 and 1943. When the Soviet foreign minister was forced, along with his German colleague von Ribbentrop, to find safety in a Berlin bunker during an air raid in November 1940, Molotov countered the Nazi's assertion that Britain "was finished" with the question: "If that's so, then why are we in this shelter and whose bombs are those falling?"[13] The deeply troubling moral conundrum of mass bombing remains unresolved.

It is easy to exaggerate the effect of intelligence gathering on the outcome of the war, but no one contests the fact that the code breakers of Bletchley Park played a key role in preventing a British defeat. The military historian Michael Howard points out that "to write the history of the war without mentioning it was like writing *Hamlet* without the Ghost."[14] German military and diplomatic ciphers were penetrated thanks to some good luck and the work of the Cambridge academic Alan Turing (1912–54). At the age of 23 he developed the idea of a theoretical machine that solved the "decision problem," a major concern of mathematical logic. The "Turing machine" became the foundation of the theory of computerized computation. His work deciphering the German Enigma code led him to formulate a massive, if primitive, computer for checking millions of permutations. The British could route convoys around waiting U-boats and send destroyers to sink them. Other vital military intelligence was uncovered and exploited.

A number of British research projects were transferred to the United States after 1941, partly for security reasons and partly due to much greater availability of funds. Howard Florey's development of Alexander Fleming's discovery of penicillin (1928) was moved there for that reason. The lives of many Allied soldiers were saved by this new medical treatment. The most important weapon to be developed during the conflict could not have been constructed without the prewar work of Thomson and Rutherford at Cambridge, and the contributions of British scientists transferred to Los Alamos, New Mexico to work on the Manhattan Project that produced the atomic bomb in 1945.

The BBC was generally allowed to report matters as they really were rather than what the government desired them to say. The credibility of the overseas news service became an important weapon in winning the war. At home few newspapers were suppressed; even the communist one was only temporarily suspended. It was possible to criticize anything and everything from the rationing system to Churchill's continuance as prime minister.

<hr>

What Britain Lost and Gained

About 382,000 British military personnel and merchant seamen died, close to half the number that perished in 1914–18. More than 67,000 civilians died in the Blitz. A further 195,500 Australians, Canadians, New Zealanders, South Africans, and Indians were lost on active service on behalf of the empire.

The state of psychological exhaustion reached in 1945 by the civilian population seems to have been greater than at the end of World War I. In 1919 a quick resumption of ordinary life and an economic boom helped recovery. In the later 1940s rationing continued and harsh conditions sustained a sense of fatigue. The bitter winter of 1947 seemed an unending nightmare of food, fuel, and financial crises. Cyril Connolly, the distinguished editor of the literary magazine *Horizon*, appealed to American readers: "If you have liked anything in it this year, send the author a food parcel: orange juice, tomato juice, butter, bacon, rice, tea, honey and tinned meats are all particularly acceptable … They take two months to arrive, so begin now."[15]

During the war as many as four million houses, almost a third of all those that existed, were damaged by bombing along with many schools, factories, and other buildings. Large numbers of merchant ships were sunk. High taxes further eroded people's sense of recovery. People's clothes looked shabby and bombed cities were ugly. World War II cost twice as much as World War I. More than a quarter of the nation's wealth was wiped out, and a huge debt and balance of payments deficit accrued. By contrast the American economy gained 50 percent in real terms. Like an organism starved of nutrients that begins to consume itself, Britain used up its financial resources to survive the last years of the war. Nothing was left to pay for imports.[16] Two-thirds of the prewar export trade disappeared, although recovery began once funds from the American Marshall Plan (1947) recreated a European market ready to consume British goods.

It is easy, however, to exaggerate the impact of the war on the British economy. In the end Britain only had to pay the United States $650 million of the $27 billion it borrowed. In 1950 Britain's GNP was the third largest in the world after the USA and USSR, and its per capita GNP was well ahead of all other countries except the USA. Russia's was only $699 to Britain's $1,393. Mass unemployment did not return. Growth accelerated. In 1945 the pound remained the second most important currency in the world after the dollar, involving close to half the world's trade. As the leader of its own monetary system on a global scale Britain retained enormous economic importance even when its financial problems caused periodic crises. Commonwealth nations in particular sought access to the London capital market. This remained true until the devaluation of 1967, when the eurodollar (dollars outside the American economy used as a major currency for international trade) replaced it. London became the principal center for trading eurodollars.

The economic recovery after the war was achieved at the cost of postponing an attempt to solve many long-term structural problems. Unhealthy dependency on traditional industries such as steel continued. Over time economic competitors would pull ahead when they experienced more dynamic growth in newer industries. Britain's share of world trade dropped from 25 percent in 1950 to 5 percent by 2000.

War goals masked differences in understandings of what was being defended and expectations for the future, largely based on political ideology. The coalition leadership included a number of notable Labour Party politicians committed to more fairness in the workplace and society, though gender and class inequalities continued. Britain gradually became a more egalitarian society after 1945 despite a continued obsession with class. Full employment, longer hours, and bonus payments meant that by 1945 real earnings were about 20 percent greater than they had been in 1938. Combined with full employment after 1945 World War II continued a process by which average real incomes rose substantially. In addition a reduction in family size produced a further gain in income per head in each household. The gap between working-class and professional incomes began to close during the war and this trend continued into the 1950s.

Even though the tax system had been taking an ever larger portion of rich people's incomes since the days of World War I and could have engendered a move to greater equality during the 1920s and 1930s, that did not happen. Gifts before death, trusts, and legal settlements allowed the avoidance of duty. The wealth of the top 1 percent was spread over only a slightly broader range. After World War II the Labour government pursued a deliberate policy of creating greater economic equality. Taxation reached unknown levels and would become virtually confiscatory for the rich: the top rate reached 97.5 percent in 1951. The pyramid of wealth became flatter. One estimate is that the pre-tax income of the top 100,000 fell by 64 percent between 1938 and 1949 while the top half fell by 37 percent.[17]

The proportion of women in the higher professions was no greater in 1950 than it was in 1914. The number of women who worked on a more or less equal basis with men in 1951 was lower than in 1918, which was largely due to the decline of the textile industry. At a time when women's formal political and social rights were more firmly established than ever, opportunities to join the skilled workforce deteriorated. Since equality in the workplace was tied to comparative equality at home, this was a double setback. Unlike after World War I, however, many women were able to hold on to their wartime jobs because of the continued vigor of the economy and the government's commitment to full employment.[18]

The aristocracy no longer controlled the state or functioned as a collective unit, while a larger portion of the working class voted Labour than ever before. The elite leadership's wartime emphasis on the equality of sacrifice could not be easily reversed after 1945. It was not just that the workers were more assertive, but also that the elite and middle class were more willing than before to acknowledge a new distribution of social status. On the other hand, workers were willing to live with commercial capitalism.

The Welfare State

The coalition broke up after the defeat of Germany, and an election (the first since 1936) was called for July 1945. Labour won a landslide, 393 MPs to 213 for the Tories. This was not a personal rejection of Churchill's leadership. He remained immensely popular and respected as a war leader, but he was not in synch with his countrymen's aspirations in peacetime.

Clement Attlee became prime minister. Churchill once called him a modest man who had much to be modest about. Orwell was reminded of "a recently dead fish, before it has time to stiffen."[19] Unlike MacDonald, he came from an upper-middle-class background. He had served as an officer during World War I and practiced as a barrister. He loved cricket, was a regular (Anglican) churchgoer, and loyal monarchist. That said, he was an ardent socialist and an exceptionally able administrator. Labour was committed to the idea of equality, which they did not see as a threat to freedom but the antidote to unrestrained capitalism that had produced fascism and communism. In his low-key way Attlee managed to get an immense amount accomplished in a very short period. Few other British leaders have changed the structure of government so dramatically or profoundly. His prosaic demeanor, probity, goodwill, and ability to harness Labour prima donnas from the left and right wings of the party into a single, effective unit was remarkable. Attlee rivaled Lord Grey as the most successful peacetime prime minister.

Attlee's ablest assistants were Ernest Bevin, who became Britain's first working-class foreign secretary, popular even among Tories, and Aneurin Bevan (1897–1960), the father of the National Health Service. Bevin was the most important union leader to become a successful politician. He rose from poverty to become a key figure in organizing the resources of the state to win World War II. His profound devotion to freedom and democracy shaped Britain's conduct in the Cold War. Aneurin Bevan's attitudes had been shaped by the suffering caused by unemployment in Wales during the 1920s and 1930s. His personal tragedy was that, with all his gifts, a quirky and impassioned personality never allowed him to build a successful bridge of trust with voters of moderate opinions. Had he been able to do so, Labour might have achieved more in the 1950s and 1960s.

The War Cabinet had commissioned a number of studies to lay the groundwork for postwar Britain. The most famous of these was the one written by Sir William Beveridge (a Liberal not a Labourite, 1879–1963) on social insurance.

The Beveridge Report advocated the restructuring of the whole welfare system and became a blueprint for a new society. Unemployment, health, and workmen's compensation insurance would be made universal. Maternity and death benefits were to be added. Indeed, it became a plan for a new Britain and was instantly popular.

Important social legislation was launched before the war ended. The Education Act of 1944 expanded funding but also further entrenched the "eleven plus" system, considered even by many Labour politicians to be a fair and efficient means of educating children. A Family Allowances Act of 1945 meant financial support to children was paid directly to mothers rather than fathers.

It is generally conceded that the greatest achievement of Labour after 1945 was the establishment of a National Health Service (NHS). Hospitals were transferred to state ownership and management. Health treatments were provided free of charge to all. A private option, however, was allowed to remain (the biggest difference that emerged over time was that NHS patients had to join lengthy waiting lists for operations). Free dental care, glasses, and drugs were also provided. The NHS was a huge step forward in creating a fairer and more humane society. Its weaknesses were the result of successive governments' inability to fund it adequately and inefficiencies that grew out of bureaucratic management.

Housing was addressed, but planners were blind to the social needs of communities. As in the United States, new public-housing tower blocks were unloved, uncared for, became infested by crime, and had eventually to be blown up and rebuilt at vast expense because their inhabitants hated them (Figure 10.2). Developments were built on the outskirts of towns, like those created in the interwar years, without amenities and adequate transportation to serve them. Old buildings were torn down that could have been renovated because "old" was associated with poverty, and local councilors could not grasp either the aesthetic or human costs of their noble frenzy to build "new."

Legal advice was made more available to the poor. Anomalies in the electoral system were rectified, and the ability of the House of Lords to delay legislation was weakened. Many Labour peerages were created in order to build a more equal balance of parties in the upper chamber. At the same time men such as Attlee and Bevin resisted calls for radical constitutional changes and uprooting of established institutions. They continued the British political tradition of maintaining continuity whenever possible. In return, after the Tories regained office, little was done to dismantle Labour reforms.

An important element in the Labour program was taking into public ownership (with compensation for shareholders) key industries (**nationalization**). The Bank of England went first on January 1, 1946, the coal industry in 1947. Many mines belonged to small owners who did not have the capital to modernize them, and there had been talk of nationalizing these pits even in the Tory camp. In 1946 civil aviation was taken over and reorganized. The electricity and gas industries, railways, canals, buses, and trucking followed. Labour left finance and commerce alone. The biggest

Figure 10.2   "High-rise public housing, 1960s."

resistance came to nationalizing the steel industry in 1949, and it was privatized again in 1953 after performing poorly under government control.

Productivity rose dramatically in the years after the war. The trouble was that Britain continued to import more than it exported. Keynes was sent to Washington to negotiate a vast loan, supplemented by a good deal more from Canada. The United States insisted on making the pound freely convertible with the dollar. Being dictated to was humiliating and yet no alternative existed to ongoing dependency on subventions from the Americans until Britain could get back on its feet. The hard winter of 1947 led to lengthy power cuts every day. Rationing did not end until 1954.

Sustained economic growth emerged, however, and continued until the 1970s, which created a kind of golden age that in retrospect was a much better time for people than might have been expected, looking at the exhausted and wrecked carcass of the kingdom in 1945. In a celebrated novel about working-class life written in the 1950s, a young factory operative described the change:

> The old man was happy at last, anyway, and he deserved to be happy, after all the years before the war on the dole, five kids, and the big miserying that went with no money and no way of getting any. And now he had a sit-down job at the factory, all the Woodbines he could smoke, money for a pint if he wanted one …, a holiday somewhere, … and a television set to look into at home. The difference between before the war and after the war didn't bear thinking about. War was a marvelous thing in some ways, when you thought about how happy it had made so many people in England.[20]

The wealthy sported new fashions and began to vacation in the Caribbean. Working-class youths, known as Teddy boys, took their name from an almost Edwardian style of fancy dress. For the first time they had some money for themselves. The advent of discretionary consumer spending among the masses was at hand.

The Cold War

Memories of unemployment, mass casualties, aerial bombing, and the threat of invasion faded. The coronation of Elizabeth II (b. 1926) in 1953 was a cathartic moment. The new reign marked for most people the final end of the deprivations of World War II and a full return to prewar civic life. It was also an assertion of British values and national identity in the face of totalitarianism past and present. Half the people in Britain watched the ceremony live on television, and most of the rest listened on radio. Ben Pimlott argues that the coronation "helped to define, not just royalty, but the British identity for the next generation."[21] Edmund Hilary and Tenzing Norgay conquered Mt. Everest. Benjamin Britten composed the opera *Gloriana* for the occasion. Roger Bannister broke the four-minute mile soon afterward. Britain seemed on a roll.

An election in 1950 significantly reduced Labour's majority and the party was riven by feuding between moderates and the left. The Tories regained office after a second election in 1951. Churchill was again prime minister and took on much the same task as Melbourne had with the young Victoria in training the 25-year-old Elizabeth in her duties. An inadequate education had left her with little but a good character and excellent French. In many respects the change in government brought no major changes in policy. Conservative governments found it hard to cut taxes due to the expenditure requirements of the welfare state, which they did not take any major steps to reverse. Most politicians, even on the right, dreaded the return of mass unemployment. Throughout the 1950s and 1960s chancellors of the exchequer from both parties proposed programs that were broadly similar, prompting the sobriquet "Butskellism," which took its name from the Tory R. A. Butler and Labour's Hugh Gaitskell.

Churchill was 77. Sadly, he could not let go of power. He once said: "Sometimes I want to do good in the world; sometimes I don't seem to care about anything but my own career."[22] A frustrated colleague observed: "We must wait and wait and see which dies first, Winston or the Conservative party."[23] His great love had always been foreign policy, and he had convinced himself that only he could walk on the world stage as an equal with American and Soviet leaders. Relations with Russia had deteriorated toward the end of the war and in the first years of peace. The spread of communist regimes throughout central Europe appalled most British people. Poland, whose victimization had precipitated World War II, disappeared behind what Churchill labeled the "Iron Curtain." Weak or broken Germany, France, and Italy were all that stood between Stalin and the English Channel. Ernest Bevin, though not as eloquent as Churchill, was as dogged in his anti-communism and, with the help of George Orwell's novels *Animal Farm* (1945) and *1984* (1949), brought the Labour Party to see that the Soviet Union constituted a mortal threat to Western democracy. This time the United States did not retreat into isolationism. When British resources could no longer sustain the battle against communism in the Greek civil war, President Truman took over the responsibility. The communist coup in Czechoslovakia in February 1948 prompted rapid moves among Western European states to form alliances, with Bevin playing a leading role. The North Atlantic Treaty Organization (NATO – 1949), a mutual defense pact, tightened the relationship between the free states in Western Europe and the USA.

Churchill liked to talk about a "special relationship" between Britain and the United States. His American parentage made this a central element in his world perspective. He requested that "the Battle Hymn of the Republic" be sung at his funeral. President Eisenhower, however, was lukewarm on the subject. Even if a special alliance was formed, could Britain be anything other than the USA's lapdog? The asymmetry in wealth and power was growing all the time. Americans joked about Britain becoming the forty-ninth state.

Attlee and Bevin made the decision that Britain should become the third nuclear power (achieved in 1952), after the Soviet Union, even though the enormous costs of the project ate into funds for further social spending. The fear that the United States might not defend Western Europe left London with little alternative other than to arrange for its own safety. Churchill hoped that the possession of an independent atomic force would give him leverage in American decision making. He decided to construct the much more powerful hydrogen bomb that was first tested in 1957. Britain and the USA finally agreed to share research and development on nuclear weapons in 1958. The Americans handed over the technological secrets needed to build nuclear submarines with ICBM (intercontinental ballistic missile) launching capability. The Polaris system was offered by President Kennedy in 1962. In 1980 Britain purchased American Trident missiles, which entailed the building of a new fleet of four giant nuclear submarines, the first of which went into service in 1994. These incredibly destructive weapons systems have remained the core of British national defense ever since. Britain developed its own fleet of nuclear attack submarines and worked with the USA to sustain its aircraft carrier force, which even in the early twenty-first century (the Labour government decided in 2007 to build two new ones) means that today only the USA and Britain can project large-scale airpower anywhere on the planet. The UK remained a leader in the design of aircraft engines, from propjets to the supersonic Concorde.

During the 1950s in Malaya Britain fought one of the few wars against a communist insurgency ever to be won by a Western power. The guerrillas were defeated by ruthless but effect counterinsurgency measures by the time Malaysia became independent in 1957. When Indonesia tried to assert claims in Borneo in December 1962 British and Commonwealth troops were deployed in jungle fighting until the invaders were repulsed. Britain supported American military operations in most parts of the world until the Vietnam War, which gave real meaning to the "special relationship." The unexpected costs associated with the Korean War in 1950–1, when Britain allied with the USA to fight what was perceived to be communist aggression, threw the finances of the Labour government out of order. Charges had to be introduced for some services in the NHS, which led to Bevan's resignation from the government and a bitter split between the left and moderate forces in the party.

Churchill suffered a stroke in June 1953. Although he recovered enough energy to make some public appearances, his performance in private seriously declined. He finally retired in 1955. The queen appointed Anthony Eden (1897–1977) on Churchill's recommendation without even consulting senior members of the Tory Party, many of who had doubts about his competence. Like Churchill, Eden was a member of the landed aristocracy, and his ancestors had been prominent in politics and the empire for centuries. He was experienced and had won respect for his objection to appeasement before the war. Eden subscribed to "Butskellism." He led the party to an easy victory over Labour in the 1955 election but soon afterward ran into a firestorm of criticism over his decision to invade Egypt.

The "Suez Crisis" of 1956, as it became known, was a profoundly polarizing event. Britain had removed its last troops from the region in June. Egypt was led by an Arab nationalist, Gamal Abdal Nasser, who seemed to be moving toward a Soviet alliance. In July he nationalized the Suez Canal, owned by a British–French company. Eden and the French leadership secretly concocted a scheme in which Israel was to invade the Sinai, giving them an excuse to send military units with which to keep the Jewish and Arab forces apart, and as if by "accident" take back the canal. This was the sort of thing Bismarck or Lord Salisbury might have done in the nineteenth century, but it did not work by the 1950s. The Anglo-French invasion force was brought to a halt by opposition from President Eisenhower. He wanted to contrast the non-aggressive, anti-imperialist stance of the West to the recent Soviet occupation of Hungary. He was also afraid Russia might intervene on behalf of Egypt and trigger a nuclear war. Eden was obliged to withdraw British forces in the most humiliating manner and lied to the House of Commons about knowing ahead of time about the Israeli invasion.[24] It was an embarrassing debacle at least in part due to Eden's incompetent diplomacy. He resigned. His health was undermined, but also he was damaged goods that the Tories needed to toss overboard. The crisis had galvanized the Labour Party and at least temporarily healed rifts. Large-scale public protests contributed to the formation of the Campaign for Nuclear Disarmament (CND), which organized popular opinion against defense policies for years to come.

Like the Reform Act of 1832 many observers have attributed significance to the Suez crisis far beyond what it can actually support. It has become an explanation for almost everything that went wrong in Britain for the next half-century. It was said that the country was operating as a great power but no longer had the will or capacity to do so. The greatest impact was probably psychological. Post-Suez, Michael Howard argues, the British sank for a time "into ironic self-flagellation."[25] Suez did not permanently break the alliance with the USA. Nor did it lead to an abrupt withdrawal from traditional military involvement in Asia and the Pacific. As late as 1965,

55 percent of the population still thought Britain should have a world role.[26] Until an economic crisis in 1967 led to drastic cutbacks in the defense budget, both Tory and Labour governments continued to project British power "East of Suez."

Macmillan and Wilson

Two candidates vied to succeed Eden: "Rab" Butler (1902–70) and Harold Macmillan (1894–1986), both formidable men. The Tory Party had yet to establish an electoral system to choose between rivals. That meant the queen had to make the selection. The last time a monarch made such a difficult choice was in 1923 between Baldwin and Curzon. Eden was not asked for, and did not give, advice on his successor. Several senior statesmen including the fifth marquess of Salisbury "took soundings" within the party and reported to the queen that Macmillan was the preferred candidate. She appointed him. Some decried the choice, but Butler was not necessarily the best man for the job. He had been a strong appeaser before the war, and his reforming urges in the domestic sphere had waned. Macmillan was a wealthy businessman who had served with distinction as a soldier in World War I and as a policy maker in World War II. Like Churchill, he had an American mother. He married a daughter of the ninth duke of Devonshire and brought his nephew the eleventh duke into the government along with other aristocratic relations. The duke's brother had married John F. Kennedy's sister, so the prime minister of Great Britain and the president of the United States were relatives.

Macmillan turned out to be a successful leader and won the 1959 election with a large majority. However, economic problems began to loom. Unemployment rose in the late 1950s and early 1960s. At the same time, people were more affluent and home ownership increased. Macmillan's campaign slogan, "most of our people have never had it so good," was true.

In 1963 Macmillan met his political demise in the Profumo scandal, which mixed sex, Cold War espionage, and lies in equal amounts. The prime minister was not directly involved, but his handling of the affair seemed inept. His health wavered, and he decided to resign. This time no single candidate stood out among a list of at least five possible aspirants. Again, "soundings" were taken by Tory senior statesmen, and during a dramatic visit by the queen to his hospital room, Macmillan took it upon himself to make the almost unbelievable recommendation of the fourteenth earl of Home (pronounced Hume – 1903–95) as his successor. He headed one of the richest and most ancient of Scottish aristocratic families. Several leading Tories refused to serve under this astounding choice, but Sir Alec Douglas-Home, as the earl quickly became after renouncing his peerage and finding a seat in the Commons, managed to cobble together a Cabinet.[27] Like Macmillan, Home came from the ideologically moderate branch of the Tory Party and had lengthy experience in government. Prejudice against the hereditary system and his slightly dotty grin led some to underestimate his skills as a politician and party leader. Indeed, he came within an ace of winning re-election in 1964 when less than one percentage point separated the vote between Labour and the Conservatives.

The Labour Party was now led by Harold Wilson (1916–95) who squeaked into office with a four-seat majority in the Commons. Wilson came from a much humbler social background than his immediate predecessors in the Labour Party. He was, however, an Oxford-educated academic and more ambitious than ideological. Wilson called for "modernization," a flashy term that ignored the long-established relationship between industry and the state in promoting research and development. The American historian Arthur Schlesinger, Jr., who met him in 1962, summed matters up: "He conveys no sense of principle whatever but a considerable sense of competence and intelligence."[28] Wilson formed a closer and more supportive relationship with the queen than any prime minister in the second half of the twentieth century.

Another election was called in 1966 in an attempt to gain a more secure government majority in the Commons. Labour did well, partly because the economy seemed on an upswing and perhaps in part because the new leader of the Tory Party, Edward Heath (1916–2005), was not popular with the electorate. He was the first Conservative to be selected by his fellow MPs by ballot, which finally removed the monarch and Tory aristocrats from the process of choosing party leaders. Under Wilson, income and other taxes rose higher. Interest rates soared, and the pound had to be devalued. Strikes proliferated. The American alliance became progressively more uneasy during the Vietnam War. Wilson, like his predecessor, lacked the political capital to break out of the existing assumptions about social welfare and full employment that began to drag the economy downward.

Labour did implement important reforms in education. After the war only 10 percent of working-class children went to **grammar school**. In the 1950s a small number of local authorities began to champion non-selective "comprehensive" schooling, which merged all secondary students into one institution. In the 1960s and the 1970s the Labour Party began actively to give a lead in this direction, both in England and Scotland. By 1979 80 percent of secondary school pupils were in some sort of comprehensive education. In areas where actively involved middle-class families existed in large numbers good schools developed, while in inner-city locations and places dominated by the poor, high schools were inadequate. Within many comprehensives, the divide between the able and the slow of the old grammar school system was preserved by tracking.

Access to full-time higher education had also long been restricted by class and gender, although many adults enrolled in evening and part-time programs. Thanks to a rapid expansion, 10 times the number of university places were made available between 1955 and 2000. Unlike on the Continent, most of the new and expanded institutions were residential in character. These were more expensive to build and maintain but provided a fuller and higher-quality college experience. Government funding rose from covering a third to more than four-fifths of the expense. The price of this reliance on the state, however, cost universities a degree of independence and submission to the dictates of transient governments. In recent decades the danger of this position, prompted by stagnant salaries, budget cuts, and irresponsible grandstanding by politicians, has led to a turn toward private fundraising.

Chronic Crises

The 1970s were a terrible time in Britain and other Western countries. People were not hit by bombs as they had been during the war, nor did they suffer decades of unemployment as they had in the 1930s. Yet it was a deeply disturbing period. Inflation began to worsen, a result largely of a steep rise in global oil prices, which spiked frighteningly during the Arab–Israeli war of 1973, and the more general rise in import prices after the pound was floated downward in 1972. The average rate of inflation in the 1970s in Britain was 13 percent, reaching a peak of 24 percent in 1975. It only began to fall after 1980. Militant trade unionists, timid government leadership, and poor business management culminated in chronic crises. Workers became disgruntled as the advances they had made in the 1950s and 1960s seemed to be slipping away due to the rise in taxes, imposition of pay restraints, and infla-tion. Membership of unions rose to a peak of 55 percent of the workforce in the 1970s, markedly higher than in the USA, Germany, and France. In 1977 Britain lost 10 million days to strikes while Germany lost only 160,000. The conventions that had governed British politics and the economy during the 1940s, 1950s, and 1960s broke down. By 1978 British per capita GNP had fallen behind that of Japan and France. West Germans were almost twice as prosperous as Britons. Only Italy and Spain among the large Western European powers still lagged behind the UK. Resentment between the rich and the poor had always been a facet of British life, but in the 1970s "the politics of envy" emerged.

To most people's surprise, Edward Heath led the Tory Party to a convincing vic-tory in the 1970 general election. He is perhaps the least attractive of all modern prime ministers. He lacked the courage to take bold measures to confront the grow-ing economic crisis. In response to massive strike actions Heath repeatedly resorted to invoking the Emergency Powers Act that allowed him to use the armed forces to carry out essential public tasks. At times the work week was reduced to three days and periodically electric power was shut down. Even the traffic lights did not func-tion. The infiltration of extremists into union leadership and among shop stewards led to concern that they were provoking an attempt to overthrow the system of gov-ernment. In Northern Ireland a sectarian civil war was being fought in the streets of Belfast and Londonderry (see Chapter 11).

Heath's ill-framed Industrial Relations Act, intended to curb union power, unleashed an unprecedented wave of unrest that culminated in the National Union of Mineworkers' refusal to accept the government's pay policy. In 1974 the prime minister had left himself no option but to call an election on the issue, "Who gov-erns Britain?" The Labour Party buried its internal differences and rallied to the call for a "social contract" with the unions and strict price controls. A "hung" parliament was elected in which no party achieved a majority.

Heath tried to form a coalition with the Liberals, who had garnered 19 percent of the vote. However, their price was enactment of proportional representation. Not only would that have greatly increased the number of Liberal MPs, but also, almost certainly, the two-party system that dominated British politics would have disappeared. Neither the Conservatives nor Labour were ready for that eventuality. Heath resigned and the queen sent for Harold Wilson, who was able to form a minority government that survived only with the votes of non-Labour MPs.

Wilson settled the immediate labor disputes, raised taxes, and tightened price controls. He promised to renegotiate Britain's terms of entry into the EEC (European Economic Community), the trade association of the Western European powers (see below). The three-day week disappeared and a sense that the crisis had passed prevailed. A second general election was held seven months after the first one in 1974, and Labour gained a majority of 42 in the Commons. Wilson managed to hold his now strife-torn party together for two years. He and the moderates favored continued membership in the EEC, but the left wing was opposed. He conducted an unprecedented national referendum on the issue in June 1975, in which nearly two-thirds of the people (64.5 percent) voted to stay in.

Inflation had not been tamed. Indeed, it had become a problem of global scope. Industrial production was lower in 1976 than 1973, and the balance of payments was severely out of alignment. Over a million workers were unemployed, a much higher number than any time since the war. The unions made further demands. The Labour Party moved more and more leftward. Marxist organizations previously forbidden for MPs to join became open to membership. The Militant Tendency, a Trotskyite group, gained support, and radicalized local constituency boards removed sitting MPs for being too moderate. It was said of one of the more radical Labour Cabinet members, Tony Benn, that he had served as a minister for 10 years "without being in any way corrupted by the slightest taint of realism."[29] The party lost credibility with many voters of all classes and became unelectable.

Wilson voluntarily decided to retire in March 1976. Candidates from across the political spectrum attempted to replace him. The moderates and right wing of the party still had enough strength among MPs to put James Callaghan (1912–2005) in power, but he only managed to defeat the most serious challenger from the left, Michael Foot (b. 1913), by a relatively small margin. Callaghan had an open and genial personality. He had grown up in Wales and sat for Cardiff for 42 years as MP, although he was not Welsh. He had never attended university and came from a poverty-stricken background. He was more conservative on social and economic issues than Wilson.

Like its predecessors, the Callaghan administration found no lasting solutions to the economic weakness of the country. The prime minister was able to bring down the inflation rate and helped persuade the unions to moderate their demands. His reputation was damaged, however, by the severe economic crisis of 1976 that forced Britain into the deeply humiliating adoption of spending restraints as a price paid for a substantial rescue package from the International Monetary Fund. In 1978 the

TUC rejected a 5 percent wage increase. A wave of strikes followed. October 1978 to March 1979 became known as the "winter of discontent." The country suffered extreme labor unrest in which even hospital workers went on strike and at one point the dead went unburied. More days were lost to strikes than even under Heath. Callaghan lost a vote of confidence 311 to 310 in the Commons. An election followed while Britain plunged into the worst recession since the 1930s.

The Good Life

Americans began to experience a much higher standard of living after the war than the British. The GI Bill moved the United States toward genuinely democratic university entrance two generations before the UK achieved a comparable level of higher education. American workers acquired automobiles long before their British counterparts. Indoor plumbing and heating were vastly superior on the Western side of the Atlantic. Even in comfortable middle-class British homes bizarre and dangerous gas-fueled "geysers" provided only small amounts of hot water to the one bathroom in houses that might have five or six bedrooms. Hot-water bottles placed between the sheets before retiring were a substitute for central heating. Showers were unheard of. The low standard of dentistry, even among the rich, could only partly be explained by addiction to heavily sugared tea. The affluent continued to put the costs of maintaining status through costly private school tuition, handmade clothing, and club memberships above comfort.

Ross McKibbin argues that up to 1950 British culture had two relatively cohesive forms, which were not integrated with each other. On the one side was the culture of the music hall and football, hobbies such as allotments and pigeon racing, and on the other side the pastimes of the middle class, such as bridge, golf, and symphony concerts. The arrival of movies and radio marked the beginning of a more integrated culture, but the major change did not come until the 1950s and above all the 1960s. Television and the growth of a distinct youth culture, cross-cutting lines of class and income, led to change. Affluence broke down rigidities within communities in industrial districts and the development of secondary education meant teenagers could more readily create their own independent identities.[30] A new "celebrity" culture among young people, epitomized by George Best (see Biography 10.1), emerged. Allotments declined but a passion for gardening became ubiquitous as more and more people owned their own houses.

"Rock 'n' roll" hit Britain soon after it emerged in the United States. Phonograph recordings, radio, film, and television began to spread mass culture between the two English-speaking countries very rapidly. It is testimony to the continued vitality of British society that native bands and music entrepreneurs quickly absorbed and then developed fresh and talented enhancements of what came from America. In the 1960s the Beatles and Rolling Stones emerged as giants in the music world. The UK rocked just as successfully as the USA. Although some people feared "Americanization,"

Biography 10.1

George Best
1946–2005

George Best was born in Belfast in Northern Ireland. He began working as an apprentice to a printer at the age of 15, when he was discovered by a scout for one of England's greatest soccer teams, Manchester United. He turned professional at 17 and by 20 was at the top of the game. He earned every accolade available including being named both British and European footballer of the year. He wore a Beatle-style haircut and became the precursor of the superstars of today such as David Beckham. He made far more money through endorsements and television appearances than previous players, although still a modest amount by today's standards. Until 1961 players had been limited to a maximum wage of £20 a week.

Best began to drink heavily, and gradually he self-destructed. At one point he was reduced to playing on a soccer team in prison where he had been sent for resisting arrest. This boy with little education played soccer with such fluid grace and courage that he became a living legend. He was an iconic part of the changing youth culture of the 1960s, but he was unprepared for fame. His reputation as one of the greatest players of the game is immortal, but he also set the trend for his successors, who were given too much too soon in a world where appetites were unrestrained.[31]

in fact British youth continued to dress and act distinctively. Pop art emerged first in Britain before moving on to the USA. The BBC remained intensely British until the later 1970s. Only in the 1980s did genuine homogenization begin. The Beatles were successful partly because some of their songs touched people in deep and powerful ways and partly because they were able to ride a wave of interest in changing forms of music and attitudes toward everything from sex to drugs. Yet they remained conventional enough to wear suits and accept honors from the queen. The Rolling Stones were more radical, although Mick Jagger was from a middle-class background and ended up with a knighthood living in the style of a successful business mogul. Their famous song "Gimme Shelter" (1969) epitomized the youth culture's revolt against the Vietnam War.

British high culture remained strong. It is not uncommon for discerning audiences to follow performances of classical music with scores on their laps. Though "Ealing" and other studios could not compete in volume with the Hollywood productivity rate in making movies, many high-quality films and television programs were created. Great actors and actresses, a striking characteristic of the British theatrical world since the 1920s, were proportionately superior in numbers, and many would say talent, to the American output. "Angry young men" such as John Osborne wrote plays in the 1950s that mocked the conventions of "old" England. Traditionalists, such as the playwright and actor Noël Coward, were dubious. He could not "understand why the younger generation, instead of knocking at the door, should bash the fuck out of it."[32] Critical assaults on hypocrisy and pomposity were launched by a string of comic reviews culminating in *Monty Python's Flying Circus* (1969–74).

No postwar British novelist towered over the era as Dickens had done a century earlier, but many writers such as Evelyn Waugh, Kingsley Amis, William Golding, and Doris Lessing produced excellent work. Though not the greatest novels of the time, two serial works by Anthony Powell and Joyce Carey comprised perhaps the finest evocations of British life during the period, contrasting creative and even anarchic forces with the strong undercurrents of conservatism that makes British society distinctive. The odd saga about hobbits by J. R. R. Tolkien, a parable about good and evil, bridged the gap between highbrow and lowbrow. Murder mysteries such as those written by Dorothy Sayers (see Biography 10.2) achieved a strange popularity in a society that had become notably non-violent.

Postwar architecture was mostly second rate. The centers of cities such as Leeds that had survived German bombs were destroyed by greedy property developers enabled by heedless local councils. Finally, in the 1980s and 1990s Richard Rogers and Norman Foster began to produce work of exceptional originality and distinction. The new skyline of the City of London and the "Docklands" revival have their critics and contain some mistakes, but there is also energy and a scale that matches the dynamism of the financial center it serves.

Though a few sculptors, led by Henry Moore, achieved international stature, only one painter did so: Francis Bacon, who produced powerful work. But that was about it. David Hockney is interesting, but his range is narrow. Lucien Freud has carried on the strong British tradition of portrait painting. Somewhere the visual arts lost their way. Michael Palin, one of the "Pythons," confessed to ennui after viewing an exhibition in 1974, finding the art "as meaningful as a tin of anchovies."[33]

The long-banned publication of D. H. Lawrence's *Lady Chatterley's Lover* in 1960 was seen as a major breach in the cultural dike. The poet Philip Larkin famously wrote in 1967:

> Sexual intercourse began
> In nineteen sixty-three
> (which was rather late for me) –
> Between the end of the Chatterley ban
> And the Beatles' first LP.[34]

Many of the developments associated with the 1960s, however, were already well under way earlier. The rate of crimes of violence rose in the 1950s. Young offenders were more aggressive and less respectful of authority, although widespread drug use

Biography 10.2

Dorothy Sayers
1893–1957

Dorothy Sayers was the daughter of a clergyman of Irish Protestant origins while her mother was descended from an old landed gentry family. Although she went to Oxford, only some kinds of jobs were available to educated women during the interwar years, including being a secretary or working in publishing. Eventually she took up writing copy for an advertising agency. She also broke with convention by having a son out of wedlock.

Wilkie Collins and Sir Arthur Conan Doyle had written mystery novels of considerable literary quality in the nineteenth century, but the genre had largely declined into popular "thrillers." During the 1930s Sayers wrote a series of detective stories that reached a high level in style and addressed wider themes than novels produced purely for entertainment. Although her hero was an aristocrat, his life was rendered difficult and complex by memories of his war service and his struggle to marry a serious woman not of his own class. *The Nine Tailors* (1934) is perhaps the best book of its kind written in the twentieth century.

Sayers stopped writing mysteries in the early 1940s and started to produce plays and poetry on religious themes. She brought her scholarly interests to bear translating medieval French and Italian literature, most famously in her Penguin edition of Dante's *Divine Comedy*. Though conventional in upbringing and strong in her Christian faith, Sayers was an independent woman who found she could make her own way in the world.[35]

did not come until the next decade. Divorces reached 10 times the prewar figure in 1947. A recent survey of British sexual behavior found "no evidence of a sexual revolution co-terminous with the decade of the 1960s." All the changes supposed to have taken place then in fact took place in the 1950s. Median age for first intercourse fell in that decade as much as it was to do over the next 30 years.[36]

Nonetheless, a remarkable wave of liberalizing legislation was enacted in the 1960s: abolition of the death penalty (1965); criminalization of racial discrimination (1965, 1968); government-sponsored family planning clinics freely distributing birth control pills (1967); legalization of abortion (1967); legalization of homosexual acts (1967); voting age lowered to 18 (1968); more liberal rules for divorce (1969, 1970); equal pay for women (1970); and special rights and compulsory assistance for the disabled (1970). Theatrical censorship was ended in 1968.

Sunday schools, so influential in inculcating "respectability" among all classes, virtually disappeared in the decades after the war. Even those who were more inclined to remain devout, such as Roman Catholics, grew impatient with the inflexibility of the church hierarchy. In a 2008 survey only 39 percent of the British professed to believe in God, compared to 80 percent of all Americans, and only 16 percent thought there was a Hell where unrepentant sinners go, compared to 54 percent in the USA.[37]

A new wave of feminism arose in the 1960s, encouraged by Germaine Greer's militant manifesto *The Female Eunuch* (1970). Much discrimination against women continued in the workplace where an increasing proportion of them were now employed. In 2000 women's wages were still 80 percent of men's. Paternalistic assumptions about the male breadwinner with wife and children as dependents remained deeply entrenched. The object of "women's liberation" was to break with male "oppression," the sexist structure of public and private institutions, and the patriarchal family. The number of women in higher education rose by a factor of five between 1970 and 1999 while men little more than doubled. By 2000 more women were at university than men. Women's participation in sports rose rapidly from the 1990s onward.

Empire to Commonwealth

In 1945 the British empire still stood intact, but the propaganda issued by Britain in World War II elevated the defense of freedom and democracy to a kind of religion, which made a mockery of continued empire. Not surprisingly, one of the most urgent steps taken by the Labour government was conceding independence to India. Britain no longer had the military will nor means to hold onto the jewel in its imperial crown, but Attlee's decision was a principled one. Most Labourites had become committed decolonizers. The controversial aspect of the process was the decision to split the subcontinent between India (predominantly Hindu) and Pakistan (Muslim). This provoked the painful forced migration of peoples due to their religion and sectarian massacres on an unprecedented scale. The government has been accused of acting too precipitately, and Attlee's choice as viceroy – the king's cousin and a former royal prince, Lord Mountbatten (1900–79) – is often portrayed as reckless in his eagerness to achieve a quick retreat. Too little preparation was made, but the Indian leaders, Gandhi, Jawaharlal Nehru (1889–1964), and Mohammed Ali Jinnah (1876–1948), were the ones who failed to find a unitary solution, and the speed of the break-up was a result of their desire for *immediate* independence. Attlee and Mountbatten, considering the British military and moral position, had no choice but to accede.

British withdrawal from Palestine in 1947 in the face of Zionist terrorism, leaving the Arab population in the lurch, was pusillanimous. Even worse was the later abandonment of Africans to racist white rule in Southern Rhodesia. In neither case,

Figure 10.3   Queen Elizabeth II and the leaders of the Commonwealth nations, 1964. Some of these leaders, such as Julius Nyerere of Tanzania (third to the queen's left) became advisors and friends of the queen. Jomo Kenyatta, President of Kenya (fourth to her right), had led the Mau Mau rising against British rule only a decade earlier

however, did the United Nations play a helpful role. The short-lived but ruthless war against the independence movement in Kenya showed the British at their worst. Decolonization took place more peacefully elsewhere: Africa in the late 1950s and early 1960s and most of the remaining colonies in the late 1960s and early 1970s. It was a remarkably rapid movement when compared to the many centuries it took to accumulate the empire in the first place. However, the British experience was hardly unique; it was part of a much wider process of European withdrawal from colonialism.

Everything, from the perceived completion of the altruistic "civilizing task" to the rise of new forms of international capitalism that no longer required colonial structures, explains the end of empire. Some argue that the increasing liberalism of British public opinion meant that support for authoritarian and racist empire disappeared. Able and charismatic leaders of liberation movements, inspired by resurgent nationalism, made it hard for Britain to resist change. It was no longer possible to count on collusion from subject peoples. Even Conservatives realized that the colonies were a liability. The task of rebuilding the economy at home after the war meant money was no longer available for overseas investment. The hostility of both the Americans and the United Nations to colonialism also helped force Britain's hand.

Unlike France, Britain experienced little angst in releasing its subject peoples. The victory in World War II made it psychologically easier to shed the empire from a position of ascendance, while France was still battling the demons of its humiliation in 1940. The argument that Britain's relative weakness as a great power after the war led to the jettisoning of many smaller colonies does not long survive comparison with the tenacious and successful imperialism that Portugal, one of the poorest countries in Europe, continued to pursue years after Britain had ceased imperial rule. With the exception of the war in Malaya and a less successful engagement in Cyprus, no British administration waged prolonged resistance to liberation movements in the way the French did. The statesmanship of Attlee and subsequent Tory governments was a realistic and largely successful attempt to depart as friends with the peoples Britain once ruled.[38] The empire morphed into the Commonwealth (Figure 10.3). The new association meant less than its staunchest upholders wanted, but it has become more important than those who are dubious tend to assume. It is a forum for cooperation, a means of staying in touch with historical associations, a wobbly but not spineless rallying point for anti-racial values, and an encourager of democracy (Map 10.2).

The Balance Sheet of Empire

The more the British looked back on the legacy of empire after their retreat from imperialism in the 1950s and 1960s the more guilty they felt. The former colonial subjects also had much that was negative to say. As time provided distance and perspective, a less one-sided view began to emerge. Recently even scholars from the colonized states have had some good things to notice about the empire. No one, however, has made a more vigorous defense of imperialism than Niall Ferguson. He argues that the imperialized countries benefited from the rule of law, transparent fiscal arrangements, investor protection, and incorrupt bureaucracies all of which encouraged free markets and cross-border capital flows. An infrastructure of harbors, docks, railways, schools, hospitals, universities, roads, electronic communications, irrigation, clean water, and public health remained behind after the British left. The English language, English forms of land tenure, banking, team sports, religion, the idea of a limited state, representative assemblies, and veneration of liberty were important legacies. Ferguson believes that the British empire was less greedy and better governed than other European colonial systems. For example, the British took away about 1 percent of trade surplus from India compared to 7–10 percent by the Dutch in Indonesia. When the British acted despotically, a critique of this behavior

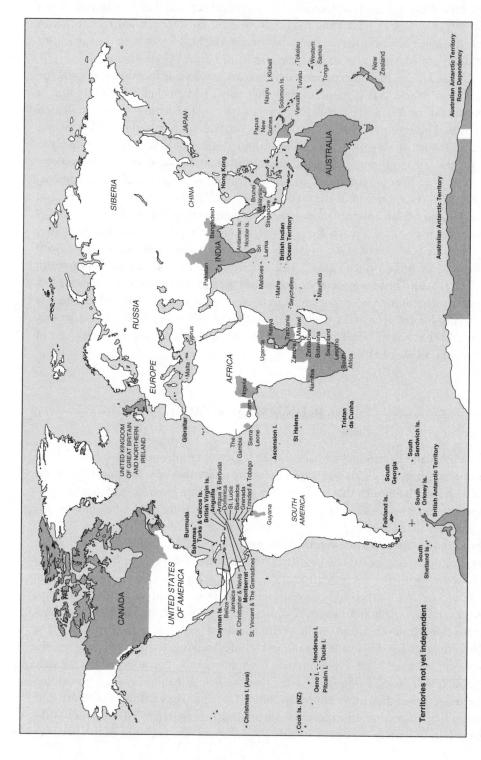

Map 10.2 The Commonwealth in 1996

emerged from within British society itself. The idea of liberty gave the British empire a "self-liquidating character."[39]

It is true that the British brought greater respect to Asian and African cultures than was once assumed. Local social structures were often left intact. Minority languages and other forms of cultural diversity have vanished at a much faster rate after 1945, when the empire began to dissolve, than before.[40] Imperialism provided peaceful relations between different ethnicities and religions, and suppressed slavery. British administrators were often more impartial in their treatment of native populations than the white colonists and sometimes offered protection against exploitation. Historians have gained a new and greater appreciation of the natives who cooperated with the British. They are no longer seen as mere collaborators but as people who had complex and rational reasons for doing so. Many saw that association with the British could bring their societies new forms of knowledge and wealth. Professional historians sometimes hyperventilate over the evils of the British empire in ways that become more and more misleading as the degree of condemnation becomes more elevated. The empire was authoritarian, but it should never be confused with the imperiums established by men such as Hitler or Stalin.

The negative side of the balance sheet on empire, however, is a long and dark one. Imperialism distorted market forces. It hurt both the colonial and metropolitan economies, was a burden on taxpayers, and was demeaning and exploitative to the colonized. Land was stolen from aboriginal peoples and attempts were made to drive them into inhospitable areas or to wipe them out. Drawing subsistence farmers into the maw of the global market turned out to be disastrous when cash crops failed or prices plummeted, leaving the farmers defenseless and starving. The colonies were used to produce raw materials and not encouraged to process or transform their products to gain added value, while the factories and businesses in Britain gained most of the profits. Borders were drawn with the convenience of the governors in mind or in ignorance of local conditions. After independence tribal, religious, and other cultural conflicts welled up in explosive and tragic episodes such as the Biafra revolt (1967–70), the reign of the psychopath Idi Amin in Uganda, or the sad experience of Iraq since the overthrow of the Hashemite monarchy in 1958. Decolonization left many fragile states in its wake. Local customs and traditions were damaged or destroyed by Christian missionaries. Educational opportunities were often provided only for a few members of the local elite. When the empire dissolved, many colonies did not have enough trained personnel to sustain their societies without outside help. The much-touted imposition of the rule of law was often not organized in a way intended to benefit the native populations. Well over one million Indians were moved as indentured migrants to other British colonies during the raj. In many places healthcare remained rudimentary at best; sanitation and clear water sources were often not developed. The advent of Social Darwinism cannot be seen as otherwise than misguided and ugly. The racism of empire would come home to roost when post-imperial immigration from Asia, Africa, and the West Indies began after the war.

Immigration

The British Nationality Act of 1948 reaffirmed the right of people from the colonies to settle permanently in the UK. The "open door" policy lasted until 1962. This was thought to be progressive and helped remedy shortages of labor. Both Labour and Tory governments blocked attempts to restrict the flow. West Indians, who had grown up in Anglicized British colonies, came in the 1950s and 1960s. They found it easier to acclimatize than immigrants from India and Pakistan who followed in the later 1960s and 1970s. By and large, all of the immigrants ended up in urban ghettos. In 2000 over half of all ethnic minorities in the UK lived in London.

Unemployment rose in the 1970s and competition for what work was available aroused racial tension. Access to scarce resources such as education, social services, and housing also caused hostility. Many immigrants turned to self-employment as shopkeepers and the like. The Indians pursued higher education most successfully, which lifted their children into better-paid jobs and the professions.

In 1962 the Tories restricted non-white immigration but did not end it. The National Front, a party that campaigned for repatriation of black immigrants, was formed in 1967. Six years later, racist sentiment was inflamed by a virulent speech given by the Conservative MP Enoch Powell. Moderate elements in both the Labour and Tory parties distanced themselves from such rhetoric, but Powell succeeded in making immigration a central political issue. An Immigration Act was passed in 1971 that placed Commonwealth citizens on an equal footing with non-Commonwealth entrants in the right to settle in Britain. This restrained the inflow, although subsequent exceptions were made for groups such as Indians fleeing Idi Amin. In 1978 a senior Conservative politician, Margaret Thatcher, spoke openly of her fear that the nation might be swamped by people of a different culture.

Legislation was passed in the 1960s and 1970s to enforce non-discrimination, but this did not necessarily reflect popular feeling. Although many black and brown citizens were now second- or even third-generation residents of Britain, people of their background were proportionately less likely to be police officers, judges, or hold other leadership positions. Even today, they cannot be said to be thoroughly integrated into British society.

Europe

Churchill delivered famous speeches in 1946 and 1948 urging a confederation of European states. What he did not state clearly at the time was that he had no intention of letting Britain be drawn away from its links to the Commonwealth and America. This was by no means a purely Conservative position. When the French offered the UK the opportunity to join the new European Coal and Steel Community in 1950, the Attlee government turned down the offer. Eden withdrew Britain's observer from a conference at which negotiations to form the European Economic Community (EEC) began. France, Germany, Italy, and some of the smaller democratic nations went ahead to form a Common Market in the Treaty of Rome in 1957. Macmillan was something of a pro-European and announced that the government would apply to join the EEC, but the Labour leader, Hugh Gaitskell, was opposed. French president Charles de Gaulle vetoed British entry in any case.

Some feel that Britain's isolation from Europe contributed to economic and psychological malaise. Others believe the UK was fundamentally different from the Continental states. It had long had a global rather than regional outlook and could not easily or safely sunder its traditional relationships. Alan Milward has argued that Britain's independent strategy after the war made sense in the context of the period in terms of playing to and maximizing its strengths in the postwar world. He rejects the notion that this policy, either joining or not joining, was a "failure."[41] In 1967 the Wilson government applied for entry into the Common Market, and Heath, who was wholeheartedly a European, successfully concluded the necessary steps for membership in 1973 once de Gaulle had departed from the French presidency. Yet membership remained a divisive issue on both the right and the left. British trade gradually shifted away from the Commonwealth to European countries. By 2000 61 percent of Britain's commerce was with Western Europe. This tied its economic fortunes more closely to what became known as the European Union (EU).

The Condition of Britain Question

Shorn of empire and bankrupted by war, the United Kingdom could not compete as a "superpower" by 1945. Corelli Barnett, John Charmley, and many others have painted a picture of paralysis and collapse.[42] C. P. Snow, in *The Two Cultures and the Scientific Revolution* (1959), argued that humanist intellectuals had undermined the power of scientists to advance economic and social progress, while the journalist Anthony Sampson, in *Anatomy of Britain* (1962), asserted that an outmoded and reactionary "establishment" was holding back progress. Above all, the cry was heard that Britain had not become "modern" and needed to be "modernized," a refrain used at one time or another by virtually every politician of the period. Reactionaries could not reconcile themselves to the loss of empire. It may be that the extraordinary popularity of Ian Fleming's fictional spy, James Bond, had more to do with anesthetizing the pain of perceived weakness than an admiration for lots of sex and fast cars that fired bullets out of the tail-lights. The idea that Britain was simultaneously trying to live beyond its means and in some sort of terminal decline became widespread and reinforced popular pessimism.

Of course, Britain's position in the world did change after 1945. The military might of the USSR and the USA was now well in advance of all other countries. The colonies disappeared, and the dominions would never again fall obediently into line behind the mother country. Periodic economic crises had punctuated the postwar era,

Figure 10.4   In 1945 Sir Bernard Lovell established the first and for many years the largest radio telescope in the world at Jodrell Bank. He investigated cosmic rays, pulsars, quasars, meteors, and other astronomical phenomena

culminating in the debacle of the 1970s. The radicalization of union leadership combined with industrial management that was at best mediocre seriously weakened the economy by the 1970s. Examples of unimaginative business practice littered the landscape.[43]

Nonetheless, the assumptions of the "declinists" are seriously misleading. The single greatest distortion built into the idea of postwar "decline" is the failure to correct for the larger populations of the emergent military and/or economic giants that surpassed Britain: West Germany, Japan, the USSR, and the USA. One needs to remember, for example, that Japan grew in population to be almost twice as large as the UK. Moreover, for almost half a century non-nuclear Germany and Japan spent much less on defense. Britain had the same per capita productivity level relative to Germany and the USA in 1989 that it had in the 1870s. It remained very near the top of the list of rich and prosperous nations of the world throughout the twentieth century. Between 1948 and 1973 the British GDP grew at the quite satisfactory annual rate of about 3 percent. The standard of living rose by about 300 percent per capita between 1945 and 2000.[44]

Postwar Britain's scientific and technical elite remained world class (Figure 10.4). C. P. Snow's analysis is belied by the disproportionate number of discoveries in medicine, physics, and chemistry achieved in Britain compared to France, Germany, and Japan, none of whose universities have ranked in the same league for academic distinction during the postwar era with Oxford or Cambridge.[45]

To focus on the decline of industry is misleading. The service sector, always a potent part of the British economy, continued to do well through most of the postwar period. The City remained at the heart of world finance. The rapid improvement made by the British economy since the 1980s, when many of the structural problems were corrected or disappeared, has brought further prosperity. Some people feared that the stresses of the 1970s might lead to extreme upheaval or even revolution. As usual, the deep-rooted popular respect for British institutions remained widespread and strong.

Contents

Tradition and change have continued to mark Britain's progress in recent decades. The country experienced the divisive era of Thatcherism that seemed to threaten consensus, but continuity ensured stability and encouraged prosperity. The unraveling of the United Kingdom, begun with the detachment of southern Ireland in 1922, continued into the twenty-first century. Wales and Scotland gained a new level of autonomy over their own affairs that could lead in the future to a looser federal structure or even independence. The Irish Republic emerged for the first time as a prosperous and happy place, and the dynamics of the Northern Ireland conflict changed decisively in a positive direction.

Margaret Thatcher

The demise of the Callaghan administration came in 1979. The winner of the election he called was Margaret Thatcher (b. 1925). She was the daughter of a small-town store owner and trained as a chemist and then a lawyer before going into politics. In 1970 she rose to ministerial rank in Heath's administration. Within five years she challenged him in an election for the leadership of the party and won. Britain's first woman prime minister was appointed in 1979. She launched a multi-pronged assault on the economic and social malaise that gripped Britain. Fundamental to Thatcher's approach was the assumption that the welfare state was evil and that unrestrained capitalism was the solution to virtually every problem facing the country. She believed that public services created a system of patronage and dependence in which unproductive, parasitical workers sucked up the wealth created by hard-working, risk-taking entrepreneurs. She wanted to rein in public expenditure and roll back the frontiers of the state. This required renouncing the bipartisan postwar consensus on the economy and society. Her ruthlessness was breathtaking. She was the equal of Lloyd George in energy. The French president François Mitterrand said she had the "eyes of Caligula."[1]

Thatcher encountered serious problems almost immediately due to the rapidly rising price of oil. A new wave of inflation reached the annual rate of 18 percent in her first year in office. Unemployment escalated from 5.7 percent in 1979 to 7.4 percent in 1980, then 11.4 percent in 1981 and 13 percent in 1983. The rate stayed at or above the punishing level of 10 percent for the rest of her premiership. Thatcher was undaunted by these numbers or by the pain they represented. She believed tough medicine was necessary to nurse the economy back to health.

If businesses could not turn a profit, Thatcher believed it was better to let them die than allow them to act as a drag on the economy even if they employed large sectors of the workforce. She was ready to see the old declining industries perish. Indeed, she believed Britain's future lay not in manufacturing but with the service sector where it was still a world leader. The number of workers employed in manual labor declined by nearly one-fourth during the 1980s and the number of unskilled workers fell by half. Manufacturing jobs were transferred to Asia where expenses

Figure 11.1   "John Bull Getting another Dose of Thatcherism," 1987

could be cut drastically. Thatcher was willing to pay for retraining of the workforce but cared little about the human costs of transition. She assumed everyone could jump from one sort of career to another, as she had done, without factoring in the effect of community values, tradition, geography, age, or luck as variables that might create situations distinct from her own. Thatcher spoke of "Victorian values" in the absurd belief that there had been a consensus among British people in the nineteenth century on moral and social issues. What she really meant was a condemnation of liberal social reforms, which she saw as "permissive," and a belief in self-reliance (Figure 11.1).

Britain was already in a serious recession when Thatcher came to power. New waves of unemployment drove up government expenditure on welfare benefits, and her power began to slip away as the economic downturn continued. Traditional Tories in the Cabinet, who had supported the "Butskell" consensus on social harmony, became restive. Thatcher contemptuously called them "wets." She was saved by two things. Firstly, North Sea oil began to flow in sufficient quantities to raise the national income and fill government coffers. A second piece of luck was the sudden attack in 1982 by Argentina on one of Britain's last colonies, a group of remote islands in the South Atlantic called the Falklands. Thatcher exploited her good fortune with the same energy and aggression with which she tackled every problem.

The Falklands were largely inhabited by sheep, although talk of oil deposits made the rounds. To date nothing but wool has ever been exported. It was not economic interests that concerned the prime minister. Nor did she care about the dreadful record on human rights accumulated by the unpopular junta of generals and admirals that had launched the invasion in a desperate bid to evoke patriotism as a means of keeping themselves in power. Thatcher was genuinely outraged that anyone would invade British territory. She was an old-fashioned patriot. A large armada of warships was quickly readied and troops were loaded onto ocean liners requisitioned by the government. The Royal Navy bristled with modern weaponry. Nuclear attack submarines were sent to infest the southern ocean. The only other power in the world that could have projected conventional military force over 8,000 miles of open ocean was the United States. Indeed, the latter made a number of useful contributions to the campaign. With the exception of a few French-made missiles, the Argentine military was heavily outgunned. The junta was driven from office as a consequence of a rapid and humiliating defeat.

Thatcher unabashedly exploited her victory for political advantage. It should be noted, however, that had the conflict gone badly her close association with the decision to fight would have quickly destroyed her career. Moreover, her belief that the Falklands battle was an example of what she had to offer the British people – forceful leadership, refusal to compromise, rigid adherence to old-fashioned values – made her "ownership" of the war a genuine triumph over which to crow. At the same time Thatcher was buoyed by a reviving economy. In the general election of 1983 the Conservatives swept to a huge majority, one of the great electoral victories of the century. Suddenly, Margaret Thatcher could do almost anything she wanted.

At Thatcher's moment of triumph a second enemy delivered themselves into her hands. In her mind the leaders of the industrial trade unions had become like overmighty feudal barons holding the country to ransom.[2] She had long sought a means of destroying their power. In 1984–5 Arthur Scargill (b. 1938), the radical head of the miners' union, who despised the existing political system, launched an assault as ill judged as that of the Argentine junta. Unfortunately for his members, he managed to throw away any moral advantage by rigging strike votes, provoking violence, and other unsavory activities. Thatcher managed to sequester union funds secreted abroad, closed pits left and right, and sent cavalry charges of mounted police against the picketers (Figure 11.2). It was a bravura performance unprecedented in its concentrated fury and effectiveness. Scargill got what the Argentine generals received, a defeat cast in terms of patriotic values and the need for decisive action against evildoers. The miners' union, which had been a great force in the land for half a century and had numbered 255,000 as late as 1974, had only 5,000 members left by 1990.

Anti-union legislation flowed from **Downing Street** like molten lava, destroying the established traditions of modern British labor relations. The closed shop was outlawed. Solidarity strikes and secondary picketing were ended. Unions were

Figure 11.2 The winding machinery operating the elevators that sank deep into the earth at this coal mine opened in 1835 stand at the center. A rail line was used to transport the product to cities, ports, and factories. On the right, rows of miners' houses formed a village close to the pit where they lived. It was closed down in 1971

required to hold postal ballots before calling strikes. Leaders had to be elected more democratically. Collective bargaining was undermined. The leaders of the Labour Party were unable successfully to disassociate themselves from the worst excesses of the radical left and thus failed to protect organized labor. The number of days lost to strikes fell from 29.5 million to 761,000 between the year before Thatcher's premiership began and the year she left office.[3]

Thatcher's attempts to remodel British society went ahead unchecked. By the mid-1980s income taxes had been radically reduced. At the higher levels of wealth they were now the lowest in Europe. The City reasserted itself as a central point in international currency dealing in the 1980s, assisted by its location between Tokyo/ Hong Kong and New York in the new 24-hour world financial market. The financial services sector of the economy surged ahead after the "Big Bang" of October 1986 when the stock exchange was deregulated and business systems modernized. The old world of gentlemanly capitalism dominated by family-owned banking houses was transformed into a more fiercely competitive place that retained and even increased its stature as a center of world finance and the economic capital of Europe.[4] Business boomed as it had not done since 1914. British foreign investment rose from 2 percent of GDP in 1963 to 22 percent in 1999. Vast new complexes of building such as Canary Wharf sprung up that changed London's skyline (Figure 11.3).

Thatcher delighted in the election of her ideological soul mate, Ronald Reagan, as president of the United States. Their personal chemistry helped reignite the "special

Figure 11.3   Cityscape, London, 2008

relationship." In spite of a few disagreements, their mutual admiration helped raise Thatcher's stature higher as a world statesperson than any other figure save Reagan himself. The new Soviet leader, Mikhail Gorbachev, arrived in London to be inspected by Thatcher, who announced that he was someone with whom she could do business. Some of the aura of victory touched Thatcher when the Cold War was won and the communist empire collapsed between 1989 and 1991.

Two of Thatcher's many mistakes failed to inflict serious damage on her reputation. She fought a running battle with the EEC over further steps toward integration. As a British nationalist, she disliked submersion in a unified Europe, and, as a Conservative, she feared the union would insinuate socialism into the UK. She was a tough negotiator with her European colleagues, and won special treatment and considerable financial advantages for Britain over the years. She left unresolved, however, her party's attitude toward Europe, which would help fragment the Conservatives in the decades after she left office. The other error Thatcher made was to fail to support sanctions imposed by the Commonwealth on the white regime in South Africa to end apartheid. It was said that the queen, whose sympathies seem to have been strongly pro-sanctions, had a worse relationship with Thatcher than with any of her previous prime ministers.[5]

A final, fatal mistake, however, destroyed Thatcher's grip on power. This was an entirely self-inflicted wound. In 1988–9 the government decided to reform the local tax system, extending the payment of **rates** to all residents, not just homeowners.

The new system was called the "community charge" but less formally named the "poll tax." She was trying to rein in overspending by local councils dominated by Labour majorities. The new system was a gift to her enemies, because it could be argued that a duke living in a 300-room mansion would pay the same fee as a poorly paid manual laborer. The idea that both received the same benefits from the police and fire service was patently absurd, and the whole conception appeared grotesquely unjust. Moreover, rates for private houses had been maintained artificially low for many years, and now people were receiving shocking tax bills. The prime minister ignored all the warning signs and steamed ahead. Many Conservatives were alarmed by the electoral effects the policy was likely to have, and anti-Thatcherite forces gathered strength. A poor showing in a leadership election led to the "iron lady's" fall in 1990.

For some, Thatcher was a figure of Churchillian stature, a savior who altered the course of Britain. She took command of a derelict wreck, decks awash and ready to sink, and guided it not just to a safe harbor but to repair, relaunching, and a new beginning. Her accomplishments were prodigious, and she led her party to three electoral victories, culminating in the final one in 1987. Her privatization policies took a dramatic turn when she moved to allow occupants of public housing to purchase their residences at a discount and become part of the vastly expanded property-owning middle class. By 1990 two-thirds of Britons owned their houses. This reflected a radically different profile than the rest of Europe. Thatcher had succeeded in making a majority of her countrymen stakeholders in the society in a new way. In addition, the sale of other state assets tripled the number of owners of stocks between 1979 and 1989. This strategy and the war against the unions decisively reshaped the class structure of Britain. "Thatcherism" split the working class into winners and losers. For some workers, the next two decades brought reduced living standards as the prevailing trend of convergence of income and wealth came to an end; for others, ownership of their own houses increased affluence and status. Poverty grew worse. The middle and upper classes were in clover.

Thatcher was actually more cautious than she sometimes seemed and less effective in putting many of her ideas into practice than one might expect. She abandoned her initial economic program in 1981 when it clearly was not working. The frontiers of the state, outside the sale of assets, were not rolled back. Welfare and expenditure on healthcare expanded during her tenure. She did not privatize the National Health Service because public opinion was too wedded to the idea of free care for any political party to abolish it, although one of her own supporters admitted her assurance of its continuance was delivered in "the listless drone of a hostage reading a statement prepared by her captors."[6] Nor did the attempt to restore the death penalty succeed. Homosexuality was not criminalized again. Immigration was not halted.

Whether the pain inflicted by Thatcher's maniacal genius – the rending of social relations – was worth the result is still a divisive issue. She deeply antagonized much of the intelligentsia, and even prosperous middle-class people felt uncomfortable about her confrontational ways and indifference to the victims of unrestrained market forces. Most people felt the new tax system was too unprogressive and fell harshly on the poorest section of society. Thatcher left behind her, Stefan Collini argues, a "deep and still bleeding gash ... cut through so many of the patiently accumulated decencies and solidarities of British society."[7]

John Major

Few observers were prepared for the surprising choice of John Major (b. 1943) as Margaret Thatcher's successor. He grew up in poverty, left school at 15, and seemed colorless except for an ardent interest in cricket, affection for goldfish, and success in cheating on his wife while living at 10 Downing Street. He entered politics late, after a career in banking, and rose rapidly to become chancellor of the exchequer. He lacked all pretension, and seemed competent – a classic compromise candidate while each of the other contenders, though more formidable men, had glaring defects. He presided over a transformed Britain. Entrepreneurship was rampant. The UK had the strongest economy in Europe.

The poll tax was abandoned. Unemployment dropped below 10 percent for the first time since 1980. The civil service became more intent on effective delivery of services. The age for consenting homosexual acts was reduced from 21 to 18. The Prince of Wales, future head of an established Church that did not accept divorce, divorced his wife. Shops were allowed to open for business on previously sacrosanct Sundays. The prime minister spoke of achieving a "classless" society. In 1992 the dual system in higher education established in the 1960s of "inferior" polytechnics and "respectable" universities was abolished, giving the former the name and status of the latter. By 2000 35 percent of 18- to 21-year-olds were engaged in higher education.

Britain signed the Maastricht Treaty of 1992 between the member states of the EEC to accelerate the process of European political integration, although Major was opposed to a common currency and the Social Charter, a policy on employment with socialistic overtones. He won the right to "opt out" on these points, and the pound remains Britain's currency today. Maastricht went too far for many Tories, who resisted the loss of sovereignty. In 1991 the government supported the American invasion of Iraq in order to liberate Kuwait.

Major won the 1992 election by a reduced but substantial margin. It appeared that Labour continued to be unelectable. However, his government lost prestige when it was forced to withdraw from the Exchange Rate Mechanism (ERM) that Margaret Thatcher had been induced to join with great reluctance. This required keeping the pound at an unrealistically high level. One historian has called the system "extraordinary and virtually insane."[8] On September 16, 1992, known as "Black Wednesday," the government was obliged to raise the interest rate 5 percent in a single day as a result of uncontrollable speculation on the pound. Before the day was over, the plug had to be pulled on the ERM in what appeared to be an incompetent series of financial maneuvers. Europhobia reached new heights. Major's reputation never recovered. Accusations of sleaze, neglect of infrastructure, and other troubles dragged down prospects for another electoral victory. Meanwhile the Labour Party had begun to transform itself.

"New" Labour

The Tories had been kept in power partly by developments within the Labour Party. First Michael Foot, who "looked like, and behaved like, an old sheep," and then the somewhat more adept Neil Kinnock made little headway in reforming the party.[9] The extreme left rampaged in the constituencies, ousting moderate MPs. The 1983 Labour electoral manifesto was called the longest suicide note in history. John Smith took over in 1992 but died of a heart attack before he could bring his formidable talents fully to bear on the situation. The party then chose Anthony (Tony) Blair (b. 1953) as his successor.

Blair came from an upper-middle-class background. He attended a Scottish boarding school and Oxford before practicing as a barrister. He was intensely religious, a high Anglican married to a Catholic wife with whom he attended mass.[10] Blair became the youngest prime minister since 1812 and the first to become the father of a baby while living in Downing Street. He was instinctively on the moderate to right wing of the party. Like his predecessors in the leadership of the Labour Party, Blair was a sincere monarchist. He was also an immensely skilled politician, a superb persuader with "a Bunsen burner smile."[11] "The history of the Labour Party is littered with nice people who get beaten," he told another politician. "I don't intend to be one of them."[12]

In 1995, Blair succeeded in overturning Labour's pledge to socialist principles, the opening shot in a strategy to make the party acceptable to the mainstream of British politics again. He sought support from middle-class voters by making Labour the party of the center. In the general election of May 1997 he delivered a landslide. The Tories did so poorly (165 MPs to Labour's 419) that some people speculated that the Conservatives might break up completely and a new political configuration in British politics would appear. The Tories failed to win a single seat in Scotland or Wales.

Blair spoke of making Britain "fair, modern, and strong."[13] In the 30 years after 1945 there had hardly been any increase in the number of female MPs. Blair pushed hard to rectify this gender imbalance, and 102 of the new Labour MPs were female. The Cabinet contained five women. He aimed at continued economic flexibility and growth in the path of the Conservative program but with a commitment to social justice. Some Labour traditionalists had trouble recalibrating, although the loyal support of the authentic working-class figures such as the deputy prime minister, John Prescott, protected Blair's flanks. Even senior ministers worried, however, that "New Labour was in danger of forgetting the poor."[14]

The economy continued to grow at or above the postwar average despite slowdowns in 2002 and 2005. The unemployment rate was the lowest since the 1970s. Further privatization took place, and the Bank of England was granted independence by the government in the setting of interest rates. Like Thatcher, Blair worked to promote a "stakeholder" society. Trade unions were given no special favors. In 2007 Britain's GDP per capita exceeded that of France and Germany.

Blair made some attempts to improve education. Spending per pupil almost doubled between 1997 and 2005. A £40 billion program to refurbish or rebuild every state-supported secondary school in Britain over 15 years was launched in 2006. He legalized new institutions akin to charter schools in the USA, which left-wing members of his own party saw as undermining public education. He pushed through regulations allowing universities to charge variable tuition fees and got the reform through the Commons only by a small margin. Loans replaced grants.

The Blair administration doubled the NHS budget between 1997 and 2005, and spending rose from 6.8 percent of GDP to 9.2 percent, higher than the average for the rest of the European Union but behind Scandinavia, Germany, and Switzerland.[15] Administrative reforms improved performance and reduced waiting lists, but he was seen as weakening the National Health Service by licensing self-governing "foundation" hospitals.

Blair devoted a great deal of time and energy to constitutional reform and reconfiguring the relationship between the four nations of the United Kingdom. High on his agenda was reform of the House of Lords, which fitted nicely into his thrust toward "modernization." All but 92 hereditary peers out of 700 or so were excluded, though titles were not abolished. Further reforms were promised. The first referendum of the Blair years was held in 1997 on the issue of **devolution**. Seventy-four percent of the Scots voted in favor of home rule. In 1999 a Parliament met in Edinburgh for the first time since 1707. A similar referendum in Wales found only 50.3 percent of the Welsh in favor of an Assembly in Cardiff. This body was granted more limited powers than the Parliament of Scotland.

Nowhere was Blair bolder than in foreign policy. He has been called a "neo-imperial prime minister who called the British people once more to a global, Gladstonian mission."[16] He tended to see problems such as those that arose in Serbia and Iraq in moral terms. The prime minister flew to Washington soon after the attack on September 11, 2001 and sat in the gallery while President Bush addressed Congress. He carried Britain into the war in Iraq with little genuine national debate. Blair was convinced the dictator Saddam Hussein possessed weapons of mass destruction, though like Bush he did not press hard for confirmed evidence. A celebrated "dodgy dossier" about Saddam's capacity to launch biological and chemical weapons was later discredited when none were discovered after the invasion. Whether the Blair administration illegitimately and knowingly "sexed up" the intelligence remains an open question.

Like Macmillan, Blair hoped to play the role of the less powerful but more experienced and wiser guide to the gauche and ignorant American leader. In the event he failed to restrain Bush and went along with everything the Americans wanted.

LEGACIES

Figure 11.4   "Legacies" by Steve Breen, 2007

He clung even more firmly to the "special relationship" than Churchill (Figure 11.4). It is a mistake, however, to see Blair as solely responsible for Britain's role in Iraq. With a few exceptions such as Robin Cook, the foreign secretary, who resigned, he carried the Cabinet and the parliamentary Labour Party with him.

Thatcher and Blair had more in common than their rhetoric suggested, and they won elections because the British people wanted most of what they had to offer. It is true that on many political and social issues the UK has moved closer to European values than American ones. Four out of five Britons have now visited the Continent and working-class fans are likely to pop over to Milan or Berlin for weekend soccer matches. However, the European model of social protection and cohesion is less attractive to the British than lightly regulated capitalism. Polls show that when it comes to the market economy Britain is more closely aligned with American ideas than it is with its partners on the Continent. A 2008 survey shows that even after years of the Iraq war, which alienated many Britons, 51 percent retain an overall favorable view of the United States compared with 39 percent of the French and 30 percent of the Germans. The British dislike the metric system and Brussels bureaucrats who modify recipes for English beer. Though many people believe Britons have gotten over their distaste for garlic and espresso, the anti-European UK Independence Party (UKIP) won 12 of 78 seats in June 2005 elections for the European Parliament. In the 2008 poll only 28 percent of Britons declared themselves satisfied with the EU and 57 percent dissatisfied.[17]

Blair was accused of changing the system by which Britain is ruled in a number of ways, most of them for the worse. His style was seen as "presidential," although focus on the leader as opposed to the party during elections has been a long-term trend. He tried to downplay the importance of the Cabinet, and some saw him acting to subordinate or circumvent the authority of the Commons. Blair was not a "House of Commons man" who hung around the bar and socialized with his colleagues in the manner of leaders as diverse as Churchill and Bevan, and this was resented. Politicized "special advisors" seeped into ministries, adding to or even replacing top civil servants as aides to ministers.

Paul Langford, taking the long view, argues that many of the characteristics of the present system can be found in the Walpolean or Disraelian years as well. Much has always depended on the ambition, energy, and skill of individual premiers, who have succeeded or failed to gain mastery according to their will and ability, and on the size of their majorities in the Commons. Margaret Thatcher, arguably the most dictatorial of all modern prime ministers, suffered an almost instantaneous political liquidation when MPs in her own party turned against her.[18] Select committees have become more active and influential than ever before, which increasingly puts pressure on government departments to act transparently and efficiently. Even the prime minister can be called to account before them. Since the expulsion of most of the hereditary peers, the House of Lords has regained stature and even peers who were members of the Labour Party showed a willingness to defy Blair. *The Economist* wryly observed: "Lacking a majority, the government has to resort to the quaint expedient of winning the argument."[19]

Blair's two closest aides, Peter Mandelson and Alastair Campbell, were image makers, and their antics marred Blair's reputation and undermined belief in his sincerity. Slick and superficial changes were sometimes trotted out without much thought. Some people believed that Blair imagined he could "spin" his way out of anything. The prime minister was right, however, considering the frenzied partisanship of the press in the 1990s onward, that "we were more spinned against than spinning."[20] He was readier than his predecessors in either party to make use of poll data, focus groups, and marketing techniques, which provoked derision, but this, it can be argued, was a move toward more genuine democratic input. Few modern prime ministers have been better at framing arguments and speaking persuasively to voters. Blair's leadership of Labour while in opposition and the electoral victory in 1997 was one of the most brilliant political performances of modern times. Although more a social democrat than a socialist, he reaffirmed the justice and viability of the welfare state.

Ireland

Perhaps the most admirable accomplishment of the Blair years took place in Ireland. The prime minister invested great effort and took enormous risks to bring the decades of terror and suffering in Ulster to an end.

After World War II the Labour government guaranteed (1949) the continued connection between Ulster and the United Kingdom out of gratitude for the contribution the province had made to victory. Only a democratic referendum in which a majority of the citizens voted to cut ties with the United Kingdom could lead to absorption into the Republic. The expansion of the welfare state after 1945 largely eliminated social rivalry within the Protestant community and encouraged cross-class solidarity. As a result, the ruling Protestant coalition of aristocrats, industrialists, and clergy were able to exercise a style of authoritarian leadership that vanished everywhere else in the Western world. Discrimination in employment and housing on sectarian lines was widespread. Intermarriage between the Catholic and Protestant communities rarely happened. Schools continued to embed the seeds of fear and religious hatred among their pupils, as did politicians on both sides. The Protestant majority used psychological and physical intimidation to terrorize the minority. At the same time, the Protestant community was crippled by a kind of siege mentality, convinced that the Irish Republic's claim of sovereignty over the whole island threatened their religious and political freedom. All this was made worse for the Catholic community by economic weakness. Unemployment was higher than in the rest of the UK, and the textile and shipbuilding industries were dead or dying. Whatever jobs there were went to Protestants.

Contemporary historians make a distinction between memory and history. No place throws the dichotomy into greater relief than Northern Ireland. Academics compiled facts and analysis that discredited many of the notions about the past held by both the **Nationalist** and **Unionist** communities. Yet, popular memory on both sides happily, often guilelessly, disregarded the hard-won achievements of historians, preferring to demonize their enemies with myths that evoked tribal loyalties. The study of popular memory in Northern Ireland suggests "that present actions are not determined by the past, but rather the reverse: that what we choose to remember is dictated by our contemporary concerns."[21] Delusional thinking also tended to prevail. As late as the mid-1990s sympathetic observers outside the inner councils of the **IRA** believed the terrorists "had overwhelmed the security forces of the British state and had won its clandestine war in England."[22] Close to the reverse had in fact occurred.

The postwar era was at first comparatively peaceful, punctuated by episodes of violence that mostly took the form of riots in which Protestant mobs attacked and burned Catholic neighborhoods. New "troubles" broke out after a Catholic civil rights movement was founded in 1967. The organizers were inspired by the success gained by African Americans across the Atlantic, and the emergence within the Unionist aristocracy of more liberal leadership. Captain Terence O'Neill (1914–90) became prime minister of the Protestant-dominated "Stormont" government in 1963. In a dramatic move, he held talks with the prime minister of the Republic in 1965. Protestants flew into new heights of paranoia.

The clubbing of civil rights marchers in 1968 by police caused much resentment in the Catholic community, but relations irretrievably broke down in January 1972 when British troops in Londonderry killed 13 protesters and wounded 17 more, many of whom were sympathizers with the IRA but apparently unarmed. The incident, known as "Bloody Sunday," made it difficult for the British government convincingly to portray itself as a mediating force, although it has never been established who fired the first shots. Sinister conspiracy theories are regularly trotted out, made credible by a heavily biased investigative report by a British judge. The major cities of Northern Ireland became war zones, and the IRA carried a new bombing campaign to Britain as well.

The moderate Nationalist John Hume (see Biography 11.1) once noted that the IRA believed Irish unity "had come to mean the conquest of one state by the other ... The pursuit of Catholic victory."[23] In fact, the tiny southern army, which was little more than a glorified police force, could not possibly have brought the Protestant community to heel. In 1970 the prime minister of the Republic realistically told a delegation of northern Catholics: "If we were given a gift of Northern Ireland tomorrow we could not accept it." He also reminded the time-warped Nationalists who clung to the illusion that Britain was the stumbling block: "The whole unhappy situation is an Irish quarrel ... [The British] are not an essential part of it. We must settle this quarrel among us."[24] Unless the Protestants could be persuaded that they had a future acceptable to them, no progress would take place. Moreover, despite egregious discrimination, the welfare state established in Britain

Biography 11.1

John Hume
1937–

John Hume was born and raised in a poor family in the Bogside district of Derry, the heart of the Nationalist Catholic community of Northern Ireland. He at first planned to study for the priesthood but altered his career path to teaching. He became a community and civil rights activist and was subjected to violent treatment by the police. He rejected the terror embraced by radical Nationalists and helped to found the moderate Social Democratic and Labour Party (SDLP), which he came to lead. In 1983 he was elected an MP. In the 1990s he initiated talks with the leaders of Sinn Fein. These negotiations widened into the peace process that included the British and the Irish governments and Nationalist and Unionist parties. His tireless and courageous lobbying, which included so many visits to Washington that he became known as the "101st Senator," helped propel Northern Ireland toward prosperity and peace. Hume remained steadfastly devoted to the view that "the answer to difference is to respect it."[25] This approach for the first time reduced the level of threat to the Protestant community in Ulster sufficiently to allow them to negotiate rationally. Along with the Unionist David Trimble, he was awarded the Nobel Peace Prize in 1998.

after 1945 gave the Catholics in Northern Ireland a better standard of living and a much wider array of social services than was available in the south. The population in the Republic continued to contract between the 1920s and the 1960s, virtually the only place in the Western world to do so, while the Ulster population expanded. By 1966 the six counties in Northern Ireland constituted more than one-third of the total population of the island.

The IRA broke apart in 1969 when the "Provisionals," traditional Nationalists dedicated to the use of terror to free Ulster from British rule, split with the Marxist-dominated "Officials," who were seen to be insufficiently dedicated to that goal. The "Provo" terrorist campaign evoked its expected response. Paramilitary organizations in the Protestant community were formed. "It is them or us," became the rallying cry.[26] Roman Catholics chosen at random were tortured and murdered. The guerrilla war became tribal and fierce.

The hunger strike in 1981 by IRA prisoners to demand that they not be treated as ordinary criminals drew international attention to the crisis. The Nationalist leadership had, however, misread their enemy. The prime minister at the time, Margaret Thatcher, was unmoved and perfectly prepared to let the strikers die in any numbers they wanted. Ten of them did so. Her intransigence deepened the bitterness in the Catholic community and strengthened the rise in the North of the political branch of the IRA, Sinn Fein. Thatcher was ignorant of the complexity of the issues in Northern Ireland. She believed toughness was the only response possible, although she did make modest concessions in the Anglo-Irish Agreement of 1985 that provoked the Protestant leader, the Reverend Ian Paisley, to call on "God, in wrath to take vengeance upon this wicked, treacherous, lying woman."[27] One can understand her hostility to the IRA, who planted bombs in a hotel where Cabinet members were lodging during a Conservative Party conference in 1984. It was the first attempt to murder the whole government since the Cato Street Conspiracy of 1820. Several prominent politicians and their spouses were killed or injured and Thatcher herself barely escaped death. Yet within a few hours she delivered a fighting speech. The violence continued. A mortar attack on 10 Downing Street when a Cabinet meeting was in session nearly pulled off the Cato Street trick in 1990.

In the end, 3,700 people lost their lives in the conflict. Numerous attempts were made to negotiate a settlement, without significant results. The British were desperate to leave. The cost of welfare payments and military occupation was a strain on the UK budget without any discernable return, but no compromise seemed possible. Tony Blair once noted: "both sides have absolute clarity about the wrongness of the position of the other side."[28]

The British government made strenuous efforts to reinvigorate the Ulster economy. The EU has also poured more than a billion and a half euros into Ulster. Prosperity and less discrimination (at least overtly) helped take the edge off the pain suffered by Catholics. Economic growth was helpful to the peace process. The European Union also had brought Britain and the Irish Republic closer together. New prosperity in the South created a more self-confident society, enabling them to break free from the myths that they had clung to in the past while shaping their worldview. Better educational opportunities were created. More realism entered into the thinking of the Provisional leadership and the efforts of David Trimble (b. 1944), a Unionist leader of exceptional courage and vision, helped create a climate for change. Both communities were exhausted by the violence.

More effective penetration of the IRA by the British intelligence service disrupted acquisition of weapons and explosives, and the 1991 collapse of the Soviet Union, which facilitated anti-Western terrorism wherever it could, helped in this regard. By one account, British spies had penetrated the IRA and Sinn Fein leadership so deeply and effectively it was holed like Swiss cheese.[29] At the same time new leadership arose in Britain, Ireland, and the United States. American money had long helped fund IRA terror. President Bill Clinton worked diligently and skillfully to support peace. The appointment of Bertie Ahern (b. 1951) as prime minister of the Irish Republic in 1997 was a critical component to making progress. Dublin was now harnessed with London in finding solutions that would leave the IRA not just out in the cold but in a deep freeze. He was dogged, realistic, and even heroic during the negotiations. That said, it was the imagination and determination of Tony Blair that put the peace process on track and kept it moving. He placed intense pressure on both sides to negotiate. Blair once told Sinn Fein: "The settlement train is leaving. I want you on the train. But it is leaving anyway and I will not allow it to wait for you."[30]

The leaders of the IRA were not new, but underground geologic shifts were taking place. Gerry Adams (b. 1948) combined pragmatic political skills and Machiavellian evasiveness with a ruthless sentimentality. His partner, Martin McGuinness (b. 1950), appeared to be made of softer material but was equally hard underneath. Due to the work of British spies the Nationalist leadership had lost the ability to operate effectively, and had to make their way to the peace table and surrender their precious goal of a united Ireland. Their helpful realism emerged out of an appreciation of the futility of deadlock.

The first part of the peace process, the "Good Friday Agreement," was concluded on April 10, 1998. Personal bitterness remained fierce. Some Unionist leaders refused to meet with Gerry Adams. One of them spurned the latter to his face with the declaration: "I don't talk to fucking murderers."[31] Bertie Ahern persuaded his countrymen south of the border to delete the claim to sovereignty over Ulster from the Republic's constitution. The repeal was supported by a remarkable majority of 96 percent in a national referendum.

Particularly controversial was the agreement to release both Protestant and Republican terrorists from prison and the supervision of the decommissioning of arms by the IRA, which provoked protracted arguments. In the words of a Blair aide: "the Republicans were florid, wordy and ambiguous, the Unionists blunt, rude and unyielding."[32] Ironically, the indiscriminate bombing by a breakaway faction of the IRA of a marketplace at Omagh on August 15, 1998, which killed 29 Catholics and Protestants including two unborn babies, was so inhuman that it forced the process forward. The IRA declared an end to their armed campaign in July 2005.

Some see that the downside of the peace process has been to marginalize middle-of-the-road parties and leaders such as Trimble and Hume. The political center weakened. Yet the process inched forward toward a viable new order. The Stormont Parliament was the first of the devolved institutions to provide home rule for one of the nations within the United Kingdom. Many are convinced, however, that the new regime in Belfast will eventually lead to a united Ireland. If that is the case, will the Parliaments instituted in Wales and Scotland by the Blair administration be the beginning of a process that will end the Union entirely?

British Identity

Never in the history of the United Kingdom had so many people felt proudly "British" as in that hour when Churchill appeared with the king and queen on the balcony of Buckingham Palace on VE Day, May 8, 1945. Never would so many feel it in the future. As times have changed, Richard Weight argues, the traditional bonds of the Union have loosened or disappeared and no compelling new national identity has emerged.[33] Ulster exemplifies the extent to which people living in a single, small area can perceive their identities in dramatically different ways. The concept of "Britishness" may not be quite so fractured, but, as we have repeatedly seen, it was by no means agreed upon by all the inhabitants of the archipelago. Moreover, characteristics of national identity have changed over time, and, to confuse things further, people have multiple, overlapping layers of loyalties. Despite strong attachments many people had to Wales, Scotland, and England, the first half of the twentieth century was a high point of *British* patriotism. The world wars intensified nationalism. For the first time all young men were drafted into a unified and homogenizing armed force. In the second half of the century, however, a trend toward more localized identities (which can be seen all over the world, not just in Britain) emerged more powerfully than at any time since the Act of Union in 1707.

A recent effort by the government to explain British history and values in a pamphlet to be given to immigrants seeking citizenship has provoked much criticism. It was riddled with errors and had airbrushed out unfortunate episodes, portraying the past through rose-tinted glasses.[34] Nonetheless, the tribal and mythic foundations of Britishness were and have remained strong: the English language, the monarchy, Parliament, liberal democracy, Protestantism, a strong civic culture, respect for authority, and a common enemy (Germany having replaced France). Outside observers often have a sense of perspective that natives lack. The art historian Sir Nikolaus Pevsner once attempted to define what made the English people distinctive. As a German who had fled Nazi persecution, he came to see stability and tolerance as the key elements in his adopted country's national identity: "England dislikes and distrusts revolutions. That is a forte in political development, but a weakness in art." Peter Mandler notes: "common sense, good temper, ordered freedom, progress ... were all qualities and traditions held in common by the English people."[35] Standing peacefully in queues and being diffident about overt displays of emotion, however, are relatively modern developments and certainly did not exist in the rollicking and undisciplined eighteenth century.

Centrifugal forces, however, were beginning to spin after 1945. Some historians have discerned a connection between the loss of empire and the detachment of Scotland from the United Kingdom. Ian Jack observes: "how odd that we thought the periphery would shrink, and the center stay unchanged."[36] Imperialism was a cement that held Britain together from the eighteenth century onwards. With the colonies that had offered so many opportunities to advance careers and bring economic prosperity gone, the ties that bound the two kingdoms became weaker.

By the 1990s a singular notion of a "British" national identity, to say nothing of Englishness and Scottishness, became more difficult to delineate because of the new social diversity created by black and Asian immigration. New religions, languages, cultures, and skin colors came to the island. Could the immigrants become British? Britain still has a smaller percentage of migrants as a percentage of the population than the USA, Germany, and France, all of which have above 10 percent, while the UK has around 8 percent. Yet in 2008 nearly two-thirds of Britons ranked immigration the top issue facing the country. Cultural clashes that once were largely based on economic fears about competition for jobs are now more grounded in cultural alienation. Here Muslims seem to be at the forefront. Four-fifths of the population feel that it would be better for the future of Britain if ethnic minorities integrated more into British culture and society.[37] Many Muslims feel unwelcome and unassimilated. Those who reject their new country in a radical way are relatively few in number, but they constitute breeding grounds for jihadi terrorism. Coordinated bomb attacks in London on July 7, 2005 left 52 dead (Figure 11.5). Fundamentalist

Figure 11.5   The London suicide bombings (July 7, 2005) killed 52 and injured 700

Muslims are troubled by religious toleration, free speech, and contemporary sexual mores. Multiculturalism may become a part of Britishness, but the continued distrust felt on both sides means that this is not so yet. Underlying and insidious prejudice against Britons of African descent can be found even in such respected institutions as the police.

Another danger to British identity comes from across the Channel. Orwell believed that the differences between someone from Scotland, Wales, or England "fade away the moment that any two Britons are confronted by a European." But in 2008 the United Kingdom, John Pocock argues, "is both threatened and tempted by absorption into a 'Europe' that is essentially a Franco-German condominium."[38] By joining a supranational organization like the EU some of the coherence of a unitary state is lost. It is still hard to assess the psychological impact of the Channel Tunnel, finally creating a land link with the Continent. Amazingly, it was Margaret Thatcher who pushed forward the long-discussed project in 1984. In 2008 it takes just two and a quarter hours to travel from London to Paris by train. Removal of barriers to labor mobility in Europe is transforming what it is to be a citizen. It is estimated that 200,000 French people now live in London.

Britain is a country "whose people, values, and institutions had spread all over the world."[39] English is now the global tongue. Unlike the French who hug their language to their chests like a precious jewel, the British cast forth their words to the winds. "What happens to a people if they cease to own their language?"[40] Some of the best writing in English is now published by children of the empire, such as Sir Salman Rushdie (born in India), Arundhati Roy (still living in India), Zadie Smith (born in London of Jamaican descent), the Naipul clan (from Trinidad), and many others. Derek Walcott from the Caribbean colony of St. Lucia won the Nobel Prize for Literature in 1992. Has "Britishness" been so diluted that it has ceased to have meaning?

"Modernizing" Britain led in the 1970s to the abolition of the traditional currency. Twenty shillings became a metric 100 pence. Ancient county boundaries were revised to accord with a more balanced population distribution. Rutland disappeared entirely while often disbelieving denizens of beloved Lancashire and Yorkshire became residents of unlovely "Greater Manchester" or only slightly more acceptable "Humberside." These removals of touchstones and markers shook people's comfort zones more seriously than officials in the central bureaucracy initially realized.

Forces favoring more localized identities can be found everywhere in Britain. The resurgence of the Welsh language is one example. The decline in identification with national Churches is another, although religion has remained a stronger force in Wales and Scotland than in England in recent years. In Northern Ireland it remains the central focus of identity but is all the more divisive because there are two competing religions in the province. Britain retains over 200 identifiable accents, probably more than any comparable country. Although syntax and inflexion mutate over time, the BBC and national curricula in schools have failed to bring about uniformity. The persistence of regional and class accents help sustain division and perhaps indicate a desire for separateness.

The Bank of Scotland continues to issue its own distinctive paper money. In 1956 stamps bearing separate symbols for the individual nations of the archipelago were printed for the first time, and this practice was later also adopted for coins. Education systems in some ways have grown further apart between Scotland and England. Funding is different, and higher education in Scotland is now cheaper. Poverty and unemployment are greater in Wales and Scotland than in England. Sports have also become ever more nationally distinctive. Now flags bearing the English cross of St. George can regularly be seen at athletic events, and "Englishness" has emerged as a powerful force.

Wales

Low emigration rates and absence of a military draft probably allowed the Welsh language to continue more strongly than it might otherwise have done up until World War I, when decline began to set in. Although Wales was granted its own regional radio station by the BBC in 1937, the homogenizing effects of time spent in the army and massive emigration during the 1920s and 1930s had a serious impact. By the 1950s the language seemed in danger of dying. A battle began to save it, which for a time included civil disobedience and political activism. English road signs were painted over, and demonstrations took place. The government responded by setting up a Welsh Office and passing legislation in 1967 that placed the Welsh language on a par with English in the principality. However, it took the threat of a hunger strike by the president of Plaid Cymru, the nationalist party, in 1979 to stop the Tory government from reneging on a pledge to establish an all-Welsh TV station.[41] The number of Welsh speakers continued to decline. In 1901 half of the population could speak the language, by 1951 it was only 29 percent, and down to one-fifth at the millennium. Then the tide began to turn, and the 2001 census showed numbers of Welsh speakers rising for the first time since 1911.

Wales had a distinctive political culture. It was more proletarian than England or Scotland. Many felt from the 1920s onwards that the "English" government was either indifferent to or actively taking advantage of the Welsh. The death of the coal industry was particularly traumatic. Even today Wales has a per capita GDP not much more than half that of London's. Allegiance to the Liberal Party gradually gave way in the 1920s and 1930s to massive support for Labour. A group of Welsh speakers founded Plaid Cymru (the Party of Wales) at the National Eisteddfod in 1925, but it did not become an effective political force until the 1960s. A referendum rejected a separate Welsh assembly in the 1970s by a vote of four to one, although non-related political issues may have affected the outcome. Plaid Cymru won only 14 percent of the vote in 2001. Leading Labour politicians such as Aneurin Bevan and Neil Kinnock were anti-separatists. The party relied on working-class votes in Wales to counteract the Tory advantage in England. It was a Labour government that arranged for the investiture of the queen's eldest son as Prince of Wales in 1969 in

Figure 11.6 Cardiff Arms Park was built in 1881. It was eventually expanded to hold 65,000 people at rugby matches. In 1884 the first international match was played on the ground between Wales and Ireland. In time it became the national stadium and one of the most important sites for the expression of Welsh national identity with the crowd singing hymns and anthems

the hope that by acknowledging a national sense of distinctiveness Plaid Cymru's influence could be blunted. Although a few protests took place, Prince Charles was welcomed warmly by the crowd at his first appearance that year at the rugby ground, Cardiff Arms Park, a sacred site of Welsh nationhood (Figure 11.6).[42] Blair's commitment to devolution can also be seen from the perspective of trying to keep the Welsh loyal to Labour.

Scotland

During the twentieth century greater and greater sensitivity was paid to Scottish distinctiveness. The Scottish National Party (SNP) was founded in 1934. The movement remained, however, obscure. Its politics were "vituperative, portentous and endlessly garrulous."[43] The BBC initiated a Scottish television service in 1952. The commercial station STV opened in 1955. A Scottish Stock Exchange was established in 1969.

A national "Covenant" was launched in 1949 that collected about two million signatures in favor of home rule, but the movement lacked a parliamentary strategy. A group of youths stole the "Stone of Destiny" from the coronation chair in Westminster Abbey in 1950. This totem, on which Scottish kings were crowned, from a period lost in the mists of time, had been seized by the English in 1296. Much nationalistic fervor was provoked by the incident, although the stone was returned in time for Elizabeth II's installation. Both the Labour and Tory parties opposed devolution.

The victory in 1967 of SNP candidate Winifred Ewing in what had been a secure Labour seat brought the issue of Scottish independence back into the political arena. In the first of the two 1974 elections the SNP won 22 percent of the vote and became a force to be reckoned with. In the second election of that year it relegated the Tories to third place in the race for Scottish seats. Scotland now had a four-party system with significant support given to the Liberals and the SNP as well as to Labour and the Conservatives.

To some degree the SNP's success was a protest against economic policies rather than support for independence. Many of the Scots who voted SNP were maneuvering for a better deal within the UK. The Scottish economy has suffered far more setbacks than the English one. Scots emigrated at a much higher rate than the English. Nearly 400,000 left during the 1920s and this outflow was sustained after the war. In 1981 the population of England was 30 percent higher than 60 years earlier; Scotland was only 5 percent larger.[44] The latter still grows at a rate slower than any other European country. Even today male life expectancy in some of the inner-city parts of Glasgow is lower than in Third World countries. Scottish death rates from lung cancer and cirrhosis of the liver are higher than anywhere else in the UK.[45] New economic policies pursued by Heath and Thatcher made things worse, as did the latter's obvious contempt for the welfare state. When "black gold" was found in the North Sea, "it's *Our* oil," became a commonly held sentiment.[46] By 1986 Scottish oil production made up 5 percent of British GNP, and London showed no signs of surrendering that income to Scotland. The hostility toward the Thatcher government became ferocious. She, on the other hand, despised the Scottish trades union movement, which since the 1970s had been led in all the key industries by professed communists.[47]

The Scots became mutinous after discovering the "poll tax" was to be levied in Scotland before England. The leaders of the three largest Scottish Churches condemned the tax as "undemocratic, unjust, socially divisive and destructive of community and family life." A massive campaign forced the issuance of 700,000 warrants for non-payment. The Scottish historian T. M. Devine summed up the problem: "The poll tax drove home the message to many Scots that they were being ruled by an alien government." "Increasingly, the problem of governance in Scotland was seen not simply as being rooted in Thatcherism but instead derived from the very nature of the British constitutional system itself."[48]

The Campaign for a Scottish Assembly now caught fire, with leadership drawn from all facets of Scottish life. The SNP moved away from radical positions and made a wider appeal. In 1990 a convention on the Scottish constitution issued a plan for a Parliament in Edinburgh. Labour embraced the idea more wholeheartedly than before. A desperate John Major voluntarily returned the "Stone of Destiny" to Edinburgh. The referendum offered by Tony Blair in 1997 for home rule won three-quarters of the votes. The new Scottish Parliament was opened in 1999 with the queen appearing in tartan. Initially, Labour formed the executive in tandem with the Liberals. However, weak leadership and outrageous cost overruns on the new Parliament building led to change. The SNP won the election of 2007, and the first minister, Alex Salmond (b. 1954), is bent on arranging a referendum on independence. His seriousness can be judged by his willingness to renounce republicanism and embrace Elizabeth II as Queen of Scots.

There is no doubt that an intensified sense of Scottishness has arisen along with a mild form of Anglophobia. The majority of people, however, continue to feel both Scottish and British. Myths and misperceptions persist. Cultural nationalists, for example, fear that insufficient attention is paid in Scottish schools to the country's unique historical development. Conversely, supporters of the Union tend to fear excessive concentration upon Scottish history and heritage. In fact, a recent study shows that the history curriculum in Scottish schools is generally evenly balanced.[49]

Scots continue to play a central role in British politics. Two recent leaders of the Liberal Democratic Party were from north of the border, as is Blair's successor in 2007, Gordon Brown (b. 1951). These and a number of other senior Labour ministers who are Scots support the preservation of the Union, which is necessary for the survival of the Labour Party as it presently exists. One unresolved issue relating to devolved government that continues to cause difficulty is referred to as the "West Lothian Question." Why should the MP from West Lothian (or any constituency in Scotland, Wales, or Northern Ireland) have a vote on issues relating to social and economic policies in England while English MPs have no comparable influence outside their borders? Some Conservatives are proposing that Scots MPs be blocked from voting on legislation that affects England alone, although ruling on what is and what is not an "English" question could be very difficult. A majority of English people now favor the establishment of an English Parliament. Polls show many Britons are pessimistic about the long-term prospects for the survival of the Union.

Other Aspects of Instability

In 2001 the population of the United Kingdom stood at 58.7 million (England – 49.1 million; Wales – 2.9; Scotland – 5.1; Northern Ireland – 1.6). Within the decade it will reach 60 million. With some ups and downs, the birth rate continues to fall. This is not just because of the arrival of the birth control pill and the legalization of abortion in the 1960s. Complex motives related to giving children a better chance in life and to women having more control over their lives drive the downward trend. At the same time life expectancy from birth has risen from 55 years for women and 51 for men in 1900 to 80 and 75 respectively at the end of the century. If present trends continue, half of all females born in Britain in 2006 will live to be over 100.[50] Most future population growth is likely to come from immigration. Britain confronts the problem of an aging population that will rely on a smaller and smaller workforce to support them in retirement. Between 1981 and 1998 the total cost in real terms of social security expenditure to benefit the elderly in Great Britain rose by over 40 percent.[51] How can this be sustained?

Families are changing not only in size but also in structure. Until the 1980s the great majority of births occurred within marriage. The illegitimacy rate was 13 percent in 1981 but rose to 38 percent by 1998. The divorce rate shot up. The number of single-parent families has quadrupled since 1971; in 1998 almost a quarter of families were headed by a lone woman. The age at first marriage began to rise in the 1970s and 1980s. In 2001 only 55 percent of the adult population was married. Sexual mores have changed and become increasingly relaxed; cohabitation before marriage is now widespread. Britain was a stable country when most marriages held together and family loyalty was taken for granted. Will the changes in the family lead to destabilization of society as a whole?

Three-quarters of workers in 1900 were manual laborers. The proportion still stood at nearly half in 1964, but by 1983 it was only 34 percent. A mere one-fifth of GDP is now contributed by industry. Today Britain has a more flexible workforce than Italy, Germany, or France. Much of what is left of industry is high-tech or in research-based fields such as aerospace engines and pharmaceuticals. Foreign investment, both inward and outward, forms a larger percentage of GDP than its main European rivals and the USA.[52] However, North Sea oil is declining in output, and long-term trends in energy could well destabilize Britain's economy.

Another unsettling force is growing economic inequality. The proportion of wealth owned by the richest 1 percent declined from just under half to about one-quarter between 1945 and the early 1990s, but most of this redistribution occurred among the top 25 percent. In the 1990s the bottom half of the population owned only 6 percent of all wealth. Poverty remained persistent and even began to grow again. Around 12 percent of the population was classified as living in poverty in the 1960s and 1970s but the figure rose to 21 percent in 1992.[53] Thatcherism/Blairism corroded the old class system. But the new meritocrats so admired by followers of "new Britain" are often more assertive in their right to rule and the justice of their privileges than the older hereditary upper class.

The toxic nature of the British press in the last two decades has weakened respect for public servants. The "**tabloids**," in particular, grew more sarcastic, self-righteous, and mean-spirited. The obsession with destroying politicians – or anyone else in public life, for that matter – by the overt invasion of privacy with information gained through bribery or other illegal means seems more pernicious every year. The rise of the 24-hour news cycle on television, which has increasingly turned journalism into entertainment rather than a public service, is driven by a desperate need to fill up time blocks with action footage and hyped stories to attract advertising revenue.

Mention has already been made of the tensions caused by immigration. The hardening of many fundamentalist Muslims against Western values makes them difficult to absorb as citizens at home and have turned some of them into enemies. The preemptive strike against Iraq violated international law, defied international opinion, was based on false intelligence, and was inadequately planned. It became one of the

Biography 11.2

Eliza Manningham-Buller
1948–

Eliza Manningham-Buller was born into a traditional aristocratic family. Her father, a **Lord Chancellor** in the 1960s, was only the first Viscount Dilhorne, but his branch of the Buller family owned 10,000 acres in the later nineteenth century and gained a title in 1790. The senior line was even richer, had been established gentry by the fourteenth century, and elected the family's first of over 30 MPs in 1555. Her mother trained pigeons that carried coded messages for the intelligence service to France and Germany during World War II. Manningham-Buller joined the security services in the 1970s. She specialized in counter-espionage and became head of the effort to penetrate the IRA. She was a senior liaison working out of Washington, DC with the CIA during the first Gulf War (1991). In 2002 she was appointed Director General of MI5, the agency in charge of home security and the anti-terrorist campaign in Northern Ireland and against al-Qaeda. She was the second woman to hold the post (**Dame** Stella Rimmington served 1991–6). She worked to make MI5 more open both in recruitment of agents and about warnings of possible terrorist attacks. She retired in 2007. Though the upper reaches of the British establishment are no longer crowded with the sons of the landed elite, neither its sons nor daughters have disappeared from power, as Dame Eliza's career illustrates.

biggest fiascoes in Anglo-American foreign policy in modern times. Its consequences in terms of terror at home and abroad are still not fully understood. Fortunately, the British intelligence services (see Eliza Manningham-Buller in Biography 11.2) have a good record of monitoring security threats, but they are not always successful.

Britain faces other threats, such as global warming, that are shared with the rest of the world. Like many countries there has been insufficient investment in new infrastructure and in properly maintaining the old. Rising crime rates make some people fearful to leave their houses, and shopping malls are killing off small businesses that anchor communities. Crimes of violence have increased to the extent that the police now often carry firearms. Public drunkenness and lack of respect for the elderly or public decency has become widespread. It still hard to say, however, whether this is a blip or a long-term trend. Today critics denounce fecklessness, selfishness, loutishness, vulgarity, and a therapeutic approach to evil that eliminates moral judgments.[54] Countervailing forces against these destabilizing factors are, however, robust.

Dynamic Prosperity

The disappearance of talk about "declinism" suggests that on balance most Britons regard the future with optimism. The dialectic of continuity and change continues to provide stability and prosperity. Britain was the only major state in Europe not to buckle and go under in modern times. France has suffered convulsion or collapse on five occasions between 1789 and 1940, to say nothing of numerous rewrites of its constitution. Italy, Spain, Germany, and Russia have also experienced revolutions and catastrophic military defeats. Britain not only avoided revolution and won a great triumph over Napoleon in the nineteenth century, but also it surmounted the three great fiscal-military challenges of the twentieth century: World War I, World War II, and the Cold War.

Britons enjoy an enormous advantage by birth of being native speakers of English, which opens commercial and cultural opportunities for them all over the world. London Heathrow is the largest international airport; Oxford and Cambridge rank among the best universities anywhere. Some of the largest and most dynamic business corporations in the world are headquartered in Britain; London remains second only to New York as the financial center of the world and also among the most desirable places on the planet to live. The Royal Navy ranks third in size and power. Only the United States has accumulated more Nobel prizes in science. The creative energy of British society in literature, music, science, and technology remains vibrant. Britain has more libraries per capita than any other country. The CAT scanner, the Dolby system for sound, and the disposable diaper are British inventions. In 1991 Tim Berners-Lee created the address system that makes it possible to operate the world-wide web. The government-funded National Physical Laboratory helped create Britain's competitive advantage in scientific application software and network management. "Dolly" the sheep, the first cloned mammal, was born in Scotland. British actors continue play a role in Hollywood films out of all proportion to their numbers. The Archbishop of Canterbury is still the leader of the world-wide communion of Anglicans, and the queen is the head of the Commonwealth with a population of two billion people. The BBC's global news service ranks well ahead of its competitors in reach and quality.

Among the top 10 economies in size in the world Britain ranked sixth in 2005, behind the USA, China, Japan, Germany, and India, and ahead of France, Russia, and Italy. Britain now leads its fellow EU members in GDP per person in real purchasing power.[55] Between 1971 and 2000 household disposable income per head doubled. Food is much better in quality and variety than it used to be. In the 1980s and 1990s Britain exploded with malls, multiplex cinemas, DIY superstores, and large-scale supermarkets. The environment is being cleaned up and planners and politicians are more sensitive to the need to recycle old buildings rather than tear everything down. Inner cities long abandoned in the flight to the suburbs are now undergoing revitalization. Britain is more egalitarian in spirit than it once was. The middle class grows ever larger and more diverse. Social and sexual stereotypes are disappearing and people are free to be themselves in ways never possible before. More students have access to higher education, and the health service, despite its faults, greatly improved during the Blair years, and it is still free. Much of the country is computer literate and people are connected ever more closely by cell phones and email.

The State of Britain

The success of J. K. Rowling's *Harry Potter* series is perhaps in part due to the darkening clouds on the world horizon that make us all wish we had some magical solution to our problems. Hogwarts, her school for wizards, bears a very strong resemblance to an elite "public" school with all its rules, games, and traditions. Comparatively few of her readers will ever have had any connection with such institutions, yet the codes of behavior in them remain distinctively British. The potent spell of tradition continues to live on in post-Blairian Britannia.

Britain is a society where custom not law determined the shape and substance of institutions. The constitution remains flexible. At its core, embedded in non-rational, traditional wellsprings of culture and memory resides the monarchy. George V, George VI, and Elizabeth II perhaps helped to moderate the pace of change. Some see this as contributing to retarded modernization and decline. Even if that was so, it also helped sustain consensus and stability. As a young man, George V wrote in his notebook after studying Bagehot's analysis of the constitution: "The existence of the Crown serves to *disguise* change and therefore to deprive it of the evil consequences of revolution."[56]

The monarchy successfully detached itself from the old court and aristocracy. Increasingly, it floated free of the Conservative Party. Recent studies by Vernon Bogdanor, Ben Pimlott, and William Kuhn have found that royal political influence continued, largely under the radar, and that by and large, in the latter's words, "it has assisted rather than thwarted discussion, liberty and democracy in Britain."[57] Brilliantly orchestrated ceremonies came to be seen as celebrations of nationhood. Even when Diana, Princess of Wales (1961–97) attempted to use her titanic star power to take revenge on her tormentors inside Buckingham Palace, it turned out that the queen possessed a more durable source of magic. Within a few years of Diana's funeral, more than a million people filled the Mall to celebrate Elizabeth II's Golden Jubilee, a crowd larger than any since VE Day. Though polls reveal ups and downs, the institution continues to receive far more popular support than any political party or other institution in British life.

The monarchy's most useful contribution remains its sponge-like quality that allows it to absorb poisons in the body politic. Ferdinand Mount argues: "There is, of course, an alternative to intense monarchism, readily available but not discussed by … any of those who argue for a republic or for a stripped down secular monarchy. The alternative is nationalism, raw and unrestrained by any higher authority.

Nationalism is not simply a dangerous possibility when customary loyalties have broken up. It is virtually inevitable."[58] The monarchy flourished over the past two centuries because it successfully linked itself to and exemplified liberal constitutionalism, and played a crucial role in defining national identity against less liberal foreign regimes.[59]

Parliament evolves just as the monarchy does. It has not lost its legitimacy. Modern British revolutions such as the Reform Acts of 1832 and 1884, the ouster of Edward VIII in 1936 and Chamberlain in 1940, the establishment of the welfare state of 1945 and the Thatcherite state of 1979 all took place *inside* the Palace of Westminster, not outside it. Much of the success of Parliament in providing effective government has been due to the two-party system. Eschewing proportional representation, which has been adopted for elections to the devolved parliaments and for MEPs (Members of the European Parliament), has provided governments with greater authority to make major reforms than Continental systems with multiple parties have been able to achieve. Almost all successful political leaders have been obliged to lean toward the center of politics, which meant avoiding republicanism, Marxism, and fascism. Even notable left-wingers, whatever their private reservations, bended their knees to the monarch; even notable right-wingers accepted as final major constitutional changes. Both the Labour and Conservative parties sought support across the class spectrum. In 1945 a third of working-class voters cast ballots for Tories and this rose to 44 percent in 1951. New Labour attracted a substantial portion of its votes from the middle class. There is some evidence to suggest that support for the two-party system is fading. Whether a new configuration will emerge or whether this is a result of less engagement by the electorate in the political system is still unclear. Changes tend to be made step by step in Britain, which leaves radicals angry but hopeful and reactionaries frightened but not despairing. Orwell put it best. The British, he said, have a preference "for doing things slowly."[60]

The civil service is an important force in the British political system, incorruptible and efficient but perhaps too powerful. The able permanent leaders of the service can become formidable roadblocks to change. The Labour minister Richard Crossman famously recorded the subtle maneuverings of his top aide, Dame Evelyn Sharp, in his diaries. The ability of the senior officials to thwart ministerial policies became even better known through the television comedy, *Yes, Minister* (1980–2). In fact, much depends on the personalities of the individuals concerned. Many civil servants were repulsed by Thatcher's ideology but tried loyally to carry out her commands. The advent of Blair's "special advisors" may fundamentally alter the system.

The British military, though reduced in size over the last half century, remains strong and experienced. It is another example of an innovative yet intensely traditionalist institution. Britain spends more on its military than any other country in the world except the USA. In 2006, while America allocated nearly half of the total world outlay on military personnel and equipment (46 percent), Britain stood next at 5.1 percent, followed by countries such as China at 4.3 percent, Germany at 3.2 percent, Russia at 3 percent.[61]

Strong forces counter the trend toward the break-up of the United Kingdom. Some people clearly do not want more local autonomy. In 2004 over three-quarters of the electorate in northeast England voted to reject the establishment of a regional assembly. The welfare state is organized on a UK basis as a single entity. The struggle the British continue to have in becoming Europeans suggests that elements in their national identity are still potent. The intense feeling of pride that many British people take in their country's role in twentieth-century history is not matched by the Germans, French, Italians, and Russians. In a 2008 poll only 2 percent of Britons thought of themselves politically as Scottish or Welsh nationalists, compared with 27 percent who identified with the Conservative Party and 34 percent with Labour.[62]

British Exceptionalism

The Whig interpretation of history portrays Britain as a unique society. It was superior to other, less favored nations in its inevitable march to democracy and greatness. This image does not jibe, however, with what we can see in the early twenty-first century: a country that went to war in Iraq against the wishes of a majority of its people; the only major state in the world to retain a hereditary aristocracy with guaranteed access to seats in the legislature; a once great commercial and imperial power now playing a modest role in world trade and without an empire; a composite state that includes four different nations perhaps on the verge of dissolution. The oak in the flowerpot could not sustain global hegemony. The rampant lion standing on the small outcropping of rock in the North Atlantic was left behind by rival giants whose population, resources, and wealth meant that the big cat seemed to have little to roar about.

Yet, several characteristics mark modern Britain as a distinct society, particularly when compared to its peers in Europe. The capitalist system has been harsh on poor people, and the law has tended to protect the interests of the rich. Again and again, however, grudging or not, most British observers, even from the working class itself, have pointed to the fact that the laboring people "were not persistently harassed by the more violent evidences of the powers above them, and felt – however severe their troubles – that the law was fairly generally applicable and authority not hopelessly corrupt."[63] This bred a reasonableness, a willingness among people to get along together in spite of gross disparities in wealth and power.

The single most important characteristic of British society in the twentieth century has been an insistence on individualism and resistance to regimentation. The British government and people had learned what G. M. Trevelyan once called "the difficult art of leaving one another alone."[64] The solitary art of fishing is the most popular hobby in the country; the individual house the most precious possession. One of the nastier epithets than a British person can hurl at someone they do not like is "nosey parker." A nosey parker invades privacy and sticks his or her nose into matters that do not concern them. Privacy is precious to Britons, and their devotion to it underpins their zest for freedom and antagonism toward bureaucracy and regulations. Communism failed to gain ascendancy over the working class; fascism left the declining and dispossessed gentry cold.

Americans find the modern British state intrusive and secretive. It is true that Britons surrender more of their freedom to the government than US citizens do. On the other hand, they are equally or even more robust in their attachment to the right to criticize those in authority and to assert freedom of speech. A modern German scholar, Ralf Dahrendorf, who knew both his own country and Britain well, judged: "There is a fundamental liberty about life in Britain which is not easily found elsewhere."[65] The tradition of dissent is deeply rooted. The British state is subject to constant scrutiny. The closest Americans have to "prime minister's question time" in the Commons is a presidential press conference. Both events can be uninformative, but the former is much more likely than the latter to lead to enlightening political debate. While Americans tend to become almost fascistic when someone uses the stars and stripes as a target of protest, in Britain monarchs have been savagely satirized and lampooned from the days of eighteenth-century cartoons to late twentieth-century TV puppetry. Jonathan Parry argues that since 1688, the Crown "is held, not just on sufferance, but as a legitimate object of popular rebuke, gossip and prurience, a symbol of a free political society."[66] That Britons aim irreverent humor and fierce criticism at their icon of nationhood is one of their most admirable qualities.

The synergy between continuity and change has allowed freedom to flourish and that in turn promoted the dynamic stability that has allowed Britain to maintain its balance while most European states experienced repeated diversions away from peace and prosperity. The fact that Britain was an island protected it from many of the forces that could have devastated both the state and the economy. The possession of a ruling class willing to bend rather than break and a laboring class that accepted much less than it deserved in order to keep the peace created a unique political atmosphere compared to that of Germany, Russia, Italy, Spain, or France. Good luck, but also good management, helped keep Britain affluent if not always happy.

Historians are often very bad guides to the future. As the underlying forces of the United Kingdom shift during the twenty-first century, new identities and ideas that we cannot possibly foresee will emerge. The odds are good, however, based on the experience of the last three centuries, that at least in outward forms the country will remain recognizable. Whether spirited resistance to incursions on personal freedom will continue unabated is another question.

Notes

1   The British Isles in 1714

1   See: L. Shaw-Taylor, "The Rise of Agrarian Capitalism and the Decline of Family Farming in England," Cambridge Group for the History of Population and Social Structure, Department of Geography, University of Cambridge, 2008, online: http://www.hpss. geog.cam.ac.uk/research/projects/occupation

2   The remaining 7 percent came from government. N. F. R. Crafts, *British Economic Growth during the Industrial Revolution*, Oxford, 1985, 16.

3   J. Hoppit, *A Land of Liberty?: England 1689–1727*, Oxford, 2000, 8, 55, 418–20, 425.

4   D. Defoe, *A Tour through the Whole Island of Great Britain*, ed. P. Rogers, London, 1971, 286.

5   C. A. Bayly, *The Birth of the Modern World 1780–1914*, Oxford, 2004, 62.

6   S. W. Mintz, *Sweetness and Power: The Place of Sugar in Modern History*, London, 1986, 39, 67.

7   J. Cannon, *Aristocratic Century: The Peerage in Eighteenth-Century England*, Cambridge, 1984, 10, 15.

8   E. Wasson, *Born to Rule: British Political Elites*, Stroud, 2000, 57.

9   D. Thomson, *Woodbrook*, Harmondsworth, 1976, 71–2.

10   Thomas Turner, *Diary, 1754–1765*, ed. D. Vaisey, Oxford, 1985.

11   W. Prest, *Albion Ascendant: English History, 1660–1815*, Oxford, 1998, 165.

12   P. Langford, *A Polite and Commercial People: England 1727–1783*, Oxford, 1989, 65–6.

13   P. Langford, *Public Life and the Propertied Englishman, 1689–1798*, Oxford, 1994, 10.

14   R. Porter, *English Society in the Eighteenth Century*, rev. ed., New York, 1990, 108.

15   Recent research suggests, for example, that it was easier to gain access to the French nobility than was once believed. M. W. McCahill, "Open Elites: Recruitment to the French Noblesse and the English Aristocracy in the Eighteenth Century," *Albion*, 30 (1999), 599–629.

16   L. Stone and J. F. Stone, *An Open Elite? England 1540–1880*, Oxford, 1984, 218, 221, 280, 402–5, 423.

17   Wasson, *Born to Rule*, 65–92.

18   J. L. Ionides and P. G. Howell, *The Old Houses of Shropshire in the 19th Century*, Ludlow, 2006, 11.

19   S. Schama, *Rough Crossings: Britain, the Slaves and the American Revolution*, New York, 2006, 24.

20   T. Barnard, *A New Anatomy of Ireland: The Irish Protestants, 1649–1770*, New Haven, 2003, 39.

21 First appointed in Scotland only from 1794; in Ireland called governors.

22 D. Eastwood, "Local Government and Local Society," in *A Companion to Eighteenth-Century Britain*, ed. H. T. Dickinson, Oxford, 2002, 40–54.

23 Barnard, *A New Anatomy of Ireland*, 329–30.

24 L. Stone, *The Family, Sex and Marriage in England 1500–1800*, abridged ed., New York, 1979.

25 M. Lenox-Conyngham, *An Old Ulster House: Springhill and the People Who Lived in It*, Belfast, 2005, 80.

26 Quoted in A. Vickery, *The Gentleman's Daughter: Women's Lives in Georgian England*, New Haven, 1998, 86.

27 Considerable progress has been made in women's studies, but our understanding of masculinity is still in the exploratory stages. See the *Journal of British Studies*, 44 (2005) 274–362.

28 L. G. Mitchell, ed., *The Purefoy Letters 1735–1753*, New York, 1973, 6.

29 P. O'Farrell, *England and Ireland since 1800*, Oxford, 1975, 15.

30 J. Boswell, *Boswell for the Defence 1769–1774*, ed. W. K. Wimsatt, Jr. and F. A. Pottle, London, 1960, 100.

31 For the importance of "Zadock the Priest," see T. C. W. Blanning, *The Culture of Power and the Power of Culture: Old Regime Europe 1660–1789*, Oxford, 2002, 268, 273.

32 Lenox-Conygham, *An Old Ulster House*, 91.

33 "Mr. Jorrocks" quoted in K. Rose, *The Later Cecils*, New York, 1975, 69.

34 J. Woodforde, *The Diary of a Country Parson 1758–1802*, ed. J. Beresford, London, 1972, 396.

35 Linda Colley and David Cannadine have called it a "British" aristocracy, a remade supra-national elite. L. Colley, *Britons: Forging the Nation, 1707–1837*, New Haven, 1992, 155–93; D. Cannadine *Aspects of Aristocracy, Grandeur and Decline in Modern Britain*, New Haven, 1994, 2, 9–36, and *Decline and Fall of the British Aristocracy*, New Haven, 1990, 5–9. But see Wasson, *Born to Rule*, 145–8.

36 L. Namier and J. Brooke, *The House of Commons 1754–1790*, London, 1964, I, 172.

37 N. Everett, *A Landlord's Garden, Dereen Demesne*, Currakeal, 2005, 5.

38 E. M. Johnston-Liik, *History of the Irish Parliament 1692–1800*, Belfast, 2002, 6 vols., I, 108.

39 Barnard, *A New Anatomy of Ireland*, 39, 146.

2   A New Beginning, 1714–62

1 Lord North quoted in R. Pares, *King George III and the Politicians*, Oxford, 1967, 34.

2 F. O'Gorman, *Voters, Patrons, and Parties: The Unreformed Electoral System of Hanoverian England, 1734–1832*, Oxford, 1989.

3 B. P. Lenman, "From the Union of 1707 to the Franchise Reform of 1832," in R. A. Houston and W. W. J. Knox, eds. *The New Penguin History of Scotland*, London, 2001, 324–5.

4 R. F. Foster, *Modern Ireland, 1600–1972*, London, 1988, 226, 228.

5 J. H. Plumb, *The Growth of Political Stability in England 1675–1725*, Harmondsworth, 1969, 182.

6   J. Brewer, *The Sinews of Power: War, Money, and the English State, 1688–1783*, Cambridge, MA, 1990, 40, 116.

7   Ibid., 65–6.

8   Ibid., 112–13.

9   P. Kennedy, *The Rise and Fall of the Great Powers: Economic Change and Military Conflict from 1500 to 2000*, New York, 1989, 99.

10 Plumb, *The Growth of Political Stability in England 1675–1725*.

11 P. Langford, *A Polite and Commercial People: England 1727–1783*, Oxford, 1989, 195.

12 T. M. Devine, *The Scottish Nation, 1700–2000*, London, 1999, 48.

13 Horace Walpole, *Correspondence with Sir Horace Mann*, III, ed. W. S. Lewis, W. H. Smith, and G. L. Lam, New Haven, 1954, 281, 296.

14 Ibid., III, 4, 286.

15 J. Black, *The Hanoverians: The History of a Dynasty*, London, 2004, 110.

16 See his autobiography: *The Interesting Narrative and Other Writings of Olaudah Equiano*, New York, 2000 [1789].

17 Joseph Knight, a slave purchased as a child in Jamaica, was later taken to Scotland. In 1776 he brought action for his liberty on the grounds that the laws of Scotland did not tolerate slavery, and finally won.

18 W. J. Bate, *Samuel Johnson*, New York, 1977, 446.

19 G. M. Young, *Portrait of an Age: Victorian England*, ed. G. Kitson Clark, London, 1977, 21.

20 He was still a slave captain at the time he wrote the hymn. The narrative of his conversion was complicated.

21 E. P. Thompson, *The Making of the English Working Class*, New York, 1963, 368.

22 B. S. Schlenther, *Oxford Dictionary of National Biography*.

23 Thompson, *The Making of the English Working Class*, 43.

24 J. C. D. Clark, *English Society 1688–1832*, Cambridge, 1985, 316.

25 Langford, *A Polite and Commercial People*, xi, 5, 68, 678, 690.

26 J. C. D. Clark, *Revolution and Rebellion: State and Society in England in the Seventeenth and Eighteenth Centuries*, Cambridge, 1986, 42–3.

27 H. Butterfield, *The Whig Interpretation of History*, New York, 1951.

28 Langford, *A Polite and Commercial People*, 4, 71, 665–6.

3   War and Revolution, 1763–1814

1   R. Middleton, *Bell of Victory*, Cambridge, 1986, 77, cited in J. Brewer, *The Sinews of Power: War, Money, and the English State, 1688–1783*, Cambridge, MA, 1990, 175.

2   J. H. Elliott, *Empires of the Atlantic World: Britain and Spain in America 1492–1830*, New Haven, 2006, 298, 306.

3   I. R. Christie, *Wars and Revolutions: Britain 1760–1815*, London, 1982, 67.

4   L. Namier, *The Structure of Politics at the Accession of George III*, 2nd ed., London, 1957, 315.

5   B. Hilton, *A Mad, Bad and Dangerous People? England 1783–1846*, Oxford, 2006, 32.

6   F. O'Gorman, *The Long Eighteenth Century: British Political and Social History 1688–1832*, New York, 1997, 143.

7   W. M. Elofson, *The Rockingham Connection and the Second Founding of the Whig Party 1768–1773*, Montreal, 1996, 8.

8   L. G. Mitchell, "The Whigs, the People, and Reform," in T. C. W. Blanning and P. Wende, eds., *Reform in Great Britain and Germany, 1750–1850*, Oxford, 1999, 25.

9   Thomas Turner, *Diary, 1754–1765*, ed. D. Vaisey, Oxford, 1985, 275.

10 J. Warner, *John the Painter: Britain's First International Terrorist*, London, 2005.

11 Two-thirds of the total of American emigrants in the colonial period – up to 250,000 people – came form Ulster. R. F. Foster, *Modern Ireland, 1600–1972*, London, 1988, 216, 241.

12 J. Woodforde, *The Diary of a Country Parson 1758–1802*, ed. J. Beresford, Oxford, 1972, 198.

13 Edmund Burke, *Reflections on the Revolution in France*, Indianapolis, 1955, 89.

14 A. Goodrich, *Debating England's Aristocracy in the 1790s: Pamphlets, Polemics and Political Ideas*, London, 2005, 56.

15 P. Langford, *Oxford Dictionary of National Biography*.

16 J. E. Cookson, *The British Armed Nation 1793–1815*, Oxford, 1997, 261.

17 A. Hochschild, *Bury the Chains, Prophets and Rebels in the Fight to Free an Empire's Slaves*, Boston, 2005, 281.

18 J. Brooke, *King George III*, Frogmore, 1974, 490.

19 M. Jasanoff, *Edge of Empire: Lives, Culture, and Conquest in the East 1750–1850*, New York, 2005, 172.

20 From his *Thoughts on the Late Transactions Respecting Falkland's Islands* (1771), quoted in R. Folkenflik, "To See Ourselves as He Did," *TLS*, April 7, 2006, 8.

4   A United Kingdom, 1815

1   M. Daunton, *Progress and Poverty: An Economic and Social History of Britain 1700–1850*, Oxford, 1995, 51.

2   L. Shaw-Taylor, "The Occupational Structure of England c. 1750–1871: a Preliminary Report," Cambridge Group for the History of Population and Social Structure, Department of Geography, University of Cambridge, 2008, online, http://www.hpss.geog.cam.ac.uk/research/projects/occupations.

3   Ibid.

4   Daunton, *Progress and Poverty*, 136, 219, 232.

5   B. P. Lenman, "From the Union of 1707 to the Franchise Reform of 1832," in R. A. Houston and W. W. J. Knox, eds., *The New Penguin History of Scotland*, London, 2001, 287; T. M. Devine, *The Scottish Nation, 1700–2000*, London, 1999, 107, 112, 152.

6   J. Boswell, *The Ominous Years 1774–1776*, ed. C. Ryskamp and F. A. Pottle, London, 1963, 6.

7   Devine, *The Scottish Nation, 1700–2000*, 150.

8   Ibid., 214.

9   D. Spring, "English Landowners and Nineteenth-Century Industrialism," in J. T. Ward and R. G. Wilson, eds., *Land and Industry: The Landed Estates and the Industrial Revolution*, Newton Abbot, 1971, and the other articles in that volume.

10 C. A. Bayly, *The Birth of the Modern World 1780–1914*, Oxford, 2004, 174.

11   P. Kennedy, *The Rise and Fall of the Great Powers: Economic Change and Military Conflict from 1500 to 2000*, New York, 1989, 149.

12   Boswell, *Ominous Years*, 289.

13   K. Morgan, *Slavery, Atlantic Trade and the British Economy, 1660–1800*, Cambridge, 2000.

14   E. P. Thompson, *The Making of the English Working Class*, New York, 1963, 67.

15   A. Vickery, *The Gentleman's Daughter: Women's Lives in Georgian England*, New Haven, 1998, 4, 7.

16   S. Tillyard, *Aristocrats: Caroline, Emily, Louisa, and Sarah Lennox 1740–1832*, New York, 1995, 201–3.

17   A. Foreman, *Georgiana, Duchess of Devonshire*, New York, 2001, 382–4.

18   J. S. Lewis, *Sacred to Female Patriotism: Gender, Class, and Politics in Late Georgian Britain*, London, 2003, 21–2, 40, 44, 75, 244–51; Foreman, *Georgiana*, 137–47.

19   B. Taylor, *Oxford Dictionary of National Biography*.

20   E. M. Johnston-Liik, *History of the Irish Parliament 1692–1800*, Belfast, 2002, 6 vols., I, 157–8.

21   M. Lenox-Conyngham, *An Old Ulster House: Springhill and the People Who Lived in It*, Belfast, 2005, 145.

22   H. Trevor-Roper, "The Invention of Tradition: The Highland Tradition of Scotland," in E. Hobsbawm and T. Ranger, eds., *The Invention of Tradition*, Cambridge, 1983, 15–41; Devine, *The Scottish Nation, 1700–2000*, has an excellent discussion, 231–45.

23   J. Morrill, "The Fashioning of Britain," in S. G. Ellis and S. Barber, eds., *Conquest and Union: Fashioning a British State, 1485–1725*, London, 1995, 13.

24   R. Porter, *English Society in the Eighteenth Century*, rev. ed., New York, 1990, 21.

25   Edward Gibbon, *Autobiography*, Oxford, 1907, 306.

26   *Richard II*, act II, scene 1.

27   A. Sisman, *Boswell's Presumptuous Task: The Making of the Life of Dr. Johnson*, New York, 2000, 22.

28   The word "liberal" did not come into use in its political sense until the nineteenth century.

29   Thomas Turner, *Diary, 1754–1765*, ed. D. Vaisey, Oxford, 1985, 239.

30   M. Jasanoff, *Edge of Empire, Lives, Culture, and Conquest in the East, 1750–1850*, New York, 2005, 247.

31   N. Ferguson, *Empire: The Rise and Demise of the British World Order and the Lessons of Global Power*, New York, 2002, 56.

32   C. W. Pasley, *Essay on the Military Policy and Institutions of the British Empire* (1810), 54, cited in L. Colley, *Captives*, New York, 2002, 10.

33   Colley, *Captives*, 11.

34   Ibid., 102–4, 116, 147, 366.

35   L. Colley, *Britons: Forging the Nation, 1707–1837*, New Haven, 1992, 5–6.

36   C. Kidd, "Integration: Patriotism and Nationalism," in H. T. Dickinson, ed., *A Companion to Eighteenth-Century Britain*, Oxford, 2002, 376.

37   M. Morris, *The British Monarchy and the French Revolution*, New Haven, 1998, 36, 147.

38   J. Brooke, *King George III*, Frogmore, 1974, 158.

39   G. Orwell, *The Collected Essays, Journalism and Letters of George Orwell, 1920–1950*, 4 vols., ed. S. Orwell and I. Angus, New York, 1968, III, 81.

40   R. F. Foster, *Modern Ireland, 1600–1972*, London, 1988, 278.

41 I. R. Christie, *Stress and Stability in Late Eighteenth-Century Britain*, Oxford, 1986, 145, 154.

42 Philip Harling has shown how difficult it was for the government to make the legal mechanisms used to suppress dissent in print work effectively. "The Law of Libel and the Limits of Repression, 1790–1832," *Historical Journal*, 44 (2001), 107–34.

43 E. Halévy, *England in 1815*, rev. ed., London, 1949, 591.

44 J. C. D. Clark, *English Society, 1688–1832*, Cambridge, 1985, 7.

45 B. Hilton, *A Mad, Bad and Dangerous People? England 1783–1846*, Oxford, 25, 27.

46 J. Hoppit, *A Land of Liberty?: England 1689–1727*, Oxford, 2000, 88.

47 D. Lieven, *The Aristocracy in Europe, 1815–1914*, London, 1992, 246.

48 W. Prest, *Albion Ascendant: English History, 1660–1815*, Oxford, 1998, 281–2.

49 G. Kitson Clark, *The Making of Victorian England*, London, 1965, 39.

5   Reform, 1816–41

1 N. Gash, *Lord Liverpool*, London, 1984, 130.

2 E. A. Wasson, *Whig Renaissance: Lord Althorp and the Whig Party 1782–1845*, New York, 1987, 85.

3 J. E. Cookson, *Lord Liverpool's Administration 1815–1822*, Edinburgh, 1975, 67.

4 David Ricardo, *On the Principles of Political Economy and Taxation*, ed. R. M. Hartwell, Baltimore, 1971, 31.

5 Which he accepted in his second edition in 1802 as a possible means of checking expansion other than vice and misery.

6 J. A. Phillips, *The Great Reform Bill in the Boroughs: English Electoral Behavior 1818–1841*, Oxford, 1992, 46.

7 N. Gash, *Peel*, London, 1976, 71.

8 T. C. W. Blanning, *The Eighteenth Century*, Oxford, 2000, 4.

9 P. Jupp, *British Politics on the Eve of Reform: The Duke of Wellington's Administration, 1828–30*, New York, 1998, 334, 377.

10 *The Morning Chronicle*, February 17, 1834.

11 W. Cobbett, *Rural Rides*, 2 vols., London, 1912, I, 31.

12 M. J. Wiener, *English Culture and the Decline of the Industrial Spirit 1850–1980*, Cambridge, 1981, 118.

13 J. C. D. Clark, *English Society 1688–1832*, Cambridge, 1985, 36.

14 E. Wasson, *Born to Rule: British Political Elites*, Stroud, 2000, 155; A. D. Harvey, *Britain in the Early Nineteenth Century*, London, 1978, 19.

15 Even in the Lords, the proportion of bishops from landed backgrounds rose from only 39 percent between 1660 and 1790 to nearly 60 percent in the period 1791–1830. D. Cannadine, *Aspects of Aristocracy: Grandeur and Decline in Modern Britain*, New Haven, 1994, 20, 23.

16 W. D. Rubinstein, *Britain's Century: A Political and Social History 1815–1905*, London, 1998, 53.

17 E. A. Smith, *Lord Grey 1764–1845*, Oxford, 1990, 259.

18 M. Brock, *The Great Reform Act*, London, 1973, 307–8.

19 See for example: N. Gash, *Politics in the Age of Peel*, New York, 1971, ix–x; D. C. Moore, *The Politics of Deference*, New York, 1976.

20 J. R. M. Butler, *The Passing of the Great Reform Bill*, London, 1964, 255.

21 Smith, *Lord Grey*, 327. A series of unintended consequences from the bill relating to registration provisions and other requirements allowed partisan electoral groups in many cases to outwit opponents on technicalities. Conservatives proved more adept than the Whigs in managing this activity.

22 G. Watson, *The English Ideology*, London, 1973, 42.

23 Clark, *English Society*; Phillips, *Great Reform Bill*; P. Salmon, *Electoral Reform at Work: Local Politics and National Parties, 1832–1841*, London, 2002.

24 Wasson, *Born to Rule*, 142, 151–5. It was once thought that the Act did little to alter the Commons' social composition. An influential but flawed study written in 1938 asserting little change after 1832 unfortunately still misleads some historians. S. F. Woolley, "Personnel of the Parliament of 1833," *English Historical Review*, LII, (1938), 240–62.

25 D. Beales, "The Electorate before and after 1832: The Right to Vote, and the Opportunity," *Parliamentary History*, 11 (1992), 139–50.

26 R. S. Surtees, *Hillingdon Hall*, 1845, chapter xi.

27 The Duke of Wellington, *The Dispatches of Field Marshal the Duke of Wellington*, London, 1834–9, vii, 451.

28 N. McCord, *British History 1815–1906*, Oxford, 1991, 7.

29 D. Spring, *The English Landed Estate in the Nineteenth Century: Its Administration*, Baltimore, 1963, 150, 168; P. Mandler, *Aristocratic Government in the Age of Reform: Whigs and Liberals 1830–1852*, Oxford, 1990; Wasson, *Whig Renaissance*.

30 Counties were empowered to do so in 1839–40 and over two-thirds did so by 1856.

31 W. L. Arnstein, *Queen Victoria*, London, 2003, 9, 58.

32 R. Owen, *A New View of Society*, ed. V. A. C. Gatrell, Baltimore, 1970, 45.

33 He ended up in one himself. His skeleton dressed up in his clothes is still kept on exhibit at the University of London.

34 G. Kitson Clark, *The Making of Victorian England*, London, 1965, 19; O. MacDonagh, *Early Victorian Government, 1830–1870*, London, 1977.

35 He also admits the possibility of the General Strike in 1926. B. Hilton, *A Mad, Bad and Dangerous People? England 1783–1846*, Oxford, 2006, 607, 611.

36 G. Stedman Jones, *Languages of Class: Studies in English Working Class History 1832–1982*, Cambridge, 1983, 109.

37 A. Briggs, *The Making of Modern England 1783–1867: The Age of Improvement*, New York, 1965, 295; Elizabeth Gaskell, *Mary Barton, A Tale of Manchester Life*, Baltimore, 1970 [1848], 125–6.

38 Elizabeth Gaskell, *North and South*, Baltimore, 1970 [1854], 96, 127.

39 Rubinstein, *Britain's Century*, vii.

40 S. D'Cruze, "The Family," in C. Williams, ed., *A Companion to Nineteenth- Century Britain*, Oxford, 2004, 254. He cites A. G. Crosby, ed., *The Family Records of Benjamin Shaw, Mechanic of Dent, Dolphinholme and Preston, 1772–1841*, Lancashire and Cheshire, 1991, 102, 103–4. For other working-class autobiographies see: J. Burnett, *Useful Toil*, London, 1974.

41 In 1831 hand-loom weaving was the largest single manufacturing occupation in Scotland. M. Lynch, *Scotland: A New History*, London, 1992, 407.

42 Lord Byron, *'Famous in My Time': Byron's Letters and Journals, Volume 2, 1810–1812*, ed. L. A. Marchand, London, 1973, 165.

43 E. P. Thompson, *The Making of the English Working Class*, New York, 1963, 197, 424, 543–9, 649.

44   H. Perkin, *The Origins of Modern English Society 1780–1880*, London, 1969, 54, 141, 175, 184, 213.

45   K. T. Hoppen, *The Mid-Victorian Generation, 1846–1886*, Oxford, 1998, 267.

46   George Rudé and Eric Hobsbawm characterized the Swing unrest of the 1830s as an archaic and improvised movement of resistance to the triumph of the capitalist cash nexus. *Captain Swing: A Social History of the Great English Agricultural Uprising of 1830*, New York, 1975, 15.

47   Thompson, *The Making of the English Working Class*, 194.

48   R. Price, *British Society, 1680–1880: Dynamism, Containment and Change*, Cambridge, 1999, 267.

49   G. Best, *Mid-Victorian Britain 1851–75*, rev. ed., London, 1973, 282.

50   George Eliot, *Middlemarch*, Harmondsworth, 1965 [1871–2], 361.

51   R. Hodgkinson, *A Lancashire Gentleman: the Letters and Journals of, 1763–1847*, ed. Florence and Kenneth Wood, Stroud, 1992, 32.

52   J. Foster, *Class Struggle and the Industrial Revolution*, London, 1974, 9.

53   C. H. Feinstein, "What Really Happened to Real Wages?," *Economic History Review*, 43 (1990), 329–55 and "Pessimism Perpetuated: Real Wages and the Standard of Living in Britain during and after the Industrial Revolution," *Journal of Economic History*, 58 (1998), 625–58.

54   G. M. Young, *Portrait of an Age: Victorian England*, ed. G. Kitson Clark, London, 1977, 89.

55   W. L. Burn, *The Age of Equipoise: A Study of the Mid-Victorian Generation*, London, 1964.

56   Stedman Jones, *Languages of Class*; P. Joyce, *Work, Society, and Politics: The Culture of the Factory in Later Victorian England*, New Brunswick, 1980.

57   N. Gash, *Aristocracy and People: Britain 1815–1865*, London, 249.

58   Hoppen, *The Mid-Victorian Generation*, 80–1.

59   F. M. L. Thompson, *The Rise of Respectable Society: A Social History of Victorian Britain 1830–1900*, London, 1988, 30.

6   Imperial Britain, 1842–84

1   The term "Victorian" was coined in 1851, and it was adopted on both sides of the Atlantic as the name for the age. G. M. Young, *Portrait of an Age: Victorian England*, ed. G. Kitson Clark, London, 1977, 96.

2   Benjamin Disraeli, *Sybil or the Two Nations*, London, 1926 [1845], 31.

3   R. Blake, *The Conservative Party from Peel to Churchill*, London, 1972, 11.

4   B. Hilton, *A Mad, Bad and Dangerous People? England 1783–1846*, Oxford, 2006, 547.

5   Earl Fitzwilliam, *First, Second, and Third Addresses to the Landowners of England on the Corn Laws*, 1839, rev. ed., 14, 44.

6   E. A. Smith, *Whig Principles and Party Politics: Earl Fitzwilliam and the Whig Party 1748–1833*, Manchester, 1975, 347.

7   M. Daunton, *Wealth and Welfare: An Economic and Social History of Britain 1851–1951*, Oxford, 2007, 35; D. Spring, "Earl Fitzwilliam and the Corn Laws," *American Historical Review*, 59 (1954), 304.

8   E. Grant, *The Highland Lady in Ireland: Journals 1840–50*, ed. P. Pelly and A. Tod, Edinburgh, 1991, 258, 260.

9   R. F. Foster, *Modern Ireland, 1600–1972*, London, 1988, 298.

10   Beginning at £20,000 in 1832, the grant rose to £100,000 by 1846.

11   R. Brent, *Liberal Anglican Politics: Whiggism, Religion, and Reform 1830–1841*, Oxford, 1987, 234.

12   R. Blake, *Disraeli*, New York, 1968, 238.

13   J. R. Greenway, "Parliamentary Reform and Civil Service Reform," *Parliamentary History*, 4 (1985), 159–69; P. Gowan, "The Origins of the Administrative Elite," *New Left Review*, 162 (1987), 4–34.

14   J. Harris, *Private Lives, Public Spirit: Britain 1870–1914*, New York, 1994, 14.

15   M. Bentley, *Politics without Democracy 1815–1914*, London, 1984, 137.

16   J. Rose, *The Intellectual Life of the British Working Classes*, New Haven, 2001, 68–9.

17   Daunton, *Wealth and Welfare*, 490–1, 499.

18   Although Salisbury calculated that the Conservatives could have won had a mere 2,000 electors across the country voted differently. J. Parry, *The Rise and Fall of Liberal Government in Victorian Britain*, New Haven, 1993, 221.

19   Up to 1914 something like 40 percent of the male householders notionally entitled to vote were absent from the electoral registers through migration, receipt of poor relief, gerrymandering, or mere negligence. W. D. Rubinstein, *Britain's Century: A Political and Social History 1815–1905*, London, 1998, 198.

20   Harris, *Private Lives, Public Spirit*, 15.

21   D. Cannadine, *The Decline and Fall of the British Aristocracy*, New Haven, 1990, 14.

22   E. Wasson, *Born to Rule: British Political Elites*, Stroud, 2000, 156.

23   J. Gallagher and R. Robinson, "The Imperialism of Free Trade," *Economic History Review*, VI (1953), 1–15, and *Africa and the Victorians: The Official Mind of Imperialism*, London, 1961.

24   D. M. Peers, in C. Williams, ed., *A Companion to Nineteenth-Century Britain*, Oxford, 2004, 68; P. J. Cain and A. G. Hopkins, *British Imperialism, 1688–2000*, 2nd ed., London, 2002.

25   P. J. Cain, "Economics and Empire," in A. Porter, ed., *The Nineteenth Century, Volume III, The Oxford History of the British Empire*, Oxford, 1999, 31.

26   C. S. Maier, *Among Empires: American Ascendancy and Its Predecessors*, Cambridge, MA, 2006, 21.

27   R. Miller, "Informal Empire in Latin America," in R. Winks, ed., *Historiography, Volume V, The Oxford History of the British Empire*, Oxford, 1999, 438–41, 446; M. Lynn, "British Policy, Trade, and Informal Empire," in A. Porter, ed., *The Nineteenth Century, Volume III, The Oxford History of the British Empire*, Oxford, 1999, 119.

28   Hilton, *A Mad, Bad and Dangerous People?*, 571.

29   N. Ferguson, *Empire: The Rise and Demise of the British World Order and the Lessons of Global Power*, New York, 2002, 144.

30   S. Schama, *A History of Britain: The Fate of Empire 1776–2000*, III, New York, 2002, 270–2.

31   J. Keay, *The Great Arc*, London, 2000.

32   M. Davis, *Late Victorian Holocausts*, New York, 2001, 7. By way of contrast, 16 million Indians died of influenza in 1918–19.

33   For a powerful critique of much of the new writing on imperialism, see: R. Price, "One Big Thing: Britain, Its Empire, and Their Imperial Culture," *Journal of British Studies*, 45 (2006), 602–27.

34   B. Porter, *The Absent-Minded Imperialists: Empire, Society, and Culture in Britain*, New York, 2004.

35   A. Thompson, *The Empire Strikes Back? The Impact of Imperialism on Britain from the Mid-Nineteenth Century*, London, 2005, 4–5.

36   T. Parsons, "Een-Gonyama Gonyama! Zulu Origins of the Boy Scout Movement and the Africanisation of Imperial Britain," in N. LoPatin-Lummis, ed., *Public Life and Private Lives: Politics and Religion in Modern British History*, Oxford, 2008, 57–66.

37   E. Said, *Culture and Imperialism*, New York, 1993, 6.

38   T. M. Devine, "The Break-up of Britain? Scotland and the End of Empire," *Transactions of the Royal Historical Society*, 16 (2006), 168.

39   Thompson, *Empire*, 41–63, 66, 83 ff., 90.

40   A. Offer, "Costs and Benefits, Prosperity and Security, 1870–1914," in A. Porter, ed., *The Oxford History of the British Empire, Volume III, The Nineteenth Century*, Oxford, 1999, 704.

41   P. K. O'Brien, "Imperialism and the Rise and Decline of the British Economy, 1688–1989," *New Left Review*, 238 (1999), 56, 65 f., 75.

42   Between 1919 and 1938 the empire got two-thirds. N. Ferguson, "British Imperialism Revisited," *Historically Speaking*, April 4, 2003, 6.

43   Offer, "Costs and Benefits," 695, 708.

44   Ibid., 709.

45   G. R. Searle, *A New England? Peace and War, 1886–1918*, Oxford, 2004, 251.

46   R. G. Irving, *Indian Summer: Lutyens, Baker and Imperial Delhi*, New Haven, 1981, 11, 18, 114, 136.

47   E. Said, *Orientalism*, New York, 1979, 40, 48.

48   D. Cannadine, *Ornamentalism: How the British Saw Their Empire*, Oxford, 2001, xix–xx, 8. For an extended critique of Cannadine see the *Journal of Colonialism and Colonial History*, 3:1, 2002.

7   New Century, 1885–1913

1   Anthony Trollope, *The Prime Minister*, Oxford, 1938 [1875–6], vol. 2, 322.

2   P. Magnus, *Gladstone*, New York, 1964, 76.

3   J. Parry, *The Rise and Fall of Liberal Government in Victorian Britain*, New Haven, 1993, 20, 224–5, 305–7.

4   G. R. Searle, *A New England? Peace and War 1886–1918*, Oxford, 2004, 156.

5   The Conservatives and the Unionists merged into the "Unionist Party" in 1912. In 1925 the party in England and Wales but not Scotland reverted to the name "Conservative," although they retained the term "and Unionist" as well.

6   P. Clarke, *Hope and Glory: Britain 1900–1990*, London, 1997, 28.

7   Searle, *A New England?*, 164–5.

8   Ibid., 269–75.

9   S. Sassoon, *The Old Century and Seven More Years*, London, 1938, 126.

10   F. Kilvert, *Kilvert's Diary, 1870–1879*, ed. W. Plomer, London, 1964, 209–10.

11   E. Hobsbawm, *Labouring Men: Studies in the History of Labour*, New York, 1964; K. T. Hoppen, *The Mid-Victorian Generation, 1846–1886*, Oxford, 1998, 67–8.

12   H. Pelling, *Popular Politics and Society in Late Victorian Britain*, London, 1968, 56.

13   G. Stedman Jones, *Outcast London: A Study in the Relationship between Classes in Victorian Society*, Harmondsworth, 1971, 313.

14   K. O. Morgan, *Oxford Dictionary of National Biography*.

15   The pact did not apply to Scotland.

16   Clarke, *Hope and Glory*, 44.

17   It was extended to all industrial workers in 1920 and to domestic and agricultural workers in 1937.

18   M. Daunton, *Wealth and Welfare: An Economic and Social History of Britain 1851–1951*, Oxford, 2007, 470–1, 522–3.

19   R. F. Foster, *Modern Ireland, 1600–1972*, London, 1988, 470.

20   R. S. Churchill, *Winston S. Churchill, Young Statesman, volume II: 1901–1914*, Boston, 1967, 360–5 and G. Best, *Churchill*, New York, 2001, 40–1.

21   D. Lieven, *The Aristocracy in Europe 1815–1914*, London, 1992, 206.

22   R. W. Johnson, "The Nationalisation of English Rural Politics," *Parliamentary Affairs*, 26 (1973), 18.

23   H. Shore, "Crime, Policing and Punishment," in C. Williams, ed., *A Companion to Nineteenth-Century Britain*, Oxford, 381–93.

24   E. A. Smith, *The House of Lords in British Politics and Society 1815–1911*, London, 1992, 39.

25   Hoppen, *The Mid-Victorian Generation*, 305.

26   D. J. Olsen, *The Growth of Victorian London*, Harmondsworth, 1979, 19, 313.

27   W. D. Rubinstein argues that the commercial and financial sectors of the British economy were always the dominant force in the economy, not industry, which seems a little extreme. *Capitalism, Culture, and Decline in Britain 1750–1990*, London, 1994, 24.

28   Daunton, *Wealth and Welfare*, 14–15, 251–2, 255, 260–1.

29   Hoppen, *The Mid-Victorian Generation*, 277–8.

30   A. J. P. Taylor, *Essays in English History*, Harmondsworth, 1976, 37.

31   M. J. Wiener, *English Culture and the Decline of the Industrial Spirit 1850–1980*, Cambridge, 1981, 14, 72, 97.

32   Rubinstein, *Capitalism, Culture, and Decline*, 135.

33   R. H. Trainor, *Black Country Elites*, Oxford, 1993; F. M. L. Thompson, *Gentrification and the Enterprise Culture: Britain 1780–1980*, Oxford, 2001, 23–44, 101–42, 154–5; J. A. Smith, "Landownership and Social Change in Late Nineteenth-Century Britain," *Economic History Review*, 53 (2000), 767–76; J. Harris and P. Thane, "British and European Bankers, 1880–1914: An 'Aristocratic Bourgeoisie'?," in P. Thane, G. Crossick, and R. Floud, eds., *The Power of the Past*, Cambridge, 1984, 227.

34   P. Thane, "Aristocracy and Middle Class in Victorian England," in A. M. Birke and L. Kettenacker, eds., *Bürgertum, Adel und Monarchie*, Munich, 1989, 93–100.

35   A. Howe, "Britain and the World Economy," in C. Williams, ed., *A Companion to Nineteenth-Century Britain*, Oxford, 2004, 29.

36   B. R. Tomlinson, "Economics and Empire," in A. Porter, ed., *The Nineteenth Century, Volume III, The Oxford History of the British Empire*, Oxford, 1999, 69, calculated from B. L. Turner and others, eds., *The Earth Transformed by Human Action*, Cambridge, 1990, Table 4.32.

37   Rubinstein, *Capitalism, Culture, and Decline*, 49, 52.

38   Daunton, 167 from A. Booth, "The Manufacturing Failure Hypothesis," *Economic History Review*, 56 (2003), 24.

39   J. Heskel and D. Dyer, *After the Harkness Gift*, Hanover, 2008, 5.

40   The cost of the naval race was not as great as is sometimes assumed: J. T. Sumida, *In Defense of Naval Supremacy: Finance, Technology & British Naval Policy 1889–1914*, Boston, 1989, 12, 193–6, 336, and Table 2.

41   P. Kennedy, *The Rise and Fall of the Great Powers: Economic Change and Military Conflict from 1500 to 2000*, New York, 1989, 230.

42   Searle, *A New England?*, 523.

43   An international convention in 1839 guaranteed Belgian neutrality.

-------------------   8   **The United Kingdom, 1914**   -------------------

1   J. Harris, *Private Lives, Public Spirit: Britain 1870–1914*, New York, 1994, 33, 37.

2   K. T. Hoppen, *The Mid-Victorian Generation, 1846–1886*, Oxford, 1998, 333; S. Koven, *Slumming: Sexual and Social Politics in Victorian London*, Princeton, 2004.

3   M. S. Lovell, *Rebel Heart: The Scandalous Life of Jane Digby*, New York, 1995.

4   J. R. Walkowitz, *City of Dreadful Delight*, Chicago, 1992, 15.

5   Scots law on divorce, custody, and property was different in the nineteenth century.

6   J. J. Norwich, *Trying to Please*, Stanbridge, 2008, 119.

7   M. Daunton, *Wealth and Welfare: An Economic and Social History of Britain 1851–1951*, Oxford, 2007, 329–30, 338–9; H. Cook, *The Long Sexual Revolution: English Women, Sex, and Contraception, 1800–1975*, Oxford, 2004, 62.

8   Daunton, *Wealth and Welfare*, 340.

9   H. C. G. Matthew, *Gladstone 1809–1898*, Oxford, 1997, 256.

10   J. S. Mill, *On Liberty*, ed. A. Castell, New York, 1947 [1859], 9.

11   Lord Byron, "Born for Opposition," *Byron's Letters and Journals, Volume 8, 1821*, ed. L. Marchand, London, 1978, 20, 146, and "The Flesh is Frail," *Byron's Letters and Journals, Volume 6, 1818–1819*, 1976, 106, 232.

12   Byron, "Born for Opposition," 13, 23.

13   S. Heffer, "The Sound of England," *Country Life*, May 14, 2008, 140.

14   G. Morton and R. J. Morris, "Civil Society, Governance and Nations, 1832–1914," in R. A. Houston and W. W. J. Knox, eds., *The New Penguin History of Scotland*, London, 2001, 359.

15   George Eliot, *Middlemarch*, Harmondsworth, 1965 [1871–2], 206.

16   T. M. Devine, *The Scottish Nation, 1700–2000*, London, 1999, 364, 368–71, 380.

17   B. Hilton, *A Mad, Bad and Dangerous People? England 1783–1846*, Oxford, 2006, 343.

18   Hilton, *A Mad, Bad and Dangerous People?*, 442, 474, 635–6.

19   E. J. Hobsbawm, *The Age of Revolution 1789–1848*, New York, 1962, 323.

20   K. Robbins, *Nineteenth-Century Britain: Integration and Diversity*, Oxford, 1988, 66.

21   G. R. Searle, *A New England? Peace and War 1886–1918*, Oxford, 2004, 425.

22   P. Mandler, *The English National Character*, New Haven, 2006, 41.

23   C. Williams, "British Identities," in *A Companion to Nineteenth-Century Britain*, Oxford, 546; Hilton, *A Mad, Bad and Dangerous People?*, 247.

24   See M. Cragoe, *Culture, Politics and National Identity in Wales 1832–1886*, Oxford, 2004; D. W. Howell, *Land and People in Nineteenth-Century Wales*, London, 1977.

25   Maud, Lady Leconfield, *Three Howard Sisters, 1825–1833*, London, 1955, 36.

26   Devine, *The Scottish Nation*, 285.

27   Ibid., 408.

28 W. M. Kuhn, *Democratic Royalism: The Transformation of the British Monarchy, 1861–1914*, London, 1996, 8.

29 Walter Bagehot, *The English Constitution*, ed. P. Smith, Cambridge, 2001 [1867], 60.

30 "The Past in Pictures," *BBC History*, October 2005, 31.

31 D. Cannadine, *Ornamentalism: How the British Saw Their Empire*, Oxford, 2001, 101–2, 118.

32 H. Nicolson, *Helen's Tower*, London, 1937, 117.

33 A. Adonis, "Survival of the Great Estates," *Historical Research*, 64 (1991), 54.

34 D. Lieven, *The Aristocracy in Europe 1815–1914*, London, 1992, 237.

35 Or succeeded before the age of 21.

36 J. Bateman, *The Great Landowners of Great Britain and Ireland*, ed. D. Spring, Leicester, 1971.

37 In 1823. Lord Byron, *"For Freedom's Battle": Byron's Letters and Journals, Volume 11, 1823–1824*, ed. L. A. Marchand, London, 1981, 35.

38 W. D. Rubinstein, *Men of Property: The Very Wealthy in Britain since the Industrial Revolution*, London, 1981, 41, 45.

39 Hoppen, *The Mid-Victorian Generation*, 283.

40 Product distribution in agriculture shifted from 47 percent in crops and 53 percent in livestock in 1870 to 29 percent and 71 percent respectively around 1910. Daunton, *Wealth and Welfare*, 45. M. Winstanley, in C. Williams, ed., *A Companion to Nineteenth-Century Britain*, 2004, 210–11. R. J. Farrelly, "The Large Landowners of England and Wales, 1870–1939: An Elite in Transition," unpublished PhD dissertation, University of Toronto, 1980, 92.

41 D. McMahon, "Ireland, the Empire, and the Commonwealth," in K. Kenny, ed., *Ireland and the Empire*, Oxford, 2004, 191.

—————————   9   **War and Peace and War, 1915–39**   —————————

1 Although the term "First World War" was coined in the 1920s, it was not much used until after war broke out again in 1939.

2 Historians are now kinder to Haig than they once were. See for example M. Gilbert, *The Somme: Heroism and Horror in the First World War*, New York, 2006, 244.

3 R. Graves, *Goodbye to All That*, New York, 1960 [1929], 133.

4 H. Strachan, *The First World War*, London, 2003, 214–15, 218–19, 292.

5 P. Kennedy, *The Rise and Fall of the Great Powers: Economic Change and Military Conflict from 1500 to 2000*, New York, 1989, 258, 274.

6 M. Daunton, *Wealth and Welfare: An Economic and Social History of Britain 1851–1951*, Oxford, 2007, 474.

7 Strachan, *The First World War*, 312.

8 A. Roberts, *A History of the English-Speaking Peoples since 1900*, New York, 2007, 107.

9 A. Thompson, *The Empire Strikes Back? The Impact of Imperialism on Britain from the Mid-Nineteenth Century*, London, 2005, 177.

10 P. Martin, *"Dulce et Decorum*: Irish Nobles and the Great War, 1914–19," in A. Gregory and S. Paseta, eds., *Ireland and the Great War*, Manchester, 2002, 39–40; E. Wasson, *Aristocracy and the Modern World*, London, 2006, 158–9.

11 G. Orwell, *The Collected Essays, Journalism and Letters of George Orwell, 1920–1950*, 4 vols., ed. S. Orwell and I. Angus, New York, 1968, II, 203.

12 D. Cooper, *The Duff Cooper Diaries 1915–1951*, ed. J. J. Norwich, London, 2006, 89, 9 December 1918.

13   "Suicide in the Trenches," in Siegfried Sassoon, *Collected Poems 1908–1956*, London, 1956, 78.

14   W. D. Rubinstein, *Twentieth-Century Britain: A Political History*, London, 2003, 112.

15   J. Stevenson, *British Society 1914–45*, New York, 1984, 92.

16   R. McKibbin, *Classes and Cultures: England 1918–1951*, Oxford, 1998, 112–14.

17   G. Orwell, *The Road to Wigan Pier*, London, 1962 [1937], 87.

18   P. Clarke, *Hope and Glory: Britain 1900–1990*, London, 1997, 131.

19   Stevenson, *British Society*, 118–19, 124, 126.

20   H. A. Clemenson, *English Country Houses and Landed Estates*, London, 1982, 120–2; B. English, *The Great Landowners of East Yorkshire 1530–1910*, London, 1990, 231–3; M. Beard, *Acres and Heirlooms: The Survival of Britain's Historical Estates*, New York, 1989, 139; E. Wasson, *Born to Rule: British Political Elites*, Stroud, 2000, 121.

21   D. Cannadine's influential book, *The Decline and Fall of the British Aristocracy*, New Haven, 1990, exaggerated the impact of the Great War on the aristocracy. See, for example, W. D. Rubinstein, "Britain's Elites in the Inter-War Period, 1918–39," *Contemporary British History*, 12 (1998), 1–18; Wasson, *Aristocracy*, 195–200.

22   H. Perkin, *The Rise of Professional Society: England since 1880*, London, 1990, 117–18, 161; A. Miles, "Social Structure, 1900–1939," in C. Wrigley, ed., *A Companion to Early Twentieth-Century Britain*, Oxford, 2003, 339.

23   The Liberals retained a stronger position in local government.

24   P. Bew, *Ireland: The Politics of Enmity 1789–2006*, Oxford, 2007, 393.

25   P. Hart, *Oxford Dictionary of National Biography*.

26   M. MacMillan, *Peacemakers: The Paris Conference of 1919 and Its Attempt to End the War*, London, 2002, 191.

27   G. Best, *Churchill: A Study in Greatness*, New York, 2001, 111.

28   Stevenson, *British Society*, 268–9.

29   R. M. Jones, "Wales and British Politics, 1900–1939," in C. Wrigley, *A Companion to Early Twentieth-Century Britain*, Oxford, 2003, 92.

30   C. Bailey, *Black Diamonds: The Rise and Fall of an English Dynasty*, London, 2007, 247.

31   R. Hoggart, *The Uses of Literacy*, New York, 1970 [1957], 70; Orwell, *Wigan*, 154.

32   Orwell, *Wigan*, 80–1 and *Collected Essays*, II, 39.

33   R. J. Overy, *Oxford Dictionary of National Biography*.

34   Stevenson, *British Society*, 131.

35   Daunton, *Wealth and Welfare*, 119.

36   Even Hitler thought Mosley was mistaken in making his movement appear more Continental than British in style. C. Mosley, ed., *The Mitfords: Letters Between Six Sisters*, New York, 2007, 89.

37   Rubinstein, *Twentieth-Century Britain*, 182.

38   Stevenson, *British Society*, 144, 165.

39   N. Annan, *Our Age: English Intellectuals between the World Wars – a Group Portrait*, New York, 1990, 52.

40   T. S. Eliot, *The Complete Poems and Plays 1909–1950*, New York, 1962, 80.

41   Thompson, *The Empire Strikes Back?*, 30; Daunton, *Wealth and Welfare*, 235.

42   A. Lascelles, *King's Counsellor*, ed. D. Hart-Davis, London, 2006, 9–10.

43   Orwell, *Collected Essays*, I, 44–8, 235–42, 306. See also his book, *Burmese Days* (1934), and the novel, *Mr. Johnson* (1939), by Joyce Cary.

44   D. Edgerton, *Warfare State: Britain, 1920–1970*, Cambridge, 2006, 330.

45   Ibid., 13–14, 23, 28–31, 74, 119; G. C. Peden, *Arms, Economics and British Strategy from Dreadnoughts to Hydrogen Bombs*, Cambridge, 2007, 141, 178.

46   J. Charmley, *Churchill: The End of Glory*, London, 1993; M. Cowling, *The Impact of Hitler: British Politics and British Policy 1933–1940*, Cambridge, 1975.

47   M. Soames, ed., *Winston and Clementine: The Personal Letters of the Churchills*, Boston, 1999, 391.

48   Best, *Churchill*, 157.

49   A. J. P. Taylor, *English History 1914–1945*, Oxford, 1965, 413.

---------   ## 10   The Warfare and Welfare State, 1940–79   ---------

1   L. L. Witherell, "Lord Salisbury's 'Watching Committee' and the Fall of Neville Chamberlain," *English Historical Review*, 116 (2001), 1134–66.

2   Historians still debate exactly what happened. See D. Carlton, "Churchill and the Two 'Evil Empires,'" *Transactions of the Royal Historical Society*, xi (2001), 331–51. J. Lukacs, *Five Days in London: May 1940*, New Haven, 1999, 146–86 is the most measured and thorough account.

3   I. Berlin, *Mr. Churchill in 1940*, Boston, 1949, 13.

4   "Finest Hour speech June 1940," typescript with manuscript annotations, Churchill Papers, Churchill Archives Centre, Cambridge, UK; http://www.loc.gov/exhibts/churchill/wc-hour.html

5   A. Potter, ed., *Transatlantic Letters between Virginia Dickinson Reynolds and Her Daughter, Virginia Potter, 1929–1966*, Athens, GA, 2006, 87.

6   A. Calder, *The Myth of the Blitz*, London, 1991, 90.

7   R. Weight, *Patriots: National Identity in Britain 1940–2000*, London, 2002, 87.

8   Some bases on British territory were exchanged for war material that was theoretically to be returned after use. The latter expectation was unlikely to be fulfilled and was rather like asking for chewing gum to be returned after use.

9   A. J. P. Taylor, *English History 1914–1945*, Oxford, 1965, 513.

10   M. Gilbert, *Winston S. Churchill, Volume VI, Finest Hour 1939–1941*, Boston, 1983, 1118–19.

11   P. Kennedy, *The Rise and Fall of the Great Powers: Economic Change and Military Conflict from 1500 to 2000*, New York, 1989, 200, 353–5.

12   J. Stevenson, *British Society 1914–45*, New York, 1984, 171, 448.

13   S. Sebag Montefiore, *Stalin*, New York, 2004, 340.

14   M. Howard, *Captain Professor: The Memoirs of Sir Michael Howard*, New York, 2006, 188.

15   C. Eden, *A Memoir from Churchill to Eden*, ed. C. Haste, London, 2007, 68.

16   Accumulated assets abroad stood at over £5 billion in 1938 and only £580 million in 1950. M. Daunton, *Wealth and Welfare: An Economic and Social History of Britain 1851–1951*, Oxford, 2007, 266.

17   Daunton, *Wealth and Welfare*, 410; Stevenson, *British Society*, 123; A. B. Atkinson, *Unequal Shares: Wealth in Britain*, 1972, 21.

18   R. McKibbin, *Classes and Cultures: England 1918–1951*, Oxford, 1998, 107–8, 521.

19   G. Orwell, *The Collected Essays, Journalism and Letters of George Orwell, 1920–1950*, 4 vols. ed. S. Orwell and I. Angus, New York, 1968, II, 426.

20 A. Sillitoe, *Saturday Night and Sunday Morning*, New York, 1992 [1958], 22.

21 B. Pimlott, *The Queen: A Biography of Elizabeth II*, New York, 1997, 217.

22 P. Addison, *Churchill: The Unexpected Hero*, New York, 2005, 35.

23 D. Reynolds, *In Command of History*, New York, 2005, 135.

24 W. D. Rubinstein, *Twentieth-Century Britain: A Political History*, London, 2003, 261–2.

25 Howard, *Captain Professor*, 167.

26 Weight, *Patriots*, 292.

27 Since 1958 people who inherited titles, like Home, have been allowed to renounce them, which remarkably few people have done.

28 A. Schlesinger, Jr., *Journals 1952–2000*, New York, 2007, 145.

29 R. Samuel, *Island Stories: Unravelling Britain*, London, 1998, 248.

30 McKibbin, *Classes and Cultures*, 527–8; Daunton, *Wealth and Welfare*, 615–16.

31 *The Economist*, December 3, 2005: 84.

32 N. Coward, *Letters*, ed. B. Day, New York, 2007, 232.

33 M. Palin, *Diaries 1969–1979: The Python Years*, New York, 2006, 196–7.

34 "Annus Mirabilis," 1967, in P. Larkin, *Collected Poems*, New York, 1989, 167.

35 C. Kenny, *Oxford Dictionary of National Biography*.

36 A. Marwick, *British Society since 1945*, New York, 1982, 64; J. Gathorne-Hardy, *Half an Arch: A Memoir*, London, 2004, 169.

37 *The Economist*, "Anglo-Saxon Attitudes," March 29, 2008, online: <www.economist.com/anglosaxon>

38 J. Darwin, "Decolonization and the End of Empire," in R. W. Winks, ed., *The Oxford History of the British Empire, Volume V, Historiography*, Oxford, 2001, 541–56.

39 N. Ferguson, *Empire: The Rise and Demise of the British World Order and the Lessons of Global Power*, New York, 2002, xxv–xxix, 215–18.

40 L. Colley, *Captives*, New York, 2002, 377.

41 A. S. Milward, *The United Kingdom and the European Community, Vol. 1: The Rise and Fall of a National Strategy, 1945–1963*, London, 2002.

42 C. Barnett, *The Audit of War: The Illusion and Reality of Britain as a Great Nation*, 1986, and three other volumes published 1972–2001. J. Charmley, *Churchill: The End of Glory*, London, 1993. For a good overview of the literature on decline: D. Coates, *The Question of the UK Decline: State, Society, and Economy*, London, 1994. For an excellent corrective to much of this writing, see: J. Tomlinson, "Economic 'Decline' in Post-War Britain," in P. Addison and H. Jones, eds., *A Companion to Contemporary Britain 1939–2000*, Oxford, 2005, 164–79.

43 For a good example, see the obituary of David Caminer, *New York Times*, June 29, 2008: 24.

44 *The Economist*, December 22, 2007: 122.

45 See D. Edgerton, *Warfare State: Britain, 1920–1970*, Cambridge, 2006, 5, 102–5, 148, 189–90, 230–69; D. Edgerton, "The Prophet Militant and Industrial: the Peculiarities of Correlli Barnett," *Twentieth Century British History*, 2 (1991), 360–79.

--- **11 "New" Britain, 1980–2008** ---

1 F. Mount, *Cold Cream: My Early Life and Other Mistakes*, London, 2008, 287. Charles Moore reports that Mitterrand said, "the eyes of Stalin." *The Spectator*, July 5, 2008: 11.

2 R. Samuel, *Island Stories: Unravelling Britain*, London, 1998, 343.

3   R. Weight, *Patriots: National Identity in Britain 1940–2000*, London, 2002, 571.

4   P. Thompson, "The Pyrrhic Victory of Gentlemanly Capitalism: the Financial Elite of the City of London, 1945–90," *Journal of Contemporary History*, 32 (1997), 283–304 and 427–40; *The Economist*, October 21, 2006: 84, and March 15, 2008: 31.

5   B. Pimlott, *The Queen: A Biography of Elizabeth II*, New York, 1997, 459–62. But it may have been that Heath was her least favorite.

6   Mount, *Cold Cream*, 331.

7   S. Collini, "Moralist at Work," *TLS*, February 18, 2005: 15.

8   W. D. Rubinstein, *Twentieth-Century Britain: A Political History*, London, 2003, 338.

9   N. Annan, *Our Age: English Intellectuals between the World Wars – A Group Portrait*, New York, 1990, 421.

10   Blair converted to Roman Catholicism after he left office.

11   A. Campbell, *The Blair Years, Diaries*, New York, 2007, 7.

12   P. Ashdown, *The Ashdown Diaries, Volume I: 1988–1997*, London, 2000, 228.

13   Campbell, *The Blair Years*, 220.

14   Ibid., 133.

15   *The Economist*, August, 20, 2005: 43.

16   W. R. Mead, *God and Gold: Britain, America, and the Making of the Modern World*, New York, 2007, 199.

17   *The Economist*, March 29, 2008: 71–3, and "Anglo-Saxon Attitudes," March 29, 2008, online: <www.economist.com/anglosaxon>

18   P. Langford, "Prime Ministers and Parliaments: the Long View, Walpole to Blair," *Parliamentary History*, 25 (2006), 382–94.

19   *The Economist*, March 1, 2008: 60.

20   Campbell, *The Blair Years*, 261, 607.

21   I. McBride, *History and Memory in Modern Ireland*, Cambridge, 2001, 5–6, 15.

22   K. Toolis, *Rebel Hearts: Journeys within the IRA's Soul*, New York, 1995, 285; J. Conroy, *Belfast Diary*, new ed., Boston, 1995, 180–224.

23   T. Hennessey, *A History of Northern Ireland*, New York, 1997, 181.

24   R. F. Foster, *Luck and the Irish: A Brief History of Change 1970–2000*, London, 2007, 72, 111, 113.

25   G. J. Mitchell, *Making Peace*, Berkeley, 1999, 101.

26   http://www.nobelprize.org

27   Hennessey, *A History*, 203.

28   D. Cooke, *Persecuting Zeal*, Dingle, 1996, 1.

29   Campbell, *The Blair Years*, 418.

30   E. Moloney, *A Secret History of the IRA*, 2nd ed., London, 2007, but see Richard Bourke's letter in the *TLS*, March 7, 2008: 6.

31   Mitchell, *Making Peace*, 137.

32   J. Powell, *Great Hatred, Little Room: Making Peace in Northern Ireland*, London, 2008, 318.

33   Weight, *Patriots*, 665–736.

34   M. Daunton, *Newsletter of the Royal Historical Society*, Spring/Summer 2006, 1.

35   N. Pevsner, *The Englishness of English Art*, London, 1956, 194; P. Mandler, *The English National Character*, New Haven, 2006, 151.

36   "Another Conundrum. Are We Inside or Outside of Europe?," *Granta*, 56 (1996), quoted in M. Griffiths, "Valedictory Nostalgia, Amnesia or New Relations: Shaping British

Studies in Australia," in W. Prest, ed., *British Studies into the 21st Century: Perspectives and Practices*, Melbourne, 1999, 6.

37   *The Economist*, "Anglo-Saxon Attitudes," March 29, 2008, online: <www.economist.com/anglosaxon>)

38   G. Orwell, *The Collected Essays, Journalism and Letters of George Orwell, 1920–1950*, 4 vols., ed. S. Orwell and I. Angus, New York, 1968, II, 64; J. G. A. Pocock, "British History: the Pursuit of the Expanding Subject," in W. Prest, ed., *British Studies into the 21st Century: Perspectives and Practices*, Melbourne, 1999, 71.

39   R. Dahrendorf, *On Britain*, Chicago, 1982, 11.

40   J. Paxman, *The English: A Portrait of a People*, London, 1999, 235.

41   G. H. Jenkins, *A Concise History of Wales*, Cambridge, 2007, 275.

42   M. Johnes, "A Prince, a King, and a Referendum: Rugby, Politics, and Nationhood in Wales, 1969–1979," *Journal of British Studies*, 47 (2008), 129–30.

43   M. Lynch, *Scotland: A New History*, London, 1992, 434.

44   P. Clarke, *Hope and Glory: Britain 1900–1990*, London, 1997, 321.

45   *The Economist*, May 20, 2006: 28.

46   Clarke, *Hope and Glory*, 323.

47   J. Foster, "The Twentieth Century, 1914–1979," in R. A. Houston and W. W. J. Knox, *The New Penguin History of Scotland*, London, 2001, 477, 488.

48   T. M. Devine, *The Scottish Nation, 1700–2000*, London, 1999, 604–7.

49   R. Dargie, "What Do History Teachers in Scotland Choose to Teach?," *Geschichtsbewusstsein-Geschichtskultur, Jahrbuch Internationale Gesellschaft für Geschichtsdidaktik*, 2006–7: 13–25.

50   J. Oeppen and J. Vaupel, "Broken Limits of Life Expectancy," *Science*, 296 (2002), 1092.

51   A. Rosen, *The Transformation of British Life: A Social History, 1950–2000*, Manchester, 2003, 116.

52   *The Economist*, February 3, 2007: 4.

53   I. Zweininger-Bargielowska, "Living Standards and Consumption," in P. Addison and H. Jones, eds., *A Companion to Contemporary Britain 1939–2000*, Oxford, 2005, 232–3.

54   See for example T. Dalrymple, *Our Culture, What's Left of It*, Chicago, 2005.

55   *The Economist*, December 22, 2007: 68, and April 19, 2008: 62.

56   J. Douglas-Home, *Dignified and Efficient: The British Monarchy in the Twentieth Century*, Brinkworth, 2000, 13.

57   W. M. Kuhn, "The Monarchy and the House of Lords," in C. Williams, ed., *A Companion to Nineteenth-Century Britain*, Oxford, 2004, 103.

58   F. Mount, "Vivat Regina?," *TLS*, February 1, 2002.

59   J. Parry, "Whig Monarchy, Whig Nation: Crown, Politics and Representativeness 1800–2000," in A. Olechnowicz, ed., *The Monarchy and the British Nation 1780 to the Present*, Cambridge, 2007, 47–75; V. Bogdanor, *The Monarchy and the Constitution*, Oxford, 1995, viii.

60   Orwell, *Collected Essays*, IV, 186.

61   *The Economist*, June 30, 2007: 30.

62   *The Economist*, "Anglo-Saxon Attitudes," March 29, 2008, online: <www.economist.com/anglosaxon>

63   R. Hoggart, *The Uses of Literacy*, New York, 1970 [1957], 74.

64   G. M. Trevelyan, *The English Revolution 1688–1689*, Oxford, 1938, 129.

65   Dahrendorf, *On Britain*, 15.

66   Parry, "Whig Monarchy," 66.

Chronology

1780	Gordon Riots in London
1781	Cornwallis surrenders at Yorktown
1783	American War of Independence ends
	Watt's steam engine installed in a factory for first time
1784	Pitt's India Act
1788	First penal colony established in Australia
1789	French Revolution begins
1790	Burke's *Reflections on the Revolution in France*
1791	Paine's *Rights of Man*
1792	Wollstonecraft's *A Vindication of the Rights of Women*
1793	Wars of the French Revolution begin
1801	Union between Ireland and Great Britain
	First census
1802	War with Revolutionary France ends
1803	Wars with Napoleon begin
1805	Battle of Trafalgar
1806	Deaths of Pitt and Fox
1807	Abolition of the slave trade
1808	Peninsular War in Iberia begins
1812	War with the United States
1815	War with Napoleon ends
	Battle of Waterloo
1819	"Peterloo" massacre
	The Six Acts
1820	Accession of King George IV
	Queen Caroline affair
1825	Stockton–Darlington railway
1828	Repeal of the Test and Corporation Acts
1829	Catholic Emancipation
1830	Accession of King William IV
	Swing riots
	Manchester–Liverpool railway
1832	First Reform Act
1833	Abolition of slavery in the British Empire
	Factory Act
	"Oxford Movement" (Tractarianism) begins
1834	New Poor Law
	Peel's Tamworth Manifesto
1835	Municipal Corporations Act
1837	Accession of Queen Victoria
1838	Anti-Corn Law League
1839	First People's Charter rejected
	Durham Report on Canada

1840	Penny post
	Treaty of Waitangi with Maori in New Zealand
1843	"Great Disruption" in the Church of Scotland
1846	Repeal of the Corn Laws
	Famine in Ireland
1848	Chartist demonstration in London
1851	Great Exhibition
1854	Crimean War begins
1857	Indian Mutiny
1858	East India Company abolished
	Jewish Emancipation
1859	Darwin's *On the Origin of Species*
	Mill's *On Liberty*
1866	First transatlantic telegraph cable
1867	Second Reform Act
	British North America Act (Canada a Dominion)
	Bagehot's *The English Constitution*
1868	Trades Union Congress (TUC) founded
1869	Church of Ireland disestablished
	Suez Canal opened
1870	Elementary Education Act
1872	Secret Ballot Act
1874	Cavendish Laboratory opens at Cambridge University
1876	Queen Victorian declared Empress of India
	Famine in India begins
1879	Land War in Ireland begins
1882	Occupation of Egypt
1884	Third Reform Act
	Fabian Society founded
	Berlin Conference establishes rules for partition of Africa
1885	Gordon killed at Khartoum
	Formation of Indian National Congress
1886	First Home Rule Bill defeated
	Crofters' Act in Scotland
1888	Elected county councils established
1892	Second Home Rule Bill defeated
1893	Independent Labour Party (ILP) founded
1895	Jameson Raid in the Transvaal
1896	Famine in India begins
1898	Death of Gladstone
	Battle of Omdurman
1899–1902	Boer War
1900	Marconi Wireless Company

1901	Accession of King Edward VII
	Australia becomes a dominion
1903	Wyndham's Irish Land Purchase Act
	Women's Social and Political Union (WSPU) formed
1904	Anglo-French Entente
1906	HMS *Dreadnought* launched
1907	Anglo-Russian Entente
1908	Old Age Pensions
1909	"Peoples' Budget"
	Airplane flies English Channel
1910	Accession of King George V
	South Africa becomes a dominion
1911	House of Lords Reform
	George V's Durbar in India
1914	Curragh Incident in Ireland
	World War I begins
	Home Rule suspended
1916	Easter Rising in Dublin
	Battle of Jutland
1917	Russian Revolutions
1918	World War I ends
	Female suffrage enacted
1919	Versailles Treaty
	Amritsar massacre in India
1922	Southern Ireland becomes the Free State
	British Broadcasting Corporation (BBC) established
1924	First Labour government
1926	The General Strike
1931	Formation of the "National" government
	Statute of Westminster grants dominions full independence
1935	Government of India Act
1936	Abdication crisis – accession of King George VI
1938	Munich crisis
1939	Outbreak of World War II
1940	Dunkirk
	Churchill becomes prime minister
	Battle of Britain
1944	D-Day invasion of France
1945	Germany defeated
	Atomic bomb dropped on Hiroshima
	Japan defeated
	Labour government elected
1947	Independence of India and Pakistan

1948	National Health Service created
	Eire (Southern Ireland) declares full independence
1952	Accession of Queen Elizabeth II
1956	Suez Crisis
1957	African colonies begin to achieve independence
1958	Campaign for Nuclear Disarmament founded
1961	South Africa leaves the Commonwealth over apartheid
1963	Beatles' first album
1972	"Bloody Sunday" in Londonderry
1973	Britain joins European Economic Community (EEC)
1979	Thatcherism begins
1982	Falklands war with Argentina
1986	Financial "Big Bang" in the City of London
1995	"New Labour" abandons socialism
1997	Hong Kong returned to China
	Referendum on Scottish Parliament
	"New Labour" in office – Tony Blair prime minister
1998	Good Friday Agreement in Northern Ireland
2003	Invasion of Iraq
2007	Gordon Brown becomes prime minister

Glossary

A note about pronunciation: The British spell and pronounce some words differently than they are spelled or spoken in North America. For example, Gloucester is often pronounced "Glouwster" in the USA but it is "Gloster" in the UK. Leicester is "Lester." Worcester is "Wooster." Warwick is "Warrick." Edinburgh is "Edinburah." Another notable example of transatlantic difference is Derby, pronounced "Darby" in Britain. Berkshire is "Barkshire" and Hertfordshire is "Hartfordshire." The River Thames is pronounced "Tems" and the triumphal avenue in central London, The Mall, is the "Mell." Ralph is "Rafe." Often the ending of a word is altered – Blenheim is "Blenum" and Althorp is "Alltrop." Sometimes pronunciation departs widely from the spelling of words: Belvoir is "Beaver," Magdalene is "Maudlin," Chomondeley is "Chumley," Mainwaring is "Mannering," Featherstonehaugh is "Fanshaw," and Leveson Gower is "Lewson Gore." Aluminum is spelled and pronounced aluminium.

A note on spelling: The royal house of Stewart of Scotland is spelled Stuart in England. Jail is spelled gaol. In Britain a "u" is usually added to words ending in "or" such as "Labour Party" or "colour." The American "z" turns into "s" as in "organisation." In Britain "er" at the end of a word is usually "re" as in "theatre."

A note on vocabulary: English is the common language by which, it is said, Britons and Americans are divided. Some terms for common items have not crossed the Atlantic. In Britain a truck is a lorry, the hood of a car is a bonnet, gas is petrol, suspenders are braces, and an elevator is a lift. The second floor of a building is the first floor, while the first floor is the ground floor. The act of enthroning and crowning a monarch constitutes "a coronation"; "to coronate" is incorrect usage. The American cartoonist Rube Goldberg designed insanely elaborate mechanisms that served no useful purpose. In Britain the name invoked as the creator of such machines is Heath Robinson.

Anglicans/Anglicanism: A name that in the nineteenth century came to be applied to the members, institution, and doctrines of the Protestant and legally established Church of England of which the monarch was supreme governor.

Ascendancy, the: The Protestant minority who ruled Ireland in the eighteenth and nineteenth centuries.

Baron: An office connected with the judiciary. Also see Lord.

Baronet: Hereditary knighthood that did not confer peerage rank.

BBC: The British Broadcasting Corporation; state-owned radio and later television service.

Borough (*Burgh* in Scotland): A town or a part of London that in the unreformed parliamentary system elected members of Parliament (MPs).

Cabinet: The body of high officials and advisors to the monarch who gradually came to perform most of the executive functions of the state. From the time of Walpole it was appointed and chaired by the prime minister. All members must be MPs or peers.

Chancellor of the Exchequer: The minister responsible for the national finances.

Church of England: See Anglicans.

Church of Scotland: See Kirk of Scotland.

City, the: The commercial, legal, insurance, and financial epicenter of London.

Commons, House of: The lower chamber of Parliament. Members were elected under varying systems of suffrage, often in two-member constituencies, until the reform acts beginning in 1832 democratized and rationalized the system. A vote of loss of confidence in the Commons ends the life of a ministry.

Commonwealth: The successor to the British empire, first comprising the white dominions from the 1920s. A voluntary association of nations, mostly former colonies, headed by Queen Elizabeth II.

Corn: Grain, not what Americans think grows on a cob. Until recently the British thought the latter only fit to feed to pigs and called it maize.

Corn Laws: Legislation regulating the import and export of grain.

Counties: Local government subdivisions also called shires. Each shire is headed by a lord lieutenant, until recently an aristocratic magnate who was responsible for the militia and nominated justices of the peace (JPs).

Cricket: An immensely complex and lengthy game played by hitting balls that are "bowled" (with a bounce) rather than pitched. Was genuinely the "national" game in England until the age of television, when soccer (football) replaced it.

Crown, the: A means of referring to royal authority and/or the government, long used in legal proceedings to designate the prosecution. In Northern Ireland the use of the term when speaking of the army or the government denotes Republican or Nationalist sympathies.

Dame: Female equivalent of the title "Sir" for those who have been knighted.

Devolution: The granting of political autonomy/home rule to Wales, Scotland, and Northern Ireland.

Dissenters: Members of Protestant sects (Baptists, Congregationalists, Presbyterians, Quakers, and later Methodists, but not Roman Catholics, referred to as "recusants") who were not members of the established state Church (Church of England or Kirk of Scotland). In the view of Anglicans they were "Nonconformists," that is, they were unwilling to accept the doctrines and ceremonies of the episcopal Church. Until 1828 they were excluded from holding public office unless they "conformed," that is, took communion at an Anglican service. Catholics were "emancipated" in 1829.

Downing Street: Small street off Whitehall near the Houses of Parliament where the official residence of the first lord of the treasury (prime minister from Walpole onwards) is located at Number 10.

Duke: The highest rank in the peerage. Sons of monarchs are princes, but usually have a dukedom conferred on them, hence the duke of Cumberland.

Earl: The third highest rank in the peerage. The title became an automatic reward for prime ministers from the mid-nineteenth century until the tenure of Harold Macmillan, the last to be granted one in 1984.

Football: Soccer.

Football pools: A legal, ubiquitous, and elaborate system of gambling on soccer matches that can produce large prizes.

gentry: Landowners without peerages but of "gentle birth." The greater gentry were wealthy and active in national politics. The lesser or "parish" gentry owned small estates and participated in local government.

Gold Standard: This applied when the paper money issued by the Bank of England could be converted on request into gold coins, thus tying the currency to the fixed price of gold.

Grammar schools: Grammar schools were academically oriented and self-governing but partly supported by state funding through accepting students on local authority scholarships. Admission was based on academic ability judged in part by the eleven plus exam. In 1975 many became independent schools while others went "comprehensive."

Grandees: Great landowners. Also referred to as "magnates."

Gregorian calendar: In 1752 Britain moved from the "old style" Julian calendar, which had been drifting apart from the seasons for centuries, to the "new style" Gregorian one, which reoriented the calendar by 11 days and kept up in future via leap years.

Habeas corpus: Legal right not to be held by government in prison beyond a short period without a charge being filed and a trial speedily prepared.

Hanover (Hanoverian): A German state over which British monarchs from George I through William IV ruled as Electors and later Kings. Hanover barred female succession, and was separated from joint rule upon the succession of Queen Victoria in 1837, when one of her uncles and his successors became the rulers.

Highlands of Scotland: The region north of the Firth of Forth except for the eastern seaboard up to Aberdeen and including the islands to the west. In the eighteenth century still predominantly Gaelic-speaking and homeland of the clans. Poor and thinly populated.

HMS: His (or Her) Majesty's Ship (a naval vessel).

Hunting: The act of pursuing foxes, otters, hares, or stags with hounds followed by riders on horseback or running on foot. In Britain "shooting" is to fire guns at birds.

IRA: Irish Republican Army. Organized to fight for Irish independence from Britain. Largely Catholic in membership and committed to the use of force. Conducted a campaign of terror in Northern Ireland and Britain during the 1970s and 1980s.

Jacobites: Supporters of the Stuart Pretenders to the throne. Attempted to overthrow the Hanoverian dynasty by violent rebellions in 1715 and 1745.

JP: Justice of the Peace, a magistrate, almost always drawn from the landed elite or clergy in the eighteenth and nineteenth centuries, who until local government was reorganized on the eve of the twentieth century functioned both as a summary judge in lesser criminal cases and as a member of a bench (panel) in charge of county government.

Kirk of Scotland: The state Church of Scotland; Calvinist Presbyterian in doctrine. No bishops ruled, and it is governed by a General Assembly. Each parish elected a "session" to supervise both spiritual and civil affairs.

Lady: May designate a noblewoman or wife of a knight.

Lobbies: When the House of Commons votes, members file out into two lobbies while they are counted like sheep passing through a gate.

Lord: As a prefix to a territorial term – "Lord Nottingham" – it designates a peer with the rank of baron, viscount, earl, or marquis, or the eldest son of a peer. Peers sat in the House of Lords; sons did not. The latter could gain election to the House of Commons, as was the case with Lord North. When the term "Lord" is attached to a Christian name, e.g. "Lord John Russell," it used to mean the bearer was the younger son of a duke or marquis. In the last few decades it has become common to refer to "life peers" in this way, e.g. "Lord David Owen."

Lord Chancellor: The head of the legal system in England and Wales. Until recent reforms he sat as a judge in the House of Lords and appointed the other judges in England and Wales (not Scotland), but he was also a member of the Cabinet and exercised political as well as judicial authority. The party political role of the Lord Chancellor was ended in 2006.

Lords, House of: The upper chamber of Parliament. Composed of the bishops of the Anglican Church, senior judges, and the hereditary peerage. The judges sitting in the Lords form the ultimate court of appeal or supreme court, confusingly also known as the House of Lords. Irish and Scottish peers met to elect a small portion of their number to represent them in the chamber. Irish peers without a British title could gain election to the House of Commons, as was the case with Viscount Palmerston.

Lowlands of Scotland: The region south of the Firth/Clyde line. In the modern period most of the population of the country settled here, especially in the urban areas of Glasgow and Edinburgh.

Loyalists: Resident sympathizers with Britain during the American Revolution, sometimes called "Tories." Also, a term used for supporters in Northern Ireland of the Union with Great Britain, but not necessarily members of the Unionist Party.

Marquess: (also spelled marquis) The second highest rank in the peerage.

MP: Member of the House of Commons (lit. Member of Parliament). MPs "stand" for election; they do not "run" for office.

Nationalists: If preceded by "Welsh" or "Scottish," denotes supporters of independence from England. Without the prefix, usually used to describe Irish people seeking independence from the United Kingdom and in the twentieth century those seeking to unify Northern Ireland with Eire (the Irish Republic).

Nationalization: The transfer of ownership of private property or companies to public ownership.

Nonconformists: see Dissenters.

Orange Order (Orangemen): A fraternal order founded in 1795 to promote and protect Protestant values and interests. It was particularly influential in Northern Ireland.

Outdoor relief: Money disbursed to poor people under the provisions of the Poor Law without their being required to enter a workhouse.

Peerage (peers): A title conferring the right to sit in the House of Lords. Also a collective term for the members of the upper house of Parliament.

Pound: The central unit of British currency; the equivalent of the dollar in the USA or Canada (see also shilling). The symbol for pound is "£".

Pretenders: Stuart claimants to the throne – James "III" (the Old Pretender) and Charles "III" (Bonnie Prince Charlie).

Prince of Wales: see Wales.

Public schools: Private boarding schools where the children of elite families were and are educated. Some of the leading ones, such as Eton, Harrow, Westminster, and Winchester, are many centuries old. Most of these schools offer scholarships to students from less prosperous backgrounds.

RAF: see Royal Navy.

Rates: Local property taxes.

Republicans: Advocates of abolition of the monarchy. In Ireland, supporters of independence from British rule and absorption of Ulster into the Irish Republic.

Royal Commissions: Committees of experts established by the government to research problems and propose remedial action or legislation.

Royal Navy: The "senior" armed service. Later the Royal Air Force (RAF) was also accorded the regal prefix. These two forces are critical to national defense and survival. The army, on the other hand, was largely an offensive force employed overseas.

Royal Society, the: Prestigious scientific society founded by Charles II.

Sepoy: Native soldier in India under European command.

Shilling: A unit of currency until the 1970s: 12 pence made a shilling; 20 shillings were in a pound.

Shires: see counties.

Tabloid: A book-like format for newspapers first used in the nineteenth century for working-class journals. Eventually, most of the "broadsheets" (formatted like American newspapers) moved to a tabloid system.

Tithe: A tax levied on agricultural produce, used to support the clergy of the state Church and understandably much resented by Dissenters and Catholics.

TUC: The Trades Union Congress was the central organ of organized labor.

Ulster: The northern province of Ireland composed of counties where in most cases Protestants form a majority of the population, mostly descended from immigrant Scots Presbyterians.

Unionists: Supporters in Northern Ireland (and for a time in the late nineteenth and early twentieth centuries in Britain) of the union of Ireland with Great Britain. For a while the party was closely allied with the Conservative party but later fragmented into a variety of groupings.

VE Day: Victory in Europe day, May 8, 1945, marked the surrender of Germany in World War II.

Viceroy: A title used informally to designate the British governor of Ireland until 1922, officially known as the Lord Lieutenant. In the nineteenth century it became the official title of the British governor of India.

Viscount: The fourth highest rank in the peerage.

Wales, the prince of: The eldest son and heir of the king or queen regnant.

West Country: Southwestern England once noted for its woolen industry.

West End: The part of London west of the City inhabited by the royal family, government offices, and the aristocracy. Gradually it became the center for cultural institutions, hotels, restaurants, shops, and the *beau monde*. The prevailing winds in London come from the west, and thus the smoke from the coal fires that heated most buildings was often blown away to the East End, where poor people lived.

Westminster: Parliament met in the remnants of the old royal palace there on the banks of the Thames, which technically still belongs to the monarch – accidentally burned in 1834 and rebuilt in the Gothic style with a clock tower known as "Big Ben." The term has come to be used as a generic reference to Parliament. The term "Whitehall," named after part of the old royal palace where many ministerial head-quarters are located, is also a collective term for the administrative machine.

Select Bibliography

Introduction

The *Oxford History of England*, the original sequence and the "New" volumes, is an invaluable starting place. Their bibliographies, lists of cabinets, etc. are very useful.

Among the printed bibliographies, always fading towards obsolescence, is D. Loades, ed., *Reader's Guide to British History*, 2 vols., 2003. It supplies bibliographical references, and brief historiographical analyses on a wide range of topics. Others include S. Pargellis and D. J. Medley, eds., *Bibliography of British History: 1714–1789*, 1951; R. C. Richardson and R. A. Smith, eds., *Late Georgian and Regency England, 1760–1837*, 1984; L. Brown and I. R. Christie, eds., *Bibliography of British History, 1789–1851*, 1977; H. J. Hanham, ed., *Bibliography of British History 1851–1914*, 1976; K. Robbins, ed., *Bibliography of British History: 1914–1989*, 1996. See also R. C. Richardson and W. H. Chaloner, eds., *British Economic and Social History: A Bibliographical Guide*, 3rd ed., 1996.

Students doing research are encouraged to use the online tools now available in college libraries. The database *Historical Abstracts* and the *Royal Historical Society Bibliography*, printed annually and searchable online at http://www.rhs.ac.uk/bibl/ are particularly useful. See also the *Bibliography for Scotland* at http://www.nls.uk and P. H. Jones, *Bibliography of the History of Wales*, 3rd ed., 1989. Much important scholarship on British history is published in the *English Historical Review, Historical Journal, Irish Historical Studies, Journal of British Studies, History, Journal of Economic History, Economic History Review, Past and Present, Victorian Studies*, and other serials. The new *Oxford Dictionary of National Biography* (2004) is a magnificent research tool. Not only are the biographies of high quality, but also bibliographical information is up to date. This is a helpful starting point for exploring many topics. It is also online at http://www.oxforddnb.com. British Official Publications Collaborative Reader Information Service helps researchers track government documents 1688–1995: http://bopcris.ac.uk.

The richness of the literature published in Britain and the United States on the history of Great Britain, Ireland, and the British Empire is extraordinary. Even a bibliography ten times as long as this one would be obliged to leave out important works. Many wonderful biographies, memoirs, collections of correspondence, and diaries exist in profusion, especially for the nineteenth century onwards. Newspapers and magazines also became prolific after the invention of steam printing in the early nineteenth century: Two million pages of British newspapers are available at http://www.jisc.ac.uk.

The following bibliography includes both works generally accepted as authoritative and landmark studies, perhaps no longer entirely up to date but "must reads" for anyone venturing into the field. In some cases more than one book is highly regarded on a topic, but in the interests of keeping this list to manageable proportions I have often included only one of them, either because it is the most fun to read or most accessible in North America. In some cases the books listed are not particularly good but are the only ones written on the subject.

There are many thousands of primary documents in print and online. A multivolume series collected many interesting ones under the title *English Historical Documents*. See also R. A. Fothergill, *Private Chronicles: A Study of English Diaries*, 1974.

Many books overlap several periods, but are listed only in one. Additional sources can be found in the footnotes.

General

Anderson, M., ed., *British Population History from the Black Death to the Present Day*, 1996.

Armstrong, A. O., *Farmworkers: A Social and Economic History, 1770–1980*, 1988.

Beckett, J. V., *Aristocracy in England, 1660–1914*, 1986.

Bew, P., *Ireland: The Politics of Enmity 1789–2006*, 2007.

Brendon, P., *The Decline and Fall of the British Empire 1781–1997*, 2007.

Cain, P. J. and A. G. Hopkins, *British Imperialism: Innovation and Expansion 1688–1914*, 2 vols., 1993.

Campbell, R. H., *Scotland Since 1707: The Rise of an Industrial Society*, 2nd ed., 1985.

Cannon, J., *Parliamentary Reform, 1640–1830*, 1973.

Cannon, J., ed., *The Oxford Companion to British History*, rev. ed., 2002.

Collini, S., R. Whatmore, and B. Young, eds., *History, Religion, and Culture: British Intellectual History 1750–1950*, 2000.

Cullen, L. M., *An Economic History of Ireland since 1600*, 2nd ed., 1987.

Devine, T. M., *The Scottish Nation, 1700–2000*, Penguin, 1999.

Finberg, H. P. R., ed., *The Agrarian History of England and Wales*, multiple vols., 1967–.

Floud, R. and D. McCloskey, *The Economic History of Britain since 1700*, 3rd ed., 3 vols., 2004.

Foster, R. F., *Modern Ireland, 1600–1972*, 1988.

French, D., *The British Way in Warfare, 1688–2000*, 1990.

Girouard, M., *Life in the English Country House: A Social and Architectural History*, 1978.

Holt, R., *Sport and the British: A Modern History*, 1989.

Hoskins, W. G., *The Making of the English Landscape*, 1955.

Houston, R. A. and W. W. J. Knox, eds., *The New Penguin History of Scotland*, 2001.

Jenkins, P., *A History of Modern Wales, 1536–1990*, 1992.

Johnson, G. and J. F. Richards, *The New Cambridge History of India*, 2nd ed., multiple vols., 1994–.

Judd, D., *Empire: The British Imperial Experience from 1765 to the Present*, 1996.

Kennedy, P. M., *The Rise and Fall of British Naval Mastery*, 1976.

Lawson, P., *The East India Company: A History*, 1993.

Lees, L. H., *The Solidarities of Strangers: The English Poor Laws and the People, 1700–1948*, 1998.

Louis, W. R., ed., *The Oxford History of the British Empire*, 5 vols., 1998–9, further supplementary vols.

May, T., *An Economic and Social History of Britain 1760–1990*, 1995.

Owen, D., *English Philanthropy, 1660–1960*, 1965.

Porter, R., *Disease, Medicine, and Society in England, 1550–1860*, 2nd ed., 1993.

Porter, R. and L. Hall, *The Facts of Life: The Creation of Sexual Knowledge in Britain, 1650–1950*, 1995.

Rosevere, H., *The Treasury: The Evolution of a British Institution*, 1969.

Royle, E., *Modern Britain: A Social History 1750–1997*, 1997.

Stone, L. and J. F. Stone, *An Open Elite? England 1540–1880*, 1984.

Thompson, F. M. L., ed., *The Cambridge Social History of Britain 1750–1950*, 3 vols., 1990.

Wasson, E., *Born to Rule: British Political Elites*, 2000.

Whyte, I., *Landscape and History since 1500*, 2002.

Wrigley, E. A., and R. S. Schofield, *The Population History of England, 1541–1871*, 1989.

Reference

Butler, D. and G. Butler, *British Political Facts 1900–1994*, 1994.

Butler, D. and D. Kavanagh, *The British General Elections*, various dates.

Cooke, C., *British Historical Facts 1830–1900*, 1975.

Cooke, C. and J. Stevenson, eds., *British Historical Facts, 1688–1760*, London, 1988.

Cruickshanks, E., S. Handley, and D. Hayton, eds., *The House of Commons 1690–1715*, 5 vols., 2002.

Deane, P. and W. A. Cole, *British Economic Growth, 1688–1959*, 1969.

Gregory, J. and J. Stevenson, *The Longman Companion to Britain in the Eighteenth Century, 1688–1820*, 2000.

Johnston-Liik, E., *History of the Irish Parliament 1692–1800*, 6 vols., 2002.

Matthew, C. and B. Harrison, eds., *New Dictionary of National Biography*, Oxford, 2004, multiple vols. and online.

Mitchell, B. R., *British Historical Statistics*, 1988.

Mitchell, B. R., and P. Deane, *Abstract of British Historical Statistics*, 1962.

Namier, L. and J. Brooke, *The History of Parliament: The House of Commons, 1754–1790*, 3 vols., 1964.

Powicke, F. M. and E. B. Fryde, *Handbook of British Chronology*, 1961.

Sedgwick, R., *The History of Parliament: The House of Commons, 1715–1754*, 2 vols., 1970.

Thorne, R. G., *The History of Parliament: The House of Commons 1790–1820*, 5 vols., 1986.

National identities

Bartlett, T., *The Fall and Rise of the Irish Nation: The Catholic Question, 1690–1830*, 1992.

Birley, D., *A Social History of English Cricket*, 1999.

Bogdanor, V., *Devolution in the United Kingdom*, 1999.

Coakley, J., B. Laffan, and J. Todd, eds., *Renovation or Revolution? New Territorial Politics in Ireland and the United Kingdom*, 2005.

Colley, L., *Britons: Forging the Nation, 1707–1837*, 1992.

Colls, R., *Identity of England*, 2002.

Connolly, S. J., R. A. Houston, and R. J. Morris, eds., *Conflict, Identity and Economic Development: Ireland and Scotland, 1600–1939*, 1995.

Ellis, S. G. and S. Barber, eds., *Conquest and Union: Fashioning a British State, 1485–1725*, 1995.

Grant, A. and K. J. Stringer, eds., *Uniting the Kingdoms? The Making of British History*, 1995.

Harvie, C., *Scotland and Nationalism: Scottish Society and Politics, 1707–1994*, 1994.

Kearney, H., *The British Isles: A History of Four Nations*, 1989.

Mandler, P., *The English National Character*, 2006.

McCrone, D., *Understanding Scotland: The Sociology of a Stateless Nation*, 1992.

Pevsner, N., *The Englishness of English Art*, Penguin, 1956.

Robbins, K., *Nineteenth-Century Britain: Integration and Diversity*, 1988.

Robbins, K., *History, Religion and Identity in Modern Britain*, 1993.

Robbins, K., *Great Britain: Identities, Institutions and the Idea of Britishness*, 1998.

Samuel, R., ed., *Patriotism: The Making and Unmaking of British Identity*, 3 vols., 1989.

Taylor, B. and K. Thomson, eds., *Scotland and Wales: Nations Again?*, 1999.

Weight, R., *Patriots: National Identity in Britain 1940–2000*, 2002.

The Eighteenth Century (1714–1814)

Overviews

Armitage, D. and M. J. Braddock, *The British Atlantic World 1500–1800*, 2002.

Cannon, J., *Aristocratic Century: The Peerage in Eighteenth-Century England*, 1984.

Clark, J. C. D., *English Society, 1688–1832*, 2nd ed., 2000.

Connolly, S. J., *Religion, Law, and Power: The Making of Protestant Ireland, 1660–1760*, 1992.

Dickinson, H. T., *A Companion to Eighteenth-Century Britain*, 2002.

Halévy, E., *England in 1815*, rev. ed., 1949.

Hilton, B., *A Mad, Bad &Dangerous People? England 1783–1846*, 2006.

Holmes, G. and D. Szechi, *The Age of Oligarchy: Pre-Industrial Britain, 1722–1783*, 1993.

Hoppit, J., *A Land of Liberty? England 1689–1727*, 2000.

Jenkins, G. H., *Foundations of Modern Wales: Wales 1642–1780*, 1987.

Langford, P., *A Polite and Commercial People 1727–1783*, 1992.

Lenman, B., *Integration, Enlightenment and Industrialization: Scotland 1746–1832*, 1981.

Moody, T. W. and W. E. Vaughan, eds., *A New History of Ireland: Eighteenth-Century Ireland 1691–1800*, vol. 4, 1986.

O'Gorman, F., *The Long Eighteenth Century: British Political and Social History*, 1688–1832, 1997.

Porter, R., *English Society in the Eighteenth Century*, 1982.

Prest, W., *Albion Ascendant: English History 1660–1815*, 1998.

Biography

Ayer, A. J., *Tom Paine*, 1998.

Boswell, J., *Life of Johnson*, 1791.

Boswell, J., *London Journal 1762–1763*, ed. F. A. Pottle, 1950.

Brooke, J., *King George III*, 1972.

Browning, R., *The Duke of Newcastle*, 1975.

Cash, A. H., *John Wilkes: The Scandalous Father of Civil Liberty*, 2006.

Ehrman, J., *The Younger Pitt*, 3 vols., 1969–96.

Flexner, J. T., *George Washington*, 4 vols., 1965–72.

Foreman, A., *Georgiana, Duchess of Devonshire*, 1999.

Gordon, L., *Vindication: A Life of Mary Wollstonecraft*, 2005.

Grundy, I., *Lady Mary Wortley Montagu: Comet of the Enlightenment*, 1999.

Hatton, R. M., *George I*, 2001.

Knight, R., *The Pursuit of Victory: The Life and Achievement of Horatio Nelson*, 2005.

Lock, F. P., *Edmund Burke*, 2 vols., 1998, 2006.

Mitchell, L. G., *Charles James Fox*, 1992.

Penny, N., *Reynolds*, 1986.

Peters, M., *The Elder Pitt*, 1998.

Plumb, J. H., *The King's Minister*, 1960.

Thomas, P. D. G., *Lord North*, 1976.

Tillyard, S., *Aristocrats: Caroline, Emily, Louisa, and Sarah Lennox 1740–1832*, 1995.

Woodhouse, R., *Locke, a Biography*, 2008.

Politics and government

Black, J., *The Hanoverians, the History of a Dynasty*, 2004.

Brewer, J., *The Sinews of Power: War, Money, and the English State, 1688–1783*, 1990.

Colley, L., *In Defiance of Oligarchy: The Tory Party, 1714–1760*, 1982.

Dickinson, H. T., *Liberty and Property: Political Ideology in Eighteenth-Century Britain*, 1977.

Dickinson, H. T., *The Politics of the People in Eighteenth-Century Britain*, 1995.

Eastwood, D., *Government and Community in the English Provinces, 1700–1870*, 1997.

Foord, A. S., *His Majesty's Opposition, 1714–1839*, 1964.

Hill, B. W., *The Growth of Parliamentary Parties, 1689–1742*, 1976.

Jones, J. R., *Britain and the World, 1649–1815*, 1980.

Langford, P., *Modern British Foreign Policy: The Eighteenth Century, 1688–1815*, 1976.

Langford, P., *Public Life and Propertied Englishmen, 1689–1798*, 1991.

McCahill, M., *The House of Lords in the Age of George III*, 2009.

Monod, P. K., *Jacobitism and the English People, 1688–1788*, 1989.

Namier, L., *The Structure of Politics at the Accession of George III*, 2nd ed., 1957.

O'Gorman, F., *Voters, Patrons and Parties: The Unreformed Electorate of Hanoverian England, 1734–1832*, 1989.

Pares, R., *King George III and the Politicians*, 1953.

Plumb, J. H., *The Growth of Political Stability in England, 1675–1725*, 1967.

Rogers, N., *Whigs and Cities: Popular Politics in the Age of Walpole and Pitt*, 1989.

Sack, J., *From Jacobite to Conservative: Reaction and Orthodoxy in Britain, c.1760–1832*, 1993.

Wilkinson, C., *The British Navy and the State in the Eighteenth Century*, 2004.

Williams, E. N., *The Eighteenth-Century Constitution, 1688–1815*, 1960.

Wilson, K., *The Sense of the People: Politics, Culture and Imperialism in England, 1715–1785*, 1995.

Economy and society

Ashton, T. S., *The Industrial Revolution 1760–1830*, 1948.

Beattie, J. M., *Crime and the Courts in England, 1660–1800*, 1986.

Berg, M., *The Age of Manufactures: Industry, Innovation and Work in Britain 1700–1820*, 1985.

Cockayne, E., *Hubbub: Filth, Noise and Stench in England 1600–1770*, 2007.

Corfield, P. J., *The Impact of English Towns, 1700–1800*, 1982.

Corfield, P. J., *Power and the Professions in Britain 1700–1850*, 1995.

Crafts, N. F. R., *British Economic Growth during the Industrial Revolution*, 1985.

Daunton, M., *Progress and Poverty: An Economic and Social History of Britain 1700–1850*, 1995.

Davidoff, L. and C. Hall, *Family Fortunes: Men and Women of the English Middle Class, 1780–1850*, rev. ed., 2003.

Floud, R., and D. McClosky, eds., *The Economic History of Britain since 1700, vol. I, 1700–1860*, 2nd ed., 1994.

Gatrell, V. A. C., *The Hanging Tree: Execution and the English People 1770–1868*, 1994.

George, D., M. D., *London Life in the Eighteenth Century*, 1966.

Hitchcock, T., *English Sexualities, 1700–1800*, 1997.

Jones, E. L. *Agriculture and the Industrial Revolution*, 1974.

Malcolmson, R. W., *Popular Recreations in English Society, 1700–1850*, 1973.

Mingay, G. E., *English Landed Society in the Eighteenth Century*, 1963.

Overton, M., *Agricultural Revolution in England: The Transformation of the Agrarian Economy, 1500–1850*, 1996.

Rosevere, H., *The Financial Revolution, 1660–1760*, 1991.

Shoemaker, R. B., *Gender in English Society, 1650–1850: The Emergence of Separate Spheres?*, 1998.

Slack, P., *The English Poor Law, 1531–1782*, 1990.

Summerson, J., *Georgian London*, rev. ed., 1962.

Thompson, E. P., *Customs in Common*, 1991.

Tranter, N., *Sport, Economy and Society in Britain, 1750–1914*, 1998.

Cultural and intellectual

Armstrong, A., *The Church of England, the Methodists and Society, 1700–1850*, 1973.

Black, J., *The English Press in the Eighteenth Century*, 1987.

Brewer, J., *The Pleasures of the Imagination: English Culture in the Eighteenth Century*, 1997.

Burke, J., *English Art, 1714–1800*, 1976.

George, M. D., *London Life in the Eighteenth Century*, 1925.

McCalman, I., ed., *An Oxford Companion to the Romantic Age: British Culture 1776–1832*, 1999.

Rogers, P., *Literature and Popular Culture in Eighteenth Century England*, 1985.

Sobel, D., *Longitude*, 1995.

Walsh, J., C. Haydon, and S. Taylor, eds., *The Church of England, c.1689–c.1833: From Toleration to Tractarianism*, 1993.

The empire

Bayly, C. A., *Imperial Meridian: The British Empire and the World 1780–1830*, 1989.
Colley, L., *Captives*, 2002.
Kidd, C., *British Identities before Nationalism: Ethnicity and Nationhood in the Atlantic World, 1600–1800*, 1999.
Marshall, P. J., *The Making and Unmaking of Empires: Britain, India and America 1750–1783*, 2005.
Wilson, K., *Island Race: Englishness, Empire and Gender in the Eighteenth Century*, 2002.

The Nineteenth Century (1815–1914)

Overviews

Briggs, A., *The Age of Improvement 1783–1867*, 2nd ed., 2000.
Burn, W. L., *The Age of Equipoise*, 1964.
Checkland, S. and O. Checkland, *Industry and Ethos: Scotland 1832–1914*, 1984.
Evans, D. G., *A History of Wales, 1815–1906*, 1989.
Halévy, E., *A History of the English People in the Nineteenth Century*, 6 vols., 1924.
Hilton, B., *A Mad, Bad and Dangerous People? England 1783–1846*, 2006.
Hoppen, K. T., *Ireland since 1800: Conflict and Conformity*, 1989.
Hoppen, K. T., *The Mid-Victorian Generation 1846–1886*, 1998.
Kitson Clark, G., *The Making of Victorian England*, 1965.
McCord, N., *British History 1815–1906*, 1991.
Perkin, H., *The Origins of Modern English Society*, 1969.
Rubinstein, W. D., *Britain's Century: A Political and Social History, 1815–1905*, 1998.
Searle, G. R., *A New England? Peace and War 1886–1918*, 2004.
Smout, T. C., *A Century of the Scottish People 1830–1950*, 1986.
Williams, C., ed., *A Companion to Nineteenth-Century Britain*, 2004.
Young, G. M., *Portrait of an Age: Victorian England*, ed. G. Kitson Clark, 1977 [1936].

Biography

Arnsetin, W. L., *Queen Victoria*, 2003.
Blake, R., *Disraeli*, 1967.
Bourne, K., *Palmerston, the Early Years 1784–1841*, 1982.
Cecil, Lord D., *Melbourne*, 1965.
Desmond, A., and J. Moore, *Darwin*, 1991.
Gash, N., *Mr. Secretary Peel*, 1961.
Gash, N., *Sir Robert Peel*, 1972.
Gash, N., *Lord Liverpool*, 1984.
Hawkins, A., *The Forgotten Prime Minister: The 14th Earl of Derby*, 2 vols., 2007–8.
Jenkins, R., *Asquith*, 1964.
Ker, I., *John Henry Newman*, 1988.
Longford, E., *Wellington: Pillar of State*, 1972.
MacDonagh, O., *Daniel O'Connell*, 2 vols., 1988–9.

Magnus, P., *King Edward the Seventh*, 1964.

Marchand, L., *Byron: A Biography*, 1957.

Marsh, P., *Joseph Chamberlain: Entrepreneur in Politics*, 1994.

Matthew, H. C. G., *Gladstone 1809–1874*, 1986.

Matthew, H. C. G., *Gladstone 1875–1898*, 1995.

Pocock, T., *Sailor King: The Life of King William IV*, 1991.

Prest, J., *Lord John Russell*, 1972.

Ridley, J., *Lord Palmerston*, 1971.

Roberts, A., *Salisbury: Victorian Titan*, 2000.

Shannon, R., *Gladstone: Heroic Minister 1865–1898*, 1999.

Smith, E. A., *Earl Grey, 1764–1845*, 1990.

Smith, E. A., *George IV*, 1999.

Stott, A., *Hannah More: The First Victorian*, 2003.

Vickery, A., *The Gentleman's Daughter: Women's Lives in Georgian England*, 1998.

Politics and government

Bagehot, W., *The English Constitution*, 1867.

Bentley, M., *Politics without Democracy 1815–1914: Perception and Preoccupation in British Government*, 2nd ed., 1996.

Blake, R., *The Conservative Party from Peel to Thatcher*, 1985.

Bourne, K., *The Foreign Policy of Victorian England 1830–1902*, 1970.

Brock, M., *The Great Reform Act*, 1973.

Chamberlain, M. E., *Pax Britannica? British Foreign Policy 1789–1914*, 1988.

Checkland, S., *British Public Policy 1776–1939*, 1983.

Cookson, J. E., *Lord Liverpool's Administration 1815–1822*, 1975.

Dangerfield, G., *The Strange Death of Liberal England*, 1935.

Daunton, M., *Trusting Leviathan: The Politics of Taxation in Britain 1799–1914*, 2001.

Dicey, A. V., *Lectures on the Relationship between Law and Public Opinion in England during the Nineteenth Century*, 2nd ed., 1919.

Gash, N., *Politics in the Age of Peel*, 1977.

Gleadle, K. and S. Richardson, eds., *Women in British Politics, 1760–1860*, 2000.

Hanham, H. J., *Elections and Party Management: Politics in the Time of Disraeli and Gladstone*, 1978.

Hanham, H. J., ed., *The Nineteenth-Century Constitution*, 1969.

Harling, P., *The Modern British State: An Historical Introduction*, 2001.

Hoppen, K. T., *Elections, Politics and Society in Ireland, 1832–1885*, 1984.

Hutchinson, I. G. C., *A Political History of Scotland 1832–1914*, 1986.

Jalland, P., *The Liberals and Ireland: The Ulster Question in British Politics to 1914*, 1980.

Jenkins, T. A., *Parliament, Party, and Politics in Victorian Britain*, 1996.

Koss, S. E., *The Rise and Fall of the Political Press in Britain: Vol. I, The Nineteenth Century*, 1981.

Lee, S. J., *Aspects of British Political History, 1815–1914*, 1994.

Lewis, J., ed., *Before the Vote Was Won: Arguments For and Against Women's Suffrage*, 1987.

McDowell, *The Irish Administration 1800–1914*, 1964.

Murray, B. K., *The People's Budget 1909/10*, 1980.

Parry, J., *The Rise and Fall of Liberal Government in Victorian Britain*, 1993.

Phillips, G., *The Rise of the Labour Party 1893–1931*, 1992.

Reynolds, K. D., *Aristocratic Women and Political Society in Victorian Britain*, 1998.

Robbins, K., *Britain and Europe 1789–2005*, 2005.

Smith, E. A., *The House of Lords in British Politics and Society, 1815–1911*, 1992.

Smith, F. B., *The Making of the Second Reform Bill*, 1966.

Steiner, Z. S., *Britain and the Origins of the First World War*, 1977.

Strachan, H., *The Politics of the British Army*, 1997.

Thomas, W., *The Philosophic Radicals*, 1979.

Economy and society

Briggs, A., *Victorian Cities*, 2nd ed., 1968.

Brown, A., *English Society and the Prison: Time, Culture and Politics in the Development of the Modern Prison 1850–1920*, 2003.

Brown, S. J., and M. Fry, eds., *Scotland in the Age of the Disruption*, 1993.

Caine, B., *English Feminism, 1780–1980*, 1997.

Clark, A., *The Struggle for the Breeches: Gender and the Making of the British Working Class*, 1995.

Clark, S., *Social Origins of the Irish Land War*, 1979.

Connolly, S., *Religion and Society in Nineteenth-Century Ireland*, 1985.

Daunton, M., *Wealth and Welfare: An Economic and Social History of Britain 1851–1951*, 2007.

Daunton, M. J., ed., *The Cambridge Urban History of Britain, Vol. 3, 1840–1950*, 2000.

Devine, T. M., *Clanship to Crofters' War: The Social Transformation of the Scottish Highlands*, 1994.

Dyos, H. J. and M. Wolff, *The Victorian City: Images and Realities*, 2 vols., 1973.

Emsley, C., *Crime and Society in England, 1750–1900*, 2nd ed., 1996.

Finlayson, G., *Citizen, State, and Social Welfare in Britain 1830–1990*, 1994.

Golby, J. M., and A. W. Purdue, *The Civilisation of the Crowd: Popular Culture in England 1750–1900*, 1999.

Harries-Jenkins, G., *The Army in Victorian Society*, 1977.

Harris, J., *Private Lives, Public Spirit: Britain, 1870–1914*, 1994.

Harrison, B., *Drink and the Victorians: The Temperance Question in England, 1815–1872*, 1971.

Hobsbawm, E. J., *Industry and Empire: The Making of Modern English Society, 1750 to the Present Day*, 1968.

Honeyman, K., *Women, Gender and Industrialization in England 1700–1870*, 2000.

Howe, A., *Free Trade and Liberal England 1846–1946*, 1997.

Howell, D. W., *Land and People in Nineteenth-Century Wales*, 1977.

Hunt, E. H., *British Labour History 1815–1914*, 1981.

Hurt, J., *Education in Evolution: Church, State, Society and Popular Education, 1800–1870*, 1971.

Jones, G. Stedman, *Languages of Class: Studies in English Working Class History, 1832–1982*, 1983.

Joyce, P., *Visions of the People: Industrial England and the Question of Class, 1848–1914*, 1991.

Kidd, A., and D. Nichols, eds., *The Making of the British Middle Class?*, 1998.

Marcus, S., *The Other Victorians: A Study of Sexuality and Pornography in Mid–Nineteenth Century England*, 1964.

Mathias, P., *The First Industrial Nation: An Economic History of Britain 1700–1914*, 2nd ed., 1983.

McLeod, H., *Religion and Society in England 1850–1914*, 1996.

Mingay, G. E., ed., *The Victorian Countryside*, 2 vols., 1981.

Olsen, D. J., *The Growth of Victorian London*, 1976.

Poynter, J. R., *Society and Pauperism: English Ideas on Poor Relief, 1795–1834*, 1969.

Purvis, J., *Hard Lessons: The Lives and Education of Working-Class Women in Nineteenth-Century England*, 1989.

Roach, J., *Social Reform in England 1780–1880*, 1978.

Rubinstein, W. D., *Men of Property: The Very Wealthy in Modern Britain since the Industrial Revolution*, 2nd ed., 2006.

Savage, M. and A. Miles, *The Remaking of the British Working Class 1840–1940*, 1994.

Smith, F. B., *The People's Health 1830–1910*, 1979.

Smout, T. C., *A Century of the Scottish People, 1830–1950*, 1986.

Steinbach, S., *Women in England 1760–1914: A Social History*, 2004.

Thompson, E. P., *The Making of the English Working Class*, 1963.

Thompson, F. M. L., *English Landed Society in the Nineteenth Century*, 1963.

Thompson, F. M. L., *The Rise of Respectable Society*, 1988.

Vincent, D., *Literacy and Popular Culture: England 1750–1914*, 1989.

Walkowitz, J., *City of Dreadful Delight: Narratives of Sexual Danger in Late Victorian London*, 1992.

Walvin, J., *Leisure and Society 1830–1950*, 1978.

Walvin, J., *A Child's World: A Social History of English Childhood 1800–1914*, 1982.

Weeks, J., *Politics and Society: The Regulation of Sexuality Since 1800*, 2nd ed., 1989.

Wiener, M. J., *English Culture and the Decline of the Industrial Spirit 1850–1980*, 1981.

Woods, R., *The Population of Britain in the Nineteenth Century*, 1986.

Cultural and intellectual

Altick, R. D., *The English Common Reader: A Social History of the Mass Reading Public, 1800–1900*, 1957.

Barrow, J. W., *Evolution and Society: A Study in Victorian Social Theory*, 1966.

Barrow, J. W., *A Liberal Descent: Victorian Historians and the English Past*, 1983.

Boase, T. S. R., *English Art 1800–1870*, 1959.

Brown, C. G., *The Death of Christian Britain*, 2001.

Chadwick, O., *The Victorian Church*, 2 vols., 1966–70.

Chitnis, A. C., *The Scottish Enlightenment and Victorian English Society*, 1986.

Collini, S., D. Winch, and J. Barrow, eds., *That Noble Science of Politics: A Study in Nineteenth-Century Intellectual History*, 1983.

David, D., ed., *The Cambridge Companion to the Victorian Novel*, 2001.

Davis, P., *The Oxford English Literary History, Vol. VIII: 1830–1880: The Victorians*, 2002.

Gross, J., *The Rise and Fall of the Man of Letters: Aspects of English Literary Life since 1800*, 1969.

Hilton, B., *The Age of Atonement: The Influence of Evangelicalism on Social and Economic Thought, 1795–1865*, 1988.

Mandler, P., *The Fall and Rise of the Stately Home*, 1997.

O'Brien, D. P., *The Classical Economists*, 1975.

The empire

Cain, P. J., and A. G. Hopkins, *British Imperialism: Innovation and Expansion 1688–1914*, 1993.

Davis, M., *Late Victorian Holocausts*, 2001.

Hyam, R., *Britain's Imperial Century, 1815–1914: A Study of Empire and Expansion*, 2nd ed., 1993.

MacKenzie, J. M., ed., *Imperialism and Popular Culture*, 1986.

Moon, P., *The British Conquest and Dominion of India*, 1989.

Porter, B., *The Absent-Minded Imperialists: Empire, Society, and Culture in Britain*, 2004.

Robinson, R. and J. Gallagher, *Africa and the Victorians: The Official Mind of Imperialism*, 1961.

Said, E., *Orientalism*, 1978.

Semmel, B., *The Rise of Free Trade Imperialism: Classical Political Economy, the Empire of Free Trade, and Imperialism 1750–1850*, 1970.

The Twentieth Century (1914–2000)

General

Addison, P. and H. Jones, eds., *A Companion to Contemporary Britain 1939–2000*, 2005.

Clarke, P., *Hope and Glory: Britain 1900–1990*, 1996.

Evans, D. G., *A History of Wales, 1906–2000*, 2000.

Harvie, C., *No Gods and Precious Few Heroes: Twentieth-Century Scotland*, 3rd ed., 1998.

Hennessey, T., *A History of Northern Ireland*, 1997.

Lee, J. J., *Ireland 1912–85: Politics and Society*, 1989.

Morgan, K. O., *The People's Peace, 1945–89*, 1990.

Morgan, K. O., *Rebirth of a Nation: A History of Modern Wales 1880–1980*, new ed., 1998.

Mowat, C. L., *Britain Between the Wars, 1918–1940*, 1955.

Pugh, M., *State and Society: A Social and Political History of Britain 1870–1997*, 2nd ed., 1999.

Robbins, K., *The Eclipse of a Great Power: Modern Britain 1870–1992*, 2nd ed., 1994.

Rubinstein, W. D., *Twentieth-Century Britain, a Political History*, 2003.

Taylor, A. J. P., *English History 1914–45*, 1965.

Wrigley, C., ed., *A Companion to Early Twentieth-Century Britain*, 2003.

Biography

Bell, Q., *Virginia Woolf*, 2 vols., 1972.

Best, G., *Churchill: A Study in Greatness*, 2001.

Blake, R., *The Unknown Prime Minister: Life and Times of Andrew Bonar Law*, 1955.

Bradford, S., *Reluctant King: The Life and Reign of George VI 1895–1952*, 1989.

Bullock, A., *The Life and Times of Ernest Bevin*, 3 vols., 1960–83.

Burridge, T., *Clement Attlee*, 1985.

Campbell, J., *Edward Heath*, 1993.

Crick, B., *George Orwell, a Life*, 1982.

Crossman, R., *Diaries*, 4 vols., 1975–81.

Gilbert, M., and R. S. Churchill, *Winston S. Churchill*, 8 vols., 1966–88; accompanied by many companion volumes of documents.

Grigg, J., *Lloyd George*, 3 vols., 1973–85.

Harris, J., *William Beveridge: A Biography*, 2nd ed., 1997.

Hodges, A., *Alan Turing: The Enigma*, 1983.

Kent, J., *William Temple*, 1993.

Marquand, D., *Ramsay MacDonald*, 1977.

Pimlott, B., *Harold Wilson*, 1993.
Pimlott, B., *The Queen: A Biography of Elizabeth II*, 1997.
Rhodes James, R., *Anthony Eden*, 1986.
Rose, K., *King George V*, 1983.
Seldon, A., *Blair*, 2 vols. 2005–8.
Skidelsky, R., *John Maynard Keynes*, 3 vols., 1983–2000.
Turner, J., *Macmillan*, 1994.
Williams, P., *Hugh Gaitskell*, 1979.
Wright, A., *R. H. Tawney*, 1987.
Young, H., *One of Us: A Biography of Margaret Thatcher*, 1991.

Politics and government

Addison, P., *The Road to 1945: British Politics and the Second World War*, rev. ed., 1994.
Dumbrell, J., *A Special Relationship: Anglo-American Relations in the Cold War and After*, 2001.
Hennessy, P., *Whitehall*, 1989.
Hennessy, P., *The Hidden Wiring*, 1996.
Hennessy, P. and A. Seldon, eds., *Ruling Performance: British Governments from Attlee to Thatcher*, 1987.
Judge, D., *The Parliamentary State*, 1993.
Kellas, J., *The Scottish Political System*, 1989.
Lukacs, J., *Five Days in London: May 1940*, 1999.
Mackintosh, J. P., *The British Cabinet*, 1962.
Milward, A. S., *The United Kingdom and the European Community, Vol. 1: The Rise and Fall of a National Strategy, 1945–1963*, 2002.
Middlemas, K., *Politics in Industrial Society: The Experience of the British Political System since 1911*, 1979.
Morgan, K. O., *Labour in Power 1945–1951*, 1984.
Olechnowicz, A., ed., *The Monarchy and the British Nation, 1780 to the Present*, 2007.
Parker, R. A. C., *Chamberlain and Appeasement*, 1993.
Pugh, M., *The Making of Modern British Politics, 1867–1939*, 1982.
Ramsden, J., *The Age of Balfour and Baldwin 1902–1940*, 1978.
Robbins, K., *Britain and Europe 1789–2005*, 2005.
Searle, G. R., *The Liberal Party: Triumph and Disintegration, 1886–1929*, 1992.
Shell, D., *The House of Lords*, 1988.
Smith, M., *The Spying Game: The Secret History of British Intelligence*, 2002.
Young, J. W., *Britain and European Unity, 1945–1992*, 2nd ed., 2000.

Economy and society

Alford, B. W. E., *Britain in the World Economy since 1880*, 1996.
Ashworth, W., *The History of the British Coal Industry 1946–1982*, vol. 5, 1986.
Benson, J., *The Rise of Consumer Society in Britain, 1880–1980*, 1994.
Berridge, V., *Health and Society in Britain since 1939*, 1999.
Blythe, R., *Akenfield: Portrait of an English Village*, 1980.
Booth, A., *The British Economy in the Twentieth Century*, 2001.
Briggs, A., *The History of Broadcasting in the United Kingdom*, 5 vols., rev. ed., 1995.

Brittain, V., *Testament of Youth*, 1933.

Burnett, J., *A Social History of Housing, 1815–1970*, 1978.

Cannadine, D., *The Decline and Fall of the British Aristocracy*, 1990.

Cook, H., *The Long Sexual Revolution: English Women, Sex and Contraception, 1800–2000*, 2003.

Daunton, M., *Wealth and Welfare: An Economic and Social History of Britain, 1851–1951*, 2007.

Emsley, C., *The English Police: A Political and Social History*, 2nd ed., 1996.

Fisher, K., *Birth Control, Sex, and Marriage in Britain 1918–1960*, 2006.

Garside, W. R., *British Unemployment, 1919–39*, 1990.

Graves, R. and A. Hodges, *The Long Week-End: A Social History of Great Britain, 1918–1939*, 1940.

Hall, L. A., *Gender and Social Change in Britain since 1800*, 2000.

Halsey, A. H. and J. Webb, eds., *Twentieth Century British Social Trends*, 2000.

Harrison, B., *Peaceable Kingdom: Stability and Change in Modern Britain*, 1985.

Hill, J., *Sport, Leisure and Culture in Twentieth-century Britain*, 2002.

Hoggart, R., *The Uses of Literacy*, 1957.

Holmes, C., *John Bull's Island: Immigration and British Society, 1871–1971*, 1988.

Lowe, R., *The Welfare State in Britain since 1945*, 1993.

Marwick, A., *The Home Front: The British and the Second World War*, 1976.

Marwick, A., *British Society since 1945*, 1982.

Marwick, A., *The Deluge*, 2nd ed., 1991.

McIvor, A. J., *A History of Work in Britain, 1880–1950*, 2001.

McKibbin, R., *Classes and Cultures: England 1918–1951*, 1998.

Middleton, R., *The British Economy since 1945*, 2000.

Modood, T. et al., *Ethnic Minorities in Britain: Diversity and Disadvantage*, 1997.

Orwell, G., *The Road to Wigan Pier*, 1937.

Osgerby, B., *Youth in Britain since 1945*, 1997.

Pedersen, S., *Family, Dependence, and the Origins of the Welfare State: Britain and France, 1914–45*, 1993.

Pelling, H., *A History of British Trade Unionism*, 1963.

Perkin, H., *The Rise of Professional Society: England since 1880*, 1989.

Rowbotham, S., *The Past Is before Us: Feminism in Action since the 1960s*, 1989.

Solomos, J., *Race and Racism in Contemporary Britain*, 3rd ed., 2003.

Stevenson, J., *British Society 1914–45*, 1984.

Supple, B., *The History of the British Coal Industry*, vol. 4, 1987.

Tomlinson, J., *Problems in British Economic Policy, 1870–1945*, 1981.

Winter, J. M., *The Great War and the British People*, 1986.

Cultural and intellectual

Annan, N., *Our Age: English Intellectuals between the Wars*, 1990.

Berners-Lee, T., and M. Fischetti, *Weaving the Web: The Original Design and Ultimate Destiny of the World Wide Web by Its Inventor*, 1999.

Edel, L., *Bloomsbury: A House of Lions*, 1979.

Edgerton, D., *Science, Technology and the British Economic Decline 1870–1970*, 1996.

Ford, B., ed., *The Cambridge Cultural History of Britain*, vols. 8 and 9, 1992.

Innes, C., *Modern British Drama 1890–1990*, 1992.

Koss, S. E., *The Rise and Fall of the Political Press in Britain, Vol. 2, The Twentieth Century*, 1984.

Marwick, A., *Culture in Britain since 1945*, 1991.

Orwell, G., *The Collected Essays, Journalism and Letters of George Orwell*, 4 vols., 1968.

Rothenstein, J., *Modern English Painters*, 3 vols., 1984.

Watson, J. D., *The Double Helix*, 1970.

Williams, R., *The Country and the City*, 1975.

Winter, J. M., *Sites of Memory, Sites of Mourning: The Great War in European Cultural History*, 1995.

War and empire

Alanbrooke, Lord, *War Diaries, 1939–1945*, 2001.

Boyce, D. G., *The Irish Question and British Politics, 1867–1996*, 2nd ed., 1996.

Churchill, W. S., *The Second World War*, 6 vols., 1948–54.

Clarke, P., *The Last Thousand Days of the British Empire*, 2007.

Darwin, J., *The End of the British Empire*, 1991.

Dimbleby, D. and D. Reynolds, *An Ocean Apart: The Relationship between Britain and America in the Twentieth Century*, 1988.

Edgerton, D., *Warfare State: Britain, 1920–1970*, 2006.

Ferguson, N., *The Pity of War*, 1998.

Fussell, P., *The Great War and Modern Memory*, 1975.

Graves, R., *Goodbye to All That*, 1929.

Grenwood, S., *Britain and the Cold War, 1945–91*, 1991.

Hennessy, P., *The Secret State: Whitehall and the Cold War, 1945–70*, 2002.

Hough, R. and D. Richards, *The Battle of Britain*, 1989.

Hyam, R., *Britain's Declining Empire: The Road to Decolonialisation, 1918–1968*, 2007.

McIntyre, W. D., *British Decolonization, 1946–1997*, 1998.

Montagu, E., *The Man Who Never Was*, 1954.

Owen, W., *The Collected Poems of Wilfrid Owen*, 1965 [1920].

Peden, G. C., *Arms, Economics and British Strategy from Dreadnoughts to Hydrogen Bombs*, 2007.

Porter, B., *The Lion's Share: A Short History of British Imperialism, 1850–1995*, 3rd ed., 1996.

Reynolds, D., *Britannia Overruled: British Policy and World Power in the Twentieth Century*, 1991.

Strachan, H., *The First World War*, 3 vols., 2001–.

Thompson, A., *The Empire Strikes Back? The Impact of Imperialism on Britain from the Mid-Nineteenth Century*, 2005.

Additional Websites

Most British newspapers and periodicals are now online, many with archival access. Political parties, devolved institutions such as the Scottish Parliament, 10 Downing Street, and the monarchy have websites.

http://ccbh.ac.uk (website of the Centre for Contemporary British History)

http://chu.cam.ac.uk/archives/ (website of the Churchill Archives Centre which holds and has put online not only much material related to Churchill but also many other important politicians of the twentieth century)

http://www.eh.net (website of the Economic History Association – has a currency converter)

http://www.history.ac.uk/ (website of the Institute of Historical Research, University of London, with links to many British history sites)

http://www.hpss.geog.cam.ac.uk/research/projects (website of the Cambridge Group for the History of Population and Social Structure that is doing much innovative research on social and economic history)

http://www.irishhistoryonline.ie (bibliography for Irish history)

http://www.oldbaileyonline.org (proceedings of London's Central Criminal Court 1674–1913)

http://www.parliament.uk (website of the British Parliament; Hansard, the record of debates, is being put online)

http://www.parliament.uk/commons/ib/research/rp2002/rp02-044.pdf ("Inflation: the value of the pound 1750–2001" a Commons research paper of value for calculating inflation)

http://www.pro.gov.uk (website of the Public Record Office where the national archives are stored. They are developing a number of collections of documents available online.)

http://www.theses.com (an index to doctoral theses)

http://www.usc.edu/ibis/ibislinks (links to many bibliographies, catalogues, images, and maps)

http://www.victorianweb.org (website devoted to Victorian history and culture)

Prime Ministers

Robert **Walpole**	1721/1730[1]–42
Spencer Compton*, 1st earl of **Wilmington**	1742–3
Henry **Pelham***	1743–54
Thomas Pelham-Holles*, 1st duke of **Newcastle**	1754–6
William Cavendish, 4th duke of **Devonshire**	1756–7
Thomas Pelham-Holles*, 1st duke of **Newcastle** (with John Stuart, 3rd earl of Bute)	1757–62
John Stuart, 3rd earl of **Bute**	1762–3
George **Grenville***	1763–5
Charles Watson Wentworth, 2nd marquess of **Rockingham**	1765–6
William Pitt (the Elder), 1st earl of **Chatham** (with the 3rd duke of Grafton)	1766–8
Augustus Henry Fitzroy, 3rd duke of **Grafton**	1768–70
Frederick North, Lord **North**	1770–82
Charles Watson Wentworth, 2nd marquess of **Rockingham**	1782
William Petty, 2nd earl of **Shelburne**	1782–3
William Henry Bentinck, 3rd duke of **Portland** (with Charles James Fox* and Lord North)	1783
William **Pitt*** (the Younger)	1783–1801
Henry **Addington**	1801–4
William **Pitt*** (the Younger)	1804–6
William Grenville*, 1st Lord **Grenville** (with Charles James Fox*)	1806–7
William Henry Bentinck, 3th duke of **Portland**	1807–9
Spencer **Perceval***	1809–12
Robert Banks Jenkinson, 2nd earl of **Liverpool**	1812–27
George **Canning***	1827
Frederick Robinson*, 1st Viscount **Goderich**	1827–8
Arthur Wellesley*, 1st duke of **Wellington**	1828–30
Charles Grey, 2nd Earl **Grey**	1830–4
William Lamb, 2nd Viscount **Melbourne**	1834
Arthur Wellesley*, 1st duke of **Wellington**	1834[2]

*   Member of a peerage family.

Sir Robert **Peel**, 2nd Baronet	1834–5
William Lamb, 2nd Viscount **Melbourne**	1835–41
Sir Robert **Peel**, 2nd Baronet	1841–6
Lord John **Russell**	1846–52
Edward Stanley, 14th earl of **Derby**	1852
George Gordon, 4th earl of **Aberdeen**	1852–5
Henry John Temple, 3rd Viscount **Palmerston**	1855–8
Edward Stanley, 14th earl of **Derby** (1844)	1858–9
Henry John Temple, 3rd Viscount **Palmerston**	1859–65
Lord John Russell, 1st Earl **Russell**	1865–6
Edward Stanley, 14th earl of **Derby**	1866–8
Benjamin **Disraeli**	1868
William Ewart **Gladstone**	1868–74
Benjamin Disraeli, 1st earl of **Beaconsfield**	1874–80
William Ewart **Gladstone**	1880–5
Robert Gascoyne Cecil, 3rd marquess of **Salisbury**	1885–6
William Ewart **Gladstone**	1886
Robert Gascoyne Cecil, 3rd marquess of **Salisbury**	1886–92
William Ewart **Gladstone**	1892–4
Archibald Philip Primrose, 5th earl of **Rosebery**	1894–5
Robert Gascoyne Cecil, 3rd marquess of **Salisbury**	1895–1902
Arthur James **Balfour**	1902–5
Sir Henry **Campbell-Bannerman**	1905–8
Herbert Henry **Asquith**	1908–16
David **Lloyd George**	1916–22
Andrew **Bonar Law**	1922–3
Stanley **Baldwin**	1923–4
Ramsay **MacDonald**	1924
Stanley **Baldwin**	1924–9
Ramsay **MacDonald**	1929–35
Stanley **Baldwin**	1935–7
Neville **Chamberlain**	1937–40
Winston **Churchill***	1940–5
Clement **Attlee**	1945–51
Sir Winston **Churchill***	1951–5
Sir Anthony **Eden***	1955–7
Harold **Macmillan**	1957–63
Sir Alec **Douglas-Home** (14th earl of Home)	1963–4
Harold **Wilson**	1964–70
Edward **Heath**	1970–4
Harold **Wilson**	1974–6
James **Callaghan**	1976–9
Margaret **Thatcher**	1979–90

John **Major**	1990–7
Tony **Blair**	1997–2007
Gordon **Brown**	2007–

Notes

1 Townsend resigned in 1730 when the ministry became entirely Walpole's responsibility.
2 Wellington was appointed titular First Lord of the Treasury during the interval while Sir Robert Peel returned from Italy.

Genealogy of the Royal Family

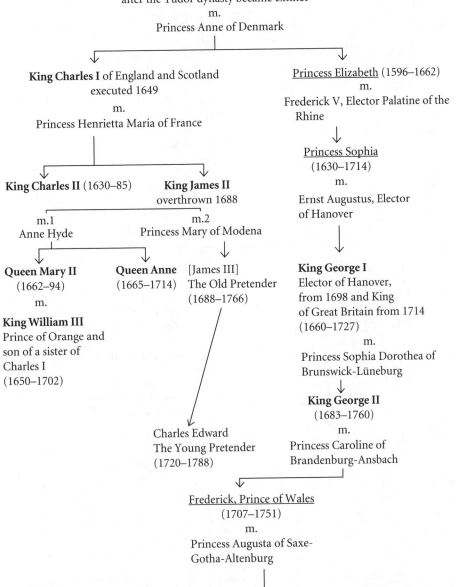

King James VI [Stuart] of Scotland, by the right of his mother, Mary Queen of Scots, daughter of a sister of Henry VIII, succeeded to the throne of England as **James I** in 1603 after the Tudor dynasty became extinct
m.
Princess Anne of Denmark

King Charles I of England and Scotland
executed 1649
m.
Princess Henrietta Maria of France

Princess Elizabeth (1596–1662)
m.
Frederick V, Elector Palatine of the Rhine

Princess Sophia
(1630–1714)
m.
Ernst Augustus, Elector of Hanover

King Charles II (1630–85)

King James II
overthrown 1688

m.1
Anne Hyde

m.2
Princess Mary of Modena

Queen Mary II
(1662–94)
m.

King William III
Prince of Orange and
son of a sister of
Charles I
(1650–1702)

Queen Anne
(1665–1714)

[James III]
The Old Pretender
(1688–1766)

King George I
Elector of Hanover,
from 1698 and King
of Great Britain from 1714
(1660–1727)
m.
Princess Sophia Dorothea of
Brunswick-Lüneburg

King George II
(1683–1760)
m.
Princess Caroline of
Brandenburg-Ansbach

Charles Edward
The Young Pretender
(1720–1788)

Frederick, Prince of Wales
(1707–1751)
m.
Princess Augusta of Saxe-
Gotha-Altenburg

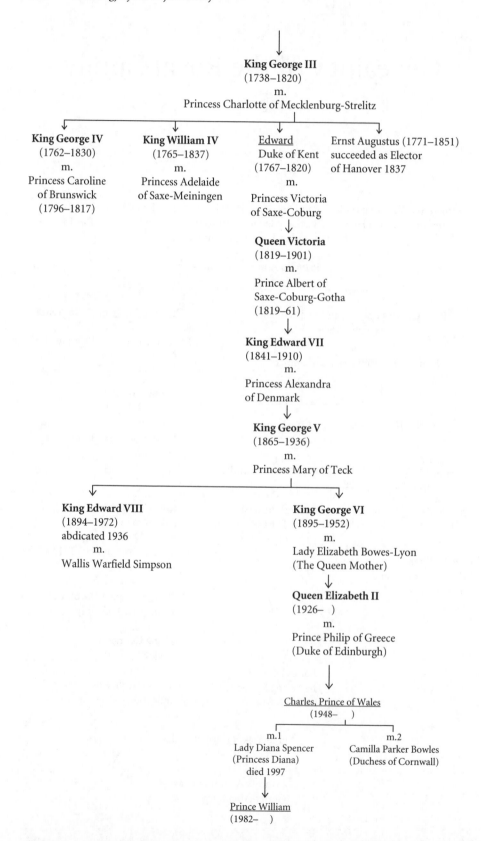

King George III
(1738–1820)
m.
Princess Charlotte of Mecklenburg-Strelitz

King George IV
(1762–1830)
m.
Princess Caroline
of Brunswick
(1796–1817)

King William IV
(1765–1837)
m.
Princess Adelaide
of Saxe-Meiningen

Edward
Duke of Kent
(1767–1820)
m.
Princess Victoria
of Saxe-Coburg

Ernst Augustus (1771–1851)
succeeded as Elector
of Hanover 1837

Queen Victoria
(1819–1901)
m.
Prince Albert of
Saxe-Coburg-Gotha
(1819–61)

King Edward VII
(1841–1910)
m.
Princess Alexandra
of Denmark

King George V
(1865–1936)
m.
Princess Mary of Teck

King Edward VIII
(1894–1972)
abdicated 1936
m.
Wallis Warfield Simpson

King George VI
(1895–1952)
m.
Lady Elizabeth Bowes-Lyon
(The Queen Mother)

Queen Elizabeth II
(1926–)
m.
Prince Philip of Greece
(Duke of Edinburgh)

Charles, Prince of Wales
(1948–)

m.1
Lady Diana Spencer
(Princess Diana)
died 1997

m.2
Camilla Parker Bowles
(Duchess of Cornwall)

Prince William
(1982–)

Index

Note: The names of modern historians are marked with an asterisk (*). Peers are listed under the title by which they are best known. Other titles referred to in the text are cross-referenced. Page numbers in *italic* refer to maps and illustrations.